Detail from U.S. Coast Survey
Map of Maine, 1859

His Glassy Essence

Also by Kenneth Laine Ketner

An Emendation of R. G. Collingwood's Doctrine of Absolute Presuppositions

Charles Sanders Peirce: Contributions to The Nation
Edited with J. E. Cook

Charles Sanders Peirce: Complete Published Works
Microfiche Edition

A Comprehensive Bibliography of the Published Works
of Charles Sanders Peirce

Proceedings of the Charles S. Peirce
Bicentennial International Congress
Edited with J. M. Ransdell, C. Eisele, M. H. Fisch,
and C. Hardwick

Peirce, Semeiotic, and Pragmatism:
Essays by Max Harold Fisch
Edited with C. J. W. Kloesel

Elements of Logic

Reasoning and the Logic of Things:
The 1898 Cambridge Conferences Lectures by
Charles Sanders Peirce
Edited with Hilary Putnam

Peirce and Contemporary Thought:
Philosophical Inquiries
Edition of the Plenary Sessions
Peirce Sesquicentennial International Congress

A Thief of Peirce:
The Letters of Kenneth Laine Ketner and Walker Percy
Edited by P. H. Samway, S.J.

HIS GLASSY ESSENCE

AN AUTOBIOGRAPHY OF

CHARLES SANDERS PEIRCE

Kenneth Laine Ketner

VANDERBILT UNIVERSITY PRESS ■ *Nashville and London*

First edition 1998
98 99 00 01 02   5 4 3 2 1

This publication is made from recycled paper and meets the minimum requirements of American National Standard for Information Sciences—Permanence of Paper for
Printed Library Materials. (∞)

Library of Congress Cataloging-in-Publication Data

Peirce, Charles S. (Charles Sanders), 1839-1914.
  His glassy essence : an autobiography of Charles Sanders Peirce
/ Kenneth Laine Ketner. -- 1st ed.
  p. cm. -- (The Vanderbilt library of American philosophy)
Largely in Charles S. Peirce's words, with additions by Kenneth
Laine Ketner.
  Includes bibliographical references (p.) and index.

  ISBN 0826513131
  1. Peirce, Charles S. (Charles Sanders), 1839-1914. 2.
Philosophers--United States--Biography. I. Ketner, Kenneth Laine.
II. Title. III. Series.
  B945.P44 A3 1998
  181--ddc21
  [B]

                                                         98-8886
                                                           CIP

Published by Vanderbilt University Press
Printed in the United States of America

Author photograph by Hershel Womack

to Robert and Marcy Lawless
with admiration and gratitude

Our day of dependence, our long apprenticeship to the learning of other lands, draws to a close. The millions that around us are rushing into life, cannot always be fed on the sere remains of foreign harvests. Events, actions arise, that must be sung, that will sing themselves.

—Emerson, *The American Scholar*,

Cambridge, Massachusetts,

31 August 1837

Contents

Illustrations

Preface

History is an abductive, guessing science. That means historians cannot avoid interpreting their data. The "story of what happened in the past" is not necessarily the same as "what happened in the past." We can never be certain that the story we have is the right one. Something new in the way of data may turn up. Or somebody may have made a mistake about how the story was told. Yet we mortals must have a story.

So history is a storytelling art. History and storytelling are intertwined such that the stories historians tell are in effect large-scale hypotheses (more or less confirmed guesses) about the truth of "what happened in the past."

In the following account, Ike, Betsey, and Roy are fictional characters whose resemblance to any person living or dead is coincidental.

The story told here arises from the life and times of Charles Sanders Peirce. Most of it is related in his own words, or in those of his family, friends, and contemporaries. Notes, signaled in the text by the [†] symbol, refer interested readers to primary sources listed at the back of the book, as explained in the Epilogue.

And now this tale begins with a letter from Ike, the narrator, who, like Peirce, has the unorthodox stylistic habit of addressing readers directly.

I

PRELUDE

1

A Mystery from Boston Unfolds

DEAR READER: My identity is significant, but ultimately of no importance. You need to understand a bit about me. I'm known as a mystery writer by trade, but I'm an amateur by inclination and instinct. I mean that I thrive on trying my hand at different things; it's fun, it preserves some childlike qualities in my mind, and it gives me a way to live one day after another. Because of those instincts and habits, I can see things, little bits of life, that most people overlook. In that respect my amateur lifestyle helps me write. But my dilettante ways, now that I reflect, are more important to me than writing. My reasonably capable detective novels are the means to finance my status as a lifelong novice in a number of other pursuits. Writing also gives me freedom for dabbling, because, thank God, it isn't a nine-to-five job. I can make up a new story when I feel like doing it. I get enough royalty checks to live as a member of the comfortable middle class in old Boston with Elizabeth and our poodle; I haven't written the great American mystery novel yet, but hope eternal springs. I might get lucky. But I'm not breaking my neck to do it—that would mean less time for my amateurism.

Today is my birthday—I'm fifty-seven, in case you're curious. I'm a Harvard man, class of 1961; Betsey is a graduate of Lady Radcliffe's Hall in the same year. We met in Cambridge. I didn't select a special field of study, as you might guess. I was interested in almost everything. I've always been that way, even as a child in Stillwater, Oklahoma, where I was "born and raised," as my family would say. From my father I received the name Louis Elisha Eisenstaat, but everyone has always called me Ike. I'm proud of my Harvard education, but I'm an Okie at bottom. I could never adopt the Cambridge ways, but I admire the folks in this region, and I live in Boston because it's a rich hunting ground for my neophytism.

One of my nonprofessional interests in the past several years in fact began to possess my life. This book, taken up at Betsey's suggestion, has been an exorcism, my way as an amateur psychologist to avoid becoming a

3

professional—which is to say, continuing to be neurotically obsessed and mildly meglomaniacal—about the topic of this volume. Physician heal thyself! That principle applies equally well to amateur physicians, otherwise known as hypochondriacs, especially those fortunate enough to live with a community health nurse.

While I'm speaking of Betsey, the growth of my preoccupation began because of her relatives. She is from Milford, a small town in Pike County within northeastern Pennsylvania on the Delaware River, near the New York border. Port Jervis, New York, is the closest larger town. It's a beautiful spot that's now for the most part incorporated into the Delaware Water Gap National Recreation Area. Even in Victorian times it was a popular vacation spot, although quite rustic. Perhaps that was part of its charm. It's not as lovely as it once was. Twentieth century blight eventually attacked in the seventies. The federal government bought most of the beautiful old country houses in the region for the Recreation Area. Many of them were torn down or have been converted for park use. Even what was formerly a famous—or infamous—honeymoon motel in the nearby Pocono mountains is now a Ranger station. You can make up your own jokes about that. But the ultimate insult came when a damnable interstate turnpike was laid right against the town. Now the natural beauty is pestered by arrogant diesel smoke and blathering truck air horns. Yet the dawn mist still rises on the river. Is that a sign?

Betsey's grandfather was William Darbey, who served as the local Episcopal minister in the first years of the second decade of the century. She is the only child of an only child, and was therefore her grandfather's darling. Shortly before his death from complications of arteriosclerosis, he called her to his bedside to tell her that she was now the owner of a large and uniquely handsome ancient wooden box she would find in a particular hiding place in his study. Because he was weak, he spoke briefly, promising to tell her more later. There was no later—he took a sudden turn for the worse and died a few hours thence.

She was still a youngster, but because the occasion was powerfully solemn, she can clearly recall the exact sounds her grandfather uttered:

In 1934 Madame Purse entrusted it to me on her death bed. Madame Purse said, "There is a fortune in it—now it's yours."

Then Grandpa added—presumably his own philosophical sentiment—suddenly in a deep tone which scared her,

"Take care! It has transforming power."

Betsey told me about it during the Christmas season of 1957, when we were freshmen, after we had become more than friends.

We met in Professor Putnam's introductory philosophy class, somehow landing in adjoining desks. At the time I was exceptionally naive regarding interpersonal relations and matters of the heart. Betsey, on the other hand, was quite the opposite—she had experience. As a matter of fact, it would be right to say that she seduced me. In the middle of October, after we had become fairly well acquainted, she asked me if I could come over to her place to help with the assignment on William James that was due in about a week. We walked from Sever Hall, past the Divinity School, and into her apartment on the second floor of an old clapboard on the edge of Somerville. Before we began our studies, Betsey asked if I would like to hear a couple of tunes from her collection of Big Band records. She put on Glenn Miller's "In the Mood," saying that the true connoisseur listened to swing music only while dancing. So we danced. One thing led to another. After considerable lovemaking, you might say that the . . . uh . . . earth moved for her, and in such an intense manner that without willing it she screamed like a banshee. This completely startled both of us, the effect being, in my case, that I fell backwards toward the floor, knocking myself unconscious on an edge of the ancient box, which she had placed near her bed as a makeshift nightstand. Had it not been covered with scattered clothing, I might have been seriously injured—as it was, the laundry softened the blow, and Betsey's emergency common-sense nursing brought me around with no permanent harm done. However, I had made an unbreakable connection with Betsey and had been introduced to Grandfather Darbey's box in a direct manner, although I took no time for examination when first my head gained an acquaintance with it.

Later I had many an opportunity to expand my musical knowledge of the swing era, all of which was facilitated by a cherished Christmas present from Betsey: permanent ear plugs in a small but sturdy gold-plated box, engraved "PROPERTY OF SWEET BETSEY FROM PIKE."

I moved into the Somerville flat within a week. In that day we were ahead of our time socially, although perhaps now that would not be so. I introduced her to what is called women's liberation, something which I never doubted because it always seemed logical to me, and she introduced me to true marriage without ceremony, which is how we faithfully live to this day. Typically folks signify the start of a lifelong relationship by exchanging rings in a church ceremony. In our case, on the eve of Christ's Mass, Betsey put on Benny Goodman's "Let's Dance," and about halfway through the number she presented me with that special gift. Sometimes one doesn't need to speak actual words for a vow to be in effect; one simply discovers that it is present.

Betsey is quite religious, but not in the sense of rituals or ceremonies. She dislikes organized religion because her grandfather was an Episcopal priest, and her mother, William's daughter, married a hardshell Baptist minister— she was overexposed, in other words. That is also one reason she took up community health as her speciality in nursing; and there were other reasons.

It's a profession that requires a finely honed spiritual sense; otherwise you burn out and die from the neck up.

Once we were settled in, our conversation inevitably returned to the fateful ersatz nightstand. She explained to me that her mother, Margaret, could tell her little about the box; she knew that he had it, but when asked, Grandpa would usually say, "I haven't decided what to do with it." It seems he never took anyone into his confidence on that topic. She did know, as do most persons who live in or near Milford, that the previous owners of the box, "Old Professor Peirce and his wife Madame Juliette Peirce," lived a couple of miles east of Milford on the Port Jervis Road in a rather large house which was later bought for a song by the Phillipses in a Sheriff's tax sale after Madame died. The Professor had expired in 1914 and his wife in 1934—both events, as it would happen, occurring when Grandpa William was the Episcopal minister in Milford. He had been in the Milford vicarage in 1914, then went to other stations but had come back to stay and to retire by 1934. Margaret could recite several local legends about the Professor and Madame, but supposedly not too much in the way of solid information was known about them.

All of this was interesting chit-chat as I learned it from Betsey on various occasions in the happy little flat in Somerville, within an easy walk to Harvard Yard from around behind. Yet with all the cares and joys of student life, somehow it didn't make complete contact with me. For instance, I didn't think to ask my teachers if they had heard of Professor Peirce—the correct spelling, by the way, but the sound is exactly like "purse," which vindicates Betsey's childhood memory. Since my studies were as general as I could arrange for them to be, I didn't really specialize in anything. So the name of Peirce never came my way, or if it did, it didn't connect. Which is ironical, since he was born a few blocks from where Betsey and I were living, and grew up in a house that was located in the heart of the Yard where Sever Hall now stands, the site of many of our classes.

We graduated in 1961. I wanted no additional formal schooling. Except for a few exceptional classes—very few—college was boring, just an exercise in lecture remembering at which any good tape recorder would excel. It had dawned upon me that my amateurism could provide a lifelong continuing education. I simply required a way to finance it. I cried "Eureka" when I sold my first detective piece for a fee that paid the bills for six months. Meanwhile Betsey had a scholarship for the Nursing School at Massachusetts General Hospital. After she graduated in 1963, we decided to move to our present apartment in old Boston. We had an opportunity to buy it. It was a wreck when we moved in, but it had character and potential that we developed over the years. Naturally, this was one of its attractions, for I'm an amateur electrician-painter-plumber-decorator-restorer.

When we moved our stuff from Somerville, the beautiful old box surprised us by reappearing from under a neglected pile of clutter in a large closet. I do recall demanding earlier that it be moved away from the bed.

I had a curious experience when it came to sight again. I was able to see it in a way I never had before; it seemed to attach itself to me. I felt that it permanently connected with my psyche. Strange. It now occupies a place of honor in my study. It's out of the closet.

Once we were settled in Boston, Betsey (who now reads my mind with ease) noticed my sudden interest. I had never opened it, although she had inspected it before I came along. So one day before leaving for work she encouraged me to look it over thoroughly. I cleared space on the big table in my writer's den. The first thing I noticed: the box was convenient to hand when placed next to my Cambridge-style reading chair. It's smaller than a steamer trunk, designed somewhat like a *Vargueno*† but without legs, of the most elegant construction in mahogany, impeccably finished in Japanese lacquer, with spectacular Moorish-style wood inlays in various subtle colors and kinds of wood.

vargueno (vär-gā'nō), *n.* [Named from the village of *Vargas*, near Toledo in Spain.] A cabinet of peculiar form, consisting of a box-shaped body without architectural ornaments, opening by means of a front hinged at the bottom edge, and the whole mounted on columns

Spanish Vargueno, 17th century. (From "L'Art pour Tous.")

or a stand at a height convenient for writing on the opened cover used as a desk. The decoration is of geometrical character, and makes especial use of thin ironwork in pierced patterns, sometimes gilded and mounted on pieces of red cloth, leather, or the like, which form a background.

1. *Vargueno*

"*Spectacular Moorish-style wood inlays*"
The Century Dictionary and Cyclopedia

I checked with some experts, who tell me that it was constructed by a famous custom builder in Alexandria Egypt in the 1890s. Every expert who examined it has immediately offered a fancy price, and each one assured me that its purchase price would have been extravagant even in 1890.

When I opened it, the intimate yet assertive aroma of cedarwood awakened my nose. There's a small compartment containing Lebanese cedar chips, to prevent insect infestation, or maybe for some other reason. Ingenious, and exquisitely tasteful. I began to tingle with attention. Just under the main lid, suspended above the larger compartments below by two side rails, was a lovely removable lap board for writing, complete with an elegant inset brass inkwell and in a handy groove a well-used pen of ebony with a fine gold-covered steel tip. Obviously, here is the elegant equipment of a master writer. The inkwell was half full of dried and caked ink. On the well was affixed a little label like the kind chemists use for samples in their analytical laboratories. In what I later discovered to be Peirce's hand were the simple words "Batch nr. 3." Maybe my subconscious had switched into a chemical context, because without warning—nearly as if someone had spoken it—"When the box is opened and prepared for the writer's hand, incense of Lebanon announces readiness to the subconscious seat of creative action." I mouthed half-silently: Damn—it's an invocation of the Holy Spirit! Those are the words Grandpa Darbey would have used. I accept the principle, but not in that language. All this reduced me to a long, musing, vacant silence. Apparently, I had been possessed by something—some character or relationship exemplified in the box and its appointments.

Finally—how much later I cannot say—I shook my head, somehow restored myself to my self, and continued the examination with an effort-free clinical eye. Below the lapboard were several sections, as in a file drawer, neatly loaded with manuscript sheets inscribed in fine black ink on an expensive and elegant high-quality laid rag paper, watermarked with "Crane's Superfine" and an image of a crane standing on one leg just above the year of manufacture. I checked the watermark instantly—another of my dilletante interests. The paper was manufactured by a well-known New England house in various years in the 1890s or early 1900s, and was in wonderful condition. Another section contained a number of photographs and illustrations, again from the nineteenth century judging by the dress.

One area on the right side, just under the lapboard, was considerably wider than the opposite supporting rail on the left. Originally I thought that was a mere construction anomaly. Yet as I began to be a friend to the box, one day it struck me that there might be a reason for the extra width. I asked an acquaintance, who is an expert on Chinese puzzle boxes, to look at it, and within an hour he opened a secret compartment that contained a smaller box. Every time I hold it in my hands, that tune my mother sang to me as a child runs through my head: "A tiskit a tasket, a little yellow casket. . . ." This box is the size of a casket, or small table-top box for storing knick-knacks. It is entirely different in style from the large box and maybe half a century or more older, according to the jewel-box expert I consulted. He thinks it was manufactured in Cordova. Certainly he regards it as in the style of master craftsmen of that city. He rates it as being of the utmost in quality of materials and artful workmanship. Basically it is a rectangle in shape flexed across one long side by means of a silver piano hinge. It is covered in tan leather, with four bands of darker leather encircling the box parallel to its short axis. On these bands, alternating two-five-five-two, are carved silver studs. Inside, the base is lined with brown velvet, with one compartment apparently intended for jewelry. This was empty when we first removed the box from its secret hiding place. There is a second compartment in the base that contained a well-used pack of playing cards in a fascinating design unknown to me at that time. These cards were nestled in a pocket specially prepared to hold them, complete with a tooled leather flap cover. On an exquisitely hand-engraved, small, solid-gold plate fastened with silver pins, the flap protecting the cards bears a crest over a name:

BACOURT

As the years went by, mystery writing became reliable, the Boston apartment became livable, so I gained more and more time for pursuits. Among these would always be the box and its contents. In the past few years, the box has approached a monopoly on my interest. I devoted a great deal of study to the manuscript. As I dug into it, I was led to many clues which I carefully ran to ground. I visited a number of sites—libraries, rare book rooms, manuscript collections—and traipsed through uncountable attics in search of materials that would illuminate. You could say the manuscript in the box led me on a merry chase through the nineteenth century. Here my experience as a detective novelist was invaluable. I'm now quite a good scholar about old Professor Peirce, his life and times; in fact I'm in mortal danger of becoming an expert on the subject, and this is causing me considerable discomfort and even neglect of Betsey, about which she has begun to fret. I really don't want to ruin my amateur standing, because I despise professionalism.

In the course of exploring the elegant box, I came to admire a way of living that was prominent in the nineteenth century but is almost gone now: the life of a gentleman scholar. Maybe I'm the last member of that nearly extinct race. And maybe this is why at the start I connected so strongly with the box and its contents. Gentleman Scholar is just another name for my dilettante proclivities. Nowadays many academics and other high priests of professionalism look down their noses at amateurs, another reason to hate this century.

I discovered that the manuscript from the file sections of the box is an incomplete draft, pretty rough in some places, of an autobiography of Charles Sanders Peirce, 1839-1914. It bears the title, *His Glassy Essence*.

That was the first puzzle I solved: an understanding of that odd title and its literary nimbus. It's an allusion to[†] Shakespeare, *Measure for Measure*, act 2, scene 2:

> ISABELLA.   Could great men thunder
> As Jove himself does, Jove would ne'er be quiet,
> For every pelting, petty officer
> Would use his heaven for thunder;
> Nothing but thunder.—Merciful heaven!
> Thou rather with thy sharp and sulphurous bolt
> Splitt'st the unwedgeable and gnarled oak,
> Than the soft myrtle; but man, proud man,
> Drest in a little brief authority, —
> Most ignorant of what he's most assur'd
> His glassy essence,—like an angry ape,
> Plays such fantastic tricks before high heaven,
> As make the angels weep; who, with our spleens,
> Would all themselves laugh mortal.

Betsey says I shouldn't forget that in the play this is a speech by Isabella. Excellent suggestion. Moreover, it's helpful to know that the plot of the play appears to have been taken from Whetstone's play of 1578 entitled "The right excellent Historye of Promos and Cassandra"; here is the hook of that work, taken from Whetstone's[†] Argument:

> In the cyttie of Julio (sometimes vnder the dominion of Coruinus Kinge of Hungarie and Boemia) there was a law, that what man so euer committed adultery should lose his head, and the woman offender should weare some disguised apparel during her life, to make her infamouslye noted. This seuere lawe, by the fauour of some mercifull magistrate, became little regarded vntill the time of Lord Promos auctority; who conuicting a yong gentleman named Andrugio of incontinency, condemned both him and his minion to the execution of this statute. Andrugio had a very vertuous and beawtiful gentlewoman to his sister, named Cassandra: Cassandra to enlarge her brothers life, submitted an humble petition to the Lord Promos.

In Shakespeare's hands Cassandra becomes a more elaborated character, Isabella, and the play on the whole becomes more complex. A nineteenth-century critic described[†] it handsomely:

> In "Measure for Measure" Shakspeare was compelled, by the nature
> of the subject, to make his poetry more familiar with criminal justice

than is usual with him. All kinds of proceedings connected with the subject, all sorts of active or passive persons, pass in review before us: the hypocritical Lord Deputy, the compassionate Provost, and the hard-hearted Hangman, a young man of quality who is to suffer for the seduction of his mistress before marriage, loose wretches brought in by the police, nay, even a hardened criminal, whom even the preparations for his execution cannot awaken out of his callousness. But yet, notwithstanding this agitating truthfulness, how tender and mild is the pervading tone of the picture! The piece takes improperly its name from punishment; the true significance of the whole is the triumph of mercy over strict justice; no man being himself so free from errors as to be entitled to deal it out to his equals. The most beautiful embellishment of the composition is the character of Isabella, who, on the point of taking the veil, is yet prevailed upon by sisterly affection to tread again the perplexing ways of the world, while, amid the general corruption, the heavenly purity of her mind is not even stained with one unholy thought: in the humble robes of the novice she is a very angel of light.

My solution was complete when I discovered that "glassy" in Shakespearean English meant "mirror-like." Also, I noted in speeches by several Shakespearean characters that mirrors often appeared as literary images for self-study or self-awareness. I also presumed that "His" was meant as Peirce's self-reference but was perhaps also meant to convey that he was but a token instance of the more general type we might name as human nature.

To come right to the point, then, the manuscript in the box should be published. You'll see why as you read it. I couldn't begin to tell you the reasons in just a few words, other than to say that Peirce was a great man in many ways, yet a mystery-man few of us have known. The manuscript is incomplete and sometimes disconnected as it stands. So I resolved to intervene from time to time—to fill in the gaps, or to provide background information. You should have no trouble discovering which piece of writing you have before you, Peirce or me: Louis E. "Ike" Eisenstaat. If Peirce's autobiographical words are rolling along in a connected manner, I'll stay out of the way. But if the passage is broken up, or if something needs explaining, I'll enter the conversation. I'm going to avoid being formal. The photos and illustrations from the box, obviously intended to accompany the autobiography, will be inserted in places that seem agreeable to my reason.

I don't want any credit for this effort. I think of my role as that of mediator, a person who stands in the background usually, whose function is to make connections and to lead forth into your attention Peirce's words and some details of his life and times. That makes me an educator in the ancient sense, for according to my copy of *The Century Dictionary*, which I routinely consult with pleasure and satisfaction, the Latin root of that word is *educare*, to lead forth, to draw out, what Socrates called the maieutic function.

After considering this quite a bit, I thought it would be appropriate and helpful to write about what happened just after Peirce's death. In the autobiography, he chose chapter headings obviously based upon lines from the book of Genesis, so from the same source I created what I hope is an appropriate heading for my introductory chapter.

I began research many years ago by visiting Milford with Betsey. There we rummaged through court house records and family attics, spoke to some persons still living who had known the Peirces, dug through some "morgue" files in the local newspaper to find some obituaries, and naturally scouted his house, which is now owned by the Park Service, complete with a historical plaque in front placed by the admiring Milfordites.

CHARLES S. PEIRCE
The noted philosopher, logician, scientist
and founder of pragmatism
lived in this house from 1887 until his death in 1914.
America's most original philosopher and greatest logician,
a great part of his work was written here.

I'll begin by showing you some of those things we discovered on that trip.

I detected a curious fact in reading these obituaries. Maybe you'll agree that the significance of a life often becomes fully clear only after it has ended. Let me explain. Herbert Spencer, the Victorian evolutionist, was known by almost everyone at the time, but no one has any interest in him today. Until recently, similar remarks were made about Josiah Royce. Peirce's case reverses that pattern. So gaining an understanding of his persona seems to require us to discover how his significance began growing shortly after he passed on. There's another reason for starting this way. It tells, as I tracked it down, why his significance is steadily increasing, which explains his greatness and indirectly why you need to read what he had to say in the handwritten papers from the box.

This is a curious tale, one I have pondered. At times it's exalting; other times it's tragic. Be patient. *Ænigma Bostoniensis evolvitur*, but it unfolds slowly. Stay with me. Betsey says I've got to get it out of my system. She claims I have become obsessed by Charley Peirce's box of papers. If she is right, I have lost my amateur standing and have to get it back. The only way I can see is the direct route, working straight through the problem, then watching quietly as it falls away from me as a devolved† sign. And it's obvious I need your help. Dis-obsession can't succeed without an honest witness.

Boston, 10 September 1996

2

For Signs and for Seasons

ANCHORET, ANCHORITE: In the classification of religious ascetics, *monks* are those who adopt a secluded habit of life, but dwell more or less in communities; *hermits*, or *eremites*, those who withdraw to desert places, but do not deny themselves shelter or occupation; and *anchorets*, those most excessive in their austerities, who choose the most absolute solitude, and subject themselves to the greatest privations.

The Century Dictionary and Cyclopedia

Estate of Charles S. Peirce, Deceased

Township of Milford (
County of Pike (
Commonwealth of Pennsylvania (

And now, January 5th, 1915, a paper writing purporting to be the last Will and Testament† of Charles S. Peirce, deceased, is presented for probate as follows:

WILL

Know all men by these presents that I, Charles Sanders Peirce, known as a logician and man of science and at present residing on the Arisbe estate, formerly Quicktown, in the township of Westfall, County of Pike, in the State of Pennsylvania, being of sound mind and memory, do hereby make this my last will and testament. I order and direct that all debts which the courts would enforce the payment of be paid. To my wife Juliette Peirce I give and devise the whole of my property without exception; but in case she should die before I do, I give all to the eldest son of my friend professor William James, the psychologist of renown, now living at 95 Irving Street Cambridge Mass.

I hereby revoke and annul all last wills heretofore made by me. I appoint C. W. Bull of Milford Pike County Pennsylvania, attorney at law, my executor or in case of his not being able to serve I appoint his son now district attorney or lately so.

In witness whereof I, the above named testator hereunto set my hand and seal this eleventh day of September in the year A.D. 1907.

Charles S. Peirce

This one may find in the Register of Wills in the Pike County Courthouse, just as Betsey and I did during a trip to Milford years ago. He had died at 9:30 o'clock Sunday evening on April 19, 1914, at his home near Milford after a long illness of cancer.

His younger sister in Cambridge, Helen Ellis, set it down a few days later in her weekly diary, just after returning from a trip to Washington, D.C.:

Charley dear[†] suffering creature died this evening and I knew not that he was sick. Son Francis saw on the public bulletin board death of C. S. S. Peirce in Milford—the first news we got of it. He had cancer! A rainy day. I stay home with my heart in my mouth.

Helen promptly sent a telegram, answer prepaid, to Juliette expressing shock at the news, inquiring about funeral plans, and offering burial in her father's lot in Cambridge. No answer. Two more telegrams. No answer.

From the Lenox Hotel in Washington, D.C., his younger brother, Herbert Henry Davis Peirce, contacted Helen on the twenty-first.

Dearest little[†] sister: You ask me to wire news as to Charley's death—I have none except what comes to me through Harry Davis in the N.Y. Herald of which I send you a copy.

The news comes as I always expected it would through newspaper sources and too late for me to get to Milford. I could be of no possible use and any meeting with that woman would result in an exchange of disagreeable expressions if we spoke at all or else in some other manner of abuses on her part of us all. I prefer to think of Charley without all this side of his vicissitudes and handicaps to the great career he ought to have had. How it came that he died of cancer is one of those mysteries beyond my comprehension. I never heard of any of our family having had it. Perhaps the poisoned atmosphere of that vile creature may have engendered it. Let us hope that he did not suffer. It is for us to remember all Charley's native sweetness and great ability which has been wasted by the alliance he formed with that vampire who has finally sucked his last drop of life's blood leaving of that life which had so great promise little but the memory of what it might have been.

Of the sweetness of his nature and his affectionate impulses you and I almost alone can have any very close associations. Some few perhaps remain.

It is not dearest sister my shrinking from meeting his widow that deters me from going to Milford. There is nothing I could do for him and I am far from having got rid of my winter's illness. Then too to sully the sanctity of death by contact with and no doubt vituperation from that creature would be sordid and useless.

Berts

With Betsey's help and a visit to the National Archives, I tracked down Herbert Peirce. He had been a pretty important man in the United States

2. *Herbert Henry Davis Peirce*
"I tracked down Herbert Peirce"
Tuttle Collection, Institute for Studies in Pragmaticism
By Permission, Harvard University Archives

diplomatic service. Here's a fast overview of his resumé. By 1914[†] he had served eighteen years. His first major position came in 1894 when President Cleveland appointed him as Secretary of Legation of the United States in Russia. The legation was raised to an Embassy in 1898, and he was made its First Secretary. In 1901 President Roosevelt appointed him third assistant secretary of state, serving for five years. During that time he was responsible for overseeing several important state visits to Washington: those of Prince Henry of Prussia, the Crown Prince of Siam, Prince Fushimi of Japan, and Prince Tsu of China. During the negotiations between Russia and Japan in Portsmouth, New Hampshire, he was in charge of the principal figures and aided materially in the eventual peace treaty that ended the Russo-Japanese War in 1905. In 1906 he was appointed envoy extraordinary and minister plenipotentiary to Norway, the top spot in the U.S. Embassy, serving until 1911. By 1914 he was doing somewhat lesser jobs around Washington. In 1881 he married Helen Nelson, daughter of Horatio Jose—quite a wealthy man—but unfortunately by 1914 Herbert and Helen had done up things so well abroad that they had consumed their comfortable fortune. Senator Henry Cabot Lodge, a kinsman of the Peirce family, was a consistent sponsor and mentor; there were probably others as well.

The *New York Herald* of April 21, 1914 did carry an obituary. It was definitely provided by[†] Juliette, but probably spiced up a bit by an editor.

MR. CHARLES S. S. PEIRCE, NOTED LOGICIAN AND PHILOSOPHER, DIES [†]

HAD LIVED TWENTY-SEVEN YEARS AS A RECLUSE IN A SMALL CABIN IN THE MOUNTAINS IN ORDER TO PURSUE HIS STUDIES WAS SEVENTY-FOUR YEARS OLD

Special Dispatch to the Herald
Milford, Pa., Monday

Mr. Charles Santiago Sanders Peirce, noted logician, mathematician and philosopher, died late Sunday night in the quaint little cabin in the mountains near here where he had been in seclusion for twenty-seven years to pursue his studies. He had been ill of cancer a long time. He was seventy-four years old.

His only companion was his second wife, who was Juliette Froissy, descendant of a noted French family, who shared his seclusion and his work. His first wife, Mrs. Melusina Fay Peirce, who lives in Chicago, is a noted organizer of Women's societies.

Following his retirement to his cabin here in Pike County his seclusion was broken only by infrequent journeys he made to lecture at Harvard on logic or to attend conferences of scholars interested in similar studies.

Mr. Peirce had gathered in his cabin what is believed to be one of the most complete private reference libraries upon the subject in which he was interested of any in the world. In his library he worked, aided by Mrs. Peirce, from dawn until dark, writing many scientific publications and contributing to several of the best known encyclopædias.

He was the author of "Photometric Researches," and also numerous articles upon logic, history of science, metaphysics, psychology, mathematics, gravitation, astronomy, map projections, chemistry and the cataloguing of libraries. He edited many of the noted works of his father, the late Professor Benjamin Peirce, of Harvard, a leading mathematician. "Pragmatism" was the name he gave to certain higher philosophical principles which he formulated.

Mr. Peirce, who was born in Cambridge, Mass. was a cousin of United States Senator Lodge and his mother was a daughter of the late United States Senator Mills. He was a brother of Mr. Herbert Henry Davis Peirce, a United States diplomatist, who represented this country in the peace deliberations of Russia and Japan at Portsmouth, N.H., and who was the then Third Assistant Secretary of State.

Some years later Benjamin Peirce Ellis, Helen's son, remembered[†] that he and his wife Bessie were the only members of the Peirce family who attended memorial services in Milford, and that Herbert had asked Ben to urge an autopsy upon the authorities, which Madame Peirce violently opposed.

Someday I may use that insinuation in the plot of a detective novel: brother suspects foul play, requests autopsy, widow refuses. But none of the evidence I have sifted suggests any such dastardly deed in this case.

Young Ben also recalled his anger with the way the popular press had handled his uncle's obituary, as his notes show.

Prof. Peirce dead in a mountain cabin, etc. He was never a "Professor," and this was in no respect a mountain cabin. He owned considerable acreage. The house was large and had numerous rooms (15 to 20) some unfinished. He added to it from time to time when he had the means, or more often when he had not the means, but could get it done. He appeared to be devoid of the ordinary common variety of "Business Logic" although his mental attainments and knowledge were vast and his especial field was "Logic." His house was well filled with many things (besides his library) and what became of them can be only known to the Harpies of Pike's County headed by Ex Governor Pinchot. His writings came into the hands of the Philosophical Dept. of Harvard by fair means, and by foul. He loved and hated, and quarrelled with almost everyone he came in contact with, wives, relatives, and associates.

I'm afraid young Ben was wrong about Charley never having been a Professor. That title was routinely conferred upon persons holding a high-level scientific position in the federal government. It was appropriately used in that sense for Peirce because of his standing near the top of the Coast Survey scientific hierarchy and because of his role as a member of the National Academy of Sciences. Indeed, Peirce had held several positions in academic and scientific circles, any one of which would have given him that appellation in the non-honorific sense, which is what I have in mind here. These thoughts led me to wonder just how much of Ben Ellis's other remarks were accurate or were hearsay.

Juliette had his body† embalmed and placed in his favorite room until all his friends and relatives could be notified. She wanted him cremated, and the nearest place where that could be done was Jersey City. To her friend Mrs. William James she confided† in a note:

> There is a chapel connected with the place where they hold service before the cremation. I am not able to decide on the date of the cremation service. Will telegraph you as soon as all arrangements are complete. In the meantime could you immediately notify his friends and relatives in Boston or in Cambridge for I have no address of them, so that they may have all opportunity, if they desire, to gaze for the last time upon his dear face.

News of his death quickly reached Paul Carus, editor of *The Monist*, a leading philosophical and religious journal in which a number of his best essays had appeared. Carus promptly requested† Judge Francis C. Russell in nearby Chicago, one of Charley's few disciples, to prepare an obituary for the next issue, and urged:

> Do not forget to mention his controversy with me in the first volume, which I intend to republish as it stands. I also intend to publish his logical papers but you had better not speak about them because I do not yet know how to bring them out and when.

Russell did act quickly to produce a tribute that appeared quite promptly—in the July issue. Excerpts from it give us some useful clues.

Concerning† genius, its advent, discovery and nurture, history informs us that with rare exceptions its worldly case is one of the utmost austerity. On reflection this appears not at all strange. *Pro re nata*, genius issues as an outlaw. It breaks over and through the accustomed rules and conceptions to the confusion and perplexity of a world otherwise comfortable in conventions regarded by it as settled possessions. Hence it is unwelcome. Hence the futility of all extant provisions in its favor. Had any Nobel Foundation been in existence in 1841, would any of its benefits find its way to Hermann Grassmann? Not in a thousand years. His case is typical of the general case of genius. Neglect and poverty are its portion in life. Then afterwards lapse of time reveals to a stupid, jealous and oftentimes spiteful world that it has conspired for the suffocation of a divine messenger.

In the late sixties the distinguished Prof. Benjamin Peirce of Harvard, lecturing before the Boston "Radical Club" on "The Impossible in Mathematics," spoke of his son Charles and of his expectations that the latter would develop and fertilize the vistas he had been able only to glimpse. On April 19, 1914, after at least a half century of assiduous probings into the most recondite and the most consequential of all human concerns, in a mountain hut overlooking the serene Delaware, in privation and obscurity, in pain and forsakenness, that son, Charles S. Peirce, left this world and left also a volume of product the eminent value of which will sooner or later be discovered, perhaps only after it has been rediscovered. For his issues have so far anticipated the ordinary scope of even professional intellectual exercise that most of them are still only in manuscript. Publishers want "best sellers." At least they want sellers that will pay the expenses of publication, and buyers of printing that calls for laborious mental application are scarce. Let me here with the utmost solicitude beg all to whom it falls to handle his books and papers to beware how they venture to cast away any script left by him.

Is this panegyric unwarranted? If so, then why should Professor James in his *Varieties of Religious Experience* call Mr. Peirce "our great American† philosopher"? Why should Professor Schröder base his great work "Exact Logic" on the prior work of Mr. Peirce? Why should the editors of the great *Century Dictionary* employ Mr. Peirce to write so many of its logical, mathematical and scientific definitions? Why should the editors of Baldwin's Dictionary make a similar draft? Why should the editors of *The New York Evening Post* and of *The Nation* for years refer their books of serious import to Mr. Peirce for examination and review? Why should Dr. Carus recognize in Mr. Peirce a foeman worthy of his steel on the fundamental problem† of necessity?

I have to admit that these comments hit me hard, for I realized that here was a prophetic voice from the past warning me about the manuscripts I now had in MY hand. When I first read this, I resolved on the spot that I would avoid suffocating any divine messengers. That experience had an uplifting effect on my principles of tolerance.

Helen despaired of having her telegrams answered, so on the twenty-third of April, she wrote a long letter to Juliette.

> I am trying to be patient† waiting for my answer to the telegram I sent you. What a terrible time you must have had. I thoroughly appreciate what you are suffering now—Poor child! I cannot go to the funeral and I have just received a telegram from Herbert and he says he cannot go. He has been very ill with pneumonia and the doctors say he ought not to go. I am too old nowadays to expose myself. I ask you in my message the day and hour of your service in Jersey City and what are your further plans. Herbert and I think it would be the best to have his ashes interred in father's lot in the Cambridge Cemetery and then together we could have a stone erected to his memory like the one we have put there for James. Does this seem nice to you? We very much hope it will. Ben could attend to the ashes being brought on. I think you have done just right in the arrangements you have made as Mrs. James tells me.

On the same day from Washington, D.C., Mrs. Henry Cabot Lodge conveyed to Helen† how her household had also acquired knowledge of Charley's death through the newspapers and of her sadness in thinking of all his wonderful gifts and talents wasted, of his loneliness and isolation during his later years. She expressed a wish that he had not suffered. And she fondly remembered Helen's visit with them a few days earlier.

Two days later, writing from Milford, Juliette unburdened herself to her friend Mrs. William† James. She expressed her love and gratitude to the James family, then lamented, "I am so broken down that I am unfit even to come to your loving sheltering arms."

She reported that arrangements had been completed for a brief service at her house at 3 P.M. on Monday the twenty-seventh of April:

> And then his dear remains accompanied by myself and the Episcopal minister that were much in touch with him, will leave here Tuesday morning at 10:28 a.m. for Jersey City and the service at the chapel there previous to the cremation will take place at 2 p.m.

The only known impression of the services at the Peirce house is recorded in a long letter from Ben Ellis to his mother Helen, writing from an inn called The Crissman House in Milford on the evening of the twenty-seventh.

I don't think† this is the best hotel in Milford altho it says it is. The driver brought us here and here we stay until tomorrow morning when we start for Jersey City in company with Uncle Charley's body, the undertaker, Rev. Mr. Darby an Episcopalian Clergyman and Juliette. Everything has happened very much as we both expected it would except that it will probably cost more than we expected. Uncle Charley's house is about 2 miles from the town here on the road from Port Jervis. We could not take the regular stage because we wanted to get some flowers which turned out well I think and we left them with your card (or rather mine with your name on it) on our way here. Then we drove back to the house again at 3. The house is by no means a cabin. It is rather upset being in the process of repair—rather had been as the work had been stopped by the illness. The service was simple and well done by the young man Darby referred to—who seems a good man with a high regard for Uncle Charley—and this by the way was one thing which could not fail to impress one—the high regard everyone seems to feel and the fine way the stage drivers and everyone you meet speak of him. There were a few neighbors in the outer parlor. Juliette, Bessie and I and the minister's wife were in the other room with Uncle Charley's body. Uncle Charley looked to me more than he ever did like Grandpa Peirce. After this service Bessie and I stayed and talked to Juliette for some time and went all over the house. The cause of Uncle Charley's death was cancer of the kidney or intestines which Juliette says she did not know was the trouble until a week or so before he died. I gather that the doctor did not tell her earlier (or when he suspected it) because his case was past relief. She certainly looks much thinner than she ever did—and I have not the least doubt that she was faithful and nursed him well. The country about here is very beautiful. Uncle Charley's house is well situated at the foot of a high hill or mountain commanding a fine view across the Delaware Valley. There appear to be about 60 acres of land with the house and an additional lot of wood land of 100 acres—the house is interesting and Bessie and I were interested in it and what Juliette had to say about it.

Ben

Receiving Ben's letter, Helen noted† in her diary that he had left his Bessie in Milford to care for Juliette for a few days. She further remarked about Ben's account of the crematory, after his arrival home, that it was very sad—in fact the whole thing most depressing. Helen had written Juliette again on the twenty-seventh, expressing hope that Bessie's presence would be helpful and including a letter she had received from Sally Rice, a friend of Charley from earlier days.

> I could hardly bear[†] to see Charley's death in the paper—it swept so much before me. Those happy days in Cambridge—and every year so many one after another going away and leaving a few with only sadness before them.
>
> Charley was such a remarkable person—that you could never think of him—except to wonder at his gifts and charm. He came with his wife to dine with us when he was last in Boston and I remember how I fell—as I always did—under the spell of his every word. How empty the world must seem to his wife with so much taken out of it and to you too who will never cease to miss him—and never cease to think of him as the great man he was.

A similar note came to Juliette from Mary Huntington in Boston, Charley's cousin:

> It is terribly hard[†] and especially so in your case as you and Charley were so much alone and so much to each other. You were truly privileged to have had such a delightful and brilliant mind and nature so near to you and in such intimate communion. When I was a child I used to enjoy my games with him more than I can say. He was so inventive and original and afterwards as I could appreciate his genius more and more he was always a most interesting and stimulating companion.

On the thirtieth, a former student from his days as lecturer in logic at the Johns Hopkins University, Fabian Franklin, in a column in *The Nation*[†] headed THE LONELY HEIGHTS OF SCIENCE, presented some thoughts about Peirce and G. W. Hill, the mathematician who had also died a few days before. While noticing that both men deliberately sought solitude to pursue their work, Franklin spoke of the remoteness of the labors of such men from the ordinary interests of mankind, of the fundamental importance of their efforts, and asked why Americans in general continued to remain unaware of the greatness of some of their fellow citizens. As a focusing example, he asked: How many Americans knew the name of Willard Gibbs? How many persons in New Haven—how many Yale students even—were aware that this modest scholar was one of the world's leaders in a great field of scientific thought?

Then Franklin added these remarks about Charley.

> It is something of a coincidence that within the few days since the death of Dr. Hill, another American man of genius has been

taken away who, different in almost every possible way from Hill, was like him in that his life had for many years been passed in extreme seclusion. A man at once of extraordinary acumen and originality, and of a phenomenal range of intellectual interests, there was in Charles S. Peirce a vein of the erratic, perhaps one may say the unstable, which seems to account for his achievements having fallen far short of what might have been expected of his unquestionably splendid powers. Even as it is, however, he left his mark on at least two branches of the intellectual activity of the age. In that modern development of the science of reasoning which is usually designated by the name of Symbolic Logic, his work well deserves to be called *bahnbrechend;* the leading German writer on the subject, Ernst Schröder, makes it the foundation of his extensive treatise. And it is from Peirce that William James derived the name "Pragmatism," and the doctrine for which that name stands in James's work; though in the interest of accuracy, it is necessary to add that Peirce repudiated James's development of his seminal idea. But the concrete fruits of Peirce's labors, many as are the fields in which he worked, are small in comparison with what those who came into contact with him could not but feel would have fallen into his hands if he had but possessed that something—constancy, balance, or whatever it may be—which nature seems to have denied him.

That there might be—that there has been in other times and other countries—an atmosphere more genial and friendly even for those strange and lofty heights in which dwells the mathematician or the abstract philosopher, we have already intimated. But these almost self-condemned exiles from "the kindly race of men" are not the only scholars who suffer from an intellectual isolation that is deplorable, and to the nature and consequences of which we seldom or never give attention. That free-masonry of the intellect which has played an inestimable part in the higher culture of Europe is almost wholly absent, as yet, in our university circles.

Herbert contacted[†] Helen in late April or early May to ask for help in getting a copy of the *Harvard Alumni Bulletin* in which an obituary was scheduled to appear. Herbert also commented:

I quite appreciate the importance of C's library being kept intact and for my own part I am strongly of the opinion that it should be sold to some learned society for the benefit of his widow but none of us can influence what course she may decide to do about this. As to his writings, which also belong of right to her, these should also be cared for with particular respect as probably important contributions to science and consequently entrusted to some body like the National Academy. But less now than ever, since she not only did not notify me of C's death but ignored my telegram asking when the funeral was to be, can I or will I meddle with affairs under her control. At the same time I beg that neither Ben nor you should be influenced by my peculiar and enforced attitude toward J. and I want you to consider that I am most deeply and affectionately solicitous regarding Charley's reputation, willing and anxious to do all in my power to communicate with that woman about whom I only know more than anyone outside of Charley's relations (and this is far more than any person now living knows). It is because of this that she dared write me the insolent letter she did. If dire need required I should tell you more but let the dead past bury its dead.

George Becker, of the U.S. Geological Survey, and a friend of Charley, wrote the obituary for the *Bulletin* which, after the urging of a number of friends and family, appeared in the issue for† 27 May. It mentioned several themes previously heard, but struck a few extra chords worthy of attention.

It would be difficult† to bring home to the average reader of American periodicals a due sense of the loss sustained by the community on April 19 in the death of Charles Peirce at the age of 75, for his work was done in the least popular realms of knowledge: Logic, mathematics, metaphysics and physics. To the worshipers of the Golden Calf his name is meaningless, but none the less he has added to the sum of human knowledge and to the fecundity of human thought, leaving the world the wiser for his existence.

Charles himself also wrote a memoir of great originality on the algebra of logic, of which the purpose is to apply the infallible mechanism of mathematics to the elucidation of logical relations, whencesoever these may be derived. Peirce was not the first to make such an attempt, but is said to have attained a far greater measure of success than his predecessors. On the whole, these memoirs and others which need not be mentioned here show that he was quite as able a mathematician as his father.

Not less important is his treatment in a series of papers, published during the last decade of the century, of the statistical method as applied to the nature of evolutionary processes depending upon the association of entities in large numbers. This method (which likewise underlies most of the very recent investigations into the properties of matter) is proving efficacious in philosophy in the hands of Professor Josiah Royce on the lines laid down by Peirce.

Genius Peirce indubitably had; he also had its eccentricities; they stood sadly in his way, diminished his intellectual output, and exposed him to privations. Though he could be very charming, he was so intensely individualistic that cooperation was for him almost an impossibility, he could not "get along" with associates, and as he grew older, ill-health aggravated his peculiarities. To his friends these were an inconvenience, speedily forgotten; to himself they were a misfortune, and this is the only considerable reason for regretting them or referring to them; they deprived him of the popularity, prosperity, and honors to which his great achievements would have entitled him.

Peirce was for many years a member of the National Academy of Sciences. His official biography will be prepared by a colleague eminently fitted for that difficult task, Josiah Royce.

Royce, Alford Professor of Natural Religion, Moral Philosophy and Civil Polity in the Department of Philosophy and Psychology at Harvard, who survived Charley by only two years, never finished a biography. An official National Academy of Sciences biography also never appeared.

In early May, Herbert and Helen collaborated[†] to prepare a notice that appeared in the *Boston Evening Transcript* for May 16; its perspective[†] is noteworthy.

SOME APPRECIATION OF A HARVARD PHILOSOPHER
FIRST AMONG AMERICAN PRAGMATISTS
WHO RECENTLY DIED IN SECLUDED RETIREMENT

Charles Sanders Peirce, second son of the late Benjamin Peirce, Perkins professor of Astronomy and Mathematics at Harvard University for forty years, and of his wife, Sarah Hunt Mills, who died at his home in Milford, Pa., on April 19 last, in his seventy-fifth year, was born in September, 1839, of a family eminent in scientific pursuits and in the higher branches of education. Beginning with Benjamin Peirce, Sr., for several years librarian of Harvard, the sum of the services of the Peirce family in that seat of learning, including that of his son Benjamin and his grandson James Mills Peirce, numbered over one hundred years.

Charles Peirce, from his youth to the end of his life, exhibited in a marked degree the family trait of mathematical ability as well as the allied sciences, his mind finally centering itself upon logic and philosophy, but never forsaking mathematical research.

Even in childhood Dr. Peirce exhibited remarkable qualities of mind and a profound love of study and research, pursued, however in his own way and by original methods. He appeared to have acquired the art of reading and writing by himself without the usual course of instruction. As a child he was forever digging into encyclopedias and other books in search of knowledge upon abstruse subjects, while discussions with his learned father upon profound questions of science, especially higher mathematics and philosophy, were common matters of astonishment, not only to his brothers and sister, but to his parents as well.

Charles however was no prig or pedant. His mirthful, contagious laugh, his keen sense of humor and ready wit made him a bright and ever welcome companion in all gatherings. He was always capable of holding his own with unconscious ease whether among his elders or with simple unpretentiousness joining in the sports of the youngest and smallest. His own choice was for intellectual games, especially chess, of which he early became a master.

Mr. Peirce was mainly fitted for college at the Cambridge High School, with one term, prior to the entrance examination, at the famous school of Mr. Epes Sargent Dixwell, in Boston. He was graduated from Harvard in 1859, among the youngest of his class, and entered the Lawrence Scientific School where he took the highest honors for research work in chemistry, which attracted the attention of some of the great German universities as valuable contributions to science. Pure mathematics, astronomy and logic, however, early attracted Peirce more deeply than the more practical pursuit which he then abandoned, and devoted himself to astronomy, passing long nights at the Harvard observatory, and, later, to pendulum observations and computations for determining the earth's density. His research regarding it was noted with warm praise by the French Academy and by other European scientists.

It was during this period of Peirce's practical work in the field of physics, that he published his book on "Photometric Research" besides many articles on the history of science, metaphysics, psychology, gravitation, chemistry, map projection and astronomy. He also edited his father's work on "Linear Associative Algebra," a mathematical contribution which was contemporaneously considered to ascend so far into the realm of pure mathematics as to make it improbable that it could ever find a reading public sufficient to warrant further publication than the one hundred lithographed copies which constituted the original edition. At this time also he was employed by the publishers of the Century Dictionary to prepare the greater part of the scientific definitions for that great lexicon.

Research in the domain of his chosen subject, logic, and the art of reasoning, had long been drawing Peirce away from the more practical and immediately profitable paths of science. He had already formulated and given to the world the principle of logic which he was first among Americans to call "Pragmatism" and which the late Professor William James of Harvard afterward amplified and carried to higher development. In 1887 Mr. Peirce, feeling the burden and friction of the busily active world too distracting for the pursuit of his studies, retired to the place he bought in Pike County, Pennsylvania, where, surrounded by his voluminous library, he immersed himself in the sea of philosophic thought from which he rarely emerged, living in Milford the life of a recluse and an anchorite.

During the pursuit of his studies this profound thinker contracted a gnawing and a progressing malady which greatly impaired the regular continuity of his labors defeating the full fruition of the brilliant promise of his life. His pursuits could not win for him popular applause, but to those who knew him well he gave a light which can never fade.

Perhaps the most interesting of all these obituary notices appeared two days before in *The Nation*, headed THE PASSING OF A MASTER MIND. It was written by his former student, Joseph Jastrow, then professor of psychology at the University of Wisconsin in Madison, subsequently the ninth president of the American Psychological Association. Obviously Jastrow was among "those who knew him well."

I desire to record† a word of tribute to one of the master minds of America. The recent death of Charles S. Peirce removes an heroic figure from the field of American learning. Living for the most part in retirement, he was known to a relatively small circle. Yet where known, his name was spoken with exalted respect; and his fame, critically appraised, placed him with the chosen few of any generation. How far he sought and failed to find the wider recognition that falls to those whose labors are in fields open to public approbation, how far he did not care to pursue the accredited steps to preferment and recognition, I cannot say. Yet this aspect of his career is significant.

My acquaintance with Mr. Peirce began in 1882 when I came as a graduate student to Johns Hopkins University. He was there lecturing on "The Algebra of Logic"—a subject which he in large measure established in this country. He had interested certain able students—all of them since distinguished in various fields—in his explorations into a broad domain of thought; and of this enterprise a volume of studies by himself and his pupils bears record. In those days there was gathered in Baltimore a group of scholars and productive intellectual workers that would have been exceptional in any scholarly community. Their names would suggest the notable contributions of American scholarship in their generation. Yet among them the impression of Mr. Peirce stands forth most prominently *primus inter pares*. The impression that I retain of his analyses of logical and philosophical problems is that of observing a plummet line descending through troubled waters foot by foot, sounding the depths, avoiding the weeds and the shoals, and reaching an undiscovered bottom; for the student many of the problems in a controversial sea seemed bottomless. It was not argument, but discovery.

It was Mr. Peirce who introduced me to the possibility of an experimental study of a psychological problem. He provided the problem, the instruments which I set up in my room, the method, and the mode of reaching the results; and these were printed over our joint[†] names. He also introduced me to the mode of attack upon larger psychological problems by methods of statistical inquiry. He gathered about him a group of five or six students and proposed a study of "great men." He drew up the questionnaire; we gathered and collated the results. The work was not finished; though I was permitted to publish one or two aspects of the material in brief papers. My personal indebtedness gave me the opportunity to gauge the measure of the man. Only one other produced upon me an equal impression of original greatness. I refer to William James. The two men may well be associated, for each held the other in high regard. Professor James recognized in Charles Peirce the true founder of Pragmatism, a way of thinking which James made popular, the significance of which he expounded. If, in addition, it be remembered that these logical, psychological, and philosophical pursuits were in a sense avocational, and that Mr. Peirce was for a long time actively connected with the Geodetic Survey, was a physicist and mathematician by profession, the scope of his attainments will be more truly perceived. In a sense he represents the American Helmholtz.

I do not know that Mr. Peirce ever held any academic position other than the lectureship for a few years at Johns Hopkins University. That his was the personal temperament that may well be called difficult may be admitted; such is the disposition of genius. It cannot but remain a sad reflection upon the organization of our academic interest that we find it difficult, or make it so, to provide places for exceptional men within the academic fold. Politically as educationally, we prefer the safe men to the brilliant men, and exact a versatile mediocrity of qualities that makes the individual organizable. All this has its proper place and is doubtless more or less inevitable, even sound; but the penalty paid for safety is too heavy, when it excludes the use of rarer gifts, the choice product of exceptional power of sustained thought. Of this lamentable lack of efficiency—to turn the sting of an abused word against itself—Mr. Peirce is not the only example. Other master minds knocked in vain at academic portals, and were refused as too elect. Or, more truly stated, the small group of their liberal-minded friends within the hallowed precincts failed to persuade the authorities to adjust methods to men. Certainly it remains true for all times that no more effective stimulus to promising young minds can be found than to give them the opportunity of contact with master minds in action. The service that a small group of such men can perform is too fine, too imponderable, to be measured; and likewise too intangible to impress its value upon the judgment of those with whom these issues commonly lie. Yet nothing would have shown better the greatness of a great University than to find a place in it for rare men like Charles S. Peirce. His memory invites not only the personal tribute, but is a reminder of our neglect of the true worth of genius.

"I wonder what Charley was like in his later years," said Betsey, probably with a clinical idea or two in mind. So I found just such an account written in 1954 by one of Charley's nephews, another son of his sister Helen:
Francis Ellis.

> My uncle James M. Peirce[†] never married and he lived in the
> house built by his father at 4 Kirkland place, Cambridge. It is very
> evident that life, in fact very existence, must have been a constant
> worry and problem for Uncle Charles and Juliette. On very rare
> occasions they would spend a few days with uncle James at 4
> Kirkland Place. And once or twice this happened when I was living
> with my uncle, as I often did while attending Cambridge schools.
> At such times I was able to see Charles, James, and Juliette together
> in friendly and cordial relationship—and it was then, and only
> then, that I was able to see and study and know my Uncle Charles.
> He was the sort of personality that demanded attention. His was a
> vivacious, commanding and sprightly nature.
>   Pictures of him that I have seen[†] do not do him full justice, as
> they cannot do more than hint at his animation, as I recall it. He
> was so alive and so alert and so full of color, that pictures are
> hardly more than drab reminders.
>   He was a fine figure[†] of a man—extremely awake at all times.
> He was, as I saw him, keen of wit and full of fun and amusement.
> He was constantly planning to do things. For instance, I can recall
> his proposal to compile an Arithmetic for the young student, with
> the object of making the subject full of wit and fun so that it would
> appeal as an enjoyment rather than a task. He would walk up and
> down my Uncle Jem's study smoking his long, thin, black
> Churchwarden pipe and expounding his theories. All of us would
> just sit and study the man and listen to his wisdom. He liked strong
> liquor, strong black coffee and smoked black pure perique in his
> pipe. I can recall his sharp high-pitched voice with a ring to it and a
> slight nasal twang. And there would be sitting apart little Juliette,
> wrapt in silent adoration and worship. She certainly was a constant,
> true and faithful companion.

Published Posthumously

Charles Peirce was dead. However, my researches showed me that his
ideas had been for several years inch by inch edging toward a life of their own.
Now this process continued and even accelerated. Working on this book has
made me an amateur philosopher, so let's get serious for a moment. I'm

tempted to speculate that in a certain sense his departure completely released those ideas to evolve and grow in stature and influence. Grandpa William Darbey developed a rather bold preaching style in his older days. I've heard disc-recordings of some of his homilies—made with his giant 1939 model 116 Philco console radio set, complete with phonograph and recording head. I'm attracted toward using his ecclesiastical tone to express my thought at this point:

> Sometimes God acts by killing persons.

I know that sounds terrible. But if you will look at it from a certain indirect angle, it won't be monstrous. If you think of that old line of scripture, "Not my will but thine be done," or of any number of other similar non-egotistical or unselfish remarks common in religion of all kinds, I think you'll see what I mean. Such thoughts one may also find in Buddhism or Taoism, or for that matter in the mind of Charles Peirce during the last decades of his life.

I began to see, almost from the beginning in working with the manuscript in the box, that one of my unavoidable responsibilities was to trace the postmortem rise of his thoughts in outline using materials that Betsey and I turned up in my amateur meanderings. That's because the release of his ideas upon the world is a vital part of the story of his life. Like Charley himself, this matter is complicated and a bit vague. It persists at this moment and is likely to do so for many more years. But we can touch the main features of its earlier history.

At the point now considered, the process began its new phase by early July of 1914. Under the leadership of William James, a number of persons some time ago had created a fund for the sustenance of Charles and Juliette, and Mrs. James had continued the project after William died in 1910. So it was natural that the question of what was to become of Charley's manuscripts and books reached the doorstep of the James household. Mrs. James developed a general strategy, which she presented to Juliette. It was simply to encourage Royce to work out a plan for proper care† of those important materials. The broad idea was well received. That is evident in a note from Juliette on the seventh of May† to Alice James, perhaps after Alice had recently visited Arisbe†—Arisbe was the name Peirce had given to his home in Milford:

> It gladens my heart to know that my dear husband's years of hard
> labor will find a place worthy of his talents. In regard to the
> manuscripts there is a great deal of it, and the library is intact. As
> soon as I am able, my Pastor a great friend of ours will assist me to
> catalogue the books. . . . I am delighted that Mr. Lowell is the head
> of the college, my dear husband and I have always greatly admired

him. If Mr. Eliot was still there, those manuscripts would never be heart of, on account of that long personal grudge he bore him. . . . I trust I may before long being able to expresse my deep gratitude to Prof. Royce whome my poor husband always mentionate to me as his dear friend.

This letter, by the way, as well as several others like it, has led me to believe that Madame Peirce had less than a masterful command of English, which may account for some of her problems. But I digress.

By late May, it appears that Mrs. James had been in contact with Joseph Jastrow, for his note of the twenty-second presented Juliette with a copy of his obituary letter to *The Nation*. He commented that among the expressions of sympathy and approval he had received was a letter from Mrs. James. His kindness was answered in early June by a message from Juliette relayed by her pastor, none other than Grandpa William† Darbey. Jastrow responded on the tenth:

In regard to the publication of the ms. it seems to me likely that Harvard University would be interested in the matter. I have reason to believe that Professor Royce would be the one who would naturally take charge of the matter. I have written to him concerning it. Naturally the rights in the ms. would be fully protected. I do not know enough of the nature of the work to say whether it would have a large appeal. . . . I am sending a note to Professor Royce and shall be very glad to cooperate with him in any way.

By early July, Jastrow had an answer from Grandpa Darbey, and responded to him† on the sixth:

Dear Mr. Darby: I have your letter and also a communication from Mr. Henry James Jr., son of William James, who has been suggested as the proper person to conduct the negotiations. Acting on this joint advice it seems necessary to proceed carefully in the matter. Professor Royce is away and is not likely to be accessible during the summer.

Joseph Jastrow

Jastrow remarked that the first step would be to give some notion of the nature and extent of the manuscript—its size, condition, readiness for publication—and then to consider whether it needed some particular care in view of immediate safe-keeping until it could be formally presented to the authorities of Harvard University. He then penned a prophetic sentence: "The procedure should be careful at the outset to avoid disappointment."

But Royce had not been inactive. Neither was the Harvard Librarian, William Lane, who had also written to Royce on the topic, perhaps at the suggestion of the James family. Royce responded to Lane on the eighth, in a long letter, important for its magisterial overview[†] of the situation.

> I suppose that you have in mind the fact that Mr. Charles Peirce (Harvard 1859) died recently at Milford, Pa., where he had been living a good many years his lonely life, and carrying on his extraordinary study. Mrs. James has taken a great interest in him and Mrs. Peirce of late years. The interest was partly humane, and partly founded on the relations which Mr. James during his life long since established with Peirce. Now that James is gone, I suppose that I am one of the principal admirers and, in a way, disciples of Peirce in this community. To say this is to make no vain boast, for Peirce's admirers and disciples are sadly few.
>
> Professor Jastrow of Madison, Wis., lately wrote an interesting letter about Charles Peirce, which was printed in the *Nation*. I enclose his letter, which I should be glad if you returned at your convenience, in order to give you some indication of the sort of interest that some of us are taking in the possible publication of the literary remains of Charles Peirce. He was, in some sense, almost our only really original logician in America. Certainly he accomplished such work as no other American has accomplished, and such as ought to live. He was incapable of finishing a large book. Masses of manuscript remain. They probably constitute a very considerable portion of the work on Logic which he planned and which for years was announced.
>
> I hope that it may be possible to edit the manuscript of the logic, as well as a good many of Peirce's other papers. Mr. Brett of Macmillan Company long ago expressed a willingness to publish Peirce's book on logic, if ever it was completed. I can no longer say whether Brett feels any such willingness at present. Of course he would do nothing unless a complete manuscript were furnished. Furthermore, I am not quite sure that the Macmillan Company or, for that matter, any commercial publishing firm would furnish the best means for putting Peirce's remains on proper record.
>
> I have thought a good deal about the question whether it would be possible to get the Syndics of our University Press interested in this matter. Of course, any appeal to the University Press, again, would have to depend on the shape into which the manuscripts could ultimately be got.
>
> As to editing the manuscripts themselves, that undertaking would have to be planned when all the materials are brought

together. Possibly a special effort will have to be made to get a fund for the publication in question. The manuscripts may prove to be in such a condition that expert work would be needed to get some of the papers referring to logical topics into shape for any kind of publication. I have in mind a possibility that, if I could ever get funds provided for the purpose, some of our younger logicians in this country could be obtained to do the work.

What under any circumstances I should be able to do some time in the matter of editorial work upon Peirce's papers, remains of course quite doubtful. At present I intend to prepare, if possible, a magazine article on Peirce. I may find it possible to edit for republication some of the older essays of Peirce which appeared long ago in the Journal of Speculative Philosophy.

In brief, here appears a large job for the future which somebody has to undertake. I have a certain responsibility for seeing as soon as I can that this job gets into good hands.

As Jastrow suggests in the enclosed letter, and as I have already suggested to Mrs. James and to Harry James, the great danger that fire or other accidents might destroy these precious papers still exists, and ought to be avoided by action taken as soon as possible. The "Mr. Darbie" whom Jastrow mentions, and who, I believe, is a clergyman of Milford, has written to me on Mrs. Peirce's behalf. I intend to propose to him, with your possible encouragement and advice, that all scientific manuscripts of Peirce, and possibly other papers of his, should be put on deposit for safe keeping in the Harvard Library. The arrangement under which the papers were deposited would, of course, have to have the approval of Mrs. Peirce. This, I suppose, could easily be obtained. The natural arrangement would be, as I also suppose, to leave the manuscripts permanently with the Library, where future editors, if such there be, may consult them under the authority of the Library. It is, of course, very unlikely that any commercial value could be attached to these manuscripts by anybody. I shall explain that aspect of the case in writing to Mrs. Peirce and Mr. Darbie.

My purpose in addressing this letter to you is, first, to ask whether at present the Library has control of any place where the manuscripts could be safely deposited, without causing too much trouble to its officers. If it proves necessary to wait until we get into our new quarters, I should, of course, be glad so to advise Mrs. Peirce. But she is aged; Milford is an insecure place; and I should be glad if it were possible to advise sending the manuscripts to any address that you choose in Harvard University as soon as possible. Second, I desire to ask whether, in your opinion, it would be possible and advisable for the Library, at any time, to take such charge of the manuscripts as I have now indicated, and to give due official attention to such plans for editorship and publication as may later come to light.

Josiah Royce

Loyal to his promise, and continuing his masterful grasp of the issues, on the same day, Royce dispatched the following[†] to Grandpa William in Milford, obviously for transmittal to Mrs. Peirce. By the way, it looks like these folks never learned to spell Grandpa Darbey's name correctly.

Dear Mr. Darbie: It would certainly seem to me advisable that Mr. Peirce's manuscripts should be placed as soon as possible in the hands of some impartial and official trustee who should be willing to act in the future with the utmost careful regard for Mrs. Peirce's rights and wishes. Such a trustee, I should suppose, would be the Harvard Library, or perhaps its librarian, Mr. Lane. The papers are precious, but in Milford they are subject to a great variety of conceivable accidents,—fire, for instance. If our library here at Harvard consents to take charge of them, with a full understanding of Mrs. Peirce's rights and of the importance of the undertaking, I believe that whatever plans for the publication of these literary remains later prove desirable, could be carried out under the best conditions.

If the papers are thus once deposited at the Harvard Library, I should be glad to do what I could, both in the way of editing or aiding in editing the manuscripts, and in the way of finding other and perhaps more effective editors for the purpose. Of course you and Mrs. Peirce both understand that scientific manuscripts are not likely to have very much commercial value. Some of these materials may prove to be much more valuable for ordinary publication than others. Some of them, and perhaps the whole or the bulk of the proposed work on logic, may be accepted for publication by the Syndics of our University Press, to whom, if you and Mrs. Peirce consent, I should be glad at an early date to submit some proposal relating to the matter. I should also propose that the Librarian should have authority to make similar proposals. If, amongst Mr. Peirce's papers, there are some that would be likely to have a more popular interest—perhaps such as the one he published a few years ago in the Hibbert Journal, entitled "A Neglected Argument for the Existence[†] of God"—I am sure that those in charge of the manuscripts would be glad, with your approval, to make as advantageous an arrangement for publication of such more popular articles as may prove to be possible. And so far as I should advise further about the matter, I should always carefully consider whether any pecuniary return for the benefit of Mrs. Peirce could be obtained.

If you or Mrs. Peirce are able, either now or hereafter, to suggest any arrangement for publication that would promise any better returns than the arrangement which I am now proposing, I think that you should be free to take such of the manuscripts again at your pleasure.

While this is the arrangement that I suggest, I have at the moment no authority to speak on behalf of the Harvard Library. I have written to our Librarian, Mr. Lane, stating to him the nature of the case, telling him what I know of the nature of the manuscripts, and asking him whether, and on what conditions, the Library would be ready to receive such a deposit of the papers as I have just proposed.

If this plan meets with approval, I will write you again, as soon as I receive a reply from Mr. Lane.

I may say that, at one time, when a very considerable portion of the manuscript of Mr. Peirce's Logic was in William James's hands for consideration and advice, I read this portion, at James's request, and was very greatly impressed with the importance of the undertaking. I have very greatly regretted the unfinished condition in which the enterprise was left by Mr. Peirce's death. I shall regard it as one of my personal and professional interests to do whatever I can to get a hearing for Mr. Peirce, in so far as he has not already obtained that hearing for himself. I hope to write some article, probably for a magazine, in which I summarize my own sense of indebtedness to the greatest logician America has produced. I have already put on record in various ways and places my acknowledgement of Mr. Peirce's contributions. But I have much more to say on the subject, if I get the opportunity.

I need not say that I have consulted with Mrs. James and with Professor Jastrow about the matter. I desire to express my very deep sympathy for Mrs. Peirce, and my hearty wish to do whatever I can to meet her desires. I trust that she is in good health. I shall be very glad of an expression of anything further that you have in mind regarding what I can do for the memory and for the rights of Mr. Peirce.

Josiah Royce

A surviving annotation in Lane's hand shows his response to Royce's suggestions: "MSS can be received at any time and Harvard College Library the proper place for them. Library's responsibility should be confined to safe keeping and proper use. Editing should be in hands of a committee of Philosophy Department. Press ought to be inclined to publish."

If we stopped at this point, everything would seem to be in good shape. Mastermind dies, friends and family close ranks to publish his *meisterstück*. But Royce passed from the scene in 1916, and matters quickly became—how can I put it delicately?—became more complex.

A Pause for Reflection

When my studies had reached this point, I explained my findings to Betsey one weekend. She said, in her most professional tone, "Ike, you have several weird puzzles here, and you're going to have to face them without flinching."

When she takes that tone—which means, "Get a grip on it, bud, or your life will get out of hand!"—I know it's time to act with determination. So, a few days later we sat down at my desk and drew up a list of enigmas.

The one that attracted my attention right off had to do with his family. Why did his brother hate his wife? Well, the word "hate" seems too mild. And probably the converse of that question would also have to be asked. How come his world-famous and influential brother, who hobnobbed with kings and potentates, who married wealth, could tolerate Charley living in what appears (certainly by Herbert's lights) to have been an unfortunate condition? Same for Senator Lodge. Herbert even seriously suspected foul play in his brother's death! With all this strong sense of Charley's greatness, why wouldn't the brother or other family members get vigorous about helping the greatness get into motion? Was Charley unhelpable or merely unhelped? If Madame Peirce was such a "vile creature," why didn't Herbert do something about that too? And by the way, what kind of vile creature? Why was sister Helen so remote from Charley? She had just travelled from Cambridge to Washington and back, but she couldn't make the trip, shorter by half—and all but seven miles by train—to his funeral in Milford. And why weren't any of Charley's friends outside of Milford to be seen?

Perhaps the most ironic conundrum lies in the following facts. For reasons that apparently could only be darkly stated in public, the living Charles Peirce had not been permitted a place on the Harvard faculty, or any other, despite the fact that he earnestly and repeatedly searched for such a position. I remember instantly wanting to know why this condition existed—had he perpetrated some major sin or faux pas? But whatever led to that state of affairs, his literary estate was *immediately* sought by the leading member of the Harvard Department of Philosophy, assisted by a number of prominent associates, friends, and colleagues. This group, which from the start grew steadily in size, vigorously pressed to obtain and publish his manuscripts and perhaps to acquire his large personal library, certainly a praiseworthy activity. But what was so unthinkable about the living Peirce teaching and studying on a university campus, and had these persons or similar ones pressed with equal vigor to acquire the living man as a university colleague? It couldn't have been his ideas that were intolerable, for now they were being aggresively sought in a spirit of deep respect and admiration. Had there been equally enthusiastic efforts to bring Charley alive onto the faculty of Harvard or another respected academy? If not, why not?

What in his published and especially his unpublished written work was attracting the admiration and respect of these bright and famous persons? I knew by now that William James had admired Peirce's thinking for decades, and James was and is a fairly well-known figure, even outside academic circles. Josiah Royce is not a name familiar to most persons today. But at this time he was recognized as the leading philosophy professor in the United States, and certainly within the international community, a highly respected figure, even in ways connected with general issues of public interest and not just with topics of narrow professional concern. Peirce's ideas were appearing at this time prominently within Royce's works that were focusing on issues of broad[†] interest. Jastrow, another name not familiar to most persons today, became a leading psychologist, and if his letter to *The Nation* is recalled, he credited Peirce with some significant contributions to the development of experimental psychology in the United States. But these contributions are not mentioned in typical histories[†] of psychology. Why is that? Royce did go on to write his magazine article on Peirce. It, along with articles by John Dewey, Christine Ladd-Franklin, Joseph Jastrow, and Morris R. Cohen appeared in *The Journal of Philosophy, Psychology, and Scientific Methods* in December of 1916. Here is another list of persons with strong ability and considerable reputation.

For another thing, writers of obituaries described his logic as path-breaking, as being wonderfully original, as having powerful and far-reaching consequences. Why is little mention of Peirce found in books that deal with such matters[†] today? He was also described as the acknowledged founder of pragmatism, the distinctive native American style of thought. Why is Peirce's role and function and contribution in that movement, which is quite healthy today, sometimes minimized[†] or misunderstood? Even more generally stated, Peirce's ideas are barely known among citizens of our age, yet everyone has some understanding of pragmatism, and (without being aware of it) many of us in daily life use principles or results[†] he developed.

As I began to put my shoulder into it, I saw that we need not limit this discussion to evaluations by Peirce's contemporaries. Each of us likely respects the sagacity of at least one current thinker or writer. Two rather diverse figures come to my mind in this capacity; I'm grateful to have met both gentlemen, one in Washington and the other here in the Boston area.

The first is Walker Percy, whose favorite self-description was simply "writer." I describe him as the best philosophical novelist of the twentieth century. With his distinctive clear-eyed surgical style, he told me when I spoke with him in D.C. a few months before his death, "Sometimes I could genuflect before Peirce, and sometimes I could kick[†] his ass." In a more formal setting, in the eighteenth Jefferson Lecture sponsored by the National Endowment for the Humanities and delivered in Washington that year (it's something like the American version of a Nobel prize within the humanities), Percy leaned heavily upon some of Peirce's ideas that he regarded as fundamental for issues we face today. There he[†] reflected, "Most people have never heard of him, but they will." If these ideas are said to be vitally important by a present-day writer and thinker of Percy's high status, why are most citizens and even most academics unaware of them, in contrast to the way—for instance—that we are aware of relativity theory, or strict constructionism, or ad hominem argumentation, or trickle-down economics, or the dictatorship of the proletariat?

"I have one too!" I was on a roll, thinking out loud, when Betsey interjected with her favorite recent sage. "Since he died in 1947, I didn't have a chance to meet him, but I have always thought very highly of Alfred North Whitehead, not as a mathematician or logician, but as a philosopher that an educated person could read with insight and inspiration. Some of his more accessible works are widely admired within Nursing. So when his biography was completed in 1990, I read it. At the end of the second volume, in one of the appendices, there is a letter from Whitehead dated January 2, 1936. It is addressed to perhaps his principal disciple in North America. There he recorded this observation":

> My belief[†] is that the effective founders of the American Renaissance are Charles Peirce and William James. Of these men, W. J. is the analogue to Plato, and C. P. to Aristotle.

"Don't you think that's nifty, Lish?"

I did; and I thanked her, and waved as she strode off to another day in the clinic. By the way, she calls me "Lish" as a rather intimate pet name, rarely on public occasions—it's a fore-shortening of "Elisha." This usually happens when she is feeling good about herself. She always pronounces it in the Oklahoma dialect of American, which makes it more pleasing to me, as she well knows. It sounds like "li" in "lice" spliced onto the "sh" from "shoo." But back to my examples.

The second judge that comes to my mind is Hilary Putnam, a mathematician and logician and philosopher with qualifications and abilities parallel to those of Charley Peirce. Betsey and I were fortunate to have been in the first class that he taught at Harvard some years ago, after he had moved over from MIT. Recently, answering some of my questions in a letter, he spoke of the monumental contribution[†] of C. S. Peirce and added that he was the first American philosopher to be known by the entire world as a "great philosopher." Paradoxically, he may be better known outside the United States than at home. . . .

Peirce's achievements would take a short book to describe adequately. In philosophy, he founded the most distinctively American school of thought—Pragmatism. As the founder of pragmatism, he was the intellectual hero of both John Dewey and William James. He also created single handed the large discipline called Semeiotic—the study of the working of signs—a discipline which engages scholars all over the world. He was perhaps the first modern Historian of Science, and he was certainly one of the great founders of Mathematical Logic. He was, in truth, one of the rare thinkers who deserves the overworked title of "genius."

Harvard has published eight volumes of the *Collected Papers of Charles S. Peirce* (1931), and an international group of scholars is cooperating to produce an expanded edition (through Indiana University) which will include many papers not in the old Harvard Edition. Harvard University also hosted the International Peirce Congress in September, 1989, which attracted scholars from twenty-eight countries, including such luminaries as Umberto Eco, W. V. Quine, and Jürgen Habermas.

But Peirce's life is of more than scholarly interest; it was full of dramatic incidents as well as periods of almost unbearable suffering.

Suppose we take these evaluations seriously. Why, then, are Charley's ideas still only known to a few specialists in a couple of academic fields, when by all accounts they are relevant and vital in areas ranging from computing to mathematics to science to business management to engineering to literature to everyday life? If they have this range of relevance, why were his ideas not taken up? Or were they taken up, but not acknowledged? To put it bluntly, why is the representative citizen unaware of Charley Peirce?

You can see my obsession starting to form. I certainly could. I saw before me a yawning gap in our knowledge of American culture, speaking as an amateur anthropologist or historian. I could see his autobiography as providing us with a survey of that matter, especially if I could succeed in beefing it up and fleshing it out. I was game: dilettantes go where angels or professionals fear to tread. I have a hunch that we are going to find out more than just what happened to Charley Peirce. I think we can also hope to gain some insights about the nature of human life in the general sense, because Putnam's last remark is entirely on the mark—in fact, deadly, admirably accurate.

But I want momentarily to delay presenting the fruits of my efforts, acquired through the stabilizing guidance of Betsey Darbey. The project will be

aided if we can now ask, how did Royce's publishing plan work out ultimately? What happened to Peirce's extensive manuscripts that had suddenly, with his passing, become the focus of strong interest by friends (and
maybe some nonfriends) at Harvard and elsewhere?

Charley Redivivus

Quite a historical document could be written, and probably will be written someday, about the saga of Peirce's papers. First of all, his friends seem
to have been thinking along the lines of a single large book manuscript on
logic, a project he certainly had been developing. But what they eventually
found was a mountain of manuscript material, on all sorts of subjects, some
parts fragmentary, but other parts fleshed out, and indeed some completed
lecture series or completed book-length projects. Royce seems to have been
the first person to make the false claim that Peirce had been incapable of finishing a book, and that false myth[†] persists to this day among academics—
the most gossip-reliant of all professional classes.

When I say mountain, I really mean it. The Harvard Peirce papers[†] alone,
which one can now purchase in microfilm, run to about 80,000 sheets. Add in
his correspondence held in the same collection, and one approaches 100,000
sheets, maybe more. Then there are other manuscript materials located in
other collections public and private—pages that were not acquired at Harvard, or which "escaped." Add on top the fact that in preparing the microfiche edition[†] of his published works, about 10,000 exposures were required,
and one realizes that he left a tremendous amount of material, most of it important in one way or another. The friends who were now seeking his papers
for Harvard were under the impression that he had not published a great
deal, and that he left a draft of a large book on logic and a few additional fragmentary scribbles.

They were about to receive a big surprise. And, as the process unfolded,
what initially was cordial became a bitter quarrel. It's an instance of Eisenstaat's Law: There will be no fights until there is something big enough to
fight over.

A turning point occurred when Royce began to transfer his efforts into
the hands of the new chairman of the Harvard Department of Philosophy
and Psychology, James Haughton Woods. I haven't discovered much information on Woods. In his book on the history of the philosophy department
at Harvard, Bruce Kuklick[†] opined that Woods was not particularly well
qualified and was appointed only because his family was prominent in
Boston. It doesn't matter. We can trace his role here quite clearly.

Grandpa William, in fulfillment of his priestly role and neighborly duties, on the seventeenth of July 1914 wrote to Royce[†] that he had visited

Madame Peirce the day before to read her Royce's long letter and its proposals about the papers.

> Mrs. Peirce wishes me to say that she is willing to leave the matter of publishing the manuscripts entirely to you. Whatever in your judgment seems best will meet with her approval. It is not the pecuniary benefit that she thinks of, but that her dear husband may have that recognition which he so justly deserves. His later manuscripts are in boxes by themselves, the earlier ones stacked on bookshelves—two tiers, six shelves high. Of the older ones we know not which are most valuable, but all have been carefully preserved. Mrs. Peirce also has all the magazines containing any of his published articles.
>
> Mrs. Peirce is far from well: she is on the verge of nervous prostration.
>
> Awaiting further communication from you, I am yours cordially,
>
> William H. Darbey

Something struck me immediately: Grandpa's phrase "all have been carefully preserved" was presumably an echo of Juliette's experience and remarks. Editorial workers in Peirce's papers in the twenties and thirties universally complained how disordered they were. If Grandpa's remark means that Charley kept them in a good order, which Juliette retained, then what happened to cause the gross disorder observed a few years later? Peirce's large corpus entails at least prima facie that he invested a great deal of himself in writing; moreover, he had a long career as a laboratory scientist in an extremely exacting experimental branch, and from an early age he had formed habits of careful scientific record keeping. Indeed, experimental science cannot succeed without such practices. All of that suggests it was quite likely that he kept his stuff in viable functioning order. I think that is indeed the meaning of Juliette's remark.

At the bottom of the letter is Royce's memo of December 1914: "Transmitted by J. R. to J. H. W. for Dep't records of the C. S. Peirce papers and of their care."

Grandpa's diagnosis of Juliette's mental state was astute, for she confided† to Mrs. James late in August that she had suffered a complete breakdown for weeks. She also commented, "Owing to my illness our minister Mr. Darbey had some correspondence with Prof. Royce and Dr. Jastrow concerning the manuscripts of my dear husband and I trust that his work will have a place in the university library."

Juliette also worried aloud to Mrs. James about money matters in this and many other letters. And Mrs. James, with the aid of interested and anonymous friends, continued to provide a small pension for Juliette, just as they had done for years when Charley was alive. The names of these generous souls appear in records I have sifted, but I will protect their desire for silence. There is a morality in such ventures, especially in New England, that should not be offended.

For the moment nothing further emerged from Royce concerning the papers, for he was busy at the University of California in Berkeley giving a series of six summer session lectures entitled "The Spirit of the Community," the first beginning at 8 P.M. on Monday the twentieth of July, the last[†] on the thirty-first.

As these lectures concluded the Great European War began. By the fourth of August, Russia, Germany, Austria-Hungary, England, Belgium, and France were exploding. The industrialization of warfare proceeded to snuff out lives by thousands, then by millions. Although depressed by the spectacle of mass warfare, Royce stayed on to give the Twenty-Fifth Anniversary Address to the Philosophical Union at the University, on Thursday August 27, 1914. Later in the published form[†] of those presentations he described their relevance to Peirce's works:

> These six preparatory lectures contained a restatement of the theory of what I had called in a recent book[†] of mine, the "Process of Interpretation," and, in particular, discussed the nature and functions of "Communities of Interpretation." . . . I had intended to continue and to summarize the main theses of these six lectures in my anniversary address before the Union. The summer session ended. The war began.
>
> My address in the form in which I had intended to read it was thus rendered useless, and was thrown aside. . . .
>
> Abandoning, then, my previous plans for the address before the Union, I wrote this present address. . . . This writing took place between August 2 and August 27, under the immediate influence of impressions due to the events which each day's news then brought to the notice of us all; and yet with a longing to see how the theory of "interpretation" which I owe to the logical studies of the late Mr. Charles Peirce, would bear the test of an application to the new problems which the war brings to our minds. . . .

I took the trouble to give you Royce's words here—from the preface of his book *War and Insurance*—because it shows one of the first public uses by a prominent figure of Peirce's ideas after his death. It seems that influential Harvard philosophy professors had a habit of travelling to Berkeley California to speak to the Philosophy Union to say a word of public praise about Peirce's thought; almost to the day sixteen years earlier, William James addressed the same organization in celebration of Peirce's pragmatism, a speech that launched the public career of the pragmatic school[†] of philosophy. Pragmatism is the first indigenous American method of philosophical reflection to have become an international movement, and it's alive and kicking even now. At the time of his remarks in 1898, James acknowledged Charley Peirce as its founder.

By late October, Madame Peirce had heard nothing further about plans for receipt of the manuscripts at Harvard, so she wrote to Mrs. James to that effect and added that there had just been a fearful forest[†] fire nearby, which her property had barely escaped. She also reported that the war had wiped out her income from Europe. This leads me to believe that she was thinking seriously about the safety of Charley's papers, perhaps because she had begun to think of realizing someday a bit of income from their publication. By the way, Juliette's post scriptum for this letter confirmed one of my earliest hunches about her, because she stated, "Excuse the poor writing and spelling for I never had a lesson in English."

The Darbey family, meanwhile, loaded their car and departed Milford. Grandpa had taken up a new church in Stevensville, Maryland. Grandma Louise Miriam Darbey described the hectic trip in a letter to Juliette[†] dispatched the fourth of November and conveyed thanks from her husband for twenty books he had personally selected from Charley's library. These have been inherited by Betsey and occupy a place of honor in our home.

The gears in Cambridge[†] meshed. Mrs. James consulted with Royce, then wrote to Juliette that the Philosophy department was proposing to send Victor Lenzen, an advanced student, to Milford to look over the books and manuscripts with an eye toward preparing them for transport. On December 9 Juliette informed Royce[†] that the envoy would be welcome. Royce then used that communication as a basis for issuing further sage guidance to Woods[†] on December 13. He particularly worried over possible future misunderstandings. He concluded:

> We have to remember, of course, that, while the papers are intended to remain with us permanently, we who undertake the enterprise are very transient, and therefore need to keep a precise record of each step of the transaction, accessible to all who in future may see these cryptic MSS, and may wonder what they mean.

On the same day, probably within the same hour, Royce penned[†] an important letter to Mrs. Peirce.

> My colleague, Professor James Haughton Woods, is now chairman of the Philosophical Department at Harvard. He has conferred both with Mrs. James and with me regarding the care which is to be given to the papers of your late husband, Mr. Charles

S. Peirce, in case you let Harvard take charge of them. He will also confer with our librarian, Mr. Lane, about how to secure that these papers, which I believe to be very precious scientific contributions, shall remain under the care of the Library, which, in future will act in cooperation with the Department of Philosophy, to the end that Mr. Peirce's papers may have permanent safe-keeping, and, in due time, as I hope, a suitable editing. Professor Woods's purpose, as well as mine, will be, to see that the care and the future use of your husband's papers shall not be dependent upon the life or the decisions of any one man, but shall be undertaken by the Harvard Library and our Harvard Philosophical Department, acting in cooperation, and consulting together when that is needed.

Professor Woods will write you further about our plans. I thank you for your kind aid and interest. I earnestly hope that we may be able to gain for Mr. Peirce's work a permanent and adequate recognition.

Josiah Royce

On the eighteenth Woods took pen in hand to write a fateful letter[†] to Juliette, a document which Royce saw the same day and approved. The first three sentences were:

Professor Royce has informed me of your very generous offer to entrust the papers of your late husband, Mr. Charles S. Peirce, to Harvard University. This gift of yours seems peculiarly fitting, in view of the many bonds of attachment between Mr. Peirce and the University as well as different members of the Philosophical Department, and we should welcome these products of his genius with the utmost loyalty.

The letter went on about details of Lenzen's proposed visit to the Peirce home before the end of the year, and about proposals for buying Peirce's library, or for receiving it as a gift to be marked in his honor.

The first thing I noticed about this document is that conceptually it moved from "your offer to *entrust* the papers to us" to "this *gift* of yours." Royce had earlier expressed care and concern for any intellectual property rights that Juliette might own in these papers. Had he now reversed himself on that point? Did he or Woods consciously plan to lead Juliette from "entrust" to "give"? Was this the sort of thing that Ben Ellis meant when he said that "Harvard acquired Charley's papers through fair means and foul"?

The fateful feature is a short annotation in Juliette's handwriting near the end of the letter in a passage that returned to the topic of Charley's papers. The note is undated, and simply reads: "Mistaken. No gift. Jllet." Did this mean that the papers or the books (or both) were not a gift? How and when did this annotation in her hand get onto the Philosophy Department's copy of this letter?

It is further puzzling because Juliette wrote by special delivery two days later to Woods[†] bubbling with enthusiasm about the prospect of the papers and books receiving a place of honor at Harvard, describing the arrangements she was making for Lenzen to stay in a small inn one-half mile from her home, and expressing that he was welcome at any time. She mentioned that she had arranged for a driver to meet him at the train and for a local workman to build the shipping boxes they would need. There was absolutely no hint of objection about a gift, only emotional relief that a heavy responsibility was about to be removed from her shoulders in a way that would bring honor to Charley. Did Royce and Woods know this and lay plans based upon such an anticipated response? In other words, were Juliette's literary property rights compromised by those means?

Woods was an active fund-raiser in this and other projects of the department—perhaps one reason he became chairman. He had already established a "C. S. Peirce fund," which by this time contained[†] more than $500.

My own opinion is that Royce was blameless in the matter of Juliette's rights. But there is evidence that Woods was not, as indicated by some of his fund-raising letters that I have examined, as well as by later developments. For instance, on the twenty-first to a colleague in another department[†] of the university:

> I had hoped to be able to boast of the acquisition of the Peirce
> papers, but now I must cry for help. . . . Will you allow me to
> violate the neutrality between the Departments to the extent of
> requisitioning a small sum from you?

The colleague declined, but offered a list of additional persons who might be contacted. To another prospective donor[†] on the same day, Woods stated:

> You perhaps know that we have an opportunity to secure the
> unpublished manuscripts of Charles S. Peirce, and probably also his
> library. William James kept the family going for many years, and
> Mrs. James has been supporting Mrs. Peirce. By getting together
> about $500 we could have a permanent memorial of Peirce in our
> library, and also publish the valuable fragments. At the same time
> we could relieve Mrs. James.

Another great myth about Charley's writings, that they were "fragmentary," appears here early in its scuttlebutt career. It just proves what I said about gossip—academics will take it over facts almost anytime. For instance, Woods could not have possibly based his remark upon an examination of Peirce's papers, for they were in Milford. At most he could have read an article Peirce had circulated to James or Royce for comment. He had never seen the entire mass of papers! So, needing an opinion in order to appear erudite, he readily repeated hearsay, of which there is always a bountiful supply in academia.

Lenzen, whose studies in philosophy were eventually interrupted by war service, departed without delay for his mission to Milford. He later wrote[†] extensively about his trip.

> As the Christmas vacation of 1914 neared, I was asked to make the journey to the Peirce home on the right bank of the Delaware River, two and one-half miles above Milford, Pennsylvania, which was seven miles below Port Jervis, New York. To make the journey, one first had to go to New York, take an Erie train to Port Jervis, 88.4 miles distant from New York, and then take the stage for the remainder of the journey.
>
> Professor James H. Woods, Chairman of the Department, gave me instructions and funds for the mission on which I started at the beginning of the Christmas vacation. My destination was the Half-Way House, on the Milford Road between Port Jervis and Milford, and which Mrs. Peirce had recommended as an Inn one-half mile from the Peirce house, in the direction of Port Jervis. In this late December, snow was on the ground, but the weather was mild during my sojourn in the area, and as an enthusiastic walker I found it no hardship to walk one-half mile or more to the Peirce house.
>
> The house faced the Delaware River toward the east, the entrance was on the south side and into a room of medium size. The morning I first met Mrs. Peirce, she was outside at the southeast corner of the house conversing in French with a dark-haired workman. As I arrived, he said, "Oui, Madame," and started up the road to Port Jervis. She turned toward me, extended her hand, and explained that he was going to New York to celebrate the New Year. The French especially like to celebrate New Year, she told me in her foreign accent, and I assumed that she was French.

These memories were written down in 1965, but many of the details are quite accurate when a comparison is made, as I have done, with material dating from 1914. Lenzen's impressions[†] of Juliette in 1914 are particularly clear.

> Mrs. Peirce was a slight woman of brunette complexion with a thin face and high cheek bones. She received me cordially. Mrs. Peirce had prepared for my task by bringing all the manuscripts and books to be packed and shipped into this one room. There were several tables stacked with manuscripts. There were also stacks of books: philosophical, scientific, and editions of Latin authors. One

thing that especially struck me was the great number of elementary books on arithmetic. I could not understand what Peirce would want with such elementary texts. I now realize that he was engaged in writing elementary texts in mathematics.

Mrs. Peirce expressed great devotion and loyalty to her late husband. She was happy that the manuscripts and library were to be preserved in a place of honor. Once, as I worked at a table beside her, she declared with great emotion that Peirce was a genius. On another occasion, I remarked that he was especially interested in logic, to which she added, "He loved logic." It was not my impression while I was with Mrs. Peirce that there was a commitment to purchase the manuscripts. It was my understanding that the manuscripts and books had been freely offered to the University through the Philosophy Department. However, Mrs. Peirce told me that she wished to complete the first two floors in the house, so that she could rent rooms and be independent. She asserted that the French workman, previously referred to, could complete the work and estimated that it would cost $500.00. She said she would accept a pension as a loan for a year merely to finish the house, for Peirce had expected to obtain money from the manuscripts. The report of the President of Harvard University for 1914-15 contains the report of the Librarian, who refers to the acquisition of the Peirce books and manuscripts. The reference includes the sentence: "His entire library of over 1200 volumes, mainly philosophical works, together with his unpublished manuscripts have been given to the Library by his widow, the manuscripts being paid for in part by special gifts and Library funds." I am unable to comment upon the reference by the Librarian to purchase of the Peirce manuscripts.

I gather that here Lenzen was saying that he had been told by the person who had sent him on this mission that the materials were a gift, but that upon talking with Juliette, she expected to make money from the manuscripts. But his reminiscences can be clarified somewhat because a letter he wrote from Milford to Woods, shortly after arriving, has survived, and gives us an amazing picture of the situation in the Peirce home, as well as a sense of desperation[†] felt by Lenzen.

> The manuscripts are packed and also some books. In all I have 5 large cases finished. But Mrs. Peirce wants to give all the University will take. She wants to give manuscripts, books, complete library. The library must remain intact. The situation for me is somewhat difficult. I wish that I could talk to you personally and give you all the details. Much that I relate must be considered

to be very private. Here are some of the facts. Mrs. P. is bitter against Harry J. and Mrs. J. because they have tried to get her from her house. Especially against Harry is she incensed because he suggested that she put her affairs in the hands of an agent and have the books auctioned off. This suggestion she rages against as barbarous, cruel, dagger in her heart, etc. She wants C. S. P.'s things to be preserved intact in a place of honor. She wants the University to have all. But it must be clearly understood that the books be not sold. She claims vehemently and passionately that she wants no money for them. She says she will accept money for the manuscripts since her husband intended to get money from them.

Mrs. Peirce's ambition is to get her house finished in order to rent it. It is a 3 storied affair—25 rooms—$25,000 spent on it. She says that $500 will enable her to finish the first 2 stories and thus to rent it. I greatly doubt it. She has a Frenchman working for her, he seems to be a hobo, but she praises him and says that with him she will be able to finish her house. I doubt it.

Mrs. Peirce is influenced by 2 strong motives. First, intense loyalty to C. S. P. When his mss and books are in safe keeping she will feel that all is well. The reason she wanted to give the library to Harry J. (as you told me) was because an earlier will had left the library to him. The last will leaves all to her. H. J. is the last person with whom she wants to do business. Second, intense pride. She wants no money favors. The pension she will accept for a year as a loan merely to finish her house. She resents having been treated in a patronizing way, etc. She wants to finish the house in order to have an independent income, so that she can tell the rest of them to go to _____ and also live in the room in which her husband spent so many happy days. She expressed herself as greatly overjoyed that the books will be taken care of. She is just beginning to live. The offer of the University is a Xmas present to her.

The whole matter is most pathetic. The library contains at least 3000 volumes. Some of the books are standard books—works of James, Royce, Santayana, Bradley, Bosanquet, Russell. There are many standard books on math, physics, chemistry, philology. Also many old books—of 16th and 17th centuries—like works of Robert Boyle—Summas, works of Duns Scotus—Tacitus, Cicero. But most of the books are in Harvard Library. Mrs. P. wants the library to remain intact. She absolutely refuses to have them put up for auction. Harry J. suggested that and put a dagger in her heart.

From what I have heard, she has told some of the villagers that she expects some cash from the University. She is very clever. I suspect she is trying "with one stone to kill two birds." That is, to raise money and at the same time gratify her heart's desire and see that her husband is given a Memorial.

Now I don't know if the University wants the books, all of them. Remember that they must be kept. But from her passionate outpourings to me, which have nearly reduced me to tears, I am fairly sure that she really places sentiment above cash. I fear that when her husband's things are cared for that she will break under the strain and pass away. She seems to be keeping up now by will power. But with this all—she has ambitions and grand ideas for the house. It is the most pretentious place around here.

After a day of most soul rending reflection I have decided to send off all the books that I am able to. To send off all would require the construction of cases—and the use of more time and money than I had planned for. Can you give me any advice about these matters. I dislike to strip the poor old lady of the books for so small a sum. Yet she protests with all the ardor of her emotional nature that money is nothing. Honor to her husband is everything. I don't feel like unloading a couple of thousand of books on the University without definite notice. But it would be a Christian act of charity to accept them. In order to finish the job I will have to stay here longer than I expected. Also I should need more money for buying lumber, paying for hauling, etc. I think you might best telegraph me. . . . I don't mind staying to finish up matters but my own work is pressing. However, with the assurance from you that the books will be gladly received and with relief from the responsibility of getting so many books for the University for so little, and with some extra cash to finish matters up, I shall be satisfied to stay and see the thing thru.

This occurred to me. The University might take the books and sell the duplicates already in library. But Peirce's books must be preserved. Mrs. Peirce might be given the net proceeds, but I doubt if she would take it. She is in a very pitiable condition.

As regards choice of books, shall I send along 9th edition of Britannica, Coast Survey reports, Smithsonian institute reports, dictionaries, log tables, pamphlets etc.

Victor F. Lenzen

Woods telegraphed instructions[†] to pack the books and send them to the Library. Royce also wrote to reinforce those directions. The books, it seems, could not be kept intact as a collection, but they could be assigned memorial book plates. One may find them occasionally today among the shelves of the Harvard College Library marked:

Harvard College Library

FROM THE LIBRARY OF

CHARLES SANDERS PEIRCE
(Class of 1859)
OF MILFORD, PENNSYLVANIA

———

GIFT OF

Mrs. **CHARLES S. PEIRCE**
June 28, 1915

One may also find that the library has sold books with such plates in them. For example, I have one that I picked up from a used book dealer, complete with plate and marginal annotations by Peirce.

Royce concluded his letter by saying, "The Peirce MSS, of course, can and will be given a place and care together, and will be kept[†] very carefully."

Lenzen reported on a postcard to Woods dated 31 December 1914: "I have shipped 24 large cases of mss. and books to Randall Hall." One of Royce's students, F. A. Woods, remembered Royce showing him the papers after they had been unpacked.

Peirce left an enormous pile of manuscripts† which his wife sent on to Royce just after his death. They formed a great pyramid in Royce's little study in Emerson Hall. Royce raising his hands in despair cried out, "Just look at the size of it. I am expected to go through all that and pick out some parts to publish. How would you enjoy going through such a mess?"

What had been Charley's working papers first became "fragments" but was now a "pile," a "mess."

Thus did the year of Charley's death come to an end.

When I first came upon Lenzen's letter, I confess to you it almost brought me to tears for another reason. Bitter herbs of miscommunication and strife were growing like weeds in a cow patch. All the kinds of misunderstandings that Royce feared and tried to prevent were steadily becoming actualized. Betsey and I had a long conversation about the whole thing.

On the one hand, there is Mrs. Peirce, who seems not to be as closely attuned to American culture as a native would be. And as her neighbors and members of the Peirce family often recalled, she claimed to be from a noble European family. Whether this claim is true I leave as an open question at this point, but suffice it to say that this is a clue to the attitudes she adopted. She certainly acted as if it were true. For instance, it is clear that she had grand plans for her residence. And she had a revulsion toward receiving gifts of money—she regarded that as contrary to her breeding. But she could haggle like a gypsy and was capable of trying to renegotiate a deal if it seemed in her interest to do so. She seemed clearly to think of the books as a gift. But in regard to the manuscripts of her husband's own works, she seemed to have the notion that she was entrusting them to Harvard for protection, care, editing, and eventual publication, from which she seemed to expect an income. After all, Charley's will had given all his property to her, including his intellectual property.

From the standpoint of the group in Harvard, there was a vigorous recognition of the importance of Peirce's ideas, and hence of his manuscripts. A number of professors, particularly Royce, regularly included Peirce's methods and results† in their courses. Royce and the late William James featured Peirce's ideas in their publications, and both had enjoyed a longstanding friendship with him. Yet somehow Royce, Woods, and associates—when the final moment of truth in regard to ownership came—did not exhibit even a minimally proper business acumen. The academic gossip mill nowadays holds that Peirce had no sense for business. Be that as it may, it is clear the group at Harvard lacked it in this case. If there had only been a simple document such as a scribbled bill of sale or a letter stating something like "We buy X items from Y for \$Z." But no such clear document has been discovered.

And a dispute between Juliette and Woods about ownership of Peirce's papers developed from the soil we have just sifted. It continued increasing exponentially in bitterness until the day she died[†] in 1934. A jurisprudentialist who studied the records would probably find the matter of the direct chain of primary ownership of Peirce's papers to be unclear; perhaps they only now ultimately vest in Harvard due to a statute of limitation[†] or other secondary legal device.

Now I began to see why she presented the box to Grandpa Darbey after she became seriously ill. The crafty old girl had held back the best manuscript, the draft[†] of Charley's autobiography. Perhaps she had planned to market it herself after some of the more technical of Peirce's works were published by Harvard. She might have thought, "When my husband's name is widely known, his own autobiography will be important and will make my fortune." That could explain her cryptic remarks to Grandpa.

How did all this end, you ask? The feud about whether the manuscripts were gifted or entrusted raged over the years. The manuscripts arrived safely in Harvard, where they were placed into the Library. Royce died in 1916. And since he was the principal driving force, particularly through his students, publication from the manuscripts was delayed. All hands were surprised, even overwhelmed, at the bulk and high quality of Peirce's unpublished writing. The onset of American entry into the European war also was damaging. But during the twenties, efforts were renewed which eventually produced six volumes of *The Collected Papers of Charles Sanders Peirce* under the colophon of Harvard University Press. The first volume appeared in 1931. The Second World War interrupted further production after volume six, but in 1958 two additional volumes appeared in this series.

Charles Hartshorne, one of the young editors of the first six volumes, in progress reports to Chairman Woods, recorded the elated impressions he and others felt as they first came into contact with this material and began to work through it.

> Peirce was a profound thinker[†] from his early teens on. The power of incisive, independent thinking which some of those early reflections show almost made my hair stand on end. There are ethical and religious reflections of great power, and sometimes of great beauty and nobility. And one magnificent prayer[†]—probably the finest (the only?) that any philosopher since the Middle Ages has given us. What an inexhaustible personality! Peirce was the only universal intellectual genius after the pattern of Leibniz in the whole nineteenth century.
>
> I call him[†] the greatest technician philosophy has had since Kant. But really he's beyond the commonplaces of praise. What he has especially & above all to give beyond all the marvelous logical

discoveries—including really a whole new[†] science, the analogue in philosophy of Newton's Calculus in physics and merely the generalization of it—beyond all such things the inestimable boon he confers is the inspiration, the élan, of the scientific spirit—an intellectual conscience profoundly at peace with itself—the spirit of cooperative inquiry instead of the impulse to defend a position one has occupied. The only position to occupy is that of the eternal advance of knowledge: "Do not block the path of experiential inquiry"—What a ring in that simple motto!

Every volume[†] will contain unpublished material of note, in almost every case of greater significance, generally far greater, than the already published stuff. Some of[†] the passages compare with Emerson or Thoreau's journals in the sense of genius it gives on every page. The existential graphs will be largely new. Lewis says they're good—after all he[†] knows more about Peirce's logic than anyone else.

But the *Collected Papers* was not the first substantial posthumous public presentation of Peirce's works. That honor goes to a smaller but effective collection of a dozen of Charley's best previously published philosophical essays edited by Morris Raphael Cohen (Harvard philosophy Ph.D. 1906). It appeared under the joint imprint of Harcourt, Brace and Company in New York and Kegan Paul Trench, Trubner and Company in London. Cohen had been involved as a worker in the early efforts by Woods to organize a team to edit Charley's papers. When he discovered the existence of Cohen's own editing project, Woods even tried to dissuade him[†] from this "unauthorized" publishing effort, but Cohen held firm and ultimately could do so because the published essays he selected required no permission from Woods. The book was successfully published in 1923. It bore a particularly accurate and charming title: *Chance, Love, and Logic: Philosophical Essays by the Late Charles S. Peirce, The Founder of Pragmatism.* It included a supplementary essay, "On the Pragmatism of Peirce" by John Dewey. In his introduction, Cohen explained his motivation:

> Besides their inherent value as the expression of a highly original and fruitful mind, unusually well trained and informed in the exact sciences, these essays are also important as giving us the sources of a great deal of contemporary American philosophy.

That was a good reason for Cohen to press ahead with his project which scooped the *Collected Papers* by eight years.

As a detective novelist, I like Cohen's book for another reason. One of my idols, Dashiell Hammett, produced a masterpiece in the field, *The Maltese Falcon.* It is a rather profound study[†] in the distinction between appearance and reality, done in the vernacular of the street instead of the prose of a seminar room. The reader is fed story after story, each of which one is at first inclined to believe, yet each of which in the end turns out false. The reasons to believe the stories escalate from politeness through greed or fear or reason and finally to undying love. Anyway, there is a famous interlude when Sam Spade tries to explain his philosophy of life to Brigid O'Shaughnessy. It is the story of one Mr. Flitcraft, who, after a chance near-disaster, abruptly left his family and took up a residence in another city. Later in the book, Flitcraft changed his name to Charles Pierce in his new life. I think, and almost all commentators agree, that Hammett read *Chance, Love, and Logic* which provided some of the meat of the philosophical stance of the *Falcon*. Probably as a tribute, he assigned the name of Flitcraft's resurrected self to Charley, but using a common misspelling. I wonder if Charley had any other effect[†] upon mystery writing.

Thus were many of Peirce's ideas released upon the world before the midpoint of the twentieth century. But many of the best ones—entombed in whole unpublished books or lecture series—still lurked exclusively in manuscript folders in the Harvard library. Research on these matters has marched ahead since the 1930s and 1950s. Texas Tech University (in Lubbock, which ain't too far from Stillwater) was first out of the gate with a four-volume edition of Charley's extensive book reviews for *The Nation*, supported by the National Endowment for the Humanities. A Texas philosopher named Charles Hardwick put together a wonderful little volume of the correspondence between Peirce and Victoria Welby that is probably the best popular introduction yet to his theory of interpretation he named *semeiotic*. An improvement upon the *Collected Papers* (also supported by NEH) is appearing in an edition published by Indiana University Press. They have developed five large volumes so far, with six times as many left to prepare. And as I mentioned before, his thought is influencing quite a diverse range of endeavors around the globe. We can readily speak of his revival as a unique American genius whose ideas are coming before us now as if from a freshly opened time capsule. (Just as I am reading galley proof on this book, word comes that Harvard University Press has published a heretofore lost set of important popular lectures[†] by Peirce, *Reasoning and the Logic of Things*.)

Yet his life has remained a mystery.

Now that Betsey and I inherited the beautiful box, after reading its contents, we have agonized over whether we should make these details known, whether we should place before you his draft autobiography and our research about it. A grain of sand tipped the scales when a few years ago my friend Walker Percy urged me to go forward.

Why all the worry, you wonder? There will be parts of it that will be unpleasant and uncomfortable. Some people who admire Peirce through his beautiful ideas may find that he had feet of clay. Or, some of his supposedly noble supporters and friends may be revealed as flawed paragons.

But after careful consideration, we decided to march firmly ahead. Our conclusion is that in the story of his life there are lessons for all of us. Everyone is fallible.

However, first, it will be helpful if you have some background information about the autobiography, knowledge that we gained the hard way but that we can freely convey.

Charley began writing down his thoughts or keeping notes and journals at a young age. The first such journal we discovered is entitled *Private Thoughts*[†] *principally on the conduct of life,* the first entry of which is dated 1853 when he was fourteen. Later, from parts of articles he had written or unfinished projects he had attempted or from his own letters or those of family and acquaintances (including scrapbook-style clippings or hand-written notes on books he had read), he added more material. And it jumps around somewhat in time sequence. The file he prepared was not a final draft but usually close to it. We found that in reading it we had to use our imagination now and then, but we also discovered that this was one of the sources of charm in these papers.

Having become an amateur student of Peirce's semeiotic, I discovered that a common pattern in biographical writing amounts to little more than an author telling a reader how to interpret the subject at hand. What one often finds is that such a biography exposes more about the biographer than about the biographee.

One of the attractions of Charley's box is that it presents him in his own words—for you dear reader to interpret. We entirely approve of that, so Betsey and I will try to stay in the background as much as possible, and certainly we don't intend to tell you how to interpret. You can't avoid it; you are condemned to interpret, to borrow and mangle[†] a phrase from Sartre.

Some of Charley's juvenile writing, especially journal entries, represent some pretty elementary youthful moralizing. Also he included some of his early Kant-style metaphysical writings. These also are rather uninteresting, except for one aspect: both categories provide a fascinating bench mark against which to gauge the charm and brilliance of those passages in his later writing which he chose to include. So be patient with young Charley.

This habit of autobiographical data gathering continued throughout his life. Roughly just before the turn of the century he began to organize this accumulation into what we now have, rearranging it, including additional comments about some of his earlier notes or journal entries, all the while continuing to write new remarks. I have been unable to decide if he meant to polish all these items into a final form, or whether he planned to leave that task to the future publisher of the work. We have left it almost as we found it, except for the addition of headings within each chapter or section.

One of his avocational pursuits was what he called "The Study of Great Men." Betsey says to tell you that she suspects the reason that near the end of his life Charley pulled all this autobiographical stuff together and started organizing it was to leave a file from which some future student might attempt to decide whether C. S. P. could be considered a great man. We agree that such questions should be answered only by posterity. All we can do is give an honest presentation of Charley's file, plus try to provide something about its broader context.

By the way, to help you keep track, our comments, as well as the letters and other comments of Charley's contemporaries, will appear in this typeface—Palatino—while Peirce's autobiography has been placed in a distinct, scriptlike face called Optima Oblique, as a tribute to the fact that he laboriously wrote out most of it by hand—the exceptions being the scrapbook-like printed clippings he also included. What can I say?—I'm an amateur typographer too!

I have hinted at my suspicion about why this file was preserved in the beautiful box and explicitly not installed among the papers that were ultimately sent on to Harvard. I think Charley entrusted it especially to Juliette, particularly in view of the difference in their ages, she being younger. That's only a guess; but it makes sense, doesn't it? Probably he hoped that she could make the best use of it when the reputation of his works began to swing upward a few years after his death. In the final analysis, the upswing didn't come during Juliette's remaining days, so she transferred it into the only pair of hands she trusted, those of Reverend Father William H. Darbey.

II

HIS GLASSY ESSENCE

3

In the Beginning

Perfect readiness to assimilate new associations implies perfect readiness to drop old ones. It is the plasticity of childhood, which if a man is going to become a teacher, or an exponent of a fixed idea, or a mechanic at any immovable trade, or a settled man in any respect, it is just in so far best that he should outgrow. But so far as a man is to be a learner, a philo-sopher, it is most essential that he should preserve; and to do so he has to battle against a natural law of growth. To be a philosopher, or a scientific man, you must be as a little child, with all the sincerity and simple-mindedness of the child's vision, with all the plasticity of the child's mental habits.

Peirce: *Reasoning and the Logic of Things*, Lecture Five

To Begin

(*I am going to write† in the first person singular, as being the sincerest and freest from everything like affectation and formality.*)

The aim which I shall endeavor in these pages to confine my pen is that of helping you who read them to reason about life better than you now do—that is, more to the purpose, more accurately, more swiftly, more ingeniously, and more solidly.

At this point you ought to feel two doubts. In the first place, you want to know who is the "you" and who is the "I." By "you," I mean you the very person who is reading this.

And I am one, Charles Santiago Peirce, now in this year of our lord 1908 about seventy years old, who has for fifty-eight years been trying to come to understand the nature of the different kinds of reasoning, and for the last twenty years has more and more led the life of a recluse in order to escape all distractions from that study. For in order that I should be of the service to you that I hold it as the first duty of my remaining years that I should try with all my might to be, this writing on my part and reading on yours, should amount to a heart to heart[†] confabulation, without any reserve that can possibly obstruct it. I, for my part, will force myself to a degree of candour to which I have all the reluctance of such half-baked souls as mine.

For these twenty years[†] (and practically longer) I have been a recluse, remote from libraries, unable to subscribe to any journals, and very rarely communicating with any philosophist. I always associated with physicists and chemists rather than philosophists. Twice a year I go to the meeting of the National Academy of Sciences of which I am a member, but I rarely get an opportunity to see anybody not in the Academy.

But logic is a science[†] that the vulgar (a word I apply, quite without[†] myoterizing, to all who have nòt passed through a certain severe and long novitiate, including people of the utmost refinement, and who indeed may be expected to catch the meaning of that last hard word, not likely to be known to readers of no other than classical Greek) the Vulgar, then, I say, passionately hate. The fact that the science calls for finer and exacter thinking than mathematics itself would suffice to make it distasteful to them. The passion of their dislike is due to the circumstance that every mother's son of the whole herd or galaxy of them is in his own conceit the sole one among them all of whom what Abelard said of Aristotle really holds good: "Doubtless Aristotle might have erred, but doubtless in his logic he never did." Now this pest, Mademoiselle Logic, on her very first introduction to him, too, has blasphemed this divine gift and exaltation by questioning its reality. The logician feels this hatred of logic in a resulting antipathy to himself that stands very much in the way of anything he may undertake; since every undertaking demands a certain good will from somebody or other. For that reason after study of the subject since 1855, rewarded by some undeniable discoveries of which nobody took the least notice, I determined to retire into seclusion and devote the remainder of my life to finding out all the logical truth I could, inasmuch as I was persuaded that no less would answer the purpose and that no other competent student would be willing so to live in neglect and universal aversion; and for considerably more years than twenty this life I have led, working daily with all my might and main (and I am a great worker) to advance my knowledge of the subject.

The result is that I can now assure the Reader, the rare Reader, who is willing to read what I write, that I have nothing in the world to gain, whether substantial or illusory, from getting listened to except the satisfaction of thinking that I shall have been of service to any Reader who shall think the matter over for himself, and who may be able to correct some of my errors, and to carry the

work further than I have had the strength to carry it. Except for that considera-
tion, I should rather devote the precious time this writing will cost me (my re-
maining days being few) to further researches in pure logic.

1839
September 10. Tuesday. Born.†

An extraordinary thing† happened to me at a tender age,—as I now reflect
upon it, a truly marvelous thing, though in my youthful heedlessness, I over-
looked the wonder of it and just cried at the pickle. This occurred 1839 Sep.
10. At that time I commenced life in the function of a baby belonging to Sarah
Hunt Mills Peirce and Benjamin Peirce, professor of mathematics in Harvard
College, beginning to be famous. We lived in a house in Mason Street. This
house belonged to Mr. Hastings, who afterward built an ugly house between
Longfellow's and the Todd's.

I regard it as <u>sufficiently</u> proved† that my name is Charles Peirce and that
I was born in Cambridge, Massachusetts, in a stone-colored wooden house in
Mason Street. But even of the part of this of which I am most assured—of my
name—there is a certain small probability that I am in an abnormal condition
and have got it wrong. I am conscious myself of occasional lapses of memory
about other things; and though I well remember—or think I do—living in that
house at a tender age, I do not in the least remember being born there, im-
pressive as such a first experience might be expected to be. Indeed, I cannot
specify any date on which any certain person informed me I had been born
there; and it certainly would have been easy to deceive me in the matter had
there been any serious reason for doing so; and how can I be so sure as I surely
am that no such reason did exist? It would be a theory without plausibility.

My father,—loved as a jovial man† within his circle, but hated by some
outside it,—announced me, in this fashion, to his sister and brother:

Mademoiselle Charlotte Elizabeth Peirce†
and
Doctor Charles Henry Peirce   at Salem

    Today at 12 o'clock was born a boy. Its mother and it are both
doing "finely" and send you their very best love. The boy would
have written, but is prevented by circumstances over which he has
no control. He does not like this blue ink he says. He hung himself
this afternoon to a pair of steelyards; but postponed the further
execution of his wicked designs upon himself, because he found he
wanted just one quarter of a pound of the nine pounds which he
regards as the minimum of genteel and fashionable suicide. At 8
1/2 this morning his mother—if she can be called his mother
before he was—his future mother, or more transcendentally, the

mother of this then child of futurity was well—or nearly so, the shadows of coming events having but slightly obscured the brightness of her countenance.

B. Peirce

And to his mother Lydia, in like manner:

Good news! Dearest[†] mother, Sarah is finely and so is the, yet anonymous boy, Sarah sends her very best love. She has had the least bad time she ever had, the least exhausting. She suffered for about two hours and at 12 was confined. The boy weighs 8 ³⁄₄ pounds, and is as hearty as possible. He offered to go out and throw the vase with me today; a certain sign that he will either make an eminent lawyer or a thief. As soon as he publishes his "Celestial Mechanics" I will send you a copy, and I have no doubt he would be glad to correspond with you about your last mathematical researches. He has two splendid optical instruments each of a single achromatic lens which is capable of adjustment!— and so wonderful is the contrivance for adjustment that, by a mere act of the will, he is able to adapt it to any distance at pleasure. But one fault has been found with these instruments and that is, the images are inverted; our new born philosopher, however, our male Minerva, contends that this is a great advantage in the present topsy-turvy state of the world. By the way, he calls himself Minervus. The first proof of his genius which he exhibited to the world consisted in sounding most lustily, a wonderful acoustical instrument whose tones, in noise and discordancy, were not unlike those of fame's fish-horn. Is not this a singular coincidence? a sure omen of his coming, almost come, celebrity?

B. Peirce

I was named after Charles Sanders, husband of my paternal grandmother's sister Charlotte. Sanders Theater at Harvard, some years later, had the same namesake.

My ancestors[†] were all of English descent, and belonged in colonial times mostly to the common folk of Massachusetts Bay. For several generations back they had mostly been professional men, attaching some value to intellectual performances as such. My mother's father was a senator of the United States, my father's father failed as an East Indian merchant, and became an author and librarian of Harvard College. My father was a distinguished mathematician and a man of remarkable force of character and of intellect. Both he and my mother were ardent natures, of great refined tastes, lovers of poetry and art, and very indulgent parents. They were Unitarians; but they were conservative, interested in the isms of New England, but not engaged in them.

3. *Benjamin Peirce, Jr., Entertains Benjamin Peirce, Jr.*

4. *Sarah Hunt Mills Peirce*
"a sure omen"
Photographs 3 and 4, Tuttle Collection, Institute for Studies in Pragmaticism
By permission, Philosophy Department, Harvard University

(1903). PEIRCE, Charles† Sanders, scientist, was born in Cambridge, Mass., 1839 Sep. 10, being second son of Benjamin Peirce, the celebrated mathematician. He was graduated at Harvard College, and likewise took a degree in chemistry summa cum laude. For over thirty years he was in the service of the Coast Survey, having at one time charge of the U.S. Office of Weights and Measures, at another of the Coast Survey Office, and for many years conducted the investigations into gravity. He has published numerous researches† relating to the figure of the earth, optics, chemistry, experimental psychology, pure and applied mathematics, logic, and philosophy. Since 1877 he has been a member of the National Academy of Sciences. He wrote all the philosophical and mathematical definitions in the Century Dictionary. He resides at his wife's country-seat, "Arisbe" near Milford, Pa., where he has a free school of philosophy, furnishing remunerative employment to such students as desire it. He also exercises the professions of Chemist and Engineer.

Old Cambridge

Although Betsey and I walked past it many times when we lived near Cambridge, we realized its significance only after beginning to study Charley's autobiography. The house in which he was born—the "Mason Street House"—is still standing, but bearing additions and renovations to the old main structure. No longer a private residence, it's the headquarters of a theological seminary, complete with a basement chapel for celebration of daily mass. Some of Charley's admirers have placed a commemorative brass plaque on the outside. Within a half block of the house, Mason Street opens in an easterly direction upon the beginning of Garden Street, directly at the west side of the center of Cambridge Common, where Washington took command of the Continental Army. Christ Church is only a block to one's right from that spot, keeping faithful guard upon the Common as it has done for centuries. Southerly and within sight is Harvard Yard. Fay House in what became Radcliffe Yard is right across Mason Street to the south. Brattle Street and the Longfellow House and other old Cambridge residences of note are near behind Mason Street to the west.

Cambridge and Harvard are well known by many persons, but picturing the city and college at the time of Peirce's birth might require some assistance to our imagination. Gardiner Day prepared a description that may surprise you:

> Cambridge in 1839† was a town that comprised three villages: Old Cambridge (Roughly the area from Harvard Square to Watertown and Arlington); Cambridgeport (roughly the section of the city in what is now Central and Kendall Squares); and East Cambridge

(the section of the city from Prospect Street east to Lechmere and the Charlestown Bridge), and these villages were largely separated by marshy land impassable save for a few roads on high ground and a half dozen canals. Between the three sections there was the keenest rivalry. For example, when in 1832 the citizens of Old Cambridge, as the village in the Harvard Square area was called, refused to allow a highway to be built across the Common and insisted on its preservation as public ground, the citizens of East Cambridge fought for and secured the removal of the County Court from beside the Common to East Cambridge where it remains to this day.

The village of Old Cambridge was separated by natural boundaries from the surrounding settlements. Beyond the Charles River on the south and west almost a mile of salt marsh lay between it and Brighton. To the north and west, Mount Auburn and Fresh Pond with neighboring swamps and clay pits separated it from Waterton and Belmont. On the north and east uninhabited and almost impassable boggy land, overgrown with woods and tangled underbrush, made communication with Sommerville (then part of Charlestown and East Cambridge) extremely difficult, and bald Dana Hill and swamp land along the river served as a natural boundary between Old Cambridge and Cambridgeport. In 1842 the citizens of Old Cambridge petitioned the General Court to be allowed to be divided from East Cambridge and Cambridgeport and be incorporated as Cambridge or Old Cambridge. After discussions at Town Meetings for several years, the proposal was defeated and the three villages were incorporated as the City of Cambridge in 1846, with a population of about 12,000 inhabitants. Of a Sunday, worshipers might choose, besides Christ Church, to attend the First Parish Church Unitarian, the Orthodox Congregational Church, which under the dour leadership of Abiel Holmes, had recently seceded from the Unitarian congregation, the Old Cambridge Baptist Church, Harvard's recently built Appleton chapel, or St. Peter's, a Roman Catholic Church, which opened for worship in 1849.

There's truth in the proverb that the first families of Boston migrated originally from Salem and Essex County in the Commonwealth of Massachusetts: the Lowells, Lawrences, Jacksons, Higginsons, Endecotts, Cabots, Hoopers, Appletons, Derbys, Phillipses, Pickmans, and Saltonstalls were already embedded in the history of Essex County[†] in the eighteenth century. If we can see Cambridge as closely related to Boston, the same proverbial rule certainly applies in the case of the Peirces. Indeed, even on a wider scale, there is an orthographic network, apparently from the same English stock, many members of which became prominent in American culture: Pearce,

Peirce, Perce, Pers, Pierce, Piers, Purs. According to *The Century[†] Dictionary,* all these forms derive from Hebrew *Cephas,* and signify "a stone."

Charley's father, Professor Benjamin Peirce Junior, had roots reaching back into the best of Salem in the peak of its splendid commercial seafaring era. The surname in America has been traced to John Pers of Norwich, England, a weaver, who in 1637 settled with his wife, Elizabeth, in Watertown, Massachusetts, a few miles east[†] of Cambridge. The line continued through their son Robert and his wife, Mary Knight, through their son Benjamin and Hannah Bowers, through their son Jerathmiel and Rebecca Hurd, then through their son Jerathmeel and Sarah Ropes. *Their* son, the father of Benjamin, Jr., was also named Benjamin. So for clarity, I identify the father of Charley (Benjamin, Jr.) as Ben, and the father of Ben (Benjamin, Sr.) as Benjamin.

Jerathmeel Peirce, Benjamin's father, one of several Salem kings of the commercial ocean-sea in post Revolutionary War days, operated half a dozen sailing vessels that traded at the major ports of the old and new world. Old Jerathmeel only emerges dimly from the records of history, but he participated in the Revolutionary War[†] with Colonel Pickering's Salem unit, and had influential contacts in many locations. The family routinely thought in terms of national and global affairs, because in such trade their fortunes were focused. Most citizens of the United States at that time, for similar commercial reasons, were concentrated at home upon the next crop or the next local business deal. Benjamin (1778-1831)[†] grew up in the house his father had built in 1772 at 80 Federal Street. It was a masterpiece of architecture then, and today it splendidly survives as the home of the Essex Institute, where enough material on the glories of old Salem may be found to fill up several lifetimes of study.

Perhaps partly as a reward for Benjamin's service for a number of years as an accountant for the shipping business, but principally because Jerathmeel was convinced of its high value, he resolved to provide his eldest son with a classical education. Whence Benjamin graduated from the Academy at nearby Andover in 1797, then departed for Harvard where he settled into room one[†] at Hollis. Promptly after arriving, he wrote his father at the end of August that he was studying Latin, Greek, Hebrew, mathematics, and rhetoric (later also Watt's *Logick,* Locke on human understanding, Algebra, plus Enfield's philosophy and Hume's essays on miracles). Somewhat later he mentioned he would be grateful to receive a parcel of cheese and crackers, and that he had sent home a "trunck of cloathes" to be washed. His sister Sally, whose responsibilities included helping with family laundry, replied by imploring him not to wear his drawers[†] so long before having them washed. Some aspects of college life haven't changed in two hundred years!

Benjamin discovered, and remarked in a letter to Sally, an enlightening attitude that was to become a family tradition.

The field of science[†] is of immense extent—the most we can gain is but a little corner in it. Yet one who has once attain'd to that little corner, has the whole open (as it were) before him, & enjoys a free air, unconfined within the narrow limits, which ignorance (with its usual attendants), vanity, self-conceit & a thousand foolish impertinences would necessarily prescribe.

Indeed, Benjamin came to think of himself[†] as a philosopher, which, in the old sense of the word, is synonymous with the above basic sentiments of *scientia*.

Another tradition of the family, at least as old as Benjamin, was the wish for an academic education for women. He expressed such sentiments to his two younger sisters, Elisabeth and Sarah, and to his maternal cousin[†] Lydia Ropes Nichols. Lydia shared this outlook and at Salem was a pupil in a controversial school for young women[†] organized by Mrs. A. D. Rogers. There are also indications[†] that Benjamin and Lydia were influenced by the feminist works of Mary Wollstonecraft, the author of *A Vindication of the Rights of Woman*, whose daughter (Mary Wollstonecraft Shelley) was the mother[†] of *Frankenstein*.

He graduated in 1801, high among[†] his class, attracting the personal approval of President[†] Joseph Willard, then returned to a merchant's life[†] in Salem with his father's shipping enterprise, the firm of Wait[†] and Peirce. At the end of October 1803 Benjamin and Lydia announced their engagement[†] and were married. Their third child and second son, Benjamin Junior (Ben), was born on the fourth of April[†] 1809.

Papa Benjamin prospered in respect, and in 1811 was elected[†] as a Federal Republican[†] Senator from Essex County to the Massachusetts legislature, where he served for several[†] years.

Young Ben[†] began formal study in the Salem Private Grammar School during his teens, where through his classmate Henry Bowditch, he came under the influence of Nathaniel Bowditch. The importance of this connection can be seen in the dedication of Ben's book (1855) on analytic mechanics more than thirty years later: "To the cherished and revered memory of my master in science, Nathaniel Bowditch, the father of American geometry." In 1824 Ben was placed in Andover academy and from there went on to Harvard in the fall of 1825. His first letter home already displayed a firm secondary interest in philosophical and religious topics examined by a fierce logical gaze[†] and intense concentration.

Cambridge, Saturday   1825 October 22

Dear Mother: I have very little time now to write to you as I have to
study a great deal. In the morning I first go to prayers, then either to
recitation in Greek or to my room and study; at commons bell I go
to breakfast. At study bell half an hour after commons bell I either
recite or study till 10 or 11 (my hour for mathematics recitation)
after which I study till 1 o'clock when I go to dinner; after dinner I
kick foot-ball till study bell at 2. From that time till prayers I study
or am at recitations; after prayers come commons, then I exercise till
eight, the evening study-bell. My time is occupied in this way every
day except Sunday & Saturday (when I exercize) from 10 1/2
o'clock, the rest of the day. On Sunday Grotius is studied.

I wish you boil me a good lot of chestnuts and send them up.

Tell Pa I wish he would write me up a permission to have
books charged in somewhat this way: "I do hereby consent that my
son Benj. Peirce jr. shall buy & charge to me classical books to the
amount of _____ (what he pleases) Benj. Peirce."

Today I dined out at Mrs. Fay's. I have been thinking of your
Trinity. Is this the way you explain it? God reveals himself to men
in three different ways. First as everlasting, omnipotent, omniscient,
as altogether good, & shortly as himself; secondly as our Saviour; &
thirdly as the Holy Ghost. In this way, I can explain everything I
now think of. Ask Pa to send me objections to this system & I will
answer them. When Christ says he is not equal to God, all he means
is the flesh is not equal to the spirit. If Pa quotes scripture let him
name the place where he finds it. Ask him if he is willing to put his
trust in a saviour less than divine. If Christ was divine he could not
have been created. If he was not created, he existed necessarie, aut
per se, & was therefore God.

Your affectionate son,

B. Peirce

In 1826, Wait and Peirce, like many similar firms in Salem, began to anticipate[†] failure—what would be called bankruptcy today. Benjamin and
Lydia quickly adjusted to these changes: near Porter's Tavern[†] in Cambridge
she opened a boarding house[†] that quickly filled with talented and scholarly[†]
boarders, while he concluded business details in Salem and began casting
around for other opportunities. The one that came his way—through the office[†] of some influential friends—was the position of head librarian[†] at Harvard. Ben's sister, Charlotte Elizabeth (Charley's Aunt Lizzie), writing from
Cambridge[†] to her aunt in Salem, noted the family's good spirits and pleasure in Benjamin's anticipated career turn toward scholarship.

All that come here are either obliged to work for us or to pay 3 dollars & a half a week, excepting Grandpa Peirce & Grandpa & Grandma Nichols. When you come we shall set you to making quilts & carpets & fixing feather beds & cleaning house.

Tell Grandpa that if Pa is librarian he will have a nice time if he comes here for he will have the best books in the world to read & that Ben and I will read to him if he wants us to. The library here is said I believe to be the best in the United States & Grandpa will admire (will he not) to come up and see it?

Benjamin was appointed to a three-year term as Librarian with the salary of a tutor by action of the Corporation on the twenty-third of August and confirmed by the Overseers[†] the following day. At about the same time, a general economic depression descended[†] upon Salem. Benjamin had successfully extracted his family just in time. The aged and deeply respected Jerathmeel was allowed by creditors to continue residence for a while in his splendid Salem mansion[†] on Federal Street.

Name, Story, and Matter

1840
Christened[†]

1841
Made a visit to Salem
which I distinctly[†] remember.

I remember nothing[†] before I could talk. I remember starting out to drive in a carryall and trying to say something about a canarybird; I remember sitting on the nursery floor playing with blocks in an aimless way and getting cramps in my fingers.

I remember early visits[†] to my grandmother in Salem, to different houses. One time in the cars with Aunt Lizzie, Miss Margaret Fuller[†] was with us and had a book with pictures about an imp in a bottle. She impressed me a good deal. She moved to N. Y. in 1844 and in 1846 left this country and was drowned on the return voyage with her husband, the Marquis Ossoli, in 1850, which event of course I remember the talk about.

I remember a gentleman[†] who came to see my mother,—probably William Story, who drew a sketch of her.

And I remember[†] an old negro woman who came to do scrubbings. I remember her because she frightened me and I dreamed about her. It is not[†] on the average, as often as twice a year that unless in grave illness I retain the slightest vestige of recollection of any dream sixty seconds after waking, for I wake up promptly. Nevertheless, I still vividly recall dreaming, when about two years old, of being carried in the arms of a negress and of biting a large piece out of her shoulder. There was, I believe, but one family of negroes in the village, and I was probably never carried in the arms of a negress. I do not recollect being scared by the dream, though I had a sort of horror at the idea of having done such a thing. It seems to me unaccountable that I should remember that dream so long. It is a mere visual picture in my memory with some skin sensation attached.

1842
July 31. Went to church† for the first time.

That the idiosyncrasy† of a man—his peculiar character—is his peculiar philosophy, is best seen in the earliest stages of its formation before those complications have been developed which render it difficult to seize upon it. The cunning speeches of children just as they begin to talk often startle one by their philosophical nature. The drawer of <u>Harper's Magazine</u> was filled for years with the sayings of "our three year old"—who seems blessed with perennial three-year-old-ness—but if all these stories are true, they are very valuable as showing the character of the childish mind in general, and particularly the philosophical tendencies of children. I shall not trouble you with the recitation of any of these funny stories—they are stale and therefore flat; but I will mention a case, which has nothing laughable in it—but which illustrates remarkably well how the peculiar differences of men are differences of philosophian method.

    I was rather backward in learning to speak,—not from dullness, but from a want of aptitude in imitating the words which I heard,—I had got to use three words only; and what were these? "Name," "story," and "matter." I said "name" when I wished to know the name of a person or thing; "story" when I wished to hear a narration or description; and "matter"—a highly abstract and philosophical term—when I wished to be acquainted with the cause of anything. "Name," "story," and "matter," therefore, made the foundation of my childhood philosophy. What a wonderful thing that my individuality should have been shown so strongly, at that age, in selecting those three words out of all the equally common ones which I heard about me. Already I had made my list of categories, which is the principal part of any philosophy. Constantly, in using these words, my philosophy became more and more impressed upon me until, when I arrived at maturity of intellect, I was able to show that it is a profound and legitimate classification. Tell me a man's "name," his "story," and his "matter" or character; and I know about all there is to know of him. Aristotle says there are two questions to be asked concerning anything: the ὅτι and the διότι, the <u>what</u> and the <u>why</u> —the account of premisses and the rational account or explanation; or as I said, the "story" and the "matter"; but Aristotle had not noticed that previous to either of these questions must come the fixing of the attention upon the object—the determination of the mind to it as an object—and the demand for this determination is asking for its "name." Here we had therefore in my childhood soul a philosophy which furnishes an emendation upon the mighty Aristotle—the leader of the thought of ages, the prince of philosophers. I dare not attempt to fathom the awful depths of that child's possibilities; when he grows up, in some way and to some degree he will manifest his character, his philosophy; then we can judge as much of it as we can see, but its intrinsic worth we never can judge; it is hid forever in the bosom of its God.

1843
Attended a† marriage.

I remember well† the Davis's wedding which took place in the house, the minister in his black gown, and my getting my leg down in the register hole and being rescued by Uncle Henry Davis. I well remember Aunt Harty before she was married and my trying to mesmerize her, I think in imitation of Jem. I remember the dining room, which had formerly been a kitchen, and eating hasty pudding for breakfast there. I remember distinctly my first taste of coffee, given me surreptitiously by the kitchen girls. No mocha will ever again have that quality for me. I remember Professor Sylvester at table there. I also remember my Aunt Helen Huntington coming and being obliged to lie at once on the bed. She died shortly after, Ned Huntington, her youngest child, being, I suppose, 2 or 3 years younger than me.

I can recall my father† reading me a story from the Arabian Nights.

"How did I slay thy son?" asked the merchant, and the jinnee replied,

"When thou threwest away the date-stone, it smote my son, who was passing at the time, on the breast, and he died forthright."

Here there were two independent facts, first that the merchant threw away the date-stone, and second that the date-stone struck and killed the jinnee's son. Had it been aimed at him, the case would have been different; for then there would have been a relation of aiming which would have connected together the aimer, the thing aimed, and the object aimed at, in one fact. What monstrous injustice and inhumanity on the part of that jinnee to hold that poor merchant responsible for such an accident! It is certainly just that a man, even though he had no evil intention, should be held responsible for the immediate effects of his actions; but not for such as might result from them in a sporadic case here and there, but only for such as might have been guarded against by a reasonable rule of prudence. I remember how I wept at it, as I lay in my father's arms, and he first told me the story.

5. *Benjamin Peirce, Jr.*
"As I lay in my father's arms"
Tuttle Collection, Institute for Studies in Pragmaticism
By permission, Harvard University Archives

Though I cannot recall it† at all, I think it very likely that in my childhood I read of a malevolent fairy who pronounced this curse upon an infant that during his whole life whatever wish he should conceive should be instantly gratified. If he wished for a drink, a drink should be instantly before him. If he wished it to taste differently, it should taste differently. If he was tired of sloth and wished he were working, he should be putting forth his strength. Only two things would be debarred. The first restriction should be that vague dissatisfaction, mere ennui at having his own way, should not be enough. He must form a definite wish. And secondly, wishing that his wishes should not be gratified should only be gratified until he made a positive wish. The instant he did that the satisfaction should come.

The Song of Ben Yamen

Charley had a somewhat unusual relationship with his father, who was a somewhat unusual man. The precise nature of that relationship is less transparent. Someday someone will write a fine book about Ben, for his life was eventful, including several major scientific and academic accomplishments. However, for the moment we need a reliable outline.

Ben graduated Harvard in the distinguished class of 1829. Even as a student he drew sparks. For example, in a widely known attack[†] upon the weakness of the mathematical professor (Hayward) who was vigorously defended by President Kirkland, Nathaniel Bowditch remarked that "Peirce of the Sophomore Class knows more of pure mathematics than he does." Among students this was roundly understood[†] to be true; one of them recalled:

Benjamin Peirce, who was born[†] with the genius for mathematics which made him afterward so distinguished a mathematician, went far beyond the college course in that direction. Each class had one day a week in which to take books from the college library; and I recollect that Peirce, instead of selecting novels, poetry, history, biography, or travels, as most of us did, brought back under his arm large quarto volumes of pure mathematics. When we came to recite in the Calculus or Conic Sections, it was observed that the tutor never put any questions to Peirce, but having set him going, let him talk as long as he chose without interruption. It was shrewdly suspected that this was done from fear lest the respective *roles* should be reversed, and the examiner might become the examinee.

Hayward was dismissed and Kirkland resigned. Bowditch, LL.D., F.R.S., A.A.S., etc., etc., was of course[†] a well-qualified judge and Ben's direct mentor in mathematics. At commencement on the twenty-sixth of August, Ben was designated to perform in the Forensic Disputation: "Whether inflicting Capital Punishment publicly has any Tendency to diminish Crime." He argued the affirmative[†] with conviction. Thence he went immediately[†] to duties as mathematics tutor in Round Hill School for boys at Northampton.

Three features of Ben's lifelong personality had emerged by this time. His student career at Harvard proved he was a very strong mathematician—yet one who worked hard constantly, on a tight schedule throughout the day and into the night. Fresh in the new year of 1830, he proudly declared[†] to his father:

I never before felt so deeply how short was time. Never before either have I kept myself more continually and zealously employed.

Indeed I never allow myself any relaxation, till I am so fatigued that I cannot possibly go on; and I find my powers of continued and intense application grow stronger every day.

A letter to home[†] shortly after arriving at Northampton shows two other traits. His health was delicate, and to strengthen his constitution he regularly engaged in vigorous exercise, including long walks in the surrounding woods: "You do not know how grand I feel[†] when I get out with my cane." Ben's exercise program was additionally reinforced by a harsh school policy: "Mr. Bancroft and Mr. Cogswell[†] have not the least feeling for a sick person. They seem to think that if a man is so ill, as to be unable to perform his duties, that he is only endeavoring to get rid of them."

Thirdly, Ben had a spectacular[†] temper, which he struggled constantly to check.

Betsey remarked one evening that a person insecure about health, who is a muscular thinker who regularly overworks, and who has a violent temper, possesses a potential to be a rather frightening parent. She also observed that Ben's attempts at self-control might explain the later loose rein upon his children: that is, he might have feared losing control of himself if he were strict as a parent, so he over-compensated in the opposite direction. I'm never sure what to think about Betsey's speculative psychoanalyses of past lives; I'm much too concrete to think successfully in that way.

Round Hill School[†] is a topic relevant to Ben Peirce, and thus also to Charley, for a number of reasons. The school gave Ben his first taste of teaching and brought him into the social orbit of the masters of Round Hill, George Bancroft and Joseph Cogswell. By 1830, ultimately through[†] those relationships, Ben could feel at home among four families in Northampton, including the household of U.S. Senator Mills (whose family were particularly strong supporters of the school) where he enjoyed the company of Sarah[†] Hunt Mills, Charley's mother-in-futuro. He called upon Sally as early as May 1830 but had met her earlier, just exactly how and where I don't know. Ben's social visits were often for the purpose of teaching mathematics to young ladies[†] of the household, a project which Ben relished: "I should much rather[†] teach a school of girls than one of boys."

Round Hill was a revolutionary educational experiment for its time, an attempt to bring the German gymnasium to American soil. Under the sponsorship of President Kirkland, Bancroft had taken a doctoral degree in history at Göttingen, but also had conducted a broad study of Germanic schools and methods of instruction while in Europe. He returned to Harvard but was not comfortable there as a tutor. With his Harvard colleague Cogswell, arrangements were completed to open their private school officially in October of 1823 to wide acclaim. Even Thomas Jefferson commented from his retirement at Monticello: "This will certainly prove a great blessing to the individuals who can obtain access to it. The only ground of regret is the small extent of its scale, in the few who can have its advantages it will lay a solid foundation of virtue as well as of learning." This prediction certainly materialized within mathematics, for Round Hill graduates were prepared through differential equations, placing them far ahead of the typical Harvard sophomore. Was that Ben's little revengeful joke?

Bancroft's European innovations included waking the boys—aged nine to twelve—at 6:00 for devotions at 6:30, study until about 8:00, then vigorous calisthenics and a mile run, then a breakfast followed by classes, and so on throughout the day. "From morning until night there is not a moment which has not its business," Bancroft proudly[†] exclaimed. To his sister he confided, "The great object with us[†] is to teach the actual application of the mind, and I think it is no object to make a play or an amusement of what should be hard work. Nor is it essential to make them find it more attractive than play; it is a lesson which men cannot learn too soon, that they are born to work, and not to while away life in pastime." In short, Bancroft had learned in Germany that it was best for his pupils that they be worked constantly, and this pedagogical doctrine was welcomed by his diligent but playful[†] young tutor, Ben Purse.

But pastimes were allowed—in their place. Along with other recreations, balls were frequently held at which faculty and students enjoyed the company of ladies from Northampton. Maybe in such a setting Ben made the acquaintance of Sally Mills.

By the time Ben joined Bancroft, the older man provided another model to his younger colleague, that of the researching teacher. Bancroft began his career as a writer of history while actively teaching at Round Hill. Ultimately he produced a monumental history of the United States while pursuing an active and successful national political career. But Bancroft is perhaps best remembered as the most influential member of the American diplomatic corps in the nineteenth century. Toward the end of his long and vigorous life he took up residence in Washington City where he was a revered and influential figure. When Ben became prominent in national affairs as Superintendent of the U.S. Coast and Geodetic Survey, friendship with his former headmaster surely did him no harm.

Benjamin Peirce[†] Senior, the Librarian of Harvard College, aged fifty-three years, died on 26 July 1831 after a sudden attack of vomiting and pain eight days earlier. Given the quack nature of what passed for the practice of medicine in those days, it is uncertain whether he was killed by the mustard plasters applied to his legs and feet "to promote circulation in the extremities" or by the physik given to "drive down his food" or by bleeding a cup of blood from his temple, or by the cause of the initial attack. The attending physician's autopsy showed a seriously thickened meninges, the normally thin membrane in which the brain rests. My classmate Bill, who is now a Boston physician, the source of forensic advice for my detective novels, mentioned that these effects strongly suggest a tubercular infection, which would have been progressive for some time but which was probably easily hidden[†] by Benjamin until near the end. Naturally, also I have my own understanding of such things arising from my detective stories; I'm an amateur physician, which is to say, a devout hypochondriac.

While reading about this in my first draft, Betsey said, "A syphilis infection can produce the same set of symptoms, Ike, including producing a thickened meninges; but I suppose we will never know, since definitive micropathology studies that would be routine today were not available in 1831."

It's too bad, for Benjamin had become widely known as the best librarian of Harvard College[†] in recent memory. In 1830 he had published a three volume catalogue of the library, which received strong praise[†] in the press. He also left a manuscript history of the university to the period of the Revolution, subsequently edited by John Pickering[†] and published in 1833. Charley had a presentation copy of that volume in his own library; it eventually was returned to Harvard through Juliette's bequest.

The following day in Northampton Ben stoically received the sad news and promptly assumed the role of eldest son and family leader, a mantle which he was prepared[†] to wear. After only a single day's respite, he continued his duties as tutor at Round Hill, while in family matters seeking the guidance of his maternal uncle, Benjamin Nichols. Ben appeared to realize the mark his father had placed upon his soul, for in an unusually stark style that was to become commonplace with him, he confided the following sentiments to his brother Charles:

> I was delighted, my Dear[†] Brother, to see from your last letter that you all view our loss in so happy a light, and we have every reason to be grateful for an affliction that has given us such a realising sense of the existence of a father in heaven, and let us so improve this chastening of God's love, that we may ever look back to it with joy, unmingled with regret except it be for the loss of so agreeable society as that of our dear parent. Through his whole life, our good father was ever striving to make his children worthy of him to prepare them for his departure. He has left us for a reason, let us show that we do not forget him. Let us pursue that path which was his delight and with which he is so closely associated in our minds—the path of truth. Here every obstacle will remind us of his precepts and his energy; & the beauties, that will surround us, will reflect to us in the purest colours the amiability and serenity of his character. Often, when I stand at my window and admire the unequalled beauties of the Northampton scenery, I feel the warmest gratitude to that classic taste that used to take pleasure in pointing

out to me the lovely hand of Nature in the works of Providence, or in reading me a striking passage from some favorite author, and never more than now that religion has taught me the value of the noble strains of moralising in which our father so loved to indulge.

The summer of 1831 was a defining moment for Ben. A number of character-forming events occurred. Besides his father's death he had received an appointment as Hollis Professor of mathematics and natural philosophy[†] at Harvard, to begin in the fall at a salary of $1000 per annum. And he discovered that he loved Sally Mills. He confided the depth of this change to her during the summer.

What was it before I felt true[†] love, that inspired me to such laborious efforts I tremble to answer. Ambition. I was resolved that I would make myself known throughout the world, and that I would bow to no living man as my superior in science. And what was my chance of success? Altered as I am, I may speak of what I was as of a different being. I do it without boasting, except that I have roused from the dream; for I now know the inferiority of intellectual to moral greatness. My hopes were, then, founded on my deeds. Again and again I had surpassed the highest anticipations of the most powerful mathematician of the present day, Dr. Bowditch. The work of what he thought months, I had finished in a week. I had gone through calculations in my head, for which he thought it necessary to resort to his pencil; and on one occasion when he had mentioned to me an elegant demonstration that had just made its appearance, I immediately proposed another that he judged in several respects to be the better one. But I will leave this disagreeable subject, and glance at my present state. My passions are no longer chained in the chilling dungeons of Philosophy. The poet's fire can now warm me into some thing like enthusiasm. The voice of Nature is not now that of mere Reason. Since I have come to love you, I feel that I have risen in the scale of being; my soul is elevated in its moral affections; it is more than gratitude that now inspires my devotions to the God of Love, to the Creator of so beautiful, so majestic, so lovely a being. God grant that I may ever be animated by this most ennobling principle; neglect shall not chill me; I am too proud for that and I feel that what would render me most worthy of your disdain is ceasing to love you.

The vanities of this life never appeared so clear to me, though they never troubled me less. I am soon going into the very marketplace of worldliness, but I do not fear contamination. Alone in the World, my wants will be small and easily gratified.

6. Benjamin Peirce, Jr., and Sarah Hunt Mills
"Not destined to be alone"
Tuttle Collection, Institute for Studies in Pragmaticism
By permission, Philosophy Department, Harvard University

A man who could write such a love letter was not destined to be alone. Ben's last summer at Northampton was closed by betrothal[†] to Sarah Mills, she one year younger[†] being born 14 September 1808. Sally moved into the Peirce household in Cambridge for a while[†] under the watchful eye of Ben's mother, in order to get acquainted with his family. A mutual friend of Ben and the Mills family made a diary[†] record on 17 April 1832, which shows the engagement had at least one rough moment.

Ben, Sally, and Elizabeth Cabot came a week last night. Ben and Mrs. Mills had a family scene Sunday p.m. Mrs. Mills reproached

Peirce with not going to her church, with offering an indignity to Sally thereby, telling him it was the worst thing she had ever known him do, and that she should mark it down against him. Ben said it must be so marked then. Mrs. Mills withdrew. Ben walked the room once or twice and then rushed out of the house in a grand passion. Sally thereupon blew up at her mother, saying she had made her engage herself to him, and that now she should treat him civilly and not insult him while a guest in her own house. Thereupon we walked off to a third service at the Episcopal, Sally talking rather loud on the way and to the hearing of divers good citizens of this commonwealth. Ben returned soon after to the front parlor. Mrs. Mills made a sort of apology and he cried and so the matter ended without a violation of the betrothment.

During 1832, due to family finances it became necessary for Benjamin's widow Lydia to seek a way to replace her husband's lost income, especially to support Ben's brother Charles who was preparing to become a physician. She accepted a position as governess to the family of Judge† Samuel Jones, a widower of New York† City. Eventually she was sent to the Judge's farm† at Rhinebeck (near Poughkeepsie), where she had full management of the farm while continuing as governess. And later she oversaw the children of the Jones family as they pursued their education in Boston. Ben thus became the head of the family in Cambridge, a duty he performed well, as Lydia confided to her parents.

Ben is well established† in life & is ready and willing to do for me & his brother & sister all we can wish him to do. But he is young & has to work more I fear than is good for his health, so that I am determined to make every exertion that he may be at no more expence than is absolutely necessary.

Ben and Sarah were married on the morning of 23 July† 1833 by Rev. Dr. Penny. Their first son James Mills, known in the family as Jem, was conceived the next month, to be born in their home at the old Dana House in Cambridge† on 1 May 1834.

Ben's professional career began to shine like a major new comet. In 1835, with his old teacher Hayward, he became mathematical consultant to the recently organized New England Mutual Life† Company; the mathematicians were employed to calculate a fresh table of life insurance premiums, based upon strictly scientific principles. With James Munroe and Company in Boston, Ben began publishing a number of mathematical textbooks in a series entitled *PEIRCE'S Course of Instruction on Pure Mathematics for the Use of Students in Harvard University*. These ultimately ranged† through basic geometry

7. James Mills Peirce
"Their first son James Mills"
Tuttle Collection, Institute for Studies in Pragmaticism
By permission, Harvard University Archives

to algebra, plane and spherical trigonometry (including navigation), analytic geometry and conic sections, differential and integral calculus, plus celestial mechanics (the mathematics of astronomy). They began appearing in 1835[†] with the title *An Elementary Treatise on Plane Geometry*. We owe one of our many clues to the pronunciation of the family name to these textbooks, for in some of them still surviving in library collections one can find this Shakespearean inscription by the original student owner: "He who steals my Peirce steals trash." One of his students[†] from the school year 1835–36 recorded his memories of Ben's classroom, which offers an insight into the way Charley might have been educated by his father.

In mathematics we had dear Benny Peirce, as we called him. His world-wide reputation was not yet made, but it was in the making. He was but twenty-six years of age. It has been the custom to say that he was not a good teacher of mathematics, because his insight was so absolute that he made one long step where a pupil needed to make four or five, and that he could not understand the difficulty of the boy who did not see what he saw. I suppose this is true: but, on the other hand, he was an enthusiast in his business, he was sympathetic and kind where he saw real interest in the pupil, and he devised the best method for the handling of a class which I have ever seen. In his case, certainly, there was no right to complain that an inferior teacher was put in charge of novices. I have never seen his exact method anywhere else. We met him for geometry in a large unused dining-hall, where the old dining-tables were still fixed. As you went in, you took a slip of paper with your own special problems on it, as he had assigned them for that day. You also took your own manuscript book, which you had left with the problem of the day before. When you opened this, if you found you had been wrong the day before, you were put back one lesson. Thus, before the winter was over, the seventy members of the class were in thirty or forty different places in the textbook. If you did not understand the thing, you were encouraged in every way to sit down by Mr. Peirce and work out the problem with him. We came to be, from that very moment forward, on terms of a certain sort of intimacy with him, which did not exist with five other teachers in college. He was very cordial and sympathetic, if anybody used his own brains enough to work out the problems in a way different from that in the book; and I doubt if I have ever received any honor in life which I prized more than the words "excellent and original," which once or twice he wrote at the bottom of my exercise. Here was Peirce, a leader of leaders, perfectly willing to take by the hand the most ignorant freshman. You felt confidence in him from the beginning, and knew he was your friend.

I have never forgotten the awful rebuke he gave to the class one day, when some fellow had undertaken to cheat at the blackboard. Peirce cut short the formal mathematics to give a lesson about truth.

8. *Benjamin Peirce, Jr., and a Harvard Mathematics Class*
"What is really meant by education"
Tuttle Collection, Institute for Studies in Pragmaticism
By permission, Harvard University Archives

The mathematics were the voice of God; we were in that room because we wanted to find out what truth was; and here was a son of perdition who had brought a lie into that room. We went out from the recitation-room sure that we had been very near God as we listened to that oracle. That sort of relation between teacher and pupil shows what is really meant by "education."

Ben became more deeply integrated within the innermost workings of the Harvard faculty. By 1838 he was an intimate member[†] of Longfellow's circle, the "Young Faculty Meeting," which also included Roelker and Felton. They held Socratic symposia—featuring songs, whist, and choice suppers—on late Monday nights, after the decorous sessions of the faculty "as such."

By the end of the summer of 1839, Professor Peirce and family had moved into the house on Mason Street where the 1839-40 academic year commenced with the advent of Charley on September 10.

Your Affectionate Son

1844
Fell violently in love[†] with Miss W
— and commenced my education.

1844 . School to Ma'am Sessions[†] with Babby Whitemore. Building of New House. Remember the Quincy's in Cambridge.

I forgot to mention[†] that earlier I remember Mrs. Harriet Gray Otis who lived next door in Mason Street and had a poodle dog; and I had a toy poodle. The Whitemore's afterward moved into that house, and Babby Whitemore,—a little girl a few months younger than me,—and I went together to Marm Session's school in the Craigie House when I was 5 years old.

I remember how angry people were when a furniture dealer cut down some elms to build a store. Cambridge was a lovely old place at that time, and people went to Boston in an "Hourly." The fare was 16 2/3 cents. The currency consisted of old worn Spanish pieces, valued at 6 1/4, 12 1/3, 25 cents and $1. Money was expressed in shillings and pence, 6 shillings to a dollar. I remember being weighed in Deacon Brown's store in a huge pair of scales.

I well remember[†] how Jem used to go to Dr. Jennison's school in a very old house under the Washington Elm; and later to Mr. Whitman at the Hopkins Academy. There I once met with him. I remember old Dr. Hedge who lived near by with two maiden daughters, and the Dixwell's. I remember old Mrs. Lowell, and Miss Louisa Greenough who lived in a house facing the Common, and her bringing me a bottle of Stuart's syrup. I remember going to see Mr. Whitemore's factory. They either made or used curry combs there. Whitemore soon failed and was made postmaster. Later he was clerk in a dry goods shop. I remember Dr. Gould coming to my father to take lessons, and he left college in 1844.

One of my earliest recollections[†] is hearing Emerson deliver his address on "Nature"; and I think that on that same day Longfellow's Psalm of Life was recited—"Tell me not in mournful numbers. . . ." So we were within hearing of the transcendentalists, though not among them.

EMERSON'S NATURE of 1836[†]
OUR age is retrospective. It builds the sepulchres of the fathers. It writes biographies, histories, and criticism. The foregoing generations

beheld God and nature face to face; we, through their eyes. Why should not we enjoy an original relation to the universe? Why should not we have a poetry and philosophy of insight and not of tradition, and a religion by revelation to us, and not the history of theirs? Embosomed for a season in nature, whose floods of life stream around and through us, and invite us, by the powers they supply, to action proportioned to nature, why should we grope among the dry bones of the past, or put the living generation into masquerade out of its faded wardrobe? The sun shines to-day also. There is more wool and flax in the fields. There are new lands, new men, new thoughts. Let us demand our own works and laws and worship.

Undoubtedly we have no questions to ask which are unanswerable. We must trust the perfection of the creation so far as to believe that whatever curiosity the order of things has awakened in our minds, the order of things can satisfy.

All science has one aim, namely, to find a theory of nature. We have theories of races and of functions, but scarcely yet a remote approach to an idea of creation. We are now so far from the road to truth, that religious teachers dispute and hate each other, and speculative men are esteemed unsound and frivolous. But to a sound judgment, the most abstract truth is the most practical. Whenever a true theory appears, it will be its own evidence. Its test is, that it will explain all phenomena. Now many are thought not only unexplained but inexplicable; as language, sleep, madness, dreams, beasts, sex.

Philosophically considered, the universe is composed of Nature and the Soul. Strictly speaking, therefore, all that is separate from us, all which Philosophy distinguishes as the NOT ME, that is, both nature and art, all other men and my own body, must be ranked under this name, NATURE.

When I was about five[†] years of age, Brattle Street, where the old royalist families had lived when the Revolution came, still retained something of its old gentility and dignity, and was bordered by the grandest and most gracious elms. Hard by the ancient mansion, known as the Craigie House, where the children went to school, was a shoemaker's (for it need hardly be said that shoes were made by hand at that time, except that they were imported for ladies, with "gauche" and "droit" written on their white kid linings). That old sage would sit at work on his low bench, muttering to himself meantime somewhat thus:

"Why ain't I in heaven? uq!"

This "uq!" stands for a syllable which began with a grunt made deep down in the throat but was quite unmodified by tongue or other mouth-parts, while the vocal chords were vibrating and the nasal passages open, and which ended by a consonant sound more like our "ng" than anything else but produced by a

violent contraction of the bronchial tubes aided by the muscles of the ab-
domen. This interjection escaped the old man every time he pulled on his
threads.

"Because man is created, uq!

"And so is under the rule of Time, uq!

"And so we can't be something and nothing at once, uq!

"Improving is the best that can happen to us, uq!

"We grow happier if we try in the right way, uq!

"But we can't try in the best way, uq!

"Because we don't know the best way, uq!

"We can only learn more and more about it, uq!

"It was lucky for me, uq!

"That I didn't know how to get what I used to long for, uq!

"I should have been a badly disappointed man by this time, uq!"

Now it is pretty clear that this talk must be much more an illusion that has
grown up in my imagination than a correct recollection, since at that tender age
I could not have comprehended an old man's reflexions. But calling it a dream,
it is nevertheless very true that every human being's likings, and energies, and
reason grow much more than his body does, and in this process of development undergoes transformations about as great as that of a caterpillar into a but-
terfly; and that on this account, what a boy ought first to acquire are those powers which are sure to be needed by every kind of man.

1845
Moved into new house on Quincy Street,
and commenced my researches†
on the physiology of marriage.

When I was about six† years old I was the devoted admirer of Miss Lizzie
Cary. I used to sit next to her in the college chapel.

I remember driving† with Father to Dr. Bache's camp at Blue Hill, in 1845.
I well remember the Quincy's who left Cambridge in 1845. I also remember a
great deal about the building of the New House on Quincy Street. I recollect
the discussion of the plans before it was begun, and the building of it. Then it
was not finished in time, and the Bartlett's who were to take the old house,
moved in and we boarded with them, and John Bartlett made a wonderful trick
cabinet of drawers out of cigar boxes. I remember eating my first meal in the
new house of oysters, seated on the back stairs. I think we must have moved in
1845. I remember in that year Judge Story's funeral, the Irish famine, the Mex-
ican War, and the retirement of Professor Treadwell. I soon after began going
to Miss Ware's school.

I remember many† other things about the old house, and often dream about
it. I remember the Isabella grapes over the piazza.

Even in my old[†] age, I still dream of my cousin Mary Huntington and of those early five-year-old days when my mother took me to her family on a long visit to Northampton. Sometimes I dream about it night after night for almost a week. It would do you good I hope to know about it. It was in the summer[†] of 1845, when we were both five years old. I was six months older than Mary, nearly six. Mother and I, Uncle Charles Mills, Aunt Anna Mills, and Charley Mills, then not quite five, stepped from the stage coach that brought us to the Huntington's door, about noon, of a hot July day. Mary's natural shyness was overwhelmed by a number of strange faces. Noticing this, Charley Mills singled her out as a victim, and began chasing her with fire crackers, and setting them off in her neck, and teasing her in other annoying ways. I took upon myself the task of defending her, and on every occasion did all I could to snub and humiliate the offending cousin. I suggested to Mary that we should make away with a drum, which was the constant companion of the spoiled darling, and which seemed to emphasize all his disagreeable qualities of conceit and self-ishness. I wanted to break it to pieces, but Mary, being less destructive in her impulses, suggested hiding it in some bushes, which separated our grounds from the next field. I told Mary of my dreams in 1910,—she also clearly recalled our actions:

> The fact that we hid that drum in bushes that were so near and yet
> so far seemed to give great zest to our satisfaction. I clearly recall
> Charley how you danced about with great glee, reiterating the cry
> D. D. D. continually. This you kept up for days, and I can see now
> your graceful dancing figure with your black elflike locks and
> bright eyes, triumphantly shouting the refrain D. D. D. This you
> kept up for days, so that it seemed strange that the elders did not
> suspect our connection with the disappearance of the drum, but it
> was not found during the whole visit, much to the satisfaction of us
> all, except perhaps the father and mother of its owner.

(1906, September 20) I must count it[†] as one of the most fortunate circumstances of a life which the study of scientific philosophy in a religious spirit has steeped in its joy, that I was able to know something of the inwardness of the early growth of several of the great ideas of the Nineteenth Century.

Reflective activity[†] was, I doubt not, native to me. Family anecdotes, daguerreotypes, and testimonies as to the impressions made upon psychologists assure me that it was so. But my environment and early education stimulated this greatly. My father was a dynamical and astronomical mathematician of great distinction, universally acknowledged to be by far the strongest mathematician in the country, who broadened as he grew old, and was at all ages remarkable for his esthetical discrimination. He was a man of great intellect and weight of character. His house might almost be said to have been a rendez-

vous of all the leading men of science, particularly astronomers and physicists; so that I was brought up in an atmosphere of science.

Agassiz came in every day without ringing, and standing in the hall, would call

"Ben!"

Alexander Dallas Bache (later Superintendent of the U. S. Coast Survey in Washington) was a particularly close friend, who came twice every year; Joseph Henry, Director of the Smithsonian only occasionally. Charles Henry Davis (at first Lieutenant in the Navy and at last Rear Admiral), whose wedding to my mother's sister I well remember, would pace up and down with my father by the hour. But my father was a broad man and we were intimate with literary people too. At the house in Mason Street, Cambridge, Mass., where I was born and lived to the age of about six, and later in our house on Quincy Street, I most distinctly recollect (besides persons whose names would mean little or nothing to most of my readers, though much for a few) old people,—among them, for example, our next door neighbor, Mrs. Harrison Gray Otis, Signor Mariotti (that is, the Italian Antonio† Gallenga, who went by a false name in America), Sylvester the poetical mathematician, Mr. Longfellow, Margaret Fuller, the sculptor William W. Story, James Lowell (possibly not in just those years), Rev'd Francis Parkman, Theodore Parker, Francis Bowen, Oliver Wendell Holmes and his more genial though perhaps less Witty Brother John, John Bartlett (whom I adored). Others whom I particularly remember were Mr. Emerson (whose address in the early forties greatly impressed me, for it was not necessary to understand Emerson or to have more than the slightest contact with him to be greatly impressed). I used to see some of the most eminent of the political people such as Rufus Choate and Mr. Webster (who took my maternal grandfather's seat in the U. S. Senate, when his weak lungs compelled him to retire). George Bancroft had been very intimate with my mother's family in Northampton. I used occasionally to see him; and Lathrop Motley was one of our friends. My father had strong contempts for certain men whom he considered shams, and among them was Charles Sumner, who was, I must say, one of the absurdest figures of vanity I ever laid eyes on.

Also near to the heart† of the family in early days were men in other lines: Frederick Dan Huntington, George Hilliard, Charles Norton, Francis Child, George E. Lanes, Dr. Thomas William Parson, and at a later date Henry James the elder. And there was Horatio Greenough, the sculptor who designed† Bunker Hill Monument, who tells us in his book that he meant it to say simply "Here!" It just stands on that ground and plainly is not movable. So if we are looking for the battle-field, it will tell us whither to direct our steps.

I was educated† by my father Benjamin Peirce, a name written in the history of American Science. He accomplished much. He advanced knowledge & he immensely stimulated all Americans who were inwardly impelled to the study of mathematics.

Nevertheless, I think of him as one of the great men sacrificed to untoward circumstance.

His tremendous analytic power of thought never came to its due fruition, partly from want of education, partly from the weight of domesticities.

He educated me & if I do anything it will be his work.

I was brought up[†] with far too loose a rein, except that I was forced to think hard & continuously. My father[†] took great pains to teach me concentration of mind and to keep my attention upon the strain for a long time. From time to time, he would put me to the test by keeping me playing rapid games of double-dummy[†] from ten in the evening until sunrise, and sharply criticizing every error. He also stimulated me to train my sensuous and esthetic discrimination, in the broadest sense of the latter adjective. He specially directed my ambition to delicacy of palate; so much so, indeed, that when I was later in France I subsequently placed myself for six months at monstrous expense, in tutelage to the sommelier of Voisin opposite the church of St. Roche, to learn the red wines of Medoc, at the end of which time I was almost fit for the profession of a wine-taster in that particular line. But as to moral self-control he unfortunately presumed that I would have inherited his own nobility of character, which was so far from being the case that for long years I suffered unspeakably, being an excessively emotional fellow, from ignorance of how to go to work to acquire sovereignty over myself.

The Florentine Academy

One of the most fortunate events in Ben Peirce's life was acquiring Alexander Dallas Bache (1806-1867) as his closest friend. It was important for Charley as well, for if he was educated by Ben, it can be said that he received his finish as a scientist in the Florentine Academy, under the eye of its Chief and its members at Cambridge and around the country. That's how Bache was known among the members of the Florentine Academy—just *The Chief.* It's an appropriate title for the leader of a group of devoted scholars, don't you think? But I'm getting ahead of myself.

In 1842, Ben had just been appointed the first Perkins Professor[†] of Astronomy and Mathematics. Ben's brother-in-law and Quincy Street[†] neighbor, Navy Lieutenant Charles Henry Davis, met Bache in Philadelphia where he gave the Baches a letter of introduction for an expected first visit to the Peirces in Cambridge. Bache couldn't come, being held at the last minute by pressing business in Philadelphia, so they finally met in May of 1843, when Ben made his debut[†] at the American Philosophical Society as member number 1173.

Bache had amassed[†] a full career even by then. As a great-grandson of Benjamin Franklin, he was related to the leading families of Philadelphia. He was a West Point man, top of his class in 1825. After two years in the Corps of Engineers, he resigned in favor of a professorship in natural philosophy and chemistry at the University of Pennsylvania. In 1836 he was called to organize Girard College. The following two years he conducted a study of European educational methods. (Several years earlier, Ben had already made a similar study at second-hand with Bancroft and Cogswell at Round Hill.) His report to Girard College on this topic eventually had considerable influence on American educational policy. Using those results, he organized Central High School in Philadelphia. By 1842, he had returned to the University of Pennsylvania, but only briefly, for in 1843, he succeeded F. R. Hassler as Superintendent of the United States Coast Survey. That agency was a small, insecure, but well-qualified body; in a few years he transformed it into the premier scientific research organization of the federal government. It also came to be well integrated into the international scientific community of that day.

Near the end of the year they were corresponding routinely, at first with a restrained tone. But they quickly became[†] much warmer, as "My dear friend" and "My dear Bache." One reason for the increasing coefficient of cordiality lay in Bache informing Ben that he was a candidate for the newly open position of Superintendent of the U.S. Coast Survey within the Treasury Department. Ben promised[†] "to leave no stone unturned, which it is in my power to turn, to obtain for you the appointment." And Ben assembled a powerful host, with the assistance of Lieutenant Davis. He persuaded President Quincy of Harvard to lobby President John Quincy Adams, and he also solicited the aid of Judge Story, Senator Choate, "some of the leading merchants of Boston," John Pickering, and George Bancroft—who by then had left Round Hill for his long and influential career in national politics.

Bache learned in December[†] that he had a competitor. Some influential figures were urging the "promotion" of Hassler's principal assistant. As strategic rhetoric Bache recommended instead that "selection" by qualified men of science ought to be the criterion for such a position, and he laid out plans whereby Ben's associates could marshall arguments along this line. Such a theme, selection of scientifically qualified officers, came to be a prime motif of Bache and his circle—"The Florentine Academy"—in opposition to what he called the present "glorious reign of mediocrity" in scientific agencies and associations by adherents to "old fogeyism." In other words, professionalism was beginning to rear its head. It worked, for Bache was appointed before the year ended.

Early next year Ben's family moved into a mansion-house on Quincy street, which had been constructed for them[†] by Harvard on University land. Sever Hall now stands on the site. It lay in a beautiful grove of trees and was a fitting setting for Ben's salon of scientific and literary men and women. Within Bache's circle where *both* fun and science prevailed, Ben eventually became known as "The Functionary" (a pun on the theory of functions in mathematics, since Ben was *the* mathematician among the Florentines) and his home as "Function Hall" or "Function Grove," the site of many social

9. *The Peirce House on Quincy Street*
"Function Hall"
By permission, Cambridge Historical Commission
(photo by Roger Gilman)

functions among The Chief's friends. And it was a great[†] neighborhood: the Feltons, Agassizs, Longfellows, Davises, Lowells lived nearby.

Ben became a close consultant for Bache's efforts to improve and expand the Coast Survey, especially in areas related to mathematical astronomy. And there were consequences of the growing relationship. For instance, in spring of 1845, The Chief easily persuaded Ben to accept a remunerated project to compute latitudes[†] by means of occultations of certain stars. I had to look that one up in *The Century Dictionary:* it means "the hiding of a star from sight by its passing behind[†] some other of the heavenly bodies." This task brought a salary to Ben and the services in Cambridge of two "computers." That's what persons were called who, with pencil and paper, ran out long strings of mathematical computations required in astronomy of the day. Of this technique, Ben was a master in both theory and practice.

Ben's family was completed when his only daughter was born[†] in December of 1845. She was named Helen Huntington in memory of her mother's sister, Mrs. Helen Huntington, who had recently passed away after a prolonged illness. Among family and friends, the new daughter was known informally as Lelly. Sarah Peirce was slow in recovering[†] from her daughter's birth, but Ben nursed her back to health. And young Helen had a rough start, suffering bouts of digestive disturbances and fevers, to the point that her parents feared[†] for her life. Sarah took her to Swamscott for healthier air and access to a wet nurse, and her health was eventually restored.

At about the same time that Baby Helen returned to Function Grove, Ben met another person who was to rival Bache in importance for his career: Louis Agassiz. The great naturalist[†] had established a distinguished career in Europe and was being courted by John Amory Lowell, member of the Harvard Corporation and prominent Boston businessman, to move permanently to America. In the winter of 1846-47 at the Temple on Tremont Street he gave a set of lectures on "The Plan of Creation in the Animal Kingdom" to wildly

10. *Helen Huntington Peirce*
"His only daughter"
Tuttle Collection, Institute for Studies in Pragmaticism
By permission, Philosophy Department, Harvard University

appreciative Bostonians in audiences as large as five thousand. Why were these lectures so well received? His biographer captured† the matter perfectly.

Besides introducing Agassiz to a wider world which he would conquer with the same determination that had seen him scale Alpine peaks and gather fossil fishes from all over Europe, the Lowell lectures were singular Landmarks in the history of nineteenth-century national culture. In an age alive and responsive to the idealism of Emerson, Agassiz gave a scientific demonstration of the spiritual quality underlying all material creation. Men might know all there was to know about the facts of nature, but if they did not appreciate the magnificence of the master plan fashioned by its Author, and the complexity of the relationship that bound all organic creation to the Higher Power, they could know the world only partially. Man's soul, his intelligence, his divine nature, provided the connective link by which he could appreciate the power of the Deity in relating him to the process of nature. "We may . . . come to a full understanding of Nature from the very reason that we have an immortal soul." The religion of nature that Agassiz illustrated by precept and by line drawings of animals demonstrated that the entire history of creation, beginning with the smallest radiated animal and ending with man, had been wisely ordained. The men and women who listened to Agassiz heard that their species was not only the highest form of vertebrates but represented the direction and the purpose to which all creation had moved from the beginning.

Agassiz had been introduced† to President Everett of Harvard, Ben Peirce, Cornelius Conway Felton the classicist, and Henry Longfellow at a luncheon arranged by Lowell shortly after arriving in the United States. Seeing the import of Agassiz's lectures, I immediately understood why Ben and he became such fast friends. That is, if one subtracted the notion of Biology from those Lowell lectures and substituted Divine Geometry (Ben's phrase) in its place, one would have something very close to the viewpoint and motivating force of the life of Benjamin Peirce, Jr., mathematician, astronomer, physicist, mystic. For such men the practice of science was much more than a profession or career. It was a way of life—a mode of communion, even communication, with the Divine Architect.

Lowell's courtship was successful: Harvard got its great biologist. Ben gained an intimate neighbor and colleague; The Chief eventually secured a distinguished member for the Florentines; and another of the formative influences upon Charley was in place.

I have become something of an expert on the Florentine Academy, also known† among themselves as the Lazzaroni—Italian for "street beggars."

This is an opportune moment to present what I have discovered, so here is a quick outline. The Florentines came to include many great figures in early American science, roughly the period of 1845-1900. Bache was *The Chief*, Ben *The Functionary*, Agassiz *The Fossilary*, Joseph Henry—Superintendent of the Smithsonian Institution—was *Smithson* or *Smithsonian*, and so on. Of course, Lieutenant Davis was part of the group, as was the Chemist Wolcott Gibbs, and many others around the country. Before the great American *Burgerkrieg*, several important figures from the South were closely involved—for instance the Le Conte brothers, John and Joseph. Their sessions and convivial dinners in the early years centered around meetings of the American Association for the Advancement of Science. The name "Florentine Academy" seems to have developed in honor of The Chief's favorite oyster bar, the exact name and location of which is lost to history.

It would be a mistake to think of this network as some happy-go-lucky bunch of revelers. This was a serious and powerful group of strong minds that had a definite and well-coordinated program aimed at enforcing professional standards in science, encouraging international scientific communication, promoting government funding for science, and creating a national research university. It was also the prototype for the National Academy of Sciences, founded by Bache, Henry, Agassiz, Ben Peirce, and others during the Lincoln administration under the political leadership of Senator Henry Wilson. Does this mean that President Lincoln and Senator Wilson were Honorary members of the Florentine Academy? My guess is, in a certain sense, yes. It would be correct to say that the National Academy of Sciences owed its very existence to the Florentines, to their power and vision, and that it was one of their best successes.

All this clearly indicates that Charley was educated within the mores of an almost monastic community of brother scientists who were the founders of American science[†] as it is organized today, who stayed in constant contact, who felt a sense of mission, and who were led by a powerful, well-informed, visionary and able chief. Their program usually succeeded. They did, however, have some defeats, especially after Bache passed from the scene in 1867. Ben became the head Florentine when he succeeded Bache to the Superintendency of the Coast Survey; from that central post he was able to continue many Lazzaroni initiatives. But with Ben's death in 1880, the zenith clearly had been passed. The group did not replicate itself into a new generation, and the last survivors were gone when the new century arrived.

From the start, the Florentines accumulated a fair number of enemies, who took pleasure in referring to them with scornful epithets[†] such as "Bache and Company" or "The Association." And I can say "brother scientists" without fear of contradiction because there were no practicing women scientists in those days; but they always included their wives in social activities and as

11. *Founders of the National Academy of Sciences*
Peirce, Bache, Henry, Agassiz, Lincoln, Wilson, Davis, Gould
"Owed its very existence to the Florentines"
Painting by Albert Herter
By permission, National Academy of Sciences

audience members during lectures and addresses. Until The Chief and Ben
passed from the scene, they were able to keep their enemies in check and to
continue forward with their plans and projects. But when these Florentine
founders of American science faded away, their enemies came forward with
a hot, intense vengence, reminiscent of the dangerous wall-busting spark one
can draw from a high-voltage Planté battery that has been constantly charged
for long years. But that is another matter for another time. And that is enough
of my amateur history of science for now.

Function Grove

1846
Stopped going to school at Marm Sessions
and began to go to Miss Ware's
— a very pleasant school
where I at once fell in love with another Miss W
whom for distinction's sake
I will designate[†] as Miss W'.

1846. Discovery[†] of Neptune. The Everett's come.

The sum total[†] of what we understand one another to be talking about is what logicians call the universe of discourse. De Morgan introduced the term on November 6, 1846. Exact logic dates from that day. I was seven, and unaware of it at the time.

1847
Began to be most seriously and hopelessly in love.
Sought to drown my care
by taking up the subject of Chemistry
— an antidote which long experience
enables me to recommend[†] as sovereign.

1847. California[†] excitement. Discovery of ether. Gam Bradford suspended. Sullivan's school. President Polk's visit.

Although I was not[†] a precocious child, at the age of 8 I took up of my own accord the study of chemistry, to which the following year I added Natural philosophy; so that by the time I went to college, I was already a fairly expert analyst. Somewhat later I became exceedingly fascinated by Lavater's Physiognomy, in which I half believed. But further than that I took no particular interest in the human mind before I reached puberty. Nor did I then read about it, although I wrote a little treatise of my own called the Dynamics of Persuasion. The first philosophical book which attracted my attention was Whately's Logic, with which as a school-boy I was delighted. At sixteen I entered college.

When I was first[†] studying chemistry, the theory was that every compound consisted of two oppositely electrified atoms, or radicles; and in like manner every compound radicle consisted of two opposite atoms or radicles. The argument to this effect was that chemical attraction is evidently between things unlike one another, and evidently has a saturation point; and further that we observe that it is the elements the most extremely unlike which attract one another.

How many times[†] have men now in middle life seen great discoveries made independently and almost simultaneously! The first instance I remember was the prediction of a planet exterior to Uranus by Leverrier and Adams in 1847 or 1848.

1848
Went to dwell in town with my uncle C. H. Mills
and went to school to Rev. T. R. Sullivan,
where I received my first lesson[†] in elocution.

1848. French[†] revolution. Sullivan's school. Cambridge High School.

Mr. Mills was in the dry goods business[†] with J. K. Mills and Company, and lived at 69 Beacon Street in 1848, but moved to 1 Park Street[†] in 1849.

Reverend Sullivan's school[†] for boys was conducted in Park Street Church in Boston. During Charley's tenure the upper floors of the church housed a school for girls kept by Miss Dwight whose pupils ranged in age from beginners to "big girls." Another school for boys, kept by Mr. D. B. Tower, was located in a large room on the ground floor. Sullivan's school was in the basement, reached from Park Street corner by a steep flight of steps. It was also a popular school, although not as large as its neighbors. A former pupil of Mr. Tower recorded the student ambience around the Church[†] and its schools:

> During the years immediately preceding the Civil War, the eastern part of the Common, especially the grass-plot alongside Park Street Hall, was a favorite playground for school-boys, hockey being then a popular feature in athletics. Many boys from the Public Latin School, then on Bedford Street, took part in these sports. In the spring and summer the game of marbles was a customary pastime. In those days the Park Street region was purely residential; the only evidence of its role as a thoroughfare being the passage of the old stage-coach in the early morning hours, and the not infrequent blocking of the road by flocks of sheep which were being driven across the city.

> *I remember in 1848[†] a vessel struck a rock in Boston Harbour, which had been an important port for more than two centuries during more than half of which it was the chief port, lying in that part of the country where such matters as surveying received the most attention. I was only a boy; but I was with the eminent hydrographer,—Uncle Davis,—who went to locate the rock, for bearings had been taken from the vessel when she struck, and considering the circumstances, they were good ones. Nevertheless, it was not until the middle of the third day's search that we found the rock.*

> *My aunt[†] Huntington, who lived near us in Cambridge, took a great fancy to me, called me a bright boy. To keep me quiet during the excessive heat of the summer day she used to supply me with boxes of black and white horn buttons of different sizes. I remember she was very much struck with the skill and ingenuity I showed in arranging them in all sorts of geometrical figures. I would lie on the floor and amuse myself with them by the hour, perfectly contented and happy.*

> *1849*
> *In consequence of playing truant*
> *and <u>laving</u> in the frog-pond, was taken ill.*
> *On my recovery, I was recalled to Cambridge*
> *and admitted as a member[†] of the <u>Cambridge High School</u>.*

1849. Macready† riot. Sparks college President. Dr. Parkman's murder.

Whoever has any practical† knowledge of chemistry, be it ever so elementary, must have such experiences of persons with mere book knowledge, that they can easily conceive of a case that will cost me very little effort of imagination, since when I was some nine years old, and had already worked nearly through Liebig's hundred bottles, a play-mate of mine of prodigious memory crammed himself with the entire contents of a treatise on chemistry; and I do not know but he was equally possessed of Rose's thick octavo on Qualitative Analysis, although his eyesight was so bad, and his scent so untrained, that I am pretty sure that if I had given him a solution of some thio-salt to analyze, and he had begun by testing it with HCL, as he probably would, so getting a precipitate of sulphur, he would have taken it to be a chloride,—argentic, mercurous, plumbic, or some other. He would not have known a floculent precipitate from a crystalline one, or one odour from another. In short, with truly great analytic knowledge, he could not have made the least use of it, as he himself was well aware. For he was no fool and only learned chemistry as an exercise of memory.

On Sunday August twelfth of 1849 young Victoria† Stuart-Wortley, later Victoria Lady Welby—one of Charley's few disciples in old age—visited Cambridge with her mother Lady Emmeline Stuart-Wortley. They called upon Harvard ex-President Everett who showed them the new Observatory, "in which there is a telescope supposed to be the largest in the world of the refractor kind, except one in Russia." The visibility was bad, so they were unable to observe. The next day they went for a walk around Boston, to Faneuil Hall, the Athenaeum, the Custom House, the State-House, and on a later day to the museum at Harvard, then to Agassiz's home. The following Wednesday evening at half-eight Victoria and her mother attended a soirée at Mr. Everett's house in honor of the American Academy of Arts and Sciences, then in Cambridge for its second annual meeting. Victoria recalled:

There I saw, of course, many learned celebrities. Among them— Professor Peirce, Professor Silliman jun., Professor Guyon, Professor Sparks (the new President of Harvard University), and Professor Agassiz, the celebrated naturalist. (I found he was a cousin, by the way, of mama's former governess, Mademoiselle Anne† Agassiz.)

1850
Wrote "A History† of Chemistry."

1850 . Coup† d'etat. Hippopotamus. Crystal Palace.

Kings and Queens;

or,

Life in the Palace:

Consisting of
historical sketches of Josephine and Maria Louisa,
Louis Philippe, Ferdinand of Austria, Nicholas,
Isabella II, Leopold, and Victoria.

BY JOHN C. ABBOTT[†]

Charles S. Peirce
with his mother's love
6 January 1850

C. S. Peirce

New York:
Harper & Bros., Publishers
82 Cliff Street

1848

A secret[†] marriage, it is commonly reported, was soon consummated between Maria Louisa and Count Neipperg, which was publicly recognized soon after the death of Napoleon. Three children have been the issue of this union: the eldest, a daughter, is married to an Italian count, grand chamberlain of Parma; a son, the Count de Monti Nauvoo, is an officer in the Austrian army; a second daughter died in infancy. Ten years ago Count Neipperg died, and Maria was again left a widow.

When I was[†] a boy of ten, I had a cousin a dear friend Charley Mills, one of the best boys that ever lived though no milksop, who grew up to be one of the noblest gentlemen that the good God ever achieved, and who gave his life for his country,—at Hatcher's Run, Virginia in 1865 after serving through almost the whole war,—though with full consciousness that he would lose it, and though he intensely desired to live. He and I had no secrets from each other. Now I had a turn for experiments and we had observed that cologne water put on my handkerchief would burn up without igniting the handkerchief. Thereupon I, who had a turn for drawing conclusions, reasoned that if I were to pour some on my hand, the cologne would burn up without igniting my hand; and my cousin, who had a turn for bringing my conclusions to naught, suggested that it would be highly desirable to verify this interesting conclusion by direct experiment. This was accordingly done, or rather was begun; for I interrupted the experiment before the result was fairly ascertained by drawing my hand between my two trouser legs after having pressed them tightly together.

My original[†] conclusion was in every way a characteristic example of the study of inferences from common observations, but it led as that often does to a proposition, which would seem to have been a study of a new phenomenon for me, namely that if a person puts his hand into the fire he will withdraw it with marked promptitude. My cousin's bent was rather artistic than scientific and he derived a delicious hilarity from my thus adding to my stock of physical cognition.

I shall[†] meet him shortly in the other world I hope. It will at any rate I am sure be a precious piece of good fortune for me if I find myself there located at all in his neighbourhood; and going as I shall with a great mass of conclusions concerning the new phenomena of the other world, I dare say I shall afford him another very hearty laugh at the experimental testing of my theories.

Somewhat later[†] I became exceedingly fascinated by Lavater's work, in which I half believed. His 'Essays on Physiognomy' is a book[†] very much discredited; and I cannot say that I am a strong believer in such notions as that a large and prominent nose is associated with push and energy. But matter of that sort makes but a small part of the work, the diligent study of which, in a good edition, will, I can testify, stimulate a young person to train the faculty of nonprecise direct observation. I should be afraid to tell what I have known this power to accomplish, because it is unpleasant to have one's veracity doubted. At any rate, ever since I read it, I have been convinced that psychology would assume its legitimate dignity among the sciences from the day on which it should be recognized as based mainly upon the pure observation of which I speak, and not before.

1851
Established† a printing-press.

1851. Kossuth. Lane† professor.

Northampton, Mass.   Sun. 17 Aug. 1851
My Dear Mother:
  I hope that you† and all the family are well. I did not go to church this afternoon that I might write you this letter. By the way while we were on the Western Rail Road a horse got in the way of the train, but they frightened him off by whistleing. We got to Springfield at 10 minutes past 11; when we got out of the cars I gave Father my check and he gave me one to the other road, and then he took me to the Agwam Bank and gave a gold dollar to pay with, then went to the Massasoit House and there we saw other gentlemen. When I got there Uncle Henry gave a first rate apple, and Dr. Bache talked with me till dinner-time, which was 12 o'clock. I never dined at a publick house before, but I think we had an excellent dinner—we had Bean Soup, and Roast Chicken, and Potatoe, and real nice Apple Pie, and Vanilla Ice Cream. Father and I eat the same. Father started from Springfield for the AAAS meeting in Albany at 12 1/2, and I waited until 2. When I got to Northampton I got out and gave my check to a Mansion House driver, and got into his stage. I got to uncle H's at 3 1/4. Neddie took me up on Round Hill and showed me everything, and when I got home Mrs. H gave me this article from the Cambridge Chronicle.

mbridge **Chronicle**   *August 9, 1851*

EXHIBITION OF THE
CAMBRIDGE HIGH SCHOOL

The third annual Exhibition† of the Cambridge High School took place at the City Hall, Saturday, August 2. The hall was filled to overflowing. The exercises consisted of speaking by the boys, reading by the young ladies, and singing. We have rarely witnessed any exhibition, not even excepting college commencement, where the speakers did themselves more credit. Perhaps, all things being considered, we may say we have never seen better performances. Usually, the style of one speaker at such exhibitions is the same as that of another, a wearisome monotony of manner and gesture. Here the majority of speakers differed from one another, and the different styles were natural and agreeable.

——Where all did well, and many remark-

ably well, it would be difficult to select the most deserving. Yet we feel that we cannot pass over one, a child of some ten or eleven summers, Charles Saunders Peirce. His part was the spirited poem of Halleck, Marco Brozzaris, and never have we heard anything more eloquently, more appropriately, more admirably delivered. Gestures the most animated and the most graceful,—in themselves, eloquence,—a voice modulated to every emotion breathed in that fine poem, an eye that kindled with lofty fire, or melted in subdued feeling, all combined to hold us spell-bound, while, we are not ashamed to say it, tears fell fast from our eyes, nor from ours alone, for many were alike deeply moved.

I went with Edie and Henry to drive the cow from the pasture, and came home and had tea and went to bed. Today is very cold and rainy here. How is it at home? As for Henry I am most agreeably disappointed in him. I have got a very interesting book today called the "Gambler." I have had a very pleasant time here as you may see. Give my love to all the family, and I would write them all letters if I could.

P.S. Tuesday. I am writeing to Lelly. Henry exclaimed the other day that he loved Jimy Peirce. Mrs. H. asked him Why? He said because he gave him Blackberries and put sugar on em. I have just got your letter. I am not afraid of being homesick for I have had a very good time. Yesterday morning I walked up to Mt. Holyoke and back. I have not got a letter from Father yet. Mrs. H sends her love and wishes I could stay longer.

    Good By

        from your affectionate son

                    C. S. Peirce

I early became interested[†] in a childish way in dynamics and physics, and my father's brother Charles being a chemist, I must have been about twelve years old when I set up a chemical laboratory of my own and began to work through Liebig's hundred bottles of qualitative analysis and to make such things as vermillion both in the dry and in the wet way and to repeat a great many well-known processes of chemistry.

Valency, in its chemical[†] sense, is a conception first brought to human cognizance by the genius of Sir Edward Frankland, in the early fifties. A certain boy who was then nourishing his mind with chemistry devoured Frankland's memoirs with avidity as they appeared in successive volumes of the 'Philosophical Transactions,'—a fact whose interest for us is that this boy having grown into the present writer, the fact goes to show how he can narrate the events of the subsequent development of the conception as matters in which he was vastly interested at the times of their occurrence. What he had previously known of chemical theory had been based upon the doctrines of the great Berzelius, with whose treatise the boy was acquainted through the French translation in six portly octavos.

It must have been late in the year 1851[†] that I remember picking up a copy of Whately's Logic in the room of my brother, five years older than myself, and asking him what logic was. On receiving his answer, I next see myself stretched upon his carpet intent upon reading the volume, and I believe that within a few days I had mastered it, as subsequent tests[†] showed; so that 6 years later, when I was, with the rest of my class, required to answer at recitations on the book, I needed no more than a slight rereading of the lessons. From that day[†] the science of logic has been my strongest passion, although my training[†] was particularly in the direction of mathematics, physics, and chemistry. In 1887, when I had attained a standing among American scientific men sufficient to satisfy a man of very little ambition, I retired to the wildest county of the Northern States, south of the Adirondacks and east of the Alleghenies, where I might have the least distraction from the study of logic.

How successful[†] my studies have been is a question to be decided by my readers, as the court of final appeal. From the time when I first began as a boy, until now, to reflect upon the question of the being of God,—not some god, but that God in whom religious people of all creeds believe in proportion as they are truly religious,—it has always seemed to me reasonable to suppose that, if He really is, there must be some good reason for believing so, otherwise than on authority of any kind, which should appeal to the lowliest mind; and whether this be good reasoning or not, I am inclined to think that the majority of those humble minds who have become persuaded by reason, in contradistinction to the weight of others' belief, that God is real, together with a large part of superior minds have, in fact, been so persuaded by an humble argument.

It seems strange[†] that at the age of twelve I didn't already know in a general way what Logic is, since the 7th edition of the Encyclopedia Britannica was in the house and for the preceding 5 or 6 years I had been poring over its pages for hours daily. But there were 21 volumes so of course I could not have read above a quarter of the whole, and doubtless much less. From that time, however, I looked upon myself (and always have) as studying nothing but logic and exercises in reasoning. The circumstance that at the age of 12 I did not know the meaning of the word "logic" even vaguely, although my father was a mathematician, leads me to mention that he had a low opinion of the utility of formal logic, and wished to draw directly upon the geometrical instinct rather than upon logical deductions from the smallest number of axioms. This disposition of his is manifest in his "Analytic Mechanics" of 1855 and still more in his interesting textbook of Elementary Geometry (of 1837). By the time[†] I was a schoolboy, his views about teaching geometry were so decided that he interfered with the course in my school to insist that before I was put into his book or into Legendre, I should go through a book containing substantially the same matter as my books on Topology and Graphics. This was one[†] of a number of allied points in which I have long disagreed with my father, mainly because I do not think instinct is an absolutely infallible source of truth. On the contrary, it must develope like every other feature of creation.

I use the word[†] <u>instinct</u> in the precise sense of an animal's faculty of acting (whether physically or psychically) in a reasonable (or better "an adaptive") manner when the animal (human or other) would be unable by reasoning to reach the requisite conclusion. It follows that, adopting this definition, I must admit that all reasoning ultimately reposes on "instinct." That is to say, it rests on a rule of logic which could not be reached by reasoning without a petitio principii, or its equivalent.

1913	The reader[†] whom I specially desire to
Aug 27	serve, and unceasingly in mind and in heart, is a
PM 2:20	young fellow with whom I am not yet personally acquainted

who is in about the same stage of culture and yearning toward understanding as I myself was on a certain sunshiny day in September, 1851 (just about 62 years ago), when I walked into my elder brother's room, and picking up from his table a newly purchased book, Whately's "_Elements of Logic_," asked him "What is logic?" and on receiving an answer,

1913	incontinently stretched myself prone upon the
Aug 27	carpet on which I laid the volume, and before the
PM 3:00	end of the week had mastered it in such fashion as I knew

how to do at the age of twelve. I value such a disciple who comes to me before the age of complete puberty, upon which follow some seven years of dense stupidity, because if he has the impulse to think and doubt for himself, no matter what offense his self-conceit may give to the small-minded, he is assuredly one of those of whom it was said, "Ye are the salt of the earth: but if the salt have lost his savour, wherewith shall _it_ be salted? it is thenceforth good for nothing but to be cast out and get trodden under foot of men," and the rest.

1913	(How sweet this genuine English is! How superior
Aug 27	to the base Greek of the original.) If you are
PM 4:00	conceited, all you have to do is to compare your crude no-

tions with the hard facts of God, and you will soon be cured; but lack of courage is less easy to surmount. You are a representative of the coming generation, whose duty it is to be a lot better in every way than the present one. Don't forget that.

The Queen of the Sciences

The Le Conte family initially entered Ben Peirce's orbit in 1850 when Joseph at age twenty-six attended his first American Association for the Advancement of Science meeting in New Haven, where he met Ben[†] and his scientific coterie, the Florentine Academy. Following the August meeting Joe proceeded to Harvard and study with Agassiz to graduate S.B. from the Lawrence Scientific School[†] in June of 1851. The Le Conte brothers were born and raised on Woodmanston Plantation in Liberty County Georgia, John five years the senior. The family was of French Huguenot stock. Their father, Louis, was both a well-to-do planter and a passionate amateur scientist, the finest kind according to me; his special interests were chemistry and botany. John and Joe enjoyed their father's large scientific library and were personally trained by Louis as naturalists. Both boys were sent to Franklin College (later University of Georgia) in Athens, and both received degrees from the College of Physicians and Surgeons in New York City. In 1841 John married Eleanor Josephine Graham, whom he had met in New York. Josephine, or Josie, was described by her contemporaries as possessed of rare intelligence, force of character, and beauty—qualities that assured social recognition. Joe commented upon John that "no other influence so greatly affected the whole course of his life as that of his wife." There were other lives affected by Josie as well.

"That's too bland," said Betsey, with whom I have a running feud on the subject of the significance of Josie. "I prefer the version of John's distant kinsman W. Le Conte Stevens, even though it is still too restrained."

Mrs. Le Conte[†] was a woman of wonderful personal magnetism, queenly in bearing, and of extraordinary beauty. Her brilliancy and wit, her quick insight and ready tact, added to her majestic presence, made her the center of attraction in every social gathering. In after-years, especially at the annual meetings of the American Association for the Advancement of Science, such men as Bache, Peirce, Henry, and Agassiz vied with each other in doing her homage. Her fame in social circles equaled that of her husband among men of science.

John and his wife probably first appeared among the Florentines at the AAAS meeting of 1851[†] in Albany, the occasion of a magnificent presidential speech by The Chief[†] in which he sketched the future development of national scientific organizations and envisaged a world union of such organizations when modern facilities of communication come to bring separate parts of the world closer. Ben, by the way, followed The Chief as president of the Association during the next year.

For a number of years after their marriage John and Josie lived in Savannah where he practiced medicine. In 1846 he became professor of physics and chemistry at Franklin College, but resigned in 1855 to accept the chair of chemistry at the College of Physicians and Surgeons. Yet he loved physics more, so within the year he accepted the professorship of Natural and Mechanical Philosophy at South Carolina College and University in Columbia. This institution enjoyed the patronage of a visionary board of trustees[†] "composed of gentlemen of refinement and culture, with a genuine sympathy for the labors of the student who strives to plant himself at the most advanced outposts of science and literature." In this atmosphere John quickly earned an international reputation through publications on his research in natural philosophy, or physics, as we would call it today.

I mention this background material about the Le Conte family by way of introducing an odd section that comes at this location in the papers from Charley's box. It departs from the usual material he inserted—his remembrances, journal entries, items he had copied from books, clippings, and the like. It is apparently a loosely-organized letter-book and diary assembled by his father that either fell into Charley's lap or was perhaps ultimately directed there by Ben's wishes. It concerns external events and inner aspects of Ben's life during the 1850s. Physically it's a collection of letters and dated loose pages bound by an elegant black silk ribbon passing through a single perforation in the upper left corner of each sheet. A number of sheets have dried flowers affixed. I surmise this came into Charley's hands sometime after the death of his mother. Probably he began assembling the box around 1900 when, so it appears, he placed this material into the sequence here. I give you this collection[†] of letters as I found it placed in the box, written in Ben Peirce's hand or that of his correspondents, introduced only by Charley's note scribbled across the blank top of the first page.

* * *

My father and The Queen ——————————— *1901 April 10*

My Dear Mrs. Le Conte   Cambridge 18 I 52

What shall I say to these exquisite presents? to this charming handicraft? to these palpable proofs that you are, as I have reported you, a true-hearted friend? What can I say? In a single mathematical formula, I could express the motions of a universe, all the past, all the future, and even all the possible motions of all possible worlds—but not a single emotion of the human heart. The only language which I can pretend to know—and what a poor master I am of that I should be ashamed to tell you—is algebra—but if I were to take my magic wand in hand, and summon to my aid all the mysterious forms of expression which the profoundest magi of my science have yet imagined they would not involve the faintest shadow of an idea of human sympathy. Were I to put on this cap and these slippers and draw around me the great astrological circle, collecting all the planets, and comets, and stars and suns and the mightiest astronomical wits from Zoroaster to Laplace, and offer them this purse provided they would convey to Georgia one ray of the light of gratified friendship of which I am so full— they would gaze upon the work of your fingers with wonder and delight, and comprehend at a glance the exact number of stitches in the curious web. There are men in this world whose whole life is a game of misery, and they lose it in the end—but as to myself, with this cap on my locks, these slippers over my socks, and my arm affectionately wound around the waist of my wife, as I fill her purse with coin fresh from the mint, I can honestly declare it as my private opinion publicly expressed that I know not misery.

Have you ever seen "Poor Pillicoddy"? I shall send it to you, by the very next mail—a dreadfully thumbed copy, because it was used in studying a part for private theatricals at this very last Christmas. And now I ask you what do you say to the President of the American Association for the Advancement of Science taking the part of Captain O'Scuttle in the farce of Poor Pillicoddy? Do not betray him for all the world.

My wife will interrupt me—For many years a proud Peirce she is now purse-proud. She commands me to thank you, in her name, most earnestly and sincerely and kindly and warmly—and a warmer heart than hers never yet loved—for your beautiful present.

Benjamin Peirce

My dear Professor   Congress Hall, Albany 19 II 52
  and very dear friend

Who would have been so bold as to wager last August, that I should receive my first letter from Athens in Congress Hall Albany? I am proud to say that I have a true friend, and a very dear friend of the feminine gender separated from me by half a continent. I came to Albany on Monday to take part in an effort to enlist the empire state in the establishment of a truly national university. This evening when I returned to my room, with the express intention of writing to my friend Le Conte (for I said I cannot leave this house with all its delightful associations without sending him a line) there lay upon my bureau your letter and hers, and I exclaimed in the overflow of my heart, "With a preestablished harmony which so mysteriously binds together Georgia and Massachusetts, the Union is safe, and I love my true friends with my whole heart." Oh that you and Josephine were here tonight—there is to be a grand ball in the dining room, and the music is already sounding through the house.

I went to the ball with Dr. Bache, staid till one o'clock, and am now closing this letter at six o'clock. It was quite a splendid affair, as was my dinner at the patroon's yesterday, whose magnificent old mansion is a wonder to be seen. Give my truest and sincerest love to Madame Josephine. Tell her I had not the heart to take the old seat at table.

Benjamin Peirce

Mrs. Josephine Le Conte   Function Hall 1 I 53

A happy New Year! My Dear Friend! All blessings be on your head. We have just had a glorious old-fashioned snow storm. I pulled out one of my gray locks and compared it with the snow, and I assure you it is not as white as snow.

Bye the bye—you almost made a conquest. The poet—not Longfellow—but the poet of Cambridge—the Batchelder—the black dwarf—Eugene (what a pretty name!) who could not keep his eyes off from you at Mrs. Dixwell's—came up to Mr. Dixwell and begged an introduction to that "stylish looking young lady." Who do you mean? said Mr. D—pretending not to take. "Why that stylish maiden." Mr. Dixwell then said "Oh she is not a maiden—she is a married lady." "Married! Is she? Well then, perhaps, I had better not be introduced."

The children are all well and send many kisses.

Benjamin Peirce

My Dear and True Friend   Niagara Falls 8 VIII 53

My presidency is over, and you were not present to support me. Hence the meeting was a sad—melancholy—business sort of affair, and we did not linger upon the spot one instant after decency permitted our departure. From one end to the other of the meeting my mouth was not opened, nor my eyes directed, nor my ears erected to a woman that was a woman. I even felt a disposition to doubt the truth of friend Haldeman's public assertion that the nature of woman was the same everywhere. My experience is not so. She who worked these lovely slippers, and whose beautiful daguerrotype has enchanted all the professors of Harvard, and set our learned friend Dr. Bache into an ecstasy of raving delight, is a totally different sort of being. It was very kind of you to send us such a beautiful likeness of yourself, and we are looking forward to your promised visit in November with the greatest impatience. You must write and let me know the very day and hour of your arrival in Boston in order that I may be at the cars, to get you to Cambridge with the least possible waste of time and temper.

Benjamin Peirce

Mrs. Josephine Le Conte   Cambridge 4 XII 53

The Sighs of Science, or the Finished Functionary

Act V, Last Scene: Function grove Dining room—breakfast table set—the morning after Mrs. Le Conte's departure.

Enter the two Benjies.

Benjie Little. I feel as lonely—Now Mrs. Le Conte has gone—As if I were ninety million miles—away from home, and knew no one—there

Benjie Big. Heaves a heavy sigh.

The curtain falls and leaves the Benjies Peirce

Blanker, by far, than Milton's blankest verse.

"Hung be the heavens with black!" began the Boston orator in his eulogy upon Washington. And I say too. Hang the Heavens!

I have found Matthew Mattucs to be the only philosopher capable of solving the inequations of life.

12 and 13. *"Enchanted all the professors of Harvard"*
Top: *Mrs. John Le Conte (Eleanor Josephine Graham) in New York, 1850s.*
Bottom: *Mrs. Le Conte in Oakland, California, post–Civil War, probably 1869*
By permission, Nancy Hopkins

Give the professor my kindest love and a Bacho-Davisian embrace. Remember me affectionately to your sister and your uncle the major. If he is angry with me for having tempted you to Cambridge, I beg his forgiveness upon my knees and am sure of obtaining it with your aid. Ask him to take a good strong look at you and then he may wonder and be angry if he can at our desire to get you here.

Benjamin Peirce

My Dearest Friend: Harvard University 3 IX 54

Soul of truth! and truest of all true friends! My heart is almost broken by your sad letter. That you should have been so ill and I not suspect it! What would I not give to be with you and help to cheer you up and restore you to your wonted hilarity and bring you home to your own joyous nature.

Next winter I shall see you at your home and see that queenly tread in its own halls. But before then, I shall see you here; for when you come north I will go to meet you unless you come to Cambridge again and again enchant us all with your loving heart. You cannot think how often the children speak of you and your beauty. Whenever they see a pretty woman—they compare her to Mrs. Le Conte, and always to her disadvantage for they have very good taste. Yes, my dear friend, we all love you in Cambridge, and the doll which bears your name is quite a pet.

Do not, I beg you, forget me—do not, I entreat you, permit the cruel words which were spoken to you at Washington to leave their poison in your pure heart.

Benjamin Peirce

My dearest, my darling friend: Cambridge 23 X 54

My friend—Mine—are you not mine? How can I tell you with what deep heart feeling I received those dear flowers—which had stood at your bedside, watching over you for so many days of sadness and sickness! I could not permit another to intrude upon such delicious a joy, and their coming is not known to others. When shall I see you, my dear Josephine, this winter? In Georgia or at the North? Mr. Ruggles has just been making quite a visit in Cambridge and spoke with great enthusiasms of the Southern beauty. He admired the Daguerrotype and the slipper—that celebrated slipper—than which none but Cinderella's was ever so well known. He was in ecstasies over its beauty.

You would feel pleased, I think, if you knew how freshly your memory was persevered in this house. The children are almost every day alluding to you and Benjie is as much your devoted page as ever he was.

Benjamin Peirce

ad Fraser Doctissimum   Clarendon Hotel, Wednesday 13 XI 54
   Omnium professorum[†] learnedissime, Tibi volo submittere questionem
difficillimam. Philosophi, qui experientia—sunt docti dicunt de diabolo
atque diabola, esse diabolos dramaticos, lyricos, politicos, scienticos,
humorosos, atque tremendos. Tibi propono investigare pro academica
scientiarum quae sit forma diabolae vestita in forma fininae, quae
hominibus est nota mimine Le Conte. Ferre conclusiones vestrae
indagationis ad Providential bonam. Ignorante sed amante.

                                                              Penetrare

Madame Josephine   Cambridge, 22 XII 54
   Dear Friend! True Friend! Beloved Friend! What a most charming time
we had at the Clarendon! I look back to it with a pleasure that swells my
heart to its fullest capacity of enlargement. The children were delighted
beyond measure at your presents and Madame would have greeted me with
a warmer smile if I had brought you to Function Grove. Yes—you are a
darling—it must be admitted—a very treasure of a friend of inestimable
value. Things do not look brighter for my going south, but rather the
reverse. The only hope I now have is that I may be able to make an
arrangement with the Smithsonian to deliver some lectures in Washington.
Yet who wants to hear a mathematician's lectures. I fear, therefore, that I
shall not be blessed again with the material sight of you till the warm sun
drives you again to the north.

                                                         Benjamin Peirce

Professor John Le Conte   Cambridge, 20 IX 55
   We have just heard that you have been chosen as Torrey's successor in
the chair of chemistry in the Med School of N.Y. We missed you at the
meeting of the Am. Ass. and lamented your absence not a little. Mrs. P. was
there and Bache, Agassiz and ourselves with Mrs. Bache and Miss Cuyler
formed quite a pleasant party at a boarding house by ourselves. Our
photograph was taken at Providence, and I have a copy for you.

                                                         Benjamin Peirce

Professor John Le Conte   Cambridge 10 II 56
   I intend to go to New York next Friday, and shall depend upon your
kindness to secure me as good a room as you can in your hotel. I shall
remain about a week at the farthest, and wish that Mrs. P would go with
me—but she positively and unequivocally declines. Give our warmest and
most affectionate greetings to the wife of your bosom.

                                                         Benjamin Peirce

Dearest Josephine   Cambridge, 28 II 56
 I am with you in heart[†] and ever shall be. God be with you, my dear friend, my heart is yours—my head is yours—I am all yours.
             Benjamin Peirce

My Dearest Josephine   Cambridge, 30 IV 56
 How I bless you for your kind letter and the sweet flowers. Your true heart was true in both and I felt the fragrance of your dear presence in the depths of my soul. I thank you for your promise to meet me in Albany.
             Benjamin Peirce

Professor John Le Conte   Function Grove, 3 VII 56
 I know not how to congratulate you upon what is such a loss to myself. But when you had come so near to us, it was tantalizing to have you torn away again. God bless you in your new situation. You will of course come with Josephine—I like to write that name—to the Albany meeting or it will be no Bene! to me. Au Revoir.
             Benjamin Peirce

To The Queen of Science,   Function Grove 11 VIII 56
Josephine Le Conte
 With what earnestness do I not look forward to our reunion at Albany next week! Although they have provided so sumptiously for our entertainment and have put us into such a fine house I almost regret the familiar old rooms of Congress Hall where we first met, and the old dining room where we so often sat side by side at the not too festive board—but in which the warmth of sentiment more than made up for the coldness of the repast.
             Benjamin Peirce

All Hail! Proud Queen of Science! Haughty Josephine   Albany 56
 Whose infinite delight it is to grind that infinitesimal heel into the ten thousand hearts of your ten thousand and one victims, and to respond to their ten thousand times ten thousand wails of agony with a ringing burst of joyous mirth!
 Will the great Queen be pleased to lay aside, for the nonce, that awful frown of indignation, whose dazzling terrors we cannot endure? Will she don the rosy garments of the dawn and meet us by moonlight alone?
             Benjamin Peirce

Philadelphia Anno Domini 1856
 We, Josephine, by the consent of the Albany Academicians, Queen of the Florentines, having established for the time being our Court in the City

of Brotherly Love, do send our friendly greetings and kindliest wishes to the tribe of Benjamin: First, to Alexander The Chief, to Benjamin the prime Functionary, Joseph to whom much is entrusted, Henry the mighty in spirit, and Louis the High Priest;—then to their consorts and their successors, and to each and to all of them, our trusty and tried servants, wherever found.

We deem it necessary to return thanks,—both we, and our grave and dignified counsel,—to the tribe, for the gift of joyous hours, and jolly good times in general, during our sojourn in that most ancient, never-rapidly-moving, always-in-a-dignified-manner-slowly-gyrating city of Albany, where in former days Dutchmen have smoked and slumbered. So long as spirits cling to our bodies, we hope to retain a pleasant recollection—not of the Dutchmen (who were defunct before we assembled our Court)—but, of the jolly good times.

Long may the scientific councils of the country be honored with your presence, and while science is advancing under your care, may an increase of friendly feelings flow in co-tidal lines of everlasting harmony, undisturbed by the earthquake waves of discord, developing ever into greater and greater complications of structure, beyond the reach of the highest Potential Arithmetic.

Lapidator, M.D. Elephantis custos, Linguisti unculus, Missinterpreter;
Johannes M.D. Subdiaconus;
Johannes M.D. Notarious;
Josephus M.D. Cubae pontifax Max!

To Queen Josephine   Function Grove 14 XII 56
I shall probably, or rather possibly, go about the middle of January to lecture at Washington. It is not quite certain, for there is a little flare up in regard to my lectures, which may end in their non-delivery. I sent my subjects to the majestic Smithsonian. They were, in general, upon Potential Physics—and the special subjects of the individual lectures were. 1st The elements of Potential Physics. The material universe regarded as a machine, as a work of art, or as the manifest word of God. 2d Potential Arithmetic or the Abacus of Creation. 3d Potential Algebra or the Logic of Creation. 4th Potential Geometry or the Music of the Spheres. 5th Analytic Morphology or the World's Architecture. 6th. The realization of the Imaginary or the mysticism of nature. 7th The powers of Justice and Love or the scientific necessity of Sinai and Christ. . . . . . . These subjects evidently frightened the immortal Smithson and made him tremble for his throne. He hurried to our dear Chief—who wrote to me at once they were a peg too high—and quite beyond the vision of a Washington audience. To which I replied that if the subjects were out of sight the lectures were much more so, and that it would not be judicious to give them at Washington. I asserted that they were not plays of fancy—but the results of all my life of investigation, and I had no desire that my audience should find them unfitted to their digestion and

should consequently turn and rend me. I answered the Great and Noble Smithson he had placed my lectures upon his programme; I begged him to withdraw them and said that I should regard them as withdrawn if I did not hear further from Washington. What will be the result, I care very little— less than I ought to care. But I had once a friend in Athens whom I believe to be the truest friend that ever a man had. Not many years shall elapse, ere I will make a pilgrimage to Athens, and meditate upon the friend who is no longer there. I have her daguerrotype which I love to look at—there is truth in every lineament. How well she used to read every expression of mine! I first found her at Albany. It was there I last saw her. Often at dusk I think of her but the dusk is not now brightened by the thought. I grieve for the fanaticism of the South, not less than for that of the North. As to myself, I am almost isolated in my political creed. My northern neighbours have gone crazy for free-soil notions.

Benjamin Peirce

1325 Spruce St. Philadelphia   July 12th 1857
Professor Peirce,

 In relation to the truly generous invitation of Mrs. Peirce, so warmly endorsed by yourself,—to pay a visit to "Function Grove" on our way to Montreal; we have been considering this proposition, and have almost concluded to do so. I presume we will find no difficulty in going directly from Boston to Montreal. As the "Chief" is in the neighborhood to Portland, he can join us on the way. But as Josephine will write to Mrs. Peirce on the subject, I shall say nothing more at present.

John Le Conte

To Queen Josephine   Cambridge 25 VIII 1857
 Well! Dear Josie! We arrived in Cambridge last night at about six o'clock and found every body well and there was an immense outburst of enthusiasm at our arrival. The city authorities were not however informed of our coming, so that we were compelled to walk in silence from the cars at the end of Quincy Street to Function Grove. After we left you at Troy we undertook to travel by coach to Albany.

 Early in the morning of Saturday Dr. Armsby called upon me and took me to the Dudley Observatory, where I found Dr. Peters and examined the arrangements and location which appear to be in every way excellent and well adapted to the high scientific duties to which they are consecrated.

 The gentlemen of this city have almost persuaded me to devote the next year after finishing my volume to the getting up of the University. Some think that I ought not to waste my time upon such a subject; but I do not feel that it would be wasting my time to accomplish the establishment of a true university upon a great scale—for I should not ask for less than a million of dollars, and none of this money should be buried in bricks and mortar nor any of it in collections of any kind. It should be exclusively devoted to salaries.

The children have been investing the funds which you lavished upon them during your visit to Cambridge.

Benjamin Peirce

My Dear Professor and true friend   Function Grove 25 VIII 57

Dr. Wyman, with whom I had a drive today, asked much about your paper and the mode in which the experiments were performed.

I send you by mail a copy of the Courier which contains my table of Harvard mortality. The articles in the Courier in defence of me were written by three persons—viz—one by Winlock who is always a trump—one by Wright—and that first one by young Newcomb who is a lad from the province of Nova Scotia and has recently been admitted to the Nautical Almanac office.

Benjamin Peirce

To The Queen   Function Grove 27 VIII 57

The book is getting ahead quite fast and I think that 6 or 7 weeks will finish it—except that I have to build Benjie a hennery—make Bache a report—provide work every day for Morrow and Newcomb—answer fifty letters from nobody about nothing—play the devil for the children—go to Lizzie Dwight's wedding—and call upon Mrs. J. R. Lowell, Mrs. Shattuck, Mr. Thingumbob and heaven knows how many others.

Benjamin Peirce

To The Queen   Function Grove 17 X 57

Mr. Yeadon called unfortunately while I was at recitation. I did not hear of this until dinner time. As soon as possible I got ready to go to Boston to see him—but before I could start Charles Mills and his wife came out to see us for the first time since his dry goods firm failed. And of course I could not leave them. The next day I found that Mr. Yeadon had left Boston in the morning train. I was prepared to receive him as your friend and John's, and your letter has given me a strong desire to know him for his own sake. These terrible times are striking down all the generous merchants of Boston. We are having a little difficulty of our own, of which you may perchance feel the effects. One of the comptrollers of the Treasury at Washington threatens to decide that I am not entitled to receive any compensation for the work which I have done for the Coast Survey—because I am at the same time an employee of the Nautical Almanac. Would it not be the height of injustice for Uncle Sam to benefit by my work and then refuse to pay for it? In case this decision is made I may be called upon to refund what I have received already—and since I have it not—I may possibly pass my vacation

in prison, instead of Columbia. The chief object of this low-lived blockhead
seems to be to give annoyance to The Chief. But I hear queer stories about
his doings in other cases, in which he has disturbed the equanimity of some
of the most distinguished members of his own party.

Benjamin Peirce

To The Queen   Function Grove 30 X 57
    Our thanks for the magnificent keg of bourbon—Oh delicious spirit—
heavenly hock! All Charley's class powdered themselves in their attempts to
exhibit the strength of their lungs cheering The Queen after each was
permitted a glass.

Benjamin Peirce

The Queen Josephine   Function Grove 3 III 58
    Here I am again in Cambridge at the North pole of the Republic after a
warm visit in Columbia. I found things at Washington much gloomier than I
expected. Fears for the dissolution of the union are gaining strength on all
sides—and there is no one of strength enough to stem the current, or has the
statemanship to divert it into the fields of harmony and discord. The
President has shown himself unequal to the situation. If the separation takes
place, remember that I am the other side of Mason and Dixon's line. I belong
to the other pole of the Republic. Take me to your hearts, my true southern
friends. My constant text now is I have seen slavery and I believe in it. You
may believe that some looks are averted—but I am persuaded that the
earnestness of my sincerity gains at least many listening ears, and I am
confident that my arguments make more or less of an impression and they
are not met unkindly. The time may come, however, when I shall be made
the object of public attack—and I know not what fear will do to those who
now listen. But I shall not shrink from what I know to be right.

Benjamin Peirce

My Dearest Friend on Earth   Function Grove, Sunday Morning, second
                                    sunday of May, 6 o'clock in the morning
    God grant that nothing may ever come between us. At Philadelphia we
were very hospitably entertained and left for New York on Thursday with
the Gibbs's and staid with them till Saturday morning. We went to the
concerts with them and the Ruggles's and Mr. R. whispered that he should
see a widow friend of mine next week and asked if I would send her a
tender message to which I made no reply.
    In returning to Massachusetts I feel more than ever the chilling
atmosphere of the north and I believe that your friend was right in his
computation of the latitude for which I was built—I would bless the day
which changed my domicile from Cambridge to Columbia. But what a task

it would be to gather around me all the appliances of labour which I now have, and which are so exactly suited to my scientific necessities.

You cannot think how you are associated with this house and how I meet you at every turn. At this place we have talked, and here you have sat, and there you have stood—and there your loveliest smile has greeted me and at this spot you have shone out in all your magnificence. Here again is your dressing gown, and here the cap and here the slippers and here the sweet likeness of yourself and last night before going to bed I took a glass of that wonderful spirit, which has not its equal in America, nor can have.

Benjamin Peirce

To The Queen   Function Grove 31 V 58

On Tuesday last the vote was taken on the re-election of the Functionary to the American Academy, to which he was nominated by the names of Josiah Quincy, Louis Agassiz and Joseph Lovering. For the election a three-fourths vote is required. When the vote was declared, the functionary was rejected. Agassiz is so wroth he has resigned his place in the academy. This is the way the Lazzaroni are honored at the north. The functionary stands ready to accept the first decent offer which comes from south of Mason and Dixon's line, and to return to his brethren of the warm hearts and whole souls.

I have been spending two days of the last week at the abolition meetings with Winlock and have heard much strange doctrine such as rarely penetrates the darkness of your black and benighted region.

Benjamin Peirce

To The Queen   Function Grove 6 VI 58

The scientific council of the Dudley Observatory are getting rapidly into inextricable difficulties. The Chief whom you do not love is resolved to sustain Gould whom you do love through thick and thin—and I can assure you there is some thick covered over with a very slight layer of thin. Gould's intention to irritate the Trustees is too plain to be mistaken. We shall be turned off. I would that I were free from this Dudley Observatory.

Benjamin Peirce

Professor John Le Conte   Cambridge 27 VI 58

The Dudley Observatory will be a hard fight and the victory will assuredly be with our opponents—but nevertheless we must die game and try to bring off Gould without dishonor from the embarrassing position in which he is placed. For my own part, I think that his course has not been characterized by any excess of wisdom and good judgment, and he seems to me rather to have sought than avoided occasions of difficulty. All the legal power is in the hands of the trustees.

A young lady has written me to inquire what is meant by the statement that salt is sweeter than sugar. I desire to reply, but my cruel wife—who is forever interfering between me and other of her sex—interdicts this tender epistle.

Benjamin Peirce

Professor John Le Conte   Function Grove 15 VIII 58

John L came to see us, and at the same time the express brought us two gallons of the most superb old Bourbon. Our house is now quite unusually dull for James and Charley have both gone to Niagara and all the society of Cambridge has dwindled to its minimum dimensions—every body being off to some watering place or other.

Benjamin Peirce

Prof. John Le Conte   Function Grove 1 XI 58

The Chief has just gone and he has been gorgeous. He was most fortunate in being present at two Clubs in one of which the best intellect of Cambridge was assembled and in the other that of Boston.

I have just completed the law of the curvature of the comet's tail. By the bye, before I tell you of my theory, you must hear how I introduced the comets at the great States-Rights-Democratic meeting over which I had the honor of presiding last evening. Now! don't be afraid that I am not going into politics—but I thought it my duty to show my colours just at this time when every patriot ought to declare himself. Our paper referred to "the very able speech of Professor Peirce."

Benjamin Peirce

To the dear Queen Josephine   Cambridge 7 XI 58

My very dearest friend in all this desolate world!

Can it be that you, who are to me the very type and soul of what is most true in human nature, have ceased to be my friend? Why then have I so long been without a word from you? Has another taken my place? If so tell me and let me die, with my face toward heaven. Oh! it cannot be. You must be ill. Could you know how you filled my heart and all my thoughts, how I am constantly sighing for Columbia.

I have just received an announcement of my election as a correspondent of the Nat. Sci. of Philadelphia—and am more pleased with it for some reason or other than I was with the election of the Royal Society.

What does her awful majesty say to my appearing upon the political arena, and presiding at a democratic meeting? It was said by a gentleman present, "I profess to be a judge of such matters, and I regard professor Peirce's speech as the best political speech that I ever heard." However, it did no good. We were beaten.

Benjamin Peirce

Dearest Queen   Cambridge 7 XI 58
Write one word, even if it be a cruel one. I would give ten million comet
tails for one hour in your parlour with you singing[†] "Vedrai carino."
Charley has been very ill, and we are exhausted with much want of sleep.
                                                            Benjamin Peirce

To The Queen of Science   Function Grove 9-10 I 59 —Just Midnight
My dearest Queen, this is the first opportunity for ever so long that I
have been able to get to write you and I have not heard from you—Oh! for
how long! Pray take pity upon me and write me. What would I not give to
see you? Do you remember the time when we first met in Albany? Do you
remember how you astonished me by your judgment of Henry? Your
judgment was a true one. Do you remember the suddenness at the head of
the stairs? Do you remember how I looked after you as you went from me
down the North River—that dreadful first parting—and every parting since!
Do you remember them all—that at the cars in Troy? That at the cars in
Columbia? That at Baltimore? Not again to meet for how long. Oh! God! Did
I think? Could I think that Josephine has forgotten me I would die. Oh! My
dear Friend! Would I not give all the world to see you! I cannot write what I
yearn to say—Could I, you would not love me less.
                                                            Benjamin Peirce

Josephine Le Conte   Cambridge 16 I 59 Sunday,
                                 Early in the morning. Nobody else up
Your letter came yesterday. You certainly know me as nobody else in this
world knows me—you have often said it and it is true. You have been the
inspiration of the most inspired portion of my life—the greatest blessing of my
existence. You have taught me to know the south, and for this I thank you. Like
yourself, though born at the north, I was made for the south—for the society of
gentlemen, and if it were possible for me in the necessary arrangements for
living, I would remove my dwelling to the land which holds you.
     You do not half realize the immense amount of work which is heaped
upon me. My Professorship—The Nautical Almanac—and the work for the
Coast Survey—are enough of themselves—especially when they involve the
arduous course of lectures which I have just completed. But there is also my
scientific labour. But then remember that of no small portion of this work
you are the inspiring genius, The Queen, the goddess to whom it is consecrated. And if you can only lift up the veil of my heart and see how it in-
spirits to feel that it is your work, you would not receive my letter with
coldness. My heart is always with you; and I always feel your presence in
this blessed studio—which you have once blessed with your presence.
     The north has hurried too fast to get rich, and it is over run with a
menial population of foreigners. But there are gentlemen here, who desire

the sustaining sympathy of their southern friends all the more that the fight is so severe.

Benjamin Peirce

To The Queen   Function Grove Sunday 30 I 59
Most earnestly do I thank you for sending me Holcombe's address. I heartily concur in its doctrines. More than ever do I feel the immense importance of Southern slavery to the permanence of the American Republic. Have you the autocrat of the breakfast table? Its author[†] has no sympathy with this northern fanaticism. The boys desire[†] to be remembered.

Benjamin Peirce

Professor John Le Conte   Cambridge April 59
I have been quite frightened this week by an event, which I keep quite secret from the family generally. It is as yet only known to Mrs. Peirce, the doctor and myself. She has raised blood—Her nights have been all this spring greatly disturbed by severe fits of coughing. Her flesh is beginning to wear off and just before her raising of blood, she was quite feverish and suffering from pain in her head—but the bleeding seemed to relieve although it left her weak.

Benjamin Peirce

To the most beautiful Queen Josephine   Quincy Street Sunday 27 III 59
I am indeed most heavy at heart—and the weight increases as I near my fiftieth birth-day next Friday First of April—for the day must[†] change. The blackness has returned upon me, and I am too sad to write to The Queen. I am all out-of-tune with all mankind and womankind too. There is nobody at my side, who can read me, and give me the food which I need to restore me to myself. I am not fit to write The Queen, and this fiftieth birth day!—I look upon it as the end of my life. Henceforth I am a mere cyphering machine, and never desire again to be roused to life.

Benjamin Peirce

Josephine Le Conte   Cambridge 30 III 59
The department at Washington has just sent to the Superintendent of the Nautical Almanac to enquire if the services of the Consulting Astronomer cannot be dispensed with. Now—you know that the possibility of an Almanac is due to my energy—and all its actual form is mine—it is my child in fact—and it is now asked if I cannot be separated from it? I am already dispensed with by The Chief of the Coast Survey. Not in form—no. Not in love—no—not the least. But as to actual service. And how have I been treated by the authorities of Harvard—you well know. Mrs. Mills, my wife's mother, asked the other day what made me so sad—Why—said Mrs.

Peirce—he has made a scientific discovery—He has discovered that the world[†] is hollow.

Benjamin Peirce

My Dear Professor   Columbia, S.C. Sun. Morning April 3, 1859
    The "Queen" received a letter from you on the lst of April, which has been the source of a great trouble to both of us. We cannot imagine what can be the cause of the extremely despondent tone of your letter. For some time she has observed such a tendency in your letters; but the last one manifests such extreme depression of spirits, that we are greatly troubled in relation to the matter.

John Le Conte

To the Darling Queen   Function Grove 10 IV 59
    Oh! My Dearest Queen! God bless you for a true-souled noble-hearted royal creature that you are! Your last three letters have all gone to the right spot—and I am now myself again. The world may surround me with all the arts of treachery and deception. With this last, most blessed, talisman from the hand of my Queen—I defy the worst it can do. The day is now clear.

Benjamin Peirce

To the dear Queen   Function Grove 6 VI 59
    Oh! My darling friend! The thousand thanks for your dear, loving letter! How delightful it is to feel after this mighty long separation that we are again drawing toward each other! Mrs. Peirce has returned home from Baltimore, and I think that her cough is very seriously mitigated. The whiskey which you sent me is now coming most happily into use for her.
    I trust that your family is well—my own family is all well except Charley, who has been confined to his room and partly to his bed for nearly a week. The doctor does not feel quite certain what is the matter with him and he is sometimes in considerable suffering and groans at night sometimes in a way which greatly distresses us.

Benjamin Peirce

Queen Josephine Le Conte   Function Grove 27 VI 59
    I cannot bear to feel that you are so near and so ill that I cannot see you and give you health and life. I have also severe illness here at home. Charley is but just recovered from one attack of intense suffering to be sick with another and you can guess how it wears upon one's nervous system to see your son suffer so cruelly.
    In a few days we meet at Springfield after fifteen months of separation! I can hardly believe that so great a joy is in store[†] for me. If Charley recovers, he will accompany us as a reporter[†] on the meeting.

Benjamin Peirce

Dearest Queen   Function Grove 21 VIII 59
    My Dearest Darling Josey. My own dear friend! How is your presence
missed! You have left your shadow everywhere—but I find you nowhere. I
went to the library, and walked all over it, and The Queen was
everywhere—looking at the busts—ascending the stairs—entering the
alcoves—standing with me in my own alcove—and yet she was not there. I
passed the point where she was introduced to the Greek Professor—both
were gone. Always when I come from town I trace my tortuous way over
the shadows which I crossed with The Queen when she said "You lead me
whithersoever you will."

                                                    Benjamin Peirce

My dear Prof.   Philadelphia August 22, 1859
    With very heavy hearts we bade adieu to you all, as we turned our faces
homeward, after having spent a most enchanting two weeks, in the
delightful society of yourself and family.
    Have you heard from Charley since his establishment at his new
quarters in Maine? Tell him he must keep his affections entire until he sees
my Lula. I fancy that they will like each other upon mutual acquaintance.
They both have a great deal of point and I am sure must attract.

                                                    Josephine

My Darling Queen   Function Grove 11 IX 59
    Last night, a son[†] of a classmate called upon Mrs. P. who spoke about
Springfield and the great levee, at which he understood that the beautiful
Mrs. Le Conte was the belle. His father, who has the class's taste for beauty
was there, and gave him an account of the affair. So she goes—conquering
and to conquer—from Georgia to Maine.
    My eyes have been delighted[†] for the last few days by observing that
Mrs. P. has had your daguerrotype open in a reclining position under
Charley's photograph on the center table. You cannot think how it cheers
me up every time that I catch a sight of that open, merry, brave, warm-
hearted countenance. Every time I look at it—I feel a new joy in having such
a friend—a new pride in having the love of so proud a nature.

                                                    Benjamin Peirce

To the Darling Queen   Function Grove 24 IX 59
    I am rejoiced to see that the prospects of the Southern University are so
good. It has long seemed to me that the only promise of a truly noble
institution of learning in America, one worthy of our great republic, was to
be found in the slave states. There alone has the question of the races been
settled on a firm and judicious footing. With us, it is evident to me, more
and more, every day that we are destined to a long and severe struggle with

the Celtic race, which may not end to our advantage. Before I die I wish I could transplant my roots to southern soil.

I am making some investigations upon tides for the Coast Survey which still continues not to pay. But The Chief says "work!" and so I work. Charley has been at the camp, and is expected home this week.

Benjamin Peirce

Regina pulcherrima et amicissima!   Function Grove 2 X 59

James has preached the two last Sundays in my own native town of Salem. Charley is home from camp, and is much pleased with that sort of life, that I shall have to let him go south with one of the triangulating parties this winter. And I shall enjoin it upon him not to show his face in Cambridge without making a visit to Columbia.

Benjamin Peirce

To the Darling Queen   Function Grove 9 X 59

The beloved Chief was here from Monday till Friday. On Thursday evening Charley and I went in with him and his to the opera of Norma, with Cortesi as prima donna—and the whole thing put upon the stage about as badly as you ever saw a thing done. When The Chief was at dinner, we drank The Queen in her own whiskey.

Benjamin Peirce

To the Darling Queen   Function Grove 16 X 59

Each nation has found for itself a set of Gods in their own image. All feel the presence of deity—but all wish to reduce this deity to the standard of their own comprehension. Hence priest-craft—whose office always has been—to substitute itself as the human side of this mediation, and make, on the one hand, the access to Deity only possible through his prime minister—whether priest or pope—or church or oracle—and on the other to give men such a kind of God as they will be willing to worship—one which shall be an available deity—one which shall not be beyond the wishes of the people. Hence it was that Aaron gave the golden calf to the Israelites—Aaron was a priest.

I am sorry that The Chief ordered Charley to Louisiana, so that he will not be able to get to Columbia.

Benjamin Peirce

My Dear Professor Le Conte   Function Grove 31 X 59

What say you in South Carolina to the Harper Ferry insurrection. We think here that it will have a good effect to wake up the good sense of the north. The abolitionists have spread their vile principles all about, and the republican party have endorsed them. How grossly they have misunderstood the southern slave! They seemed to think that if you could only put weapons into the hands of the blacks—the work was done. How little they know the fidelity of these cherished servants to whose very feelings I have observed that the Southern gentlemen were so politely considerate.

Benjamin Peirce

Josie Le Conte, my dear friend   Cambridge 28 Nov. 1859
I think for the present, while the affairs of your University remain undeveloped, and the Observatory a thing of the Future, Ben ought to content himself with saying that an "Extraordinary Professorship" if such are established, which he could hold in conjunction with his place here, lecturing during the months of our Summer Vacation, would be highly acceptable to him.

Dear Charley is far away but I hope in a good position for the establishment of his health & his improvement in other ways.

Yours, S. M. Peirce

Professor John Le Conte   Function Grove 11 XII 59
The tone of public sentiment has greatly disgusted Mrs. Peirce, who is one of the truest lovers of her country that I know, and she is every day, more and more, reconciled to the thought of going to the great University of the South.

Benjamin Peirce

To Her Imperial Majesty,   Function Grove 21 XII 59
The Queen of Science and of Sense
You can have no idea, what uncomfortable times these are for those of us who love the South—and now there is one great comfort to me in it, for Sarah is quite warmly upon our side, and fights the battle of the South against every body who ventures to insinuate a word against you or rather us; she even gave her dear Dr. Wyman a heavy pommeling last Monday, because he ventured to suggest that the south could not leave the Union if it would, saying "we mean to leave and go South." She is every day more and more favorably disposed to leave the North and go to your noble University. I have left a club in which some of the most accomplished scholars of Boston were accustomed to meet and have a good dinner once a month—because as I honestly told them, they had become such desperate abolitionists.

Benjamin Peirce

My Dear Professor: Columbia, S.C. Jan. 8th 1860
It does our hearts good to see the true fraternal and patriotic sentiments uttered at the great Union Meeting in Boston. We know that your best and truest men are loyal to the Constitution. All of your reflecting men must see,

that unless this spirit of abolition fanaticism is checked, it must necessarily end in agrarianism, and a total obliteration of all distinctions in society. This would be attended by fierce civil discord and anarchy in its most appalling forms. In fact, the more I reflect upon the subject, the more I am fortified in the conviction, that such a result is the legitimate and logical sequence of the exercise of universal suffrage under your free labor system. In Europe, the laborer recognizes his position in society: is contented, satisfied and happy. The shoe-maker expects to live and die a shoe-maker:—his sons expect to be shoe-makers after him.

John Le Conte

To the beautiful Queen   Function Grove 8 I 59
    I had quite made up my mind to stay quietly at home this winter and vegetate with the exotics, when yesterday the cruel old Chief sent me orders to repair to the Capitol of the Country and there lecture to the Smithsonian Institution. Perhaps I shall do them good, for I shall lecture upon the "Diversities in Mathematical power of the various Races and Nationalities of Man." Who ever heard of a nigger mathematician? He might do for a black[†] board!

Benjamin Peirce

Professor John Le Conte   Function Grove 19 II 60
    When I was in Washington and Baltimore, I was so much occupied with my lectures, attendance at the house and senate, and parties that I could not get one instant for writing to any body. My visit in Washington was unusually pleasant partly because The Chief was lovelier than ever, and partly because your southern gentlemen were so very civil to me. A little boy of Colonel Jefferson Davis was christened while I was there and after the services we were invited to the house of the young baptized where there was a nice party, with cake and wine, and President Buchanan toasted the youthful Mississippian.

Benjamin Peirce

Professor John Le Conte   Function Grove 11 III 60
    Charley is somewhere in the Gulf of Mexico—getting lazy and fat. James got home last Monday, and was especially delighted with his visit to Columbia. He has brought us a picture of the Inauguration of the Dudley Observatory in which I am delighted to see that The Queen is conspicuous.
    What say you to Darwin? What does Joe say? I cannot think that his observations have anything to do with the larger and more radical transformations which taken place in the transitions from one geologic age to another. Agassiz insists that the geologic changes are thorough and complete, and that there is no instance of a species common to two

successive epochs. The transitions of the successive ages of geology have their own laws, which are to be studied by themselves. They came from God, and so did gravitation. Both are divine messages, intended for man.

Benjamin Peirce

My Dear Professor: Sunday Morning, Columbia, S.C. Feb. 3d 1861
                                   Southern Confederacy of States

It has been a long time since I wrote to you; but, I presume you are aware of the causes of this delay. On the first Sunday in January,—when I should have written,—I was absent on a visit to Georgia to look after the interests of my plantation. Since that time, I have been so much occupied with the opening of the college term,—with the multifold excitements incident to the successive secession of the several states,—that I have scarcely had time to think. But, I am happy to report, that matters have now assumed a more permanent and satisfactory character. The formation of a Southern Confederacy is now a *certainty*. It is true, Fort Sumter is not yet in our possession: but it *will* and *can* be taken whenever it is deemed necessary. The preparations for a successful assault are so complete, that we hope Major Anderson will not tarnish his military reputation by ultimately surrendering the Fort, and thereby avoiding the effusion of blood. If otherwise, its capture, will, probably, cost the lives of his whole command, as well as 200 or 300 of our best citizens:—but it will be taken whatever the cost.

We hope that it will be but a short time before *all* the slave-holding states will be with us. As soon as this is consummated, it will give an immense impulse to the cause of the great University of the South. The Queen says, that she expects to live to see the "good Chief" as Chancellor of the great University of the South, with his true and faithful friends around him! As the dissolution of the Union will break up the "Coast Survey," would it not be glorious for the great Chief and his friends to spend the evening of their days at such a post? It will be the persistent policy of the Southern Confederacy to induce the good and true men of the North to take up their abodes with us.

What say our Northern friends in relation to attending the Meeting of the "Scientific Association" at Nashville next April? Will they attend? Does Lovering expect to attend? I see no reason why the Meeting should not take place. Science is *Universal*,—she is not circumscribed by geographical lines. We met as an "American Association" in Canada, and we can meet as such at any point on the Continent.

The Queen unites with me in much Love to Mrs. P, yourself, and each of your household,

Most Devotedly, Your Friend, John Le Conte
Professor of Physics, University of South Carolina
Confederacy of States

As Betsey and I finished going through this part of the box, I turned to her and asked if she thought . . . whether . . . er . . . uh . . . if, . . . ah. . . . Ben and The Queen had ever, . . . uh . . . consummated their . . . ah . . . *feelings* for each other.

"Probably," she said. "At least I like to think they did."

I respect Betsey's judgment in such matters, but for myself, I don't know. I can't say.

In Another World

1852
Joined a debating⁺ society.

1852. Death⁺ of Wellington.

Today's composition of the class⁺ of New Yorkers differs amazingly from what it was when I first looked the town over in 1852.

Charley, you recall⁺ I went to stay with your mother in 1852. I hadn't seen you for two or three years. You lived in a delightful house on Quincy Street, which was since moved to Frisbie Place. It stood on a raised terrace and had a lawn in front and many beautiful trees and was the scene of many exciting games you invented. You were busy perfecting a cypher and also had made up a new language which you taught me, so that we could talk together, without being understood by outsiders. You would also make up all sorts of tricks to puzzle me, which was very easy, and altogether you made my visit a very delightful one and further gratified me very much and made me feel proud by sending me, soon after, an original poem for Valentine's Day.

Your cousin,

Mary Huntington

THE BEAUTIES OF EBRATUM⁺
By C. S. Peirce
The Ebratum language is spoken by a tribe of Gews,—a peculiar people, whose ways are certainly not those of the common "herd." Here is a specimen of poetry by the melodious Nezol Beetho:

Quotol, Quotol, quincfum hoatol,
Ad ha yuko, hand pierd met goat ol.

O quit ol hum ha quincfum shorr,
Hand zom o goat ol joluh yorr.

Ebratum can easily be translated without a dictionary, provided we have a thorough acquaintance with the grammar; and this is not difficult to acquire, because while the grammar of every other tongue consists of Orthography, Orthoepy, Etymology, Syntax, and Prosody, that of Ebratum has only Orthography,—for the language has neither orthoepy, etymology nor syntax, and very little prosody.

The principal rule of orthography is that in order to translate Ebratum into Hombrush it is necessary to write G instead of B, etc, according to the table.

Cambridge Chronicle August 17, 1852

EXHIBITION OF THE
CAMBRIDGE HIGH SCHOOL[†]

The exercises of the exhibition at the High School, will take place to-day, at the Athenaeum Hall to commence at 9 o'clock. Hon. Edward Everett, and other gentlemen will be present, and make addresses.

The following is the order of exercises on the occasion. The exercises are confined to the members of the senior class.

10. "Speech of Sergeant Buzfuz," An Extract from Dickens, by Charles Sanders Peirce.

1853
Set up for a fast man[†] and became a bad school-boy

1853 . My first visit[†] to New York in the Autumn. Jem graduated.

Private Thoughts[†]
principally on the conduct of life

Charles S. Peirce
Cambridge, Massachusetts

Procul, o procul[†] este, profani!

I

Everyone's mind has a certain basis, which can't be decreased or enlarged. This can be filled, covered with <u>mind</u> or with <u>memory</u>. And everyone can take their choice and cover their Foundation with MIND or MEMORY; or PASSION or GENIUS. But here I mean mind in contradistinction to memory. Ought mind to be used in contradistinction to memory?

II

Genius is the result of thinking 'till__ 'till__ 'till Genius 'till you turn a corner and find yourself in another world. Genius is above reasoning. The principle of Genius holds good with the passions. Its principle is this —

III

Love is the foundation of everything desireable or good.

IV

Impudence __ Grace __ .... These three are requisite for everything.

V

Witty people have the least sympathy.

VI

Every truth may be infinitely extended, but when all truths are expanded to universal principles they make a parallelogram of forces which can't be calculated. Hence the need of particular rules.

VII

Grace consists of
    Energetically bold magnificence and easy neat simplicity, variously combined.

IX

Poets see common nature.

X

A style in writing, if formed, should be a very varied one and have all the constituents of grace.

XIII

Music and Oratory are opposite things.

XIV

Literature to please must be so lively that it will be music and painting.

Order of Exercises[†]
at the
Fifth Annual Exhibition
of the
Cambridge High School
August 6, 1853

4. "The Passions." An Ode by William Collins..........Charles Sanders Peirce

Great claps

Cambridge Chronicle   *August 13, 1853*[†]

EXHIBITION OF THE
CAMBRIDGE HIGH SCHOOL

Gray's Ode on the Passions was delivered by Charles Sanders Peirce
with his usual grace, energy and effect.

In 1853† October, went to New York with my Mother, Jem, and Louisa Greenough, to see the World's Fair. We had a special interest in it because my uncle, C. H. Davis, had been detailed by the U. S. Government, as an officer of the Navy, to assist in the arrangement of it, and had been in New York at work upon it for a good many months. We then stayed in Amity Street, at a boarding house, kept if I remember the name rightly by the Misses Castle. Mr. and Mrs. George Ripley, old friends of my Mother, lived there. We went often to the theatre, seeing Burton as Micawber in Copperfield. I think it was on another visit, possibly in '52, that I saw Burton in Toodles. Jem went to King's at Hoboken and passed a whole day and brought home to Mother the most magnificent bouquet you ever saw. I was at the Palace alone several hours. I enjoyed the trip as much as I had anticipated, and it was really pleasant to experience such unalloyed delight. Louisa was very pleasant and amiable and found everything to her mind.

1854
Left the High School, finally;
after having been turned out several times.
Worked at Mathematics for about six months
and then joined Dixwell's school† in town.

1854. Crimean† war.

Theories
of C. S. Peirce's†
First set of Theories—General and Abstract

My life is built upon a theory; and if this theory turns out false, my life will turn out a failure. And just in proportion as my theory is false my life is a failure. Well, my theory is this. But first, I am not to be an old fogey or go by any rules that other people give me—if I should turn old fogey or obedient lad, my life would in truth and indeed be a failure. For on my not doing it is my whole Theory built.

XI†
Will will .... Fill up the blank with what you will.

XII
Genius and conversation are vice versa, yet sworn friends.

XLVII
It is almost impossible to conceive how truth can be other than absolute; yet man's truth is never absolute because the basis of fact is hypothesis.

It has been proved that the probability of the premisses is always greater than that of the conclusion, or that these starting hypotheses are the truest of facts. How the consciousness humbles the arrogance of intellect that the most plausible truths at which it has arrived are the ones at which it has guessed.

XLVIII

Notes on Heaven

The seeker after divine truth will agree that faith is the test of truth. The highest truths cannot be proved.

There are two classes of men who err, those who are convinced too easily and those who are not convinced at all.
The first are infinitely superior to the second.

Let us start then with a reasoning which is above Logic, state truths that have only to be conceived to be believed; and do not say, if you do not understand "It is foolishness" as the Greeks did of Paul and Luther of the Apocalypse.

All through the animal and vegetable Kingdoms, the great end of life is generation. Is it not so with man?

Man is made in the image of his creator. That is to say, he is what God is, but that he is finite. Man then has the qualities (tho' not the quantities) of his creator-creator. He creates. This is not subtilty nor sophistry. Now what is the soul!

What is matter?

Every thing material, physical, objective, is creature. The soul is creator. All else is creature.

Space and Time are creature.

Now let us suppose that God has created an infinite universe of space. He could create another infinite universe of space which would bear no relation whatever to the first. None of distance for distance is a creature if space is a creature, and none has been created between them. None of direction, etc.

But you, inexperienced reader, do not understand this; you think that space has always, everywhere, existed. What then are the dimensions of your soul? In other words, is not your soul without the universe—yea, infinite universe of space?

When man gets to heaven, he is made perfect. He was already in the image of his God; then he is made perfect. He is the son of God arrived at manhood. And Christ says he is put over ten cities. What are these ten cities? Is he to be put to govern a part of God's creation?! And shall he never exercise his own creative powers? Shall not God govern his own creation? Whose creation shall an angel govern but his own?

There are ten thousand creations which bear no material relations to each other and whose Gods are angels of God, less than God yet infinite, to the creature differing but in personality. And why is not our God one of these? Or shall not God have a higher office than his angels. The Angels of God are in no universe of space. But they are in heaven. And is not that the Kingdom of the God of Gods?

Dear Charley: April 1912

When I was first entering† upon my fifteenth year, I went to live in your family, while attending school in Cambridge, and for five or six months you and I were constant companions. You helped me with my Latin, taught me chess and were my escort at all the simple, little parties, or sociables, which met at the houses of neighbors and friends. They lasted through the winter and spring months, but were at last broken up by a tragic occurrence, when a young man, very much in love with a cousin of the lady at whose house we met, shot himself outside the window of the young lady. We were dancing the old-fashioned reel called "Pop Goes the Weasel," when just as the note sounded "Pop" a shot was heard and almost all the young men rushed from the room, leaving the girls struck with consternation. Later, they returned with pale and solemn faces and the party broke up, but without disclosing the fact that a suicide had been committed. As we walked home together, you succeeded in eluding my curiosity, but probably some of the older ones knew what had happened and it was only my youth and ignorance that kept me from the truth.

Our games of chess were of daily occurrence, because you demanded it. I had no aptitude for the game, though I liked to play with you to please you, but would often have liked to escape; though I never dared to refuse but once. Then, you showed such displeasure, that I was glad at the end of a few days to play as often as you wished. This was the only occasion when you showed toward me your violent temper, but I knew it was there and instinctively avoided any danger of rousing it.

You were famous, at this time and when you were much younger, for your powers of elocution and often a charmed circle of family and friends would listen to your declamation of Edgar Poe's "Raven" and other blood-curdling poems. Your voice was thrilling and your eyes wonderful in their brilliancy and penetration and you really were a beautiful and striking figure, as you stood in our midst. The whole family were noted for their dramatic talent and would get up on the spur of the moment an amusing travesty, or a serious scene from Shakespeare, and you, Charley, were one of the foremost in the frolicking fun. Many an evening hour I passed enjoying these impromptu plays and charades, and as good acting as I have ever seen on the stage.

You asked for my memories of that visit, and asked that I be straightforward. I hope this is what you require.

Mary Huntington

Cambridge Chronicle   *August 5, 1854*

CAMBRIDGE HIGH SCHOOL
ANNUAL EXHIBITION[†]

The exercises consisted of nineteen original pieces by the young gentleman, and three by the young ladies.

"School Life" (an original poem by Maria Carter Warland) was read admirably by Charles S. Peirce.

Edgar A. Poe's Poem, "The Raven," was recited by Charles S. Peirce, in a most superior manner. For effective reading and speaking, probably this young gentleman stands at the head of the school.

I was not listed among those receiving a diploma

I recall my father[†] telling me a story about meeting Thomas Wentworth Higginson in the street in 1854. Higginson had been indicted for the attempted rescue of a fugitive slave, and prison seemed imminent. He mentioned humorously that he would have time to read the Peirce translation of La Place's Mechanique Celeste *if he were imprisoned. "In that case," said father, who abhorred the abolitionists, "I sincerely wish you may be."*

A Theory or a Life?

1855
Graduated at Dixwell's and entered College.
Read Schiller's Aesthetic Letters
and began the study[†] of Kant.

(1903). The first year[†] of my serious study of philosophy, in 1855-56, forty seven years ago, was devoted to esthetics. My good angel,—Mrs. Anna Cabot[†] Lowell, who was known for an interest in stimulating young minds,—must have prompted me to take up first that branch of philosophy which ought immediately to follow the study of the categories, and to study it in a German book which though it was too old to be sensibly influenced by Hegel was nevertheless one of those books in which the three categories, in an almost unrecognizable disguise, played a great part. It was Schiller's Aesthetische Briefe,—a very good book for an infant philosopher.

After that I passed to Logic and the analytic part of the Critic of the Pure Reason, and I am sorry to confess that I have entirely neglected esthetics; so that, though I am now obliged to say a few words about it, I am constrained to preface them with the acknowledgement of my incompetence.

It is a pity that the English language has no more accurate term for esthetic goodness than beauty, which does not seem to me to convey that idea so purely as even the French beauté. That a word for esthetic goodness is still more strikingly absent I do not regret so much, because I do not feel sure that there is any such quality. Of course, some will say that there is no such Quality as beauty either.

(January 1898). Having been bred[†] in a highly scientific circle, I came to the study of philosophy not at all for the sake of its teachings about God, Freedom, and Immortality, concerning the practical value of which I was very dubious from the outset, but intensely curious about Cosmology and Psychology. In the early sixties and before, I was a passionate devoteé of Kant, at least, of that part of his philosophy which appears in the Transcendental Analytic in the Critic of the Pure Reason. I believed more implicitly in the two tables of the Functions of Judgment and the Categories than if they had been brought down from Sinai. Hegel, so far as I knew him through a book by Vera[†] repelled me.

I spent two[†] years, absolutely solid, on nothing but the study of Kant,— chiefly the C.d.r.V. Later I read every medieval scholastic work that I could procure, after I had read everything of a logical or philosophical nature that has been preserved of the Greeks.

XV[†]
You may do anything with a person who is in love with you.

XVI
Argument is contrary to Conversation. One is without and one is with Sympathy.

XL
1855 July 21
The art of Love has for its object, not Love, but the Enjoyment of Love. This enjoyment of love is produced by the mixing of body and soul. In order to do this it is necessary:
1st that the soul should have an eager desire and unquenchable burning love for this enjoyment.
2nd that the soul to be mixed with should be loved and seem divine.
3rd that nothing should hinder the desire from charging the volition.
4th that there should be no External hindrance.
That the soul should be in an excited state it is necessary that it should be put into a sensitive state.
1st to be divested of Callousness.
2nd to have the attention directed to the part to be excited.
For the last it is necessary:
1st that the attention be not in the slightest degree distracted.
2nd that the attention be kept up & the excitement produced by an aesthetic alternation of arsis & thesis.

From MS Pharmacopoeia of uncle C. H. Peirce, M.D., † 1855 June 16[†]
Opium *is the concrete or inspissated juice of the poppy—papaver somniferum. Good opium, when broken open, has a fine fawn or reddish brown color, and when damp is easily compressed into a compact structure which takes a smooth & emulsive surface under the moist finger; it has a heavy narcotic odor & disagreeable bitter taste. When dry it becomes brittle & breaks with a shining fracture and yields a yellowish brown powder. It should contain 9 percent of pure Morphia. Opium is by many medical men regarded as the most important of all therapeutic agents; and indeed it affords to suffering & distressed humanity an incalculable amount of relief and even bliss. It acts as a cordial in restoring strength in low typhoid & continued fever, in the exhaustion consequent upon long periods of bodily pain and mental anguish, in the debility of reformed inebriates, and in some cases of prostration following hemorrhages and severe surgical operations. It is the great anodyne, which is resorted to in most painful disorders, as cancer, neuralgia, rheumatism, gout, strangury, colic & lead colic, stone in the bladder, painful wounds, all painful organic diseases, toothache, earache,*

and all painful ulcerations. It is the principal <u>narcotic</u> *for inducing sleep in watch-fullness of fever &c., in delerium, in nervousness, in the inability to sleep which effects some individuals after making severe or unusual mental efforts or those suffering from anxiety of mind & grief, and in delerium tremens or horrors of drunkards. As a* <u>sedative</u> *for allaying irritations it possesses active powers. It is given in the irritation and restlessness of typhus fever, in the restlessness which so commonly attends severe accidents, in irritating coughs, in uterine irritation.*

Function Hall   *1855 June 20*
Father's brother Charles† died in his arms last Saturday after years of excruciating suffering. Uncle Charles's sufferings and his mother's anguish at witnessing them have preyed upon our spirits.

Notes on father's scientific account of the six days of creation† in the first chapter of Genesis, recorded by his student Rev. Thomas Hill of Waltham, later president of Harvard, from a conversation, as published in the <u>Christian Examiner</u> *in 1855 November:*

The first account† of creation in Genesis,—what has been called "the Elohim document"—is an extended statement of the fact that all things were created by one Almighty will. It declares Him to be the creator of matter, and the author of those forces by which it is governed; the maker of the heavens above, and of the earth beneath; the intelligent framer of all the complicated machinery of the physical world; and the maker of all the tribes of vegetable and animated beings to which that world is adapted; the Creator of man, with all his powers, to which he has appointed a work and for whom he has provided a rest.

If mathematical analysis† will allow Laplace's hypothesis to stand, there was a chaos in the beginning. And the creation of light as the first fruit of the Spirit moving over chaos, was primarily intended as a declaration that God was the author of all those forces of nature for which there was then no general term, but which was expressed in a figure, light.

This first chapter of Genesis† implies a correct knowledge of the world, so far as we yet know it, and yet is so written as to be entirely independent for its interpretation upon the discoveries of human science. It was not written by a philosopher or a man of science. The language is all simply the description of phenomena, as they appear to every eye. The philosophy is the absence of all philosophy.

Everything which is obscure† in the world is intelligible—for it was the work of intellect. Hence science is safe.

The material world was made by an infinite intellect. It contains the element of infinity, and its study cannot be exhausted even by the archangel. Science must be one of the occupations of heaven and is, therefore, a duty upon earth.

At sixteen[†] I entered[†] college. All I knew of ethics was derived from the study of Jouffroy's Ethics, a very interesting book, the first year under Dr. Walker, of Kant, and of a wooden treatise by Whewell[†]—Elements of Morality. Before I entered college Mrs. Anna Cabot Lowell, with her admirable discernment of the needs of young minds, lent me a translation[†] of Schiller's Esthetic Letters. That book made the most profound impression upon me: so much so, that to this day it seems to me almost divine, and acute pain is excited by hearing people speak of it as no doubt it deserves.

When I got to be[†] a college[†] Freshman, the fact that we were seated in the class-rooms in alphabetical order brought me into intimacy with a noble-hearted, sterling-charactered young gentleman, Horatio Paine, almost the only real companion I have ever had, in the sense of not only being interested in the ideas that interested me but also disposed to think along the very paths of thought that I myself pursued. He and I occupied almost all our leisure together in reading and discussing Schiller's Aesthetische Briefe, which being the first philosophical work I ever read, made an indelible impression upon me.

Schiller's letters[†] naturally awakened Horatio's and my curiosity about Kant's Critik of Pure Reason; and we began the study of that great work and of the Prolegomena. Indeed, I was almost entirely absorbed in the two editions of the Critik and the Leibnizian, English, and other works to which the Critik relates, for several years. I almost knew the Critik by heart in both editions. It was little short of a Bible to me; and if my father had not exposed the weakness of some of its arguments, I do not know to what lengths my worship of it might not have gone. The point of view of the Prolegomena did not satisfy me near so well.

I read very carefully[†] Schiller's Aesthetische Briefe. A great part of my time was taken up by a most painstaking study of it, which was my first dip into philosophy, and its mark is still on my soul. It produced so powerful an impression upon me, that I am unable to this day to disabuse myself of it. That naturally led me to a humble and passionate study of Kant's Critic of the Pure Reason. The C.d.r.V. chiefly occupied my mind for three years; and it was several years more before I began to see that it was in the main mistaken. Before I left college, I almost knew the book by heart; and certainly no day passed without my spending two or three hours in hard thinking about it. I always write "Die Critik der reinen Vernunft," and I spell "Critik" with a C, partly because Kant himself did so (at any rate in the first edition) and partly because the word was borrowed from Locke's English word "critic," meaning the science of criticism,— and it should be remembered that Kant is emphatic in declaring that he does not want it confused with the word we spell "critique." The title of the book ought to be translated as "Critic of the Pure Reason," and by no means as "The Critique of Pure Reason," since in the first place we do not in English put an *article before names of sciences, such as Logic, Rhetoric, etc., and since in the second place it would be ridiculous to criticize* reason, *the whole subject of criticism being to subject reasonings, or in Kant's case the human reason, to reason. "The Reason," in good English, means the human faculty of reason; but "Reason" without the article,—and* a fortiori, *"Pure Reason," means reason in the abstract, reason in its perfection. Kant's great work was my study until, without the least intention of doing so, I found I knew it almost by heart in both editions. I interpreted it, however, as I thought it ought for the sake of its truth to be interpreted, often departing from usual interpretations, and sometimes recognizing that I was departing from Kant's own meaning. I now see that my interpretations were often much more precise than Kant's thought. The more I studied it, the further from Kant I grew. I never accepted the Transcendental Dialectic, as a whole, though I often thoroughly did accept passages thought by most students unsound or even to be insincere, such as the Refutation of Idealism, which I thought and still think one of Kant's greatest performances, notwithstanding its having been suggested by Reid. But what struck me even in my first stage of puppilage to Kant, and struck me more the more I studied the work,—and on that single page I worked for a good many years, all told,—was that notwithstanding the fundamental importance of the part played throughout the whole work by Kant's list of categories, yet the study of formal logic on which the list is built is so extremely superficial as to be simply despicable. There is no milder word to fit it.*

I began the study† of logic in 1855, and it has been my principal occupation ever since.

∴ Harvard in 1850† was popularly regarded as reactionary, pro-slavery, and an obstruction to the Spirit of the Age. But as the ancient Greek philosopher Heraclitus said, things change. Over the next ten years, the abolitionists became dominant in politics. As a sign of this development, in disgust Ben Peirce quit the discussion club† he had attended for years, because its luminaries had become abolitionists.

To gain an understanding of educational matters during Charley's years as a student—1855 through about 1863—it would be tough to find anyone who has described this period better than Sam Morison, the great historian of Harvard.

The Lawrence Scientific School† was full of sparkle, with Agassiz denouncing and Gray defending Darwinism, and Jeffries Wyman giving a course of lectures on Comparative Anatomy and Embryology with the facts so cunningly arranged that the audience supplied the "missing links." In Harvard College Benjamin Peirce was "giving instruction which nobody understood, to a select audience of students who were trying to become mathematicians"; but they could go for guidance to the great man's son, James Mills Peirce, who had just given up the ministry to be Assistant Professor of Mathematics. Lowell was helping Longfellow and Norton to translate Dante, and discussing it with a delighted if somewhat handpicked class of seniors. "Fanny" Bowen was delivering rather deadly lectures on his own textbooks in Logic and Economics. "Stubby" Child was devoting what energy he could spare from correcting themes to Anglo-Saxon; Lane, Goodwin, Gurney, James B. Greenough, and Evangelinus Apostolides Sophocles sustained the classical programme; and the Divinity School counted among its lecturers George Rapall Noyes the orientalist and the Reverend Frederic H. Hedge, transcendentalist, hymn writer, and exponent of German culture and of Biblical criticism. Sibley and Ezra Abbot were the librarians. "There has never been in any American college a corps of teachers equal to this one," declared an old member of the Class of 1866; and a perusal of the University Catalogue for his senior year bears him out. Excluding the medical and law professors, proctors and stewards, there were thirty-two "officers of the University"; and twenty-six of them have attained a certain immortality in the Dictionary of American Biography. One naturally asks: Why, then, was the University so in need of undergraduate reform? A '69 man gave the answer:

> These competent and learned instructors did not give us of their best, but having listened to our stumbling recitations and inscribed an estimate of our blunders, would then withdraw to the congenial companionship of erudite neighbors, contented if collegiate discipline had been reasonably secured. We realized that we were in the presence of distinguished men, but they moved in a higher sphere and tolerated undergraduates as the unruly subjects of official discipline.
>
> And there was no graduate school or other means for training scholars.

Charley's particular intersection with the statutes of Harvard can be divided in two classes: Harmless and Serious. In the prior category I found that in 1856 he was privately admonished[†] for neglect of Latin and for[†] 2 absences and 7 times tardy; in 1857 he received a private admonishment[†] for 3 absences and 3 times tardy, for which he was assigned[†] ten prayers then ten again on 7 December 1857[†] followed on the fourteenth by another admonition for 7[†] absences; in 1859 he was privately[†] admonished and once again assigned ten prayers as penance for stated delinquencies.

In the second class, in the Faculty Reports[†] I found an incident of 13 January 1857; the official entry stating that "Paine and C. S. Peirce, Sophomores, came out of Boston in a state of intoxication." They were sentenced to public admonishment, and "the father of Peirce" was advised to withdraw him from college—a temporary condition milder than dismissal. From his perch in Washington, D.C., where he was giving a series of lectures at the Smithsonian, Ben urged his son[†] to "strive to make yourself a thorough scholar in chemistry, at least, and that the more rigidly you devote yourself to it, the better shall I be satisfied and the more likely will you be to succeed in life." It must have been a gloomy moment for Charley. The month of January for Ben, on the other hand, was a triumph: he concluded his lectures at the Smithsonian, was admitted to the floor of the Senate, which was a high honor in those days, attended a Presidential reception, and dined with the Supreme Court, as well as with various Florentine[†] buddies. Charley did not buckle down quite as readily as Ben hoped, because on the thirtieth of March, Charley again appeared in the Faculty Reports[†]—he and a classmate were fined one dollar each for cutting benches in Mr. Eliot's Chemistry recitation room.

1856
SOPHOMORE.
Gave up the idea of being a fast man,
and undertook the pursuit[†] of pleasure.

I remember in my college days[†] that the Statutes of Harvard defined a "group" as <u>three</u> *persons or more convening together.*

I was an early and late[†] friend of John Fiske and a particular friend of Tom Perry—and a very early friend of Mrs. Perry with whom I remember going up Monadnock[†] in 1856 or 1857,—Susan Hale was of the party & the life of it, but I particularly devoted myself to Perry's destiny.

I remember when[†] a sophomore sitting in the dark room of my class-mate, Albert Stickney, he having just carried away the lamp, I believe. I suddenly saw everything lit up and quickly looking out the window I caught sight of a great meteor. Objectively, my memory of it is of an intense light; subjectively, it is very dim.

I remember about 1856[†] calling upon my physician Dr. Morrill Wyman (brother of the comparative anatomist Jeffries Wyman) and he called my attention to a young fellow of about 16 years old one side of whose face was entirely insensible though it moved when he smiled or made other movements while the other side of his face remained motionless & he could not move it although its sensibility seemed normal. This proved to me that there is no feeling in Molition [endeavor] & countless experiments I have made myself confirm me in this.

Glen House, New Hampshire[†]   Wednesday 6 1/2
Dear Mother:

I still live. The night which I passed on the boat was tremenjous
for one of those small craft, so that I didn't sleep a wink. In the
morning (3 1/2 A.M.) I sauntered forth into the streets of Portland and
it by no means seemed to me that paradise of delights which it did
when I visited it with father. All this time you will observe that I
hadn't had anything to eat, that I couldn't see my hand before my
face by reason of the fog. I went down to the U. S. Hotel however
and indulged in my favorite pastime of spilling an egg on the
tablecloth after which I felt better. In the railway cars I formed the
acquaintance of an exceedingly gentlemanly young man who is
travelling with his wife and also an old fellow who sees how the
country looks with regard to politics. Arrived at Gorham I sent my
baggage over to the Glen and then—mind you it had turned out the
most glorious day that ever charmed these parts—but then I went into
the house, scrubbed down to within an inch or two of my face and
hands, looked at the book found Ames & Draper of my class had
been there and that the Wyman's had left for the Glen in the very
coach I might have gone in for nothing. No one worth speaking to
remained in the house. It was now 11.30 and they had dinner at the
Glen 8 long miles off at 1 but I thought I could get over by that time
and I did which I consider quite a feat for me considering: —

1st how little I slept the night before

2nd that I had had nothing to eat worth mentioning since that
honey

3rd that it was done half of it—at the two ends—under a
meridian sun and the rest under a most terrific thunderstorm.

The Wymans are here and are delighted to see me as Aunty
Margaret says, a class-mate of mine Preston has just appeared from
the summit of Mt. Washington and all goes merry as a marriage-ball.
Only it is raining silently pensively determinately.

Love to father, Benjie, Lellie and Bertie &c &c

Excuse any defects or faults in the matter style & chirography of
this letter as I am running a race with Annie Wyman. That's all.

Your loving son, C. S. P.

XVII[†]

"Genius" has come—from the multitude of its uses—to mean nothing at all.

XLI

1856 August 12

The "soul" is that which can move. According as a soul is <u>greater</u> or <u>less</u>, *it possesses more or less of this power. According as at any time it is exercising that power or moving, it is more or less "excited."*

When the soul is in an active state the repetition or continuance of the same thought or notion (to be distinguished most carefully from many notions which leave to each little weight) will pass that notion naturally <u>up through</u> the soul.

But what puts the soul in this active state? <u>Beauty</u>. In this (which I shall term the <u>Automatic</u>) method of excitement, it is necessary that the <u>patient</u> notion should outweigh all others—which can happen in two ways:—First, by the superiority of the Notion itself (a thought is <u>caeteris paribus</u> to an idea) and

2nd by the attention given to it.

In order that our Automatic Attention may be of any use it will be necessary to devise some means by which in practice

All superior notions may be expelled.

The principal part of the attention may be given to the <u>patient</u>. That is to say

1st That the attention† may be drawn from all other notions

2nd to the patient notion.

Now then we have decided that 3 things are to be done, 1 to render the soul sensitive and active, 2 to empty the attention, 3 to put the Patient Notion in.

1856 August 21   *Function Hall*

I have been reading Kant† all day—and all yesterday and the day before that &c and I must have acquired a little of his detestable style—so that a multitude of admirable thoughts crowd into a very small space. I like it very much when I've dug out his meaning. Here is an example:

Transcendental Exposition of the Conception of Space

The representation of space is an intuition and not a conception. For, geometry is a science which determines the properties of space synthetically and yet <u>a priori</u>. What then must be our representation of space, in order that such a cognition of it may be possible? It must be originally intuition and not conception, for from a mere conception, no propositions can be deduced which go out beyond the conception, and yet this happens in geometry, &c. &c. &c.

1856 August 26   *Function Grove, Cambridge*

Cambridge is awaking† from the dead—freshmen are arriving in great numbers but I have seen few of the class who were Freshmen last year. I went over to the Library this morning. They were scrubbing it. There has been a great barbecue in Waltham or Watertown or somewhere and "lots and lots" of people have gone over there. It's a Fremont and Freesoil barbecue, I believe.

XLII[†]
1856 September 3

Excitement in two ways
    1st by an irritant
    2nd by an allayer of irritation
<u>*Note*</u> *The same object may belong to both classes.*
    As to the 1st see XL.
    2nd Way. It is necessary
        1st that the exciteability should be great
        2nd that the subject should be conscious of the Narcotic
powers of the object.

Sophomore Theme Number 1
Fall 1856[†]
Professor Francis James Child

Assigned Topic:
When the people of Crete, in times past, had a mind to curse any one, they prayed the gods to engage him in some evil habit.

    If there be a single fact, with regard to life and human nature, with which we might presume that one with the experience of a Sophomore would be acquainted, it seems that it is the curse of evil habits. He has seen one classmate get weak eyes and a weak brain from novel-reading; another turned sallow by smoking; another ostracized for "button-holding"; another lose untold marks by want of punctuality; another ruined, really, if not financially, mentally at least, by extravagance; another of his bosom friends die in a drunken fit;—perhaps someone has fallen in love (an evil habit when indulged in too incessantly). He himself has been besieged by these evil habits for a year; and is not without scars. Bad habits do not assail the conduct alone, they pervert the intellect, the imagination, the will. I say, therefore, that he cannot have passed a year in college, not only without being aware of the fact, but without appreciating the truth, that evil habits are heavy curses; and nevertheless, he is or has been their slave.

    But the influence of habits by no means begins with college life; children, it is true, are less ruled by them, than adults. Children are geniuses; at least they have that readiness at taking new ideas and new ways which is an important attribute of genius. If this use of the term be allowed me, I shall add that they derive their first ideas from no other source than this "genius." When they think anything or do anything for the second time, it is easier, to be sure, than at the first, but its freshness and genius have vanished. Thus as habit grows upon the child, his genius generally dies out. If some very few retain the latter, no one escapes the former; and he is fortunate and gifted who is not to some degree its slave.

Should we not then be freer, if we could abolish habits entirely? In writing, for example, is it not a desideratum to be without any fixed style, but to vary one's manner as the theme varies? I ask this question, because it often is asked by young men of a certain stamp, and because it will afford me an opportunity of defining habits. Habits are modes of being. Now applying this definition to the above question, it reads: "Would it not be preferable to live without living in any settled manner?"—which, overlooking the impossibility of the thing, is certainly not desirable. Without those innumerable & mostly minute habits which make one person different from another, there can be no beauty; and certainly, there is no one who would like to shut off from himself mental and moral beauty, and every possibility of being loved. The above question, therefore, is decidedly to be answered in the negative; and having so answering it, considered habits merely as under the general heading of modes of being, I wish now to exhibit that point in which they differ from others of the same class.

This point regards the origin of habits, for no habit is born but from itself, and it is also true that every habit does constantly reproduce itself. An evil habit seems to live like a parasite, and if left to itself, is sure to multiply; but it differs from a parasite, inasmuch as it becomes a part of its victim, eating the life out of him; so that eradicating it is like cutting off a hand or plucking out an eye. If this be not done, it not only eats out that part of the soul or body which was its legitimate prey, but it corrodes the will; and then it can no longer be cut out. Sometimes it does more, and begins to dissolve the very wish to destroy it; then our only hope is that what desire for freedom yet remains may increase enough to get foreign aid. Slender hope! To think that our salvation depends—I should say upon accident if there were such a thing.

But the people of Crete, I suppose, prayed the gods to avert this contingency.

Mrs. Anna Lowell's[†] _Seed-Grain for Thought and Discussion_ of 1856
The foundation stone[†] of all religion is a sentiment in the breast of man of disproportion or disunion between him and God, between him and the Infinite. Hence it is[†] that you see the religious life, under whatever skies it may flower, involves more or less of asceticism.—Henry James

Would'st with thyself[†] be acquainted? Then see what the others are doing. But would'st thou understand others, look into thy own heart.—Schiller

Rank exists[†] in the moral world also—commoner natures pay with what they do; nobler with what they are—Schiller

1857

JUNIOR
*Gave up the pursuit of pleasure
and undertook to enjoy[†] life.*

XVIII [†]

1857.

Volition
arises from
Desire
which originates in
-Appreciation & Passion
arising from   arising from
exercise of   exercise of
Imagination   Sensation
in order to get which
moving, there is necessary
a certain amount of
Reasoning[*]
which always originates in
an exercise of the
Perceptive Intellect.

———

[*] To be exercised in the inverse ratio of the
Credulity. Be careful not to get too little or too much.

XVIII.

Concomitants in Audience †

In oration

Action.

Life

BEAUTY.

Character

Rest

Life increases and Rest decreases.

Rhetoric Poetry Logic ——

Faculty
Impulses } the Soul

I — Reason Faith Goodness Love of Order Unity Quality Permanence,

THOU — Affection Beauty Love Love of Totality Individation Causality IX †

IT — Sensation Notion Truth Love of Quality Negation Community World

1857.

Emerson's Over-Soul[†] of 1841
In youth we are mad for persons. Childhood and youth see all the world in them. But the larger experience of man discovers the identical nature appearing through them all. Persons themselves acquaint us with the impersonal. In all conversation between two persons tacit reference is made, as to a third party, to a common nature. That third party or common nature is not social; it is impersonal; is God.

Swedenborg's Treatise on Influx[†] of 1794 (Boston)
Three different opinions or hypotheſes have been advanced, to account for the communication between ſoul and body, and for the operations of the one on and jointly with the other. The firſt hypotheſis attempts to ſolve the matter from phyſical or natural Influx, that is from body acting on ſpirit: The ſecond, from a contrary Influx, or from ſpirit acting on body: And the third, from a ſettled law of ſympathy or harmony between both, eſtabliſhed at the creation, called by the author, <u>Harmonia praeſtabilita</u>.

Swedenborg's Divine Love & Wisdom[†] of 1851
There is unceasing influx out of the spiritual world into the natural world. He who does not know that there is a spiritual world, or that it is distinct from the natural world, as what is prior is distinct from what is subsequent, or as cause from the thing caused, can have no knowledge of this influx.

It must have been[†] 1857 when I first made the acquaintance of Chauncey Wright, a mind about on the level of J. S. Mill. He was a thorough mathematician of the species that flourished at that time, when dynamics was regarded (in America) as the top of mathematics. He had a most penetrating intellect. There were a lot of superior men in Cambridge at that time. I doubt if they could have been matched in any other society as small that existed at that time anywhere in the world. Wright, whose acquaintance I made at the house of Mrs. Lowell, was at that time a thorough Hamiltonian; but soon after he turned and became a great admirer of Mill. He and I used to have long and very lively and <u>close</u> disputations lasting two or three hours daily for many years.

(1897). One of the books[†] which I have been working at all my life, having begun when I was in College and steadily pursued it since,—although of actual writing upon it I have done little,—is what I have called an <u>Index Raisonneé of Words and Ideas</u>. It is, if you please, like a Roget's Thesaurus.

I returned to this point in Charley's box of papers after I had achieved an understanding of his categories. When I first read these pages I hadn't grasped why he might have expended quite a bit of study upon creating an *Index Raissonnee of Words and Ideas.* I thought it was unrelated to his interests in the logic of science. I guessed it must have been something like a hobby or a pastime. I was wrong. This early word study was a solid preparation for his categorial theory, which emerged fully only later.

The Synonyms[†]
of the English Language
Classified
according to their meanings
on a definite and stated philosophy
by
Charles S. Peirce
Begun Oct. 13, 1857

Preface

Most works of this kind have proved to be little better than failures, and the reason seems not very difficult to point out. The differences of the only synonyms one would ever take the trouble to refer to a vocabulary for are of such a delicate and evanescent character that, like the flavor of a fine wine, when we try to notice them they are gone; so that when a man sits down to write about them he is puzzled about words which he could never use amiss. The differences no longer suggest themselves to him, but he has to suggest them to himself. Now as it is commonly said that no two words have exactly the same meaning so it is also true that none have exactly the same force in any respect. Of course, then, the writer no sooner suggests a difference to himself than he finds it accords with the facts; but in this way he entirely misses the object of the work which is to note the important differences.

Moreover writers do not make it sufficiently clear in each case whether the two words refer to different objects, or to the same object regarded as a function of different variables, or whether their differences consist merely in the style of the words themselves.

In looking in a dictionary under some common word, we are struck by the great diversity of meaning there laid down though we had never observed the slightest ambiguity in the use of the word. If the dictionary were arranged on the principle of Passow's Greek Lexicon—that is, if the meanings were arranged in chronological order with dates of arising and disappearance, a synonym-vocabulary would hardly be required. But as it is the dictionary serves rather to confuse than instruct and a book of synonyms becomes necessary in order to make a synthesis of the meaning which has been analyzed in the dictionary. How is this to be done? We have only to look out the same word in two books of Synonyms and then compare it with our own impression to be convinced that no guess-work however plausibly sustained in its results by facts will do here, but a strict scientific induction is necessary.

The process I have followed was this. The first thing to be done was to select words. I began with Metaphysical terms taking the transcendental philosophy of Kant throughout but in cases of importance explaining them *according to other systems also. I then took up the arts & sciences, grammar, rhetoric &c, & miscellaneous terms. Then I proceeded to words expressive of our feelings, and lastly considered the conjunctions, prepositions &c. After having got a word to be explained I generally looked into Roget's "Thesaurus" for as large a number as possible of words of similar meaning. Next I made general sentences like those above under is and exist, only of the greatest possible variety for each word, and from those inferred the differences in the meaning of the words. (If we say "not only that, it is" evidently "it may be" has been suggested, if we say "not only that, it exists" "it seems to be" has preceded, if we say "at any rate, it is" whether there is any argument or necessity for it or not. "At any rate, it exists" does not suggest anything as having very certainly preceded.) I then looked up examples in modern authors where I could of the different words and tested my result by them. Lastly I traced where I could the way in which the words came to have the signification I had given to them.*

BEING
LIFE & SOUL
CONSCIOUSNESS

I	*THOU*	*IT*
Ideas	*Thought*	*Perception*
	BEING	

Of things in themselves we know nothing, but only of the effects they produce on our receptivities. Before speaking of any kind of cognition we can only consider the words for things in themselves.

Noumenon. (νέος, νόος) That of which we can know nothing except by thought. Some philosophers thought we could become acquainted with neumena by thinking on them.

Substratum. (Sub sterno) That which lies behind and underneath what is presented to our senses.

Substance. (sub. sto) Literally that which supports accidents. That which can never be predicate but must always be subject. But that which is presented to our senses may be regarded as predicate of its substratum.

These three (preceding) words denote the same thing but they have different definitions, nevertheless. That is they view things in themselves in different lights.

Thing in itself. (Ding) Literally that which has weight. The substratum of a single object.

Matter. (materia, Welsh mater, mad) Literally, that which produces the substratum of the outward world. In the outward world we see matter and form, it is commonly said. Matter contains no mind and can therefore produce no effect and cannot even affect us, Therefore, it is noumenal.

stuff. (Danish *stof*) That which fills out. In that thought, lies its distinction from matter. It is seldom used neumenally.

Subjective. (*subjectus*) That which, whether it actually exists or not, is considered in itself and not in its relations.

Substantial. See Substance.

Self-existing(-existent). (*self-exist*) That which has an independent existence.

Positive. (I. *positivo* L. *pono*) Existing.

Real. (*realis, res*) That which produces an impression on our sensation. Opposed to vague and unreal.

Actual. (F. *actual* L. *actus, ago*) That which coheres with the material conditions of experience. More than possible, less than necessary, just as *is* lies between *may* & *must*.

Absolute. (L. *ab solvo*) Phenomenally self-existent, total necessary &c. I say phenomenally for the following reason. Only one kind of bodies present themselves to us as absolute, namely those which we get from that spiritual sense by which we see God; in short, only ideas are absolute. This thing alone is sufficient to make us suspect that these things are not in themselves absolute, but when we consider that we are in God's likeness, that consequently we can reason about his nature from ours, while absolute perfection in him would shut off all possibility of progress, we infer that those things which phenomenally are absolute really belong to the order of ∞^∞.

Internal. (*internus, intus*) relating to the neumena of phenomena; the adjective corresponding to *substratum*.

Transcendent. Beyond human knowledge.

Existence. (*ex sisto*) Applied to phenomena and neumena.

Entity. (*ens, sum*) Applied only to neumena but both to things & forms.

Being. (*be*) Applied only to neumenal things & phenomenal living things.

Subsistence & *to subsist*. see Substance.

To exist. See Existence.

Positively, In itself. The former implies actual existence, the latter does not.

Subjectively. See Subjective.

Negatives of the Above

Concrete nouns: Unsubstantiality, nothingness, nothing, bought, nullity, zero, nothing at all. A shadow, phantom, phantasm, dream, vision, air, void, inanity, &c.

Adjectives: Nonexistent, unsubstantial.

Abstract nouns: Nonexistence, nonentity, no such thing, abeyance.

LIFE AND SOUL

Life & Soul are really different but the distinction is hardly made in the language.

<u>Life</u>. *The Immaterial of beings.*

<u>Soul</u>. *That which the life animates.*

<u>Spirit</u>. *(spiritus, spero) Literally, breath. Life & Soul.*

<u>Person</u>. *(persona, per sonus) A living being whether with or without a body.*
    Not applied to the lower animals.

<u>Individual</u>. *(invidiuus, individo) More stress is laid on the unity of the soul than*
    in the word person. It is also applied to animals.

<u>Inner man, Ghost</u> &c.

Sciences: Psychology, Pneumatology (Metaphysics)

<u>Spiritual</u>

1858

SENIOR.

Gave up enjoying life† and exclaimed
"Vanity of Vanities! saith the Preacher, All is Vanity!"

(1913). I organized the Harvard Orthoepy Klub† with fourteen other classmates. First meeting of the Harvard O.K. was in Holworthy 21, 1858 September 16, to be organized on the assumption that the group would disband at the end of the year. However, we enjoyed our elocutions so well that I was asked to prepare a constitution for continuing the organization into the indefinite future. I provided† for the election of sixteen members from the senior class and four from juniors. The meetings were to be private and the proceedings secret. The exercises were strictly literary and oratorical in nature and in accordance with the statutes of the College. The Secretary was required to have care of all books, papers, periodicals, maps, and other wealth of the society. In 1859 these consisted of The Library—which was one copy of Bogie's Orthoepy *plus papers of former members—and funds consisting of $3.25 and one new cent minted 1859. You may wonder why such a high and mighty position was dedicated to this single volume. It was because the book represented much that was right and wrong about Harvard in those days. Dear old Bogie was James Jennison, instructor in elocution, and tutor in history, philosophy, and other subjects in the 'fifties. His privately printed book,* Lessons in Orthoepy *of 1856, was widely used in classes. Orthoepy is the art† of uttering words with propriety. Jennison was not a good instructor, hence the sobriquet meaning "an evil spirit." While he was a good man, with some elements of knowledge, he never had much respect. I remember asking my father why Jennison was retained on the faculty. He answered, "Compassion." In 1869 the society was in danger of dying, so we spliced together a rump group of alumni, which we quite logically designated as the X.O.K., who convened at my house in Arrow Street. Our efforts*

succeeded, for the O.K. survives to this day. Some of its better-known members over the years—which I can recall—were Theodore Roosevelt, Alanson Houghton, Charlie Tower, Josiah Quincy, Wm. Everett, R. H. Dana, Wendell Garrison, George Santayana, and my classmate Frank Abbot. My piece† on Shakespearean Pronounciation, written with J. B. Noyes, was inspired by our exercises.

XXIX†
Opposite evils are sometimes concomitant without amelioration. Sensuality is bad enough, Transcendentality is bad enough, but Free Love is worse than either. The rake is at least not transcendental; Emerson is at least not sensual but Walt Whitman has no good trait to be mentioned.

XLIII
When a child burns his finger at the candle, he has not only excited a disagreeable sensation, but has learnt also a lesson in prudence. Now the mere matter cannot have given him a notion since it had none to give; therefore, it must have been God who at the creation of the world put this thought into nature. Now this heat was a form, and all powers are forms. And matter we know nothing of.

All forms are also powers, since to affect is to effect, & are therefore spiritual manifestations. If this is so every form must have a meaning. But since all phenomena are forms, all things must have meanings. The transparency of the drop of water must actually convey a meaning to our conscious <u>affections</u> as truly as the Whole Sea itself.

My essay† for <u>Harvard Magazine</u>
THINK AGAIN!
by THE NORMAL MAN (C. S. PEIRCE, '59)

A writer in the Magazine has already awaked to the fact that Shakespeare is not what he is cracked up to be, and proclaims himself a reformer accordingly. But his business will be no very difficult task, if undertaken with characteristic modesty; for few of us either love or read the works of Shakespeare much. As for the Iliad and Odyssey, they have long been detested by Juniors and Freshmen generally, and the Vedas are now held up by professors to be laughed at by students. Yet these three have been considered the sublimest poems out of the Bible.

A young man feels sure he sees something unreasonable in Milton or Bacon, or else in the study of natural science in general, and he is tempted to admire too much his own imitation of the pig's squeal. This ought to be a sign to him that he does not comprehend the author or the science, and he should throw himself into the study of him or it with the more *abandon*.

The argument of the critic of the Taming of the Shrew is this:

> Shakespeare makes a radical change occur in the character
> of one of his heroines.
> Radical changes of character never do occur in real life.
> *Ergo*, Shakespeare is not true to nature.

I deny his major premise. Radical changes of character are certainly improbable, but it is unnatural for improbabilities never to occur. They are extraordinary, but a play in which there are no extraordinary workings of character is simply commonplace. Every one of Shakespeare's plays contains something improbable or extraordinary. The delineation of Hamlet's character, which this critic seems to approve, is so extraordinary, that its meaning is not now settled.

His argument would have applied very well to the parable of the Prodigal Son. Thus Paul by his own account, even before his conversion, still acted according to his ideal of right, and, as he thought, to the glory of God.

Now, if Shakespeare brought about an extraordinary result, he also used extraordinary means; namely, the power of love, which has worked a miracle with every Christian.

We condemn the writer's verbal criticisms as much as his general one. People who like gaudy poems had better shelve Shakespeare, and take up Alexander Smith, the Brownings, and Tennyson. And I am afraid they will be disgusted to find that even these poets, except the first, try to avoid showiness, and have a real sympathy with Homer and Shakespeare and the Vedas.

XLIV

I think the secret of the sea is this: A noble nature of entire unity yet infinite variety, which everywhere follows after the moon as its ideal. And the black rocks against which that placid body dashes with such force are the circumstances of life.

XLV

Rise early in the morning and be profitably employed the whole of your time. And don't say you can't do anything—you can. You agree with me that this is the secret of life.

In eye be clear; in reason, profound, in heart earnest, in will bold, in hand skillful, in foot swift.

Be great, and beautiful and good; and don't say you can't—you can!

THE CLASS OF 1859† OF HARVARD
By Charles S. Peirce
Begun February 4, 1858

Abbot, Francis Ellingwood. *Supremely conscientious. Wants some elements of good taste. Ability mediocre. Gentleman slow & religious. Engaged. A poet. Very popular. Going to be a* <u>Rev</u>. *Hasty Pudding Club.*

Ames, Felham Warren. *The Representative Man; the man peculiarly like everyone else. Little honor enter his composition. Gentleman. Was fast as a Sophomore but has since subsided. Has been engaged to Mary Felton off and on for 12 years. H.P.C.*

Barrett, William. *Utterly wanting in conscience. Vulgar. Scheming. No gentleman. Keeps quiet. Quietly seduces.*

Blake, George Baty. *Avaricious. Fine manners but all show. Gentleman. Fast. Gambler. Fond enough of ladies.*

Bond, William Sturgis. *Must drink a good deal. Gentleman. Somewhat faster than his brother. Irreligious.*

Bradford, Samuel Dexter. <u>Absolutely unprincipled</u>. *Gentleman. Fast. Religious. Married. Kept a mistress while he was in college.*

Carpenter, Chapin Howard. *Very strict religionist & moralist. No gentleman & I hope I sha'n't meet him in heaven unless he improves.*

Gray, John Chapman. *Damned reserved.*

Greenough, Francis Boott. *Ever on the selfish system but the result is very pleasant.*

How, Henry Jackson. *Undeveloped mind. Straight forward. Perfect drunkard.*

Locke, George Lyman. *Talks very well, but hardly ever says anything of his own; he rather expresses what you have said in different language. Talks so well he doesn't say anything.*

Newell, William Wells. *Common-place kind of talent. Nervous. Practical. Deficient in power of abstract reasoning altogether.*

Paine, Horatio. *Remarkable for docility. Could seize upon a mode of reasoning, of pronouncing, of feeling &c very easily. Was very quick at learning languages. Tact. Vacuity & idleness. Don't know what he is about, half the time. Can't take a firm stand. Can't put a matter requiring boldness through. Has no valor in short.*

Peirce, Charles Sanders. *Vanity. Snobbishness. Incivility. Recklessness. Laziness. Ill-tempered.*

Shurtleff, Nathaniel Bradstreet. *Has principles but they are very bad ones. Hypocritical. Jesuitical & is a Jesuit. Some slight popularity in college. Fast rather. Gentleman.*

Stickney, Albert. *Fellow of sense, knows what he wants to do, perseveres & does it. No great breadth of mind. Snarling. Unpopular in college.*

Somewhat a gentleman. Hates ladies. Slow & religious. Unitarian I think.

Vincent, Strong. Selfish, aristocratic, dashy fellow. Has some sense & some want of it. Gentleman. Fast. Unpopular.

Winn, Abel Theodore. Good in a discussion. No delicacy & no gentleman. Smart & pleasant. Slow but he has nevertheless seduced a girl since he has been in College. From which I judge he is fond of ladies' society. Somewhat religious of the Catholic kind.

During one of Betsey's terrific chili suppers one evening I wondered out loud about the meaning of the word "fast" as Charley had applied it to himself and his classmates. I surmised that it must have been a common colloquialism at that time.

"That has to be easy, Ike. Even in Milford it meant 'sexually active.' In my high school conversations, we always assumed that the expression had probably arisen as an allusion to the velocity with which male subject *A* produced a seduction of female subject *B*. Wasn't there a similar kind of expression at Stillwater High School?"

There was, but I declined to revive it, preferring to concentrate on the chili and the little green chunks of jolly-peenos, and listen.

"Of course if a female had engaged in that kind of activity, she was probably described as 'loose.' That wouldn't have been a problem in college in Charley's time, because there were no female college students.

"It seems clear that several of Charley's classmates were fast. In my community health practice, I have seen enough evidence to convince me that the story one hears about strictly diminished sexual activity in the Victorian era is one of the biggest myths that ever was perpetrated. Humans are pretty similar in basic things in every epoch."

Betsey swiped a bit of chili sauce off the side of my cheek where it had strayed, then smacked it onto her lips.

I said nothing, just ate more flaming chili liberally splattered with Llano Estacado jalapeños shipped in special to Betsey on Southwest Airlines. Hot mouth. Dos Equis beer fire extinguisher. Chilled out. Shacked up. Fast.

Father's letter† from his visit in Columbia, S.C.　　　　　　*1858 February 22*
My Darling son:

Washington's Birthday! Your eloquent epistle rejoiced my heart and made vivid, to my internal vision, the charms of that sweet house in Cambridge, whose doors will open to my embrace in a week from today. May nothing ever come to damp the ardour of your enthusiasm! May the love of science spread through your whole life. May you ever hear it, in the simplicity of an earnest spirit, as the voice of God, speaking through nature! Religion, my dear son, is all of life, which is worth living for, and it is but the other side of true science—or rather, science is the worst of guides if it does not lead to the God of the gospel.

Here I am in the centre of slavery, and I should not know that I was not at home, except that the domestics are so universally well-mannered and never disgust by their excess of servility any more than by their impertinence. Should the slave question ever be presented to you for your discussion, come to the South and judge for yourself before you commit yourself. I am now fully satisfied that we Democrats were right in the last election, and that if Fremont had been successful, the Union would have disappeared.

This day has been celebrated in Columbia by the parade of the soldiery, and I can assure you that they are a very military looking set, and since all the officers are gentlemen, you cannot but watch their evolutions with interest. The bands of music are composed of negroes, so that when they come to blows with the enemy, the blacks will obviously be the most skilfull, and will take every trick with a trumpet. The Queen and the Professor send you their best love.

Your loving father, Benjamin Peirce

When I was in† college, the merest start had been made upon gaining the right procedure for science. The stereoscope was a novelty. The first photograph on paper,—an albertype,—was a surprising thing. There was a crane in our kitchen at the "old house" on Mason Street. The railway and telegraph weren't many years old. The spectroscope was unknown. The undulatory theory of light was disputed. The mechanical theory of heat, when put forward at the American Academy, by Uriah Boyden, so frightened the fogies that they would not print his paper any more than Poggendorf would print Mayer's great paper and the poor fellow went mad with his pent up truth. Anesthetics did not exist, and when a woman was in labour, all the neighborhood heard her cries. Of course you yourself can remember the sensation made by the Holtz machine and the other made by the dynamo. The book of Genesis seriously interfered with paleontology and geology. Therefore it is not surprising that all we know is an infinitesimal fragment. But nowadays how many fools there are who think that laboratory experience measures what goes on in the world, who are cocksure of the doctrine of energy, etc., etc. That great Canadian Rutherford with J. J. Thompson on the other side are in a fair way to show that the three laws of motion are not true. If they succeed, the effect on men's minds ought to be salutary though no doubt the race of fools will not become quite extinct. So much then for science.

During my college years† I read a good many philosophical books other than Kant and Schiller, among which I remember James Mill's Analysis of the Human Mind, Hume's Treatise of Human Nature, and a large number of logical treatises. But I retained, all the time, a decided preference for chemistry. I had thoroughly mastered almost everything that was known of inorganic chemistry, besides having read the masterpieces in the organic branch, and I endeavored to keep up with all the new discoveries.

Kant's Deduction of the Categories[†]
Kant's Critic of Pure Reason
Doctrine of Elements
Part II, Book I, Chapters 2nd & 3rd
Translated
from the 1st German Ed.
By .
Miss C. E. Peirce & Mr. Charles S. Peirce 1858

I'd arrived in Cambridge in 1957 as an Okie, and still am proud that my mind was formed in that great state—under the guidance of my grandfather who was a travelin' man, and my father who was superintendent of the school system I attended. However, I didn't have to live long in Cambridge before I noticed something that was socially different from my upbringing. I didn't really understand the blue-blooded tendency in some persons from around Boston—of which Charley was a specimen, certainly in his college days and probably for some years later as well—until Betsey told me a particular joke. I don't know if it is a true story. It seems that Eliot Richardson, a Bostonian, was running for office sometime after his infamous dismissal by President Nixon as Special Counsel for the Watergate scandal. Richardson was shaking hands at a local factory as folks left their shift. One worker, after receiving a greeting, scratched his head, then walked over to a member of Richardson's staff and asked,

"I have always thought well of Mr. Richardson, but I am puzzled about this particular election. After all, why should I vote for him?"

The staffer's reply was unhesitating and full of conviction:

"Because he is better than you!"

Betsey and I think it is well established that Charley felt, at this time in his life, that he and his family and associates were clearly better than the great mass of humanity. My view, with which Betsey disagrees, is that something happened to him later in life that burned this attitude out of his soul. Consideration of that will have to wait.

But casting aside any animadversions about the color of his blood, it's easy to see how other factors might have led him to be a self-described insouciant student[†] in college. For one thing, by stepping across the back hedge of Function Hall—which was built by the college to house Ben's family—he was in Harvard Yard! Another reason might lie in his literally having been educated by his father, one of the best minds in the world at that time, member of the Royal Society, the American Philosophical Society, past president of the American Association for the Advancement of Science, soon to be a founder of the National Academy of Sciences, who moved widely and freely among the best scientists, artists, literatti, and politicians of the day. Through Ben, Charley was in the presence of, and became the student of, these other leading minds and talents. Why then should he, we might easily imagine him thinking, be concerned with dull recitations and sophomoric discipline?

"Why don't you cut to the heart of the matter, Ike?"

It's invigorating when—speaking metaphorically—Betsey throws water in my face.

"As an undergraduate Charley was one of the junior companions of his erudite neighbors—the inner circle of the great Harvard faculty at that time. And after 1859, he was a coworker in their projects who soon developed a distinctive research program of his own. No wonder he was an insouciant undergraduate—almost anyone would be, given the same situation, especially in the atmosphere of indoctrination that passed for organized education at that time!"

With that, for a fact, we agreed. We grabbed our portable does-it-all boom-box CD player and a couple of toothbrushes so we could celebrate the fact by driving out to Lynn for a weekend of goofing off on Nahant peninsula. Within a cozy rendezvous I played Harry Connick Jr.'s *Just Kiss Me* for Betsey. This is on an album I had bought for her swing collection. Since it is brand new big band music I thought it was particularly suited to express my side of an emotional dialogue I wanted to have with her. Betsey's response surprised me. She pulled out a new remake of an old standard, *Killing Me Softly* by the Fugees. Thus did we exchange recordings.

If you want to guess about our conversation, you will have to buy at least two CD's to admit into evidence.

Nahant is a magical spot for agreeing. We had a lot of agreements that weekend.

The Amatorious Verse of Charley Peirce

1859
Wondered what I would do in life.
Appointed Aid on the Coast Survey.
Went to Maine† and then to Louisiana.

XXXVI†
It is impossible for a man to act contrary to his character.
    It is foolish for him to try to do it; He would be no better man for doing it since the character makes the man.
    The Very Law of the Growth of Character is contained in the Character.

XLVI
Prayer
I pray thee, O Father, to help me to regard my innate ideas as objectively

valid. I would like to live as purely in accordance with thy laws as inert matter does with nature's. May I, at last, have no thoughts but thine, no wishes but thine, no will but thine. Grant me, O God, health, valor, and strength. Forgive the misuse, I pray of thy former good gifts, as I do the ingratitude of my friends. Pity my weakness and deliver me, O Lord; deliver me and support me.

XLIX

On the Classification of the Human Faculties

Who will give us the true one at last? Here is one I offer as presenting some merits.

Man		
	1	awakens and rouses himself
	2	he sees
	3	he thinks
	4	he desires
	5	he does
	6	he enjoys and suffers
	7	he respects and loves.

I have elsewhere advanced the classification of the I-impulse, the It-impulse and the Thou-impulse, but that is not a classification according to faculties. That the present classification includes everything needs no proof, everything is there which has been inserted into any other system.

2 Every faculty is a real one

3 No faculty is the same as another, for arousing is not volition, nor enjoyment perception.

LI

However immense our science may become, we are only burrowing light into an infinitude of darkness. Once an infinitude, always an infinitude.

Valentine to Miss Anna Lillie Greenough†

I

Cheeks where rose and lily blend,
Coral lips, and eyes which send
Lightening glance or liquid beam —
These but poor attractions seem
Till the soul their grace inform
And these outward beauties warm,
Thou in whom all charms combine.
Be thou but my Valentine! —
What could maddest bard or boy
Dream beyond this crowning joy!

II

Nor wintry sky, nor chilling air,
Nor frost, nor sleet, nor snow,
Congeals my truest love for thee —
I laugh at 5 degrees below.

The flame that within my heart
Ah! let it reach thine own.
'Twill make all seasons warm for thee —
Blot out the frigid zone.
Plant a fair tree of living green
On every frozen heath.
Verdure will hang upon the boughs,
And roses bloom beneath.

III

Aurora is thy name, fair maid
Around thee vapors fly,
And roseate hues of light pervade
Earth, ocean, air, and sky.

IV
For Rosy Paper
When flowers bloom in summer
We ask no reason why
Far shores of willing answers
Are in the smiling sky.
What marvel, then, if round your path
In winter flowers appear?
Since smiles of such a charm as yours
Make summer all the year.

V
For Rosy Paper
Through wintry airs, o'er snowy plains
Whence comes the blushing Rose?
The only flower that fairly mates
The fair to whom it goes
O lady where such flowers bloom,
Your smile makes sunny weather,
And it is always winter
We cannot be together.

VI

Give back, O maid, give back my heart,
That thou, with necromantic art,
Hast slipped away from careless me!
Grant to one victim liberty.
       Of all thy slaves free one.
Enchantress thou a spell hast wove,
That all who see thee can't but love;
O, then, a kindly fairy prove;
Endow some victim with thy love.
       Make me the blessed one!

11 May 1859   *Cambridge*

    I am of a meditative[†] and silent turn of mind and even when I do speak my conversation is very grave and serious. If I am so particular about what I say as to think few things worth saying you may imagine that I have an almost uncontrollable modesty. For instance, now, I do not wish to talk about the weather interesting as that topic may be.

    If I cannot write either the news or my own thoughts, the former because it is <u>stale</u> and the latter because it is <u>unprofitable</u> and if this somewhat long preface is becoming <u>flat</u>—then I do not know what better I can do than to give a short account and analysis of Dr. Walker's sermon last Sunday. This being Wednesday doubtless I could do it. Last Sunday was very hot so was Saturday, and I began to be a little in despair about not having thin clothes. I was afraid to take off my flannels. And winter clothing when the temperature ranges from 80 to 90 degrees F is apt to make a person who is not a Salamander a little irritable. Jim had invited that Gates out to <u>his</u> room and on returning from Boston where I had been for the sake of taking in grandmother Peirce & putting her into a carriage at the Revere & then not having anything else to do I had gone to the Museum to see Lord Timothy Dexter which is pretty good, not that the plot is anything, in fact as I got in a little late, I did not think that worth listening to, but on account of Warren's doing Lord Timothy to perfection and several other of the characters being excellent, as the Poet— Lord T's poet laureate—with a gentle and absorbing conceit &c &c so that altogether it makes a pretty good play. I say having returned from Boston whither I had been for the aforesaid purpose and where I had indulged in the aforesaid amusement coming out pretty tired I found <u>that</u> Gates in my room. I do not like him. He is a bore. He has neither conversation to make him agreeable nor is he able to keep still to make him harmless; and I suppose that a person who puts you into a state of nervous irritation without conferring any pleasure is the <u>beau ideal</u> of a bore. A person who is agreeable may be a bore, but a person who can keep still and not sit on the edge of his chair and twitch and change his position every moment nor constantly change the subject nor *be unwilling to let you do any of the talking if he has nothing to say himself, cannot be. I don't object to talking. I think it is a highly necessary and pleasant medium of exchange; but I would not give a snap for a man who could not go a week without talking. Gates stayed in my room all the evening and only left when I reduced to a pitiable state of exhaustion. To make the matter a little more so John Noyes came. Now he and Gates haven't a point not the smallest dot in common, and the only way I had of amusing them both, as John Noyes talked about a certain old quarto of Love's Labor Lost all the time & Gates about nothing, was to begin a sentence about Shakespeare for John and to end it about nothing for Gates or to begin about nothing for Gates and to end about Shakespeare for John. The conversation progressed delightfully. After Gates left Noyes remained for about an hour still talking about the authenticity of this quarto which I knew all about already and was too sleepy to give my views upon. Time rolled on and I was just about to give up my dying gasp, when he left. Next morning early Gates appeared and stayed all day, restless and tiresome. Dr. Walker as I said preached on Sunday; from the text—I forgot what. He began by saying that religion was a want not a science, just as society was. There might be a science of society but society itself was not a science but a want. That was the best religion which best satisfied that want. The best religion absolutely was that which was the best for the best men, but that was not necessarily the best for all. They must be educated up to it, hence the arrogance & presumption of creeds, declared to be the only true one.*

Although it was so hot on Sunday, since then it has been cool enough. I do not go out without my coat at all. Last night I went to see Burton, but I do not think he is so good as Warren.

Charley's new class photograph† pleased his friends and family. Betsey says it is her favorite likeness. His younger brother, Benjamin Mills—Benjie— remarked it in a letter to his mother† who was visiting in Baltimore during May:

> Have you seen the new photograph of Charley? It is one of the handsomest likenesses I ever saw. It is much like him when he is discussing or talking profoundly. It is splendid—perfectly splendid—glorious.

"Ike, stop staring at that photograph. Your laziness is no excuse for failing to identify J. B. Noyes, the student who seemed to be one of Charley's friends. Didn't you say he was a collaborator† on the publication about Shakespearean pronunciation?"

Betsey splashed me again, right in the kisser, with another bucket of icy metaphorical water. I bonded with her in part, no doubt, because of her candid way of going after the truth. Dreamers like me need something shocking from time to time. I did my duty.

John Buttrick Noyes was one of seven children of George Rapall Noyes[†] (1798-1868) who in 1840 Harvard elected to an unusual joint appointment as Hancock Professor of Hebrew and Oriental Languages as well as Dexter Lecturer on Biblical Literature and Theology, posts which he held in the Divinity School until his death. He had a high reputation as a scholar of sacred literature. In fact, he was so good that he often danced with the Devil, which is to say that his contemporaries sometimes viewed his clear eye and strict observance of an honest critical method as heretical. For instance, one of his leading hypotheses—that there were no Old Testament prophecies of the Messiahship of Jesus—earned him consideration for prosecution under an old statute about blasphemy. Also, he might be the source of Charley's familiarity with the Vedas, but I haven't confirmed it.

Thus John Buttrick—J. B. Noyes—was Charley's fellow Harvard brat.

Having completed these brilliant sentences, I was going to give Betsey a snide reply, as she came over to view my findings. I gave up the plan because while she read, the tip of her left ring finger floated in a random whorl delicately and ever so slowly down the back of my head and upper neck, the result being that I completely forgot about any form of revenge. In the whist game of life, some trumps are higher than vengeance.

19 May 1859   *Cambridge*

In the past[†] few days I have read a Volume of Knight's History of England—a large part of Mansell's Limits of Religious Thought—Coleridge's Lectures (1818) on Shakespeare & Milton. Besides that I have got all my lessons, have written a report to the OK Club, have written a Speech, have written a forensic, have written a letter, have written my life for the class book, have written an essay on the conceptions of Totality, Infinity, Substance & Necessity, which are the four moot points of metaphysics.

Mother wants me to invite Keighler, Lawrence & Loring to the house. With regard to Keighler, I should be most happy. Lawrence I have never been intimate with but can invite him. But Loring I black-balled for a Society. And as that is saying not merely that I don't want him as a member but that he shall not belong,—I think it would be rather adding insult to injury to invite him to the house.

21 May 1859   *Cambridge*
Dear Mother:

There are several[†] topics in which the written word has every advantage over word of mouth. I think for instance if I was about to offer myself in marriage I think I should find it much more difficult to clasp my hands, bring them up to my chin, throw myself frantically on one knee & exclaim
"Lillie! Take me to your bosom!"
than I should in going down to Bartells, purchasing a sheet of paper, a bottle of ink, and a tin pen holder, coming home, placing the paper upon the centre-

table, dipping the pen carefully in the ink-stand & writing as follows:

Harvard University May 21, 1859

Madam:

> *I have three times attempted to give you a verbal relation of the contents of this letter but my heart has often failed me. I am about to make a proposal upon your answer to which will depend a large portion of my happiness in this tearful vale. Marriage has been denounced by the wisest of the sages as being the beginning of all the trouble that humanity is heir to. You will, nevertheless, my dear Madam, do me a great injustice in supposing that any motives of mere temporal happiness could for a moment deter me from paying a young lady's board.*

> *We seize our ruin in our bliss. You have already seen some of my relations, particularly my mother, with whom I now live. My circumstances are independent, my character hitherto unblemished, and my capacity undoubted. I shall await your answer with the utmost impatience and am, madam,*

> *Your devoted admirer, Charles S. Peirce*

So likewise when Napoleon wanted to give up the slave-trade he might have said so, but no indeed that would not do, because no one would hear it but the man he was speaking to. And the Hon. Anson Burlingame when conversing with his friend Henry Wilson upon the wrongs of the North, thinks of an argument which is very pat. Does he state it at once? No. He goes home and indites this epistle:

Messrs. Wilson, Banks &c

Gentlemen:

> *When human policy fastens its chain of slavery around the ancle of the slave, divine justice rivets the other end around the neck of the master.*

>> *With great respect*
>> *I remain*
>> *Your obliged servant*
>> *Editor of Boston Advertiser, Henry Wilson*

Your affectionate son,

C.S.P.

VALENTINE†

'Twas in a thronged hall
There to rich music's sound
Warm youths and maidens through the hall
Traced the light dances round.
Were gathered then the fair,

The beauteous, and the wise;
But the fairest maiden there
Was the maid with the dark blue eyes.
Those blue eyes through my soul
Shot a bewildering ray
And never has my heart been whole
Since that disasterous day.
Give back O maiden mine
Give back my rifled peace
And take this heart, it shall be thine
Till all its pulses cease.

ANACREONTIC VALENTINE†
As in the woods I spent my hours
I came upon a bed of flowers.
In some fairy's mystic hall
Lofty elm trees formed whose wall
Round encircled fanned the sky
Then sweet silver poplar trees
Ruffled by the kissing breeze
Little fountains wept hard by
Singing a sweet lul-a-bye.

Lying in a bed of roses
Sweeter far than all the posies
Slept a maiden all unconscious
Of the odors breathing round
There she lay so simple beauteous
Sleeping on the pillowed ground
That complexion! That complexion!
Oh in sooth I see it now
There the rose with snow is mingled
In those cheeks and on that brow
See her hair so rich contrasting
With that lovely brow of snow
Perfumed with the primrose blossoms
Half ashamed that lay below.
Then that lip so rich in blisses
Panting nest of bland persuasion
Sweet petitioner for kisses
Ripely sueing love's invasion
Then that neck in grace descending
To the line which bounds the sight!

How that vision soul entrancing
Burst upon my wondering sight
Long I gazed, I gazed and pondered
On that form of virgin light
Thus I gazed until the noon day
School-bell called me from the dove
But e'er since that sight delicious
I have been a boy in love.

1859   *Cambridge*

Proper Domain of Metaphysics[†]
    Metaphysics it is acknowledged is all science truly entirely <u>a priori</u>.
Hence no obtaining of facts—for no making of observations—is metaphysics.
Even picking up the <u>a priori</u> conceptions—as they are not to be observed in
their unmixed state, but only are obtained so by analysis—is out of the sphere
of metaphysics.
    Reasoning, then, or in other words analysis—the analysis of concep-
tions—is the synonym for metaphysics. Theology, Cosmology, Psychology are
eminently metaphysical sciences, but they are not pure metaphysics but ap-
plied metaphysics. The whole of metaphysics, because the whole of reason-
ing, is contained in the analysis of conceptions without any reference to their
objective validity.

On the last day of May, Charley became seriously ill[†] and was confined
to his room. I've shown the little evidence I have about it to Betsey and my
classmate Dr. Bill; neither have any hope of identifying his ailment from that
information alone. But it was serious, for both parents were quite concerned.
In a letter to The Queen, Ben remarked that Charley had been seriously ill
and "was confined[†] to his room and partly to his bed for nearly a week." Apparently Ben and The Chief[†] had planned for Charley to join The Chief's field
party on the Coast Survey during the early summer after Harvard Commencement. On the twenty-seventh, Ben noted[†] to The Queen that Charley
had just recovered from one attack only to suffer another.

Also, Ben was anxious about Josephine because she had become ill during her travels from Columbia, South Carolina. She and her husband planned
to visit Cambridge during August on occasion of the American Association
for the Advancement of Science meeting in Springfield, Massachusetts.

Ben informed The Chief[†] that Charley's illness would prevent him from
being present, as planned, at the opening of the Superintendent's field station
in Maine on the ninth of July. Whatever ailed Charley, he was catheterized[†]—
don't ask for more details because I have found none, and like you I can only
guess. He recovered sufficiently to attend the AAAS meeting and join The
Chief's surveying party in Maine by mid-August.

June 1859   *Cambridge*
Metaphysics as a Study†

  All proveable propositions have for their ancestors a major premiss & a minor premiss, a major premiss & a minor premiss, a major premiss & a minor premiss, until we come to their progenitors which are original truths and they too must be universal propositions (having a distributed middle) & particular ones, particularly the former. Where do these original truths come from? Some come from experience; but the original major premisses cannot come to us so, for a major premiss distributes the middle term, and must therefore be either universal or negative. Now experience <u>unreasoned upon</u> (which has no ancestry) cannot be universal. Neither can it be negative; for instance, the proposition "This is not Green" cannot be a universal experience, for it is a thought of green & and that thought of green, experience did not give by the statement; or to put it more plainly Nature or Experience does not in her account to me predicate Green of This, neither does she predicate Not-green of This; the Not-green produces not excitation of my optic nerves; no negative excites my sensorium; Nature is not in the habit of calling out,

  "Charles!"

  "What?"

  "Nothing."

A negative quality does not exist in nature and if you turn the sentence about "Green is not This," I have to say that a disembodied quality cannot be the subject of a thought.

  It is only the minor premisses then that Nature affords us; for all Universal, Negative, Permanent, & Necessary Truths exist & have their truth in the mind. They being true without proof can have but one basis & must be independent of nature.

  Nothing can be more important therefore than that they must be tested by normal minds; but lamentably most minds are upon most subjects or upon most subjects about which there is any question, abnormal. Nothing is more certain than that salt junk† does not go with molasses. No salt junk ever can. This is not derived from experience merely but is a truth founded on the constitution of the human mind. Yet most eaters of salt-junk are heretics on this point.

  No one doubts that the shortest way between two points is a straight line because the ideas of the whole world are perfectly clear upon this point. The Sailor's judgement on the salt junk is falsified not only by his inaccurate distinctions of taste but by his uneducated aesthetic ideas.

  Humanity always agrees upon these <u>a priori</u> when the ideas are perfectly analyzed; when they have not been they have occasioned the most fruitless controversies.

  To learn how to analyze ideas, therefore, and to analyze them—in short to study metaphysics—will be <u>par excellence</u> education.

  But I will† go further than this and say that all wisdom is derived from the study of Metaphysics. For what is the study of metaphysics but reflection, med-

itation? And what is wisdom? Knowledge is that which we get empirically, but wisdom is wrought by the unfolding of the mind. Now the terms of every proposition are presupposed to be comprehended; therefore, no proposition can give us a new conception, & wisdom is not learned from books.

You cannot read Metaphysics. It isn't in the books, but in the mind.

July 1859   *Cambridge*
Definition of Metaphysics†

Metaphysics is the philosophy of the elements of all that we are conscious of. A definition of any science or philosophy must not be expressed in terms of that philosophy, but must contain those ideas which suggest the science; thus the idea of material substance joined to that of quality suggested the science of chemistry. We therefore define chemistry as the science of the qualities of material substances.

A philosophy differs from a science in as much as observation is no part of its procedure. The philosopher as such† only reflects upon the results of science.

That which is the subject of apperception we call soul. *The apperception itself may become an object of thought & is then called* consciousness.

Finally, to end my account of what metaphysics is, since there are in the idea of apperception three parts—Subject, Act, Object—so there are three sorts of perception & consequently three objects of metaphysical inquiry, namely:

1. Self & the qualities of self or feelings
2. Volitions
3. Representations.

Such is pure *metaphysics. Now of any science, observation, the collection of the facts, forms but a small part. The rest consists not in adding to the notions we have but in clarifying them, setting them in order, moulding the elements anew; but this is the business of metaphysics. It is easy to see therefore that metaphysics is an organon for every science, a general particular logic. Those sciences into which metaphysics enters largely constitute applied metaphysics which has three parts:*

1. The metaphysics of the soul or that which consciousness believes in or Psychology
2. The metaphysics of the world or that which understanding believes in or Cosmology
3. The metaphysics of the supernatural or that which reason believes in or Theology.

1859, 25 July   *Cambridge*
Comparison of our knowledge of God & of other Substances†

All that we are conscious is conditioned. All that we are conscious of *is unconditioned. The* noumenon *tree we never can know. The phenomenon God we can always apprehend. If this simple distinction be kept in view, where is the puzzle, where is the contradiction of the infinite & the absolute? Is space infinite? The understanding cannot complete the successive synthesis. What does that prove? That that space that we are conscious is conditioned. But has space a corresponding neumenon? There are no innate ideas. Is it then a thing out of us? It is an innate idea. It will be seen that I take a realistic view of this subject. Many paradoxes of God's attributes are too foolish for philosophy; all disappear when we remember,*

All unthought is thought of.

It is not that Realism is false; but only that the Realists did not advance in the spirit of the scientific age. Certainly our ideas are as real as our sensations. We talk of an unrealized idea. That idea has an existence as noumenon in our minds as certainly as its realization has such an existence out of our mind.

List of Horrid Things I am:
Realist, Materialist, Transcendentalist, Idealist.

It was arranged that I attend[†] the annual meeting of the American Association for the Advancement of Science in Springfield as a special reporter for the Boston Daily Evening Traveler, *for which I prepared six articles before leaving for Machias, Maine as an aid in Professor Bache's Coast Survey party.*

SCIENTIFIC MEETING ATTRACTS PROMINENT SPEAKERS
The thirteenth Annual Meeting of the
American Association for the Advancement of Science

From Our Special Reporter
Springfield, Mass. August 2, 1859

The thirteenth annual meeting[†] of the American Association for the Advancement of Science commences in this city to-morrow forenoon. Already a very large number of members have arrived from all parts of the country, and the meeting promises to be the most interesting that the Association have ever held. Several of the most prominent scientific celebrities are already here, and their number is augmented by the arrival of every train.

Every exertion has been made for the comfort of members, but it is a matter of some doubt whether the hotels will be of sufficient capacity to accommodate all the late arrivals; however, should any be so "shut out," Springfield is a good sized place, and its citizens have the reputation of being hospitable to a fault.

MEETING OF THE AAAS

From Our Special Reporter
Springfield, Mass. August 4, 1859

The meeting of the Association[†] commenced at 10 $1/2$ o'clock yesterday, in the City Hall. For two or three days past the members, many of them bringing their families, have been arriving by every train, until the city now presents quite a thronged appearance.

Before the time for commencing the proceedings, a large number of the Association, with many ladies, had assembled in the beautiful hall, where half an hour was pleasantly spent in the renewal of scientific acquaintance among the members from the various parts of the Union.

At the hour above-named the permanent officers for the year ascended the platform, and the Association was called to order by Prof. Alexis Caswell, the late President, who introduced his successor, Prof. Stephen Alexander of Princeton College.

On taking the chair, Prof. Alexander called on Rev. George B. Ide, D.D., to offer prayer.

Dr. Ide then made an appropriate address to the throne of grace, fervently invoking the divine guidance in the deliberation of the Association.

President Alexander, at the close of the prayer, delivered the usual opening address.

At the close of the address of the President, His Honor Mayor Calhoun, who, by the way, bears a strong resemblance to the late Hon. John C. Calhoun, offered a welcome. On closing, the speaker was warmly applauded. The number of papers on the docket was then announced by the Permanent Secretary, to be forty-one.

It was then moved by Prof. Caswell, that the Association proceed to elect six members of the Standing Committee, and this being carried, nominations took place; after which a ballot was taken, and the following were declared elected:—Profs. Benjamin Peirce of Cambridge, A. D. Bache of Washington, Benjamin Silliman, Jr., of New Haven, Rev. J. W. Foster of Monson, Prof. W. Gibbs, of the New York Free Academy, and Dr. Joseph Le Conte of Columbia, S.C.

The meeting then adjourned until 4 o'clock P.M.

On coming to order in the afternoon, prompt to the time, a large company was present, the ladies again showing in full force.

Prof. Peirce read a paper upon the theory of the comet's tail, after which the meeting adjourned till 10 o'clock this morning.

Hon. George Bliss, Chairman of the Local Committee, gave a levee† to the members of the Association, and the ladies accompanying them, last evening, at his mansion in

Chestnut street, and a large number accepted his polite invitation.

MEETING OF THE AAAS
From Our Special Reporter
Springfield, Mass., August 4
Second Day—Thursday

The members assembled[†] for business shortly after 10 o'clock and after the meeting had been called to order by President Alexander, the Permanent Secretary read the names of seventeen gentlemen who were recommended by the Standing Committee for election as members of the Association.

A motion being made that they all be elected, was carried. The only Massachusetts names on the list are Messrs. R. Beal of Gill, and Simon Newcomb and Truman H. Safford of Cambridge.

It was announced by the President that the Standing Committee advised the acceptance of an invitation from the Western Railroad and the Amherst and Belchertown Railroad to the members of the Association and the ladies accompanying them, to take a free excursion to Amherst on Saturday next, thus enabling the party to remain two hours in Amherst to examine the Shepard Cabinet of collections in Natural History. It was also stated by the President, that the students of the College had volunteered an escort from the cars to the grounds, and that the ladies of Amherst had politely invited the company to partake of a collation[†] on the College grounds. It was voted to accept the invitations.

The Proceedings terminated at seven o'clock.

The levee at the residence of Hon. George Bliss was a brilliant affair, and was attended by about six hundred ladies and gentlemen, among them Gov. Morgan and wife of New York. Last evening, the beauty of Springfield put its best foot forward, and a levee, such as it has seldom been our good fortune to be invited to, was given by them to the scientific visitors and their families. The reception took place in the City Hall, and a more brilliant scene when the company assembled, much heightened by the gorgeous coloring of the interior of the hall, could scarcely be imagined. The most delicious music, an unlimited quantity of the choicest refreshments, and a profuse display of the most fragrant flowers, were only secondary to the exquisite beauty of the fairest daughters of Hampden County, the whole providing an appropriate and pleasing welcome to the men of science.

MEETING OF THE AAAS
From Our Special Reporter
Springfield, Mass., August 6 1859

In accordance[†] with annual custom, the retiring President of the Association, Prof. Alexis Caswell, of Providence, R.I., delivered his valedictory address in Hampden Hall on Friday evening. Before the hour announced, (8 o'clock) the hall was filled by the most literary and scientific audience that has ever assembled there.

On Saturday at 12 1/2 P.M. the members of the Association and their ladies, in the number of four hundred, proceeded by railroad to Amherst, where they were met by the Undergraduates of the College. The students gave three mild cheers for science, and then, preceded by a band of music and a banner inscribed "Honor to Science," escorted the company to the beautiful grounds of the college. Here, without any speeches or other formalities, the ladies and gentlemen scattered over the place, wherever fancy led. The paleontologists soon filled the room of the Appleton Cabinet, where Professor Hitchcock explained to them the "footprints on the sands of time." The chemists were all to be found in the Octagonal Cabinet, warmly discussing points of mineralogy. Here also were astronomers examining meteorites, and the antiquarians buried themselves in a small room, all the appointments and furniture of which was brought from the ruins of Nineveh. Many were to be found admiring the beautiful telescope, which was made by Alvan Clarke, Esq., of Cambridge, while the Williston Laboratory was filled with the curious about retorts and crucibles. At 5 o'clock all assembled in Williston Hall, where a sumptuous collation was provided. After the collation had been disposed of, the company were addressed by Mr. Dickinson representing the citizens of Amherst, by President Stearns representing the College, by President Alexander representing the Association, and by Prof. Hitchcock representing the geological collection they had come to see. At six the Association again proceeded to the railroad station, whence after more cheers from the students, rather more heartily than those given earlier in the afternoon, they were hurried back to Springfield, where they arrived safely at eight o'clock, charmed by the pleasure of the trip.

Besides attractions to the man of science, Amherst affords many attractions to the eye of taste. From the eminence on which the college stands we have a glimpse of that lovely valley of the Connecticut, which on Saturday afternoon shone with glorious freshness and tenderness of beauty. The arrangements of the day were simple and delightful, and the collation of sandwiches, ice cream, and various kinds of delicious "home-made" cake was enough to create an appetite for the most fastidious.

MEETING OF THE AAAS

From Our Special Reporter
Springfield, Mass., August 8. 1859
Fifth Day—Monday

The Association met[†] this morning at 10 o'clock in the City Hall, about the usual number being present.

President Alexander announced that the Standing Committee had recommended that the rule of the Association, as adopted at Montreal, in relation to the publication of papers offered at the meeting of the Association in the report of the same, be not changed, a motion for such a change having been made by Prof. Coffin of Penn.

This gave rise to considerable discussion, in which several members took part, and this became somewhat warm in its character, Prof. Peirce of Cambridge evidently supposing those who took part in the discussion intended to cast reflection on the manner in which the Standing Committee accepted and rejected papers offered to them, and he defended the action of that committee in an able manner.

On being put to the vote the amendment was lost by a very decided vote.

Mr. Wm. R. Prince, of Flushing, L.I., said he had a preamble and resolution to offer, and he would read it to the meeting. He said learned societies had been assailed as composed of Atheists and Infidels, and he desired to give the Association an opportunity to set this calumny at rest. Furthermore, he desired that the Association should give to the world a proof that its object is to elucidate and not to suppress investigation. The subject I shall introduce, said Mr. Prince, is Mental Power or Spiritualism. He stated that he did not consider that the Association has any thing to do with the isolated fact that spirits do communicate with man, but the Society is certainly bound to recognize Mentalism and Spiritualism, so far as they form a medium for the communication of knowledge to the human race.

You may refuse Spiritualism a hearing, said Mr. Prince, but if this spiritual science courts investigation and you evade it, the world will form its own opinion, and my purpose will be answered.

When Mr. Prince had got thus far, the President called him to order, and requested him to confine himself to the reading of the resolution.

Mr. Prince said he had a preamble to offer with the resolution and he wished to explain it. He then recommenced his remarks where he had left the subject, but was stopped amid cries of "Order" from all parts of the hall.

The President then told him that he must confine himself to the reading of his resolution, without the preamble, when Mr. Prince said his object in offering the resolution was to have it referred to a committee with instructions to examine the subject thoroughly and report at the next annual meeting, and he wished to read the preamble in order to give his ideas on the work before such committee.

The meeting showed unmistakable signs of objection to hearing the preamble. Mr. Prince read the resolution as follows:

Resolved, That a committee composed of six members be now appointed to take into consideration the claims of Spiritual communications to be ranked among the Sciences,—the most exact of sciences too, and that said committee report at the next annual session of this Association.

After some delay, a gentleman seconded the resolution, when it was moved to lay the resolution on the table, and this was carried by a large vote, thus laying Spiritualism at rest for this year at least.

MEETING OF THE AAAS

From Our Special Reporter
Springfield, Mass., August 9, 1859
Sixth Day—Tuesday

The general meeting† was held at 10 o'clock, and notwithstanding many of the members had left town, there was a good attendance.

The Standing Committee recommended Newport, R.I.,

as the place for holding the next annual meeting. This was accepted, and Newport decided on, the time to be hereafter fixed.

The same Committee reported the following list of officers for the next annual meeting:

> *President*—Prof. Isaac Lee of Philadelphia.
> *Vice President*—Dr. B. A. Gould, Jr., of Cambridge.
> *Secretary*—Prof. Joseph Le Conte of Columbia, S.C.
> *Treasurer*—Dr. A. L. Elwyn of Philadelphia.

The list, as reported by the Committee, was elected unanimously.

In the evening the Association met in general session at Hampden Hall, after which the Association adjourned to meet at Newport on the First of August, 1860.

Solitude

Machias, Maine   Eastern Hotel   Friday P.M. 8 1/2 1859, August 19

Camp life† I am perfectly fascinated by. The domestic arrangements are very good. My tent at the mountain I share with Mr. Toomes, aid and assistant to Dr. Gould. It is a nice new tent with a fly & a floor with a tarpolin on it & is about 14 by 10 feet. The beds are very narrow & the nights are so cold that I sent for a Night-cap. At 7 1/2 we get up and have breakfast at 8. Our mess consists of Mr. T. McDonnell, formerly carpenter, now Quartermaster, who is an old man and I believe has been upon the Coast Survey since its establishment. His delight is to save a dime, and he shows great ingenuity in doing it. He is not mean, but he feels the importance of his position and anxiety is his element. He sits at one end of the table; at the other end is Mr. Hugh McHenry, The Chief's Secretary. He has an enormous memory and a wig. Then on one side is Goodfellow, Talcott a very nice young man whom I am working under, & Toomes. On the other side is Mr. Dunn assistant-in-charge, Halter, & I. The eating was not superb. The bread above all was invariably heavy & sour. Nevertheless we all eat it with a very hearty appetite.

As for the air it is a delicious combination of sea air & mountain air. The views are very numerous & various & superb. There was the sea & the hills & the promontory of Machias-port, and the beach, & the woods, & some grand caves—the best by far I ever saw.

They used to bring 40 lbs. of raspberries to camp every day—and 7 dozen eggs.

The neighbors too very very amusing. But here in town at Machias I am perfectly ennuï. The eating is very good (and by the way I notice one smart Yankee girl waits on 12 people much better than we got waited on at home). I have the best room in the house &c, &c. But it is too stupid for existence. No one will be here tomorrow but Talcott & Goodfellow and one isn't much better company than the other. As for the people Miss Erwynes is an extremely unsophisticated young lady I should judge who talks about Wabbits and chwonometers. Henny is a booby. McDonnell I have a great aversion for. Talcott reminds me very much of Story Greenough, Lillie's brother. Still he is preferable to Goodfellow. Halter is very good company. McHenry is amusing and funny. Mr. Dean I like very much, and I consider myself as very fortunate in getting Toomes for a chum, as he fits me to a T.

Percy Frazer a boy of 15 who is a Sophomore in College, is very much like his father, and I like him very much. Mrs. Bache out-Herods Herod up here. I stay in Machias till Wednesday or Thursday.

I have to borrow a drawing pen, but I think I better not have these expensive instruments up here. I have plenty of time to read the _Bible_, & that & Kant _Critik_ are the only books I have got. I am remarkably well. I shouldn't be surprised if I was not back in Cambridge till November. There is much more regard for appearances than I thought here. My new shirt created just about as much sensation as it would have done in College. I am on the "Astronomics" as they call them. My work at present is easy though there is plenty of it. I have had to buy all sorts of things.

Machias, Maine   1859, August 21†

The town of Machias has little that is attractive about it. The houses are mostly one-story white askew looking things. There are no pretty views in town; it is cold all the time; and there are very few pleasant people here. When I first came to this part of Maine I could not imagine how the people got their living, the ground is so barren. The observatory at Howard is on a rock 100 feet high which is nearly destitute of soil or even of moss. All around there seems to be as much rock as ground. Wheat is not ripe yet. Raspberries are in the height of the season; so are blueberries. Blackberries are still green. In such a country as this, of course the people cannot live by farming; they support themselves by fishing, woodcutting, and coast navigation.

At Machiasport, or rather at that part of it where I was, they are all fishermen. My friend Mr. Thompson has a wife, a daughter, and three sons George Washington, Benjamin Franklin, and John LaFayette. He seems to support them all without difficulty by going out to fish once or twice a week.

Fishing, however, only supports the poorer class of people. The rich men here are all lumber-merchants. Even in the towns it is easy enough to cut down trees enough to make a fortune on; and then there is a great deal of unsettled country in Maine. Here we are in a large town with two hotels, a courthouse, a jail, a telegraph, a railroad, a library &c &c and the next 3 townships as you can see by the map are unoccupied. That is 150 square miles of wilderness. On a wood as large as 2400 Mt. Auburns one can imagine there is lumber enough to support a good many people. Machias is one of the towns they bring the wood to be sawed up. There is a natural water power here to move the mills, *and I suppose there are a dozen of the saws, down at the river. The machinery is very simple.*

Mr. Walker of the class of 1844, nephew to Dr. Walker called on me today, and is going to take me to ride to-morrow. I am going to call on C. S. Hillard to-night with him.

My address here is Charles S. Peirce, C.S. Station Western Ridge, near Lane's Brook, Washington Co., Maine. It will be the same till the middle of October.

1859 August† 26

Moved to Cooper, north of Machias. Got over to the camp & reconnoitered. Nice tent nice location & a nice sun shiny day which makes camp a paradise—a thing which it has not resembled during the past week. Read letters from brother and Rickets. Saturday August 27: Dined with the Baches. Finished week work. Arrival of Mr. Dean, Dr. Bache, & Mrs. Goodfellow. In the morning went to see Mrs. Sawyer, a good old soul—wife of a farmer about. Everybody likes her as she is amusing and talkative. I like Helen Davis except perhaps she smokes a pipe. Took tea and spent evening with the Baches. Tuesday August 30: Sent letter to Mother.

I think Charley was shuffled around to several Coast Survey camps in the area so he could get the big picture. These were north of the town of Machias. Because he was not officially a member of the Coast Survey in August, Charley apparently was given an initiatory or orientation period before receiving his official appointment as Aid on the twenty-first of September.

Station Western† Ridge, Machias, Maine   *1859, August 30*
Mrs. Prof. Peirce, LL.D., F.R.S., &c
Dear Mother:

I received the box (expressage $1.00) and your note this afternoon and was delighted to get it. Everything was there and all right, and it is particularly fortunate that Chalk mixture has such a nice smell as various pieces of linen are impregnated with it. What was left of it is all right and well shaken up to be taken if wanted immediately. My last letter was written under somewhat trying circumstances as I had long been looking to Dr. Bache for sheets of blotting-paper, & writing-paper & cotton as well as nightcap & pillow-cases and pens &c. Now however all these are supplied & I am in extasy. That dressing gown I have longed for more than a little. The night-cap is a gem & a much better one than I expected. Another would be a good idea.

So you met Frank Hopkinson—and I can easily picture him got up in his cleanest walking forth to view the world & especially his neat & elegant sentence about the waif & the stray.

My dear mother the amount of letter writing I have to do up here is perfectly appalling; you must therefore expect a costiveness of ideas to manifest itself occasionally unless I should copy one letter into another which I hope I sha'n't be driven to.

Your affectionate Son,   C. S. Peirce

Thursday, September[†] 1
First term begins. Went to walk with Baches. Showed 'em a wood very beautiful I had found out. Took tea with 'em. Percy Frazer left, & Mr. Cooper— clerk, queer character, dispeptic—arrove. Friday, September 2: Acrora Rainy. Monday, September 5: In AM went to walk with Irwyn. Dined with Baches. Began recording Vertical Angles & taking corresponding meteorologies. Wednesday, September 7: Evening at Baches. Thursday, September 8: Began Magnetics. Friday, September 9: Came into my tent just after breakfast. Hall there. I said good morning when instead of answering he rolled onto the floor in a fit. Foomer left. Saturday, September 10: In evening went & called on some girls with Halter. Wednesday, September 14: Hail storm. Thursday, September 15: Wrote to Lelly. Friday, September 16: Water in wash basin was frozen. Sunday, September 18: Dr. Gould arrived. Went to church in AM. Tuesday, September 20: Miss Pike arrived. Wednesday, September 21: Took tea at Baches. Saturday, September 24: Went down in evening at houses of the nobility. Sunday, September 25: Dr. Gould left.

As for remaining on the Survey. Reasons Pro. 1 Have no money to do anything else. 2 If I was sent to Pacific could save $500 in 3 years. 3 Time to study. 4 Pleasant life for young man. 5 Opportunity to travel and knock round. 6 Really see more of character of people and of any place in this way than any other. Reasons Con. 1 Shan't have energy to leave it. 2 Lazy habits. 3 Put me back. I don't imagine I come back much stronger, for on this party the life is sedentary—altho the air is of course great. Besides the eating makes us all sick.

I have about made up my mind not to go to Chamkook as it will be cold & rainy & few persons in camp & the whole thing carried on with the strictest regard for economy. Anyone would say that was done here. Our cook is a frenchman & a queer fellow. Some of his conceptions "make one's head ache." We had had bad eggs for some time & also bad blueberries. There was no way of getting either of them eaten. What does our hero do but produce blueberry-omelette. Need I say it was devoured? The croquettes Dr. Gould knows are really very nice. Pickles and soup however are the greatest staples.

1859 Sept. 27   *Cooper, Maine*
I leave here[†] today for Calais—Spend the night & Wed—proceed to Cherryfield Thurs. To Bangor. Fri. To Portland where I wait till next day. And am home Saturday night.

Charley was back home in Cambridge where he remained through October. The Chief ordered him[†] to join a survey party in Louisiana. He departed in November. He surely noticed that Mrs. Greenough and her daughter

Lillie had begun their trip to Europe. What did he do immediately upon arriving home from Maine? He began writing metaphysics† again: about types of thinking, about the nature of infinity and how one can reason about it, the nature of objects, and on pantheism. This shows where Charley's heart lay, and it was to be a love that would not desert him. By the way, here is Bache's appointment letter and Charley's reply.

Coast Survey† Office, Washington D.C.   28 October 1859
Dear Sir: Having served with my party† during the month of August, and until its departure from Section I, you are hereby appointed an aid in the U. S. Coast Survey from the 21st Sept. ultimo. Your compensation will be at the rate of $15 per month with an allowance of 60 cents per day for subsistence.
                                        Yours respy, A. D. Bache   Supt.
Charles S. Peirce Esq. U.S.C.S.

Cambridge, Mass.   31 October 1859
Dear Sir: I have the honor† to acknowledge the receipt of my appointment as aid and also my instructions both dated Oct 28. I shall report to Mr. Harris in Mississippi by the same mail that takes this letter.
                                        Vr, Charles S. Peirce
Prof. A. D. Bache, Superintendent U. S. Coast Survey

By November, Charley was on station with the Coast Survey vessel *Twilight* in Pascagoula, Mississippi. One of his first letters home was for Benjie, his younger brother.

Pascagoula, Miss.   Thursday 24 November 1859
My Dear Benjie:
    I haven't yet written† to Aunt Sarah or The Chief to thank them for their hospitality & kindness. Yet this being thanksgiving-day, you cannot think that I should be so forgetful of things at home as not to write to you my dear Benjie & tell you what I had for dinner and to give slight sketches of other dinners I have had since I left home—what nice oyster-pie I had at the Bache's one day & only cold corn beef the next. The wonderful hock you wouldn't so much appreciate, I suppose.
    Today I am sorry I had dinner on board the steam-boat from Montreal here, but it was as fine a boat as ever I was on & I had a very jolly dinner. I began with calves head soup which was very fine. Then I had some Red Fish a large ichthiological specimen, the natural history of which, I dare say you know as much about as I do, but if it is not stated in your zoological compendiums I desire you would make a note of it in the margin & promulgate it in your lectures, that it is if anything more delicate to the palate than anything else I ever tasted in that line. Next I had some oyster-pies. Are

the oysters of the Gulf of a different species from those of the north or are they merely a different variety? At any rate they have a much higher flavor than any I ever tested before. Harris says I shall get tired enough of them before the winter is over. But I very much doubt it.

Harris by the way is a splendid fellow & every day he reminds me more & more of Jem. Of course, he hasn't Jem's genius, but I believe he is quite as good & he looks a good deal like him & has a good many of his ways. Today I came near having my dinner in Mobile where there is a very fine hotel and would you know the reason why? It is kept by a couple of Bostonians, as all the best hotels in the country are. Yes, my dear sir, I have travelled over a large portion of the civilized globe in my time. I have seen most cities of any note & those that I haven't seen I have heard of, and I sincerely believe that for a power of making themselves in a quiet way eminently comfortable the Bostonians are unrivalled.

Well I had my thanksgiving breakfast at this Hotel & knew what it was & of course I didn't fancy much the idea of having my thanksgiving dinner on board Steamer X on the way to Pascagoula—(the real name of the boat was Florida but she was an unknown quantity to me).

C. S. Peirce

(1909 Jan 28[†]). Magnificent as were the teachings of the doctrine of chances to physical science, no intelligent physicist can hesitate to admit that they are far out shone by the heliac effulgence that has been emitted from Darwin's immortal <u>Origin</u>. It has always been a matter of personal regret to me that I missed the first impressions the work made in Cambridge, Massachusetts, where I lived, owing to me having set out on the tenth[†] of November, before its appearance on Nov. 24 1859, to go under instructions from the Superintendent of the Coast Survey to take part in triangulation on the east coast of Louisiana. Once arrived in the field of work, I spoke absolutely with no soul except two Coast Survey officers not particularly interested in biology, a densely benighted sailing master, half a dozen men before the mast, a negro cook and a cabin boy until April. However, in the course of the winter, a letter from my mother told me what a sensation the book had made; and thereupon I wrote to my friend Mr. Chauncey Wright that I felt confident that Darwin had received a hint of his idea from Malthus <u>On Population</u>. Long after, Wright inquired of one of Darwin's sons whether this was the case; and reported the answer to be that it was nearly certain the father had never looked into Malthus's celebrated book. But I believe it has since transpired that he really did derive just such a hint as I surmised from that very quarter. I mention this circumstance as evidence that that element of the theory that at the time of its broaching struck a non-biological young chemist as the most novel idea in it was the proposition that the very existence of species is continually at stake in a desperate struggle.

1859 December 12, Schooner Twilight, Pascagoula, Miss.

The views here† are of three kinds. The most beautiful is the prime forest which is all just alike—hot, unshady. The second kind of view which is also comparatively refreshing is a marsh backed by distant trees; the third & commonest kind is a marsh unbacked by anything.

We are still aground here and I am tired of it. The bow of the schooner is on slides, & we expect to buoy up the hinder part by two large mud-flats. For my part, I have my private doubts whether they will lift the schooner, which draws 4 3/4 ft. of water & we cannot hope to get more that 10 inches. Moreover I don't believe 2 pine logs would bear the weight of the vessel long. However last night she seemed to be raised a very little. This morning our sailing master arrived.

We had a Nor-Wester this last week and the weather felt really very cold & some water in pails out doors froze.

1859 December 15, Schooner Twilight, Pascagoula, Miss.

Our schooner is still aground† and at present appearances it will remain there at least till the New Year. This is distressing as there is no work to be done but go to the P.O. and I am approaching the end of the schooner's library. Pascagoula is as nice a place as there is here I suppose, but I see it is such a gossiping little town, that I like to keep out of the people's reach. Yet it is an excellent place to learn chess.

This week I have had a bad cold in my head for we had considerable rain last week which leaked through a hole in the deck big enough to put my hand in directly down into my berth & wet the matrass through & through. It is getting a little better now, however, & this morning, I started off in a "peerague"— which is the name they call dories by here,—and got reeds enough for pipestems to last me and all my descendants to the ninth generation.

As I expected before leaving Cambridge, Halter and I do not get on very well together. My opinionatedness (not of course on matters relating to our work, as I never offered any opinion about that) troubled him excessively, and he consequently began to snub me &c which as I did not immediately resent gradually grew to a head until finally he used language which was outrageously insulting. As I shall take nothing less than an apology, & as he will not render that, things will continue in statu quo, which of course will be anything but agreeable to me. He now takes the manly course of lying about me behind my back, which he can well afford to do as he is not much dependent upon my good will, as I, of course, am upon his when I am under his orders.

I shall write to father in a month or so as to what I am to do in respect to my profession but I am not ready to do so at present.

Schooner Twilight   Pascagoula, Miss.   *1859 December 18*
Dear Jem:
    I would like to have† a little conversation with you before I write to father

about the choice of a profession as after I have asked his advice I cannot well go to any body else for it.

As I suppose you know, he has always been pressing and urging me to devote myself for science, for which I have a <u>gout</u>, to be sure, although for sundry reasons I hesitate much about making it my trade. In the first place, the first business of a man, in my view, on this terrestrial orb is to live—to earn his bread & salt. It is certain that the most of our time has to be devoted to refreshment—to eating, sleeping, &c., and it appears that as the world goes most of our working hours must go to supply our material wants. If a fellow goes and commits matrimony, as most fellows do, why that is all the more true. Now a <u>savan</u> is supposed to be doing that which he most delights to do and he does it as the impulse of his rational nature directs and simply in order to satisfy his intellectual desires. Now it seems both out of fact and out of reason that people should take the trouble to pay a man for that. Science may happen to fill popular wants or it may not. But if it does certainly scientific men will not & do not rest from useful discoveries because they are not paid for them. We cannot, therefore, expect people to pay for what they can have just as well without pay. To be sure there are certain devices & inventions which though not science, it is generally scientific man who makes that are to be had for pay. Very well, as I have said, a man must devote his working hours to what will pay; his leisure he may give to science if he will. Now although I like science very well, it is rather doubtful whether it is desirable or not to be a scientific inventor. So with the educational dodge. The fact is science is meant for leisure. Man is put on earth and chained to it; he has to spend most of his time in sleep and eating, then he has to support existence and avoid pain with almost all the rest of his time. And what on earth rewards him for all this, but ideas? Take a day laborer: 3 great ideas, perhaps, pass through his brain in a lifetime and they make life pay. Isn't it Utopian to suppose that a man may make his pay—his advance wages—support him—and make it needless for him to work. Men of science enough have been farmers-general, merchants & what not, is there any necessary connection between science and education or invention. Isn't there a necessary connection between making a sole pursuit of play and slip-shodity or else affluence?

Now if the pursuit of science were a sacred duty, all this argument would be very flimsy. And so Tom Hill etc. represents it to be and makes a kind of goddess of truth—a kind of Juggernaut before which mortal men are bound to sacrifice themselves. But after all ideas are man's, man is not ideas'; truth is good so far as it is good for man, no further. Science is not a supreme good; nor is the pursuit of science the noblest of occupations, and as for its utility, it is little for present generations, and let future generations get their own.

In short, I am not bound to sacrifice my worldly welfare to science; neither am I prepared to do so voluntarily. And science won't pay, and it is irrational to expect it can be made to. The big bugs in every thing get along well enough in this world, but second rate men only come off second best if they have not material goods to sell. I hope you will let me have your opinion on my opinion at once and greatly in debt,

Your ever affectionate brother, Charles S. Peirce

1859 December 18, Schooner Twilight, Pascagoula, Miss.

I just got up† at 9 1/2—for the Southerners are not early risers—dressed myself in my thin drab clothes and just emerged upon deck when a little nigger rushed up to me with a number of letters one among others from The Chief & I have read several sentences in it already! I took the letters together with some for Mrs. Sarrazin from the little fellow who evidently expected a remuneration if not a gratuity, and was extremely unwilling to let me carry Mme. Chefe's letters, but I had no change so he had to go without. The woods here are just as full of birds as they can be but I haven't yet got a single specimen for Mr. Agassiz owing to the fact that there is no fresh water here, and I have very little room for anything.

Our sailing-master has come. His name is Capt. Bentley. He is called Capt. Mozambique for short. He is a great character & has a great quantity of yarns, about shipwrecks, and digging gold in California, and going for niggers to Africa & being offered the hand of an African princess together with the command of 100,000 warriors, all of which are extremely amusing. He has gone to N.O. now and it is quite dull here without him.

1859 December 20, Schooner Twilight, Pascagoula, Miss.

This style of writing† is as stupid as the life here is, but I will write a full account of everything I did yesterday.

Yesterday morning I got up about 8 1/2 AM and arrayed myself in gorgeous display—consisting of my red shirt, my dirty yellow pantalons and vest and my last red coat which cost $22 together with my molucca joint and went to breakfast. For breakfast, we had as usual wild ducks. We have wild ducks for breakfast, for dinner and for tea every day. But they are not so epicurean when you have them three times a day as when you have them three times a year. Besides that, they eat them fresh here and then they are not so very highly flavored. Besides ducks we had of course cafe au lait. I had some conversation with Mrs. Sarrazin relative to the coffee which I noticed was of a different kind from what we had hitherto had which was very fine. Mrs. Harris thought the difference was occasioned by the sugar's being brown instead of white but I was sure the difference was in the coffee & was confirmed by Mrs. Sarrazin. What other conversation we had I do not now recollect but I have no doubt it concerned the schooner and the hopes which we might entertain of getting her off before the new year. We have made many attempts at getting off the schooner, without success, whenever there was a high tide which happens whenever the wind is SE which is equivalent to saying it is now NW. Indeed we had one hard pull at her yesterday afternoon and that I shall describe in this minute narration. After

*breakfast I sat talking with Mrs. S for a half hour or so and then took my cane
and went down to the P.O. which is about 3 miles off through the pine forest.
On my way down I was thinking of something, it's of no necessity of saying
what, even if I could remember. When I got to the sea-shore I visited one or
two acquaintances and then started to come back. On my way I met my wash-
erwoman to whom I pay 75 cts a dozen—Mr. Harris's bargain—and told her I
would send her my clothes by a nigger Frank that night. When I got back I commenced ruling a duplicate book which occupied me till dinner. When I went
up to dinner I noticed the tide was rising very high and preparations were in
progress for another attempt to haul the schooner off. For dinner we had pork
stuffed with garlic & wild ducks with coffee after dinner as always. The conversation was not particularly lively. After dinner I came back to the schooner
and put on my rough clothes for work. The apparatus by which we proposed
getting off the schooner consists of two large mud flats on each side of her stern,
over which is chained a large beam which is blocked up from the flats at low
tide and thus lifts the stern of the schooner at high tide. Under the bow have
been placed ways, in which are notched for jacksdraws by which it is proposed
to push off the bow. Then there is a single anchor in the middle of the stream
which is attached by its chain to the capstan on the bow of the schooner. Then
there are two other anchors dropped from a flat which is connected by tackle
with the schooner and a large capstan on shore. There is also another anchor
connected by tackle with the stern of the vessel. Now come a gang of darkies
and commenced heaving, & hollaring, shoving and singing, working and playing & creating a general rumpus—but still making the vessel move somewhat
owing to the great height of the tide. Now goes yr obd't sv't up to his middle in
the water and bears a hand at the screws, and then the schooner begins to move
still more. And now we begin to think we shall really get her off, and Mr. Sarrazin sends for some whiskey for the men. And then we keep on hauling &
heaving till seven o'clock when a Nor Wester comes up sharp in the teeth of
the SE wind and the tide begins to run down 2:40 and our hopes begin to be
dashed and the darkies begin to work a little less hard and it all begins to seem
like the story of the old woman whose ox won't go over the style and we should
have given up in despair of the schooner just that moment hadn't got afloat so
we began to rouse the men and the men began to pull at the ropes and the
ropes began to pull the schooner and so the old Twilight got fairly anchored in
the middle of the river that night. Next morning we sent for the Capt. who has
gone to Mozambique or Mobile or somewhere. And now we have got the old
schooner ballasted and I hope to pass Christmas but certainly New Year in
Biloxi.*

    *I have long had an abhorrence of the doctrine† that any proposition what-
ever is infallibly true. Unless truth be recognized as <u>public</u>,—as that of which
<u>any</u> person would come to be convinced if he carried his inquiry, his sincere
search for immovable belief, far enough,—then there will be nothing to prevent*

each one of us from adopting an utterly futile belief of his own which all the rest will disbelieve. Each one will set himself up as a little prophet; that is, a little "crank," a half-witted victim of his own narrowness.

It is said there is a "Faith" the object of which is absolutely "certain." Will someone have the goodness to tell me what could be meant by this "certain"? Does it mean anything more than that one is personally obstinately resolved upon sticking to the proposition, ruat caelum?

This reminds me of an anecdote that was told me late in 1859 by a southern darky.

You know, massa, said he, that General Washington and General Jackson was great friends, dey was (the fact being that the latter was an irreconcileable opponent of the former). Well, one day Gen'l. Washington, he said to Gen'l Jackson, "Gen'l, how tall you think that horse of mine was?"

"I don't know General," says General Jackson, "How tall is he, General Washington?"

"Why," says General Washington, "he is sixteen feet high."

"Feet, General Washington," say General Jackson, "feet, General Washington. You means hands Gen'ral!"

"Did I say feet, General Jackson," said General Washington. "Do you mean to say that I said my horse was sixteen feet high?"

"You certainly said so, General Washington."

"Very well, then, Gen'ral Jackson, if I said feet, if I said feet, then I sticks to it!"

Is your "sublime certain faith" any more "sublime" than that? How?

Now I will tell you the meaning that I would, in my turn, attach to the word faith. The New Testament word is πίστις, which means, in its most proper sense, trust; that is, belief in something not as having any knowledge or approach to knowledge about the matter of belief, but "implicit belief," as the catholics say, that is, belief in it derived from one's belief that a witness who testifies to it would not so testify if it were not so.

XX[†]
1860 January 15

Never be ill-paid. Better be well-paid for something poor, than well-paid for something excellent. Otherwise excellent things will never be well-paid.

In 1860, to pass the time[†] on a survey ship where I was stationed, I cooked up a melange of effects of most of the elementary principles of cyclic arithmetic; and ever since, occasionally exhibited them in the form of a "trick" (though there is really no trick about the phenomenon) at the end of an evening's sitting at card-play, with the uniform result of interesting and surprising all the company, though their mathematical powers might range from barely enough to care for cards at all, up to some of the greatest mathematicians of the nineteenth century, who with a little reflexion would easily discern the rationale of the thing.

1860 February, Quarantine Station, Mississippi Delta, Schooner Twilight
The bad seeing† we have lately had makes this Delta connection work hold on in the most provoking way. I long to be over on the Isle au Breton, Grand Gosie, & Chandeleurs both because they are much cooler & pleasanter than this inner place which whatever may be its excitements in the way of seeing the ship go up the river & down, I am now beginning to be a little tired of and also because from the fact of their extended length and slight breadth, the triangulation of them will be a difficult problem that I am anxious to see solved.

Here is a curious fact. There is some land here which is always growing larger. Other land which is always growing smaller. The latter seems to be the securest place for a scaffold.

Half the mail doesn't come through here. Scandalous! This New Orleans P.O. is the most shiftless, uncontrollable unpunishable den of thieves that remains from the Dark Ages. Mr. Harris gave an account of the way he saw them distributing mail there that ought to be made a campaign document of by the Republicans & I have no doubt if they would put Postal Reform into their Chicago platform they would put in their candidate.

1860 February 18, Buras Settlement, Mississippi Delta Schooner Twilight
When Mr. Harris† first visited the Quarantine Station near here, he asked the doctor what sickness was there.
"Nothing but a few cases of small-pox."
"Small-pox? Where did that come from?" Mr. Harris said the doctor seemed perfectly astonished that he didn't know where the small-pox came from.
"Why from Boston of course," said he, "All the small pox comes from Boston."

Politics! It seems strange enough to me sitting down in this cabin to see to what a point of phrenzy men will work themselves to on serious & grave topics. Here I have the facts & am entirely removed from all bias & heart-biting. That's one advantage. I haven't seen a slave since I left Pascagoula. I think the abolitionists & the republicans who are the self-deceived abolitionists are injuring the North, the South, the slaves, and Canada. However nobody can expect them to cool down. We might as well prepare ourselves to make the best of a dissolution. But I cannot think that the dissolution will last forever. At any rate, all is for the best. This abolitionism is tending to the same result that Socialism has in France.

Our stove is down long ago & the weather hasn't been cold enough to make us shut the hatches for a long time. Almost always we like to lie down in the shade out doors & we go into the water if the wind is Southerly.

My mother thinks I have discarded my boyish habits. Good trait or bad trait, it isn't so, since I am looked aboard here as a marvel of boyishness.

1860 March 18, Oyster Bay, Schooner Twilight,
We had a good deal† of rain on the 16th which after the seams had been well opened by hot weather came directly through into the cabin. If I ever venture to complain of any little inconvenience Mr. Harris seems to think the complaint is against him. Now that night there wasn't a dry place in the cabin. After I had gone to bed the water came pouring down into my bunk & made it sopping wet. I mentioned it next evening as something of a hardship, but Mr. H. thought that was preposterous. Yet I am on quite good terms with H.

We play chess a good deal now there are four of us who play. There is very little danger of my wasting much time at it, as I may say with truth I never did. But lately I haven't played so much since I learned father was anxious on the subject.

Thinking of father, he is considering letting me go to N.Y. to study. Of course, I can't help seeing in the present financial condition of the family it is full as much as I can expect to be allowed to study in Cambridge & if the question is between sending me to N.Y. or Benjie to a better school I wish it may be decided that the latter shall take place. At the same time I should value going to N.Y. so highly as to be sure it would put me into a higher grade of science.

U.S. Schooner Twilight, Bird Island, North Oyster Bay,   *1860 March 25*
My dearest Mother:
I was very sorry† to hear by your last letter which I received on the 26th inst. that you were no better than you were a fortnight before. Before this letter gets to you however you will have got nicely through the month of March & will be recovering I hope from this troublesome rheumatism. For the last few days we have been having some extremely cold weather down here. Last night at tea time the thermometer was at 64º in the cabin, & you can easily imagine that we all had on our thickest clothes & were well right frozen at that. I am happy to say that it is a perfectly healthy country, except near the river where the Captn. Halter, & the cabin-boy are immediately seized with fever & Ague & all of us feel more or less under the weather. This you will think strange as people in general are not affected so at this time of the year (tho' you remember that a few years ago when I went to pay a visit to the Huntingtons in Northampton, the proximity of the river made me sick) but it appears that living in the marshes gives one a peculiar aptitude to these complaints at least so the doctors say. For my part I was quite unwell during a somewhat protracted stay at the river but I wound up with a violent neuralgia, during which the only mail left the schooner which has not carried a letter from me home, which was the upshot.

When I say living at the river I mean living in Buie Ronde where the strip of land between the river & the sea is only 10 ft. wide or the width of our house from study to parlor.

We have likewise been having a great deal of lazy weather this month when no observing was to be done and when nothing was to be done & when we all felt listless & ennuï. This is provoking. You see I have written no more letters to you meantime but how can one write letters when one is ennuï & besides I have had several to write to classmates.

I didn't get my Punch and Ill Lond News last time; perhaps it was lost in the Hungarian.

Your affectionate son, C.S.P.

XXI†
1860 April 1
USCS Schooner Twilight, Isle au Breton
The Use of Solitude

O, they who know what it is, feel its use! But who does know it? The poet or sentimentalist who shuts himself up for an hour or a day or three days seems to himself to feel the excellence of solitude. But he is mistaken; his condition is not solitude; this: to live in the desert after the two months home-sickness, thoughts of home, and care for home are over, and before any prospect of return to the world has brought them back, this is solitude.

And these are its properties:

Negatively, it is a soothing absence of all care for appearances,—it is the normal absence of all thoughts of the fictitious and the factitious.

"Sleep, sleep, today, tormenting cares
Of earth and folly born."

Positively, everybody knows it is drawing nigh unto the personality in nature, and that it is, in an humble sense, walking with God. It is a calmness preparatory to enthusiasm on those things worthy of enthusiasm & the enthusiasm it makes is of calm and noble, unpartizan nature. Thus, rightly used, Solitude has a reference to the world, and if it is rightly used, the mind grows under its climate. Man, certainly, was not made for solitude; hence taken as an end in itself, it only hurts. It enervates. The mind just emerged from it lacks that hardihood which pertains to those who have been grappling with circumstances & exposed to the storms of life. It is, in fact, a green-house and a nursery.

The Important portion of this earth consists of variegated land, with inland seas (the Atlantic, the Mediterranean, the Indian, the Arctic) all made for the promotion of intercourse. This is man's workshop. But a full half the globe is nothing but a polynesian ocean—all isolation—with nothing out of the monotony, either to think of or to care for. Thus we see that the idea that man should sometimes be solitary is expressed in the very contour and face of the planet.

THE MIND, too, is constructed in its contemplative, concentrative faculties, with the same thing in view; and people who live in cities and who violate this physical and mental law of nature, are doomed to a degeneracy, in consequence; and, in my opinion, it should be made one principal point in a boy's or a girl's education, besides instructing them in literature & philosophy & in the accomplishments of discernment and readiness, to teach them also the depth, the power, and the use of solitude.

Emerson's Nature of 1836[†]

TO GO into solitude, a man needs to retire as much from his chamber as from society. I am not solitary whilst I read and write, though nobody is with me. But if a man would be alone, let him look at the stars. The rays that come from those heavenly worlds will separate between him and what he touches. One might think the atmosphere was made transparent with this design, to give man, in the heavenly bodies, the perpetual presence of the sublime. Seen in the streets of cities, how great they are! If the stars should appear one night in a thousand years, how would men believe and adore; and preserve for many generations the remembrance of the city of God which had been shown! But every night come out these envoys of beauty, and light the universe with their admonishing smile.

The stars awaken a certain reverence, because though always present, they are inaccessible; but all natural objects make a kindred impression, when the mind is open to their influence. Nature never wears a mean appearance. Neither does the wisest man extort her secret, and lose his curiosity by finding out all her perfection. Nature never became a toy to a wise spirit. The flowers, the animals, the mountains, reflected the wisdom of his best hour, as much as they delighted the simplicity of his childhood.

> Crossing a bare common,
> in snow puddles,
> at twilight,
> under cloud sky

In the woods, we return to reason and faith. There I feel that nothing can befall me in life,—no disgrace, no calamity (leaving me my eyes), which nature cannot repair. Standing on the bare ground,—my head bathed by the blithe air and uplifted into infinite space,—all mean egotism vanishes. I become a transparent eyeball; I am nothing; I see all; the currents of the Universal Being circulate through me.

1860 April 2, Isle au Breton, Schooner Twilight,

We have been at Isle au Breton[†] where we got through work 3 days ago but the schooner being aground we had to wait till we could get her off which was a good deal of work. I thought the ballast would have to be taken out of her, but they finally succeeded in working her bow off the shoal & then by ballasting down her level head worked her off this AM.

When I visited Isle au Breton before, in the dead of winter (If the winter had any dead), I was already favorably impressed by it; the beautiful beach & irregularities of surface giving it a character that compared very favorably indeed with the other localities here. But now in the spring when it was blooming with flowers, lillies, oleanders, morning glories, daisies, besides hundreds of other flowering plants some of which aspired to the dignity of trees, the names of which I know not, made it a perfect paradise. The temperature was just warm enough to make the air quite delicious & the water a little better still; & a fine surf came up on the beach. In addition to the flowers there were a variety of pretty shells, of which I am sorry to say I had no leisure to collect, though they were scarcely handsome enough for ornaments tho' pretty on the beach. The cook by the way got a large number of pearls of good size & shape but bronze colored.

There was also a deserted garden and the remains of a house on the island, the inhabitant of which died two years ago. It was really a beautiful place & in front of his house he had two of the most finely shaped & splendidly colored trees I ever saw. They were dwarf palms or palmettos, & their flowers beyond description beautiful.

I hope to be home early in June.

U.S. C. S. Schooner Twilight   *Bird Island South,*   *1860 April 4*
Dear Jem:

I ought long ago[†] to have answered your two very nice letters. Your first contained some suggestions which happened to be just what I wanted to settle my mind on that subject of profession & put the matter in a point of view I hadn't thought of.

I haven't heard that you have any particular desire to be settled at present, which I am not greatly surprised at, good sermons not being writable off hand & I suppose nothing could be pleasanter than living in Cambridge & be able to give as much of attention as ever you wish to what you are engaged on. For my part, I look back upon Cambridge as a miracle of beauty & am very apt to consider the houses as of stupendous height. I think I shall have a feeling of disappointment when I go back to find them no higher than our tripods, a momentous truth which I can hardly realize at present.

You needn't think by anything that I say that I am in the least homesick. I think for the first six weeks after setting sail, I thought the places rather lonely & the times rather slow. However, I have long got over that & I find a great many peculiar pleasures & advantages in this style of life. To be sure it is quite absurd to try to convince you or anybody living in civilization that this is so, but you do not know how much keeping appointments, having to hurry, regarding appearances actually weighs upon you & how delightful it is to have rid of them. I get up in the morning half an hour before sunrise. If there is no "seeing" I take a boat & go off on a sail till breakfast. After breakfast, I have almost always some computing, duplicating, plotting or something to do. After that I play a few games of chess & then dinner. After dinner we generally do nothing but talk till it is good seeing or if there is no seeing, I go a-swimming, a-fishing or a-shooting. In the evening for the last month we have had reading aloud. We have already accomplished Bleak House & are now on Quentin Durward.

Yr. Affectionate brother   Charles S. Peirce

1860 April 8, Bird Island South, Schooner Twilight,

My wardrobe† is reaching fast a climax of delapidation. The thick pants are about as good as ever, except that the best pair I went overboard in one day, but those of course were long ago laid aside. For my thin clothes, I held on as long as I could to that buff waistcoat & pants that I got 18 mos ago at Cull & Tuttles, but they are now too bad to wear even down here & that beautiful maroon coat, it wrings my heart to see, is getting to look shabbier & shabbier everyday. I have confined myself as much as possible to one pair of blue pants but I think they will disappear as dew before the summer sun ere long & then— I shudder at the thought—I shall have to begin on the only suit I have to be decent in. Linen clothes I wear as little as possible on account of the expense of washing and besides they come back all spotted & scrubbed to pieces. As for the blue plain shirt I had sent it to the wash one day & it came back about large enough for an infant in arms & with the color so washed out as not to be white without suggesting at all that it could ever have been blue. But the most mournful havoc is among my cotton clothes. They are always too damp to put on & have suffered from mildew, despite the care I have taken to have them frequently put out in the sun.

Here is a sample of the way clothes go. Yesterday, I started off with Mr. Harris to go to Bird Is. N. to observe. Bird Is. has a break in the middle over which there is water enough at high tide for one of our boats, & there is also another place covered at high water but bare at low. We were—that is the vessel lay within the bay; but in order to obtain a better landing (the tide being high) Mr. H. took the boat through the break. After observing all the P.M. we started to come back. The sun was hardly set even in this high latitude of 29° before it is pitch dark & the consequence was that Mr. H. passed the break without seeing it. I saw it, but the tide now being pretty low I considered it more than doubtful whether the boat could be got through, & supposed Mr. H. was going to adopt the wise plan of going around the Island. We soon however got to the second low place & through that Mr. H. determined to go. The result was that we all had to get out of the boat & pull the boat over the Is. & of course got every rag upon us completely loaded with salt water. I mention this as the handiest instance of how clothes are ruined. If good seeing comes you know we can't stop to change our clothes but must go off at once & take advantage of it.

I hope everyone at home won't be disappointed at my shabby state when I return.

1860 April 10, Raccoon Point, Schooner Twilight
I was not surprised[†] at hearing mother had been so very sick with
erysipelas, as I was fully persuaded she would be so if she was sick at all. I was
somewhat composed by hearing she was better, but I have begged Jem, in case
she is not so well again, to let me know by telegram as it will much relieve my
mind. I am thankful I was not at home when mother was sick & that I didn't
hear of it till I could hear she was better for I could have done no good there.
Jem has been very kind to write me as much as he has this winter.

Charley had a number of vitally important topics on his mind during this time. For one thing, he had received news that his mother had erysipelas (from the Greek: rosy-skin), a particularly nasty disease as Betsey has informed me. It was even more grim in Charley's day, when therapeutic options were virtually nonexistent. As a period reference work[†] reported, it produces a peculiar rose-colored eruption of the skin, whence the name. The highly painful inflammation—also known in Europe as St. Anthony's Fire—was little understood at that time; it could terminate on the surface of the skin—in those days thought to be a more or less favorable resolution—or less favorably by abcess (which is apt not to be limited to a particular spot and thus very dangerous). Or it can terminate in gangrene and death of the patient. Pure air, a milk diet, and the use of quinia and iron with stimulants were mentioned as treatment over a sustained period. In this case, she was stricken in mid-March, passing through a terrible fortnight. When this news eventually arrived, Charley could do little more than write comforting letters to his parents, of which result his elder brother[†] gave assurance.

Ben shouldered the supporting burdens of the attack. He confided to The Queen[†] that Sarah almost died:

> Sarah has been at death's door with Erysipelas in the head. It is a frightful disease, with its violently wild delirium[†] and its horrid distortion of the face. But The Queen is always the blessing of her friends.
>
> One day, Sarah gave me in the coolest way, full directions what I should do when she was dead. Fortunately her eyes were so glazed with disease that she could not witness my contortions and I was able to command my voice. This was the day after the fainting fit—and seemed to be the first decided manifestation of the wildness of her mind.
>
> At the instant of greatest danger—when her pulse was scarcely sensible, and the doctor was anxious lest she was right in her assertion that she was fast sinking out of the world—it was The Queen's glass of hock which saved her. There was nothing else in the house which she could take for a stimulant and it was long past

midnight. When she first began to recover gleams of reason, The Queen's letter came, and we both blessed it. And Sarah's heart was never more warm towards The Queen—whom she calls "the sweetest creature in the world." Of course I was with her night and day, till—none too soon—I was compelled to resign my place to a nurse. But strange to say, the nurse proved to be ill herself, was obliged to leave and I restored to the care of her.

By the end of April Sarah was clearly recovering, although her hair fell out and she suffered with[†] crossed eyes for awhile. But now Ben became ill[†] and generally run down from nursing. He had been invited to the British Association meeting in June, and had debated[†] whether to go. His friends urged him to make the trip. It was settled when Sarah improved and Ben's physician absolutely insisted that he give up university duties for six months[†] and take a sea voyage to recover[†] his own health. Ben had dropped a chunk of coal on his foot when Sarah was desperately ill. He walked about too much, so it became inflamed. Eventually he was in violent pain. His physician prescribed inhalation of ether vapor and a great deal of laudanum plus leeches for the swelling. Betsey mentioned that it was well that Ben took the trip because if nothing else he escaped his doctor. It was now more than thirty years since Ben brought his strenuous work habits first to Round Hill then to Harvard, and all hands demanded[†] that he take a long vacation.

Any financial objections to a leave were eliminated when Ben's supporters presented him with a fund of $1200 for the trip, with stops to be first at London and the British Association, then to Paris[†] for further scientific consultations. Ben's teaching duties at Harvard were assumed by Jem[†] (who was paid by Ben).

The trip was a marvelous experience, for Ben witnessed the Wilberforce/Huxley debate over Darwin's Origin of Species, met Charles Babbage to discuss mechanized computing, and did a number of other interesting things connecting him strongly[†] with European scientific circles.

A Man of Science

During these hectic times in Function Grove, back on the *Twilight* Charley made some further decisions about his career. He proposed to accept a Harvard Proctorship (Proctors were college disciplinary officers, somewhat like Student Resident Assistants in contemporary college dormitories). He would live at home and study science[†] at Harvard, especially chemistry.

Yet Charley had made an important bit of progress within his soul as a result of a kind of study for which one needs no university. Indeed, his location on the *Twilight* surrounded often by raw nature, placed him in the ideal venue to receive the lessons of solitude, to draw nigh to the personality in nature through his own experience instead of through descriptions of the experiences of others.

U.S. C. S. Schooner Twilight   Raccoon Point,1   1860 April 23
Dear Mother:
Jem says† you are getting well but that you don't by any means take the most hopeful view of yourself, which I should not be surprised to hear of any body but you; but I am convinced you have energy enough to get well about twice as quick as any other lady so I have my mind at rest on that point. Jem says you want me to come home without unnecessary delay. Tell me how fast you want me to come. By travelling night & day and arriving a living skeleton, I could get home in four days. He says however that you would like me to come home direct by ship. This would certainly take 10 days. That is the least possible time. I might take 3 weeks. I should like the mode very much but for one thing. You remember when I came South, you asked me not to spend but one day in New York, tho' I wanted very, <u>very</u> much to stay longer. When I woke up in the morning I departed, I debated for some time if I wouldn't stay. In the first place I knew very well that the reasons you wanted me to leave for were based on false facts, that therefore they were no reasons at all, & that moreover you didn't know why or how much I wanted to stay. When I got down stairs & found I had got to go without breakfast & almost without dinner I was still more tempted not to go. Ever since I have been in a miserable state of mind for losing the opportunity. In going home I am going to make up for it to stay in New York a week.
I hear from Jem who has had the goodness to write regularly to me since you have been ill that Father has been unwell. I hope by next letter to hear something better. What on earth has got into all the Cambridge people! Love to all.
Your Aft. son, Charles Peirce

1860 April 23, Raccoon Point, U. S. Schooner Twilight
I am delighted† to learn from Jem that mother is getting well & am also glad to hear that father has been invited to the meeting of the Brit. Ass. I think he really needs the trip & shouldn't be surprised if he came back refreshed enough to commence of his Celestial Mechanics. At any rate I think it would do him good & I hope he can be persuaded to go whether he has any papers to present or not. Of course, he would have as none of his papers before the Am. Ass. have been properly preserved. How anyone so fond of travelling should persist in refusing all invitations to go to Europe, I really can't see.
My plan for coming home. If any body is sick or if there is any other grave reason for coming right home, of course, I desire to do so. Otherwise, I have no desire to see much of New Orleans & as for Mobile, except that there is such a

comfortable hotel there, nothing would induce me to visit such a mean and austere-looking place again. Washington I should like to see more of but I shall have other chances to do that & as far as Baltimore & all other places where I know anybody my wardrobe will keep me away from them. Therefore, I shall go to N.Y. by steamer via Havana since it is certainly as quick & most probably quicker than going to Boston direct, however pleasant that might be. And moreover I shall in that way spend a few hours in Havana which of course I wouldn't miss. Also, I shall spend a day or two in N.Y. because in coming down here, I sacrificed a very earnest desire to do so because mother asked me to, thinking I never should regret it much, but now instead of that I have been ready to pile ashes on my head for doing it all winter. I mean therefore to see several things in New York before I leave it viz:—Abbot's Egyptian Museum, which may be taken out of the country any time. The Astor Library, of which I want to have a correct idea, without delay. The Düsseldorf Gallery. The Central Park. The city generally & the churches or a few of them. This ought to take a week. So for the expense, it needn't be great, & accordingly I have made up my mind to stay there as long as by economy I can. These southern cities are nothing to see, & the expenses are enormous. Washington and New York are the two places I want to see. As father & mother want me not to delay unnecessarily, I omit Washington. New York I am not prepared to forego, but I am probably quite as anxious to get home as anyone there is to see me, I might say a thousand times more so, reasonably.

I wonder if there is any news from Mrs. Greenough & Lillie.

There is a small bundle of scraps in Charley's box probably gathered late in his life, tied with a rosy ribbon, concerning Lillie Greenough. It appears that Charley kept track of her off and on over the years. Betsey urged me to summarize most of that material here. The first item is a set of genealogical notes that Charley jotted down, to which I added one date.

Greenough, Anna† Lillie, June 18, 1844–March 17, 1928
   wife (1) of Charles Moulton. †
   wife (2) of Johan Henrik de Hegermann-Lindencrone.
Daughter of Harriet Howard Fay (daughter of Samuel P. P. Fay) and William H. Greenough.
Named Anna Lillie in honor of her maternal grandmother, Anna Lillie Howard.
Her brother, Joseph Story Fay G., January 1, 1837—March 20, 1906.
Henry Greenough, Architect of the Peirce and Davis houses on Quincy Street.

Perhaps the most informative of Charley's scraps is a page clipping of a long note, probably by Lillie, in the front matter of a book published in 1914 collecting correspondence from her career—it's entitled *The Sunny Side of Diplomatic Life.*

Madame de Hegermann-Lindencrone, the writer[†] of these letters, is the wife of the recently retired Danish Minister to Germany. She was formerly Miss Lillie Greenough, of Cambridge, Massachusetts, where she lived with her grandfather, Judge Fay, in the fine old Fay mansion on Mason Street, now the property of Radcliffe College.

As a child Miss Greenough developed the remarkable voice which later was to make her well known, and when only fifteen years of age, her mother took her to London to study under Garcia. Two years later Miss Greenough became the wife of Charles Moulton, the son of a well-known American banker, who had been a resident in Paris since the days of Louis Philippe. As Madame Charles Moulton, the charming American became an appreciated guest at the court of Napoleon III. Upon the fall of the Empire Mrs. Moulton returned to America, where Mr. Moulton died, and a few years afterward she married M. de Hegermann-Lindencrone, at that time Danish Minister to the United States, and in later periods his country's representative at Stockholm, Rome, Paris, Washington, and Berlin.

> Washington, 1875–1880 Paris, 1897–1902
> Rome, 1880–1890 Berlin, 1902–1912
> Stockholm, 1890–1897

Probably much later in life, Charley added the following two bits, the first a loose page from one of his journals (quite late) and the second is a few lines he cut from a letter written by his brother, Benjamin Mills—Benjie—in 1865 from Paris where he was attending college.

In 1859[†] I had a tremendous love affair with a great beauty, a wonderful singer, who was taken abroad by her mother to prevent the catastrophe of a marriage with a poor man. When cured of that I married while still a young man her cousin, Melusina Fay, and settled down to the business of earning a living.

Paris,   November 5, 1865
My dear Friend,
        I have refused an invitation to go out to Vincennes to see Mrs. Moulton, formerly Miss Lilly Greenough of Cambridge—then a flame of my brother Charley's, now one of the grand Parisian flirts and a friend of the Emperor's, to write you my usual Sunday epistle.

Madame Moulton indeed became a flashing figure in the court of Emperor Napoleon III. The wife of a fabulously wealthy banker, she was widely sought for her beautiful voice and her charming social skill; she became a virtual member of the French nobility, as her memoirs[†] clearly trace.

Betsey and I speculate that Charley met Lillie Greenough, with whom he fell hopelessly in love, as an indirect result of her attending the Agassiz School for Young Ladies, which Agassiz, his son Alexander, and his new second wife Elizabeth Cabot Cary Agassiz opened in 1854 in their new home next door[†] to Function Hall. A number of Harvard Professors and students who were interested in the principle of equal educational opportunities for women lectured there. That was a doctrine at least two generations old in Charley's family. This school was the germ from which Radcliffe College grew, nourished by Mrs. Agassiz's astute leadership over the years. Lillie recorded impressions of her classes there in a letter to her mother[†] dated 1856, at age twelve. Charming is the only appropriate word for Lillie's personality and style—even at this young age.

Dear Mother,—You say in your last letter, "Do tell me something about your school." If I only had the time, I could write volumes about my school, and especially about my teachers.

To begin with, Professor Agassiz gives us lectures on zoology, geology, and all the other ologies, and draws pictures on the blackboard of trilobites and different fossils, which is very amusing. We call him "Father Nature," and we all adore him and try to imitate his funny Swiss accent.

Professor Peirce, who is, you know, the greatest mathematician in the world, teaches us mathematics and has an awful time of it; we must be very stupid, for the more he explains, the less we seem to understand, and when he gets on the rule of three we almost faint from dizziness. If he would only explain the rule of one! The Harvard students say that his book on mathematics is so intricate that not one of them can solve the problems.

We learn history and mythology from Professor Felton, who is very near-sighted, wears broad-rimmed spectacles and shakes his curly locks at us when he thinks we are frivolous. He was rather nonplussed the other day, when Louise Child read out loud in the mythology lesson something about "Jupiter and ten."

"What," cried Mr. Felton, "what are you reading? You mean 'Jupiter and Io,' don't you?"

"It says ten here," she answered.

Young Mr. Agassiz teaches us German and French; we read Balzac's *Les Chouans* and Schiller's *Wallenstein.*

Our Italian teacher, Luigi Monti, is a refugee from Italy.

No one takes lessons in Greek from long-bearded, fierce-eyed Professor Evangelinus Apostolides Sophocles, so he is left in peace.

Cousin James Lowell replaces Mr. Longfellow the days he can't come. He reads selections of "literary treasures," as he calls

them, and on which he discourses at length. He seems very dull
and solemn when he is in school; not at all as he is at home.

I consider myself a victim. In recess, when the other girls walk
in Quincy Street and eat their apples, Mrs. Agassiz lures me into the
parlor and makes me sing duets with her and her sister, Miss
Carey.

There are about fourteen pupils now; we go every morning at
nine o'clock and stay until two o'clock. We climb up the three
stories in the Agassiz house and wait for our teachers, who never
are on time.

Mrs. Agassiz comes in, and we all get up to say good morning
to her. As there is nothing left for her to teach, she teaches us
manners.

I don't wonder that you think it extraordinary that all these
fine teachers, who are the best in Harvard College, should teach us;
but the reason is, that the Agassiz's have built a new house and find
it difficult to pay for it, so their friends have promised to help them
start this school, and by lending their names they have put it on its
legs, so to speak.

Charley left for Maine probably thinking that he was successfully courting Miss Greenough and had even hinted to his mother that he was near to a
proposal. He knew the external details of their trip, but the full significance
of it for his courtship was made a clear idea only after he returned home from
Louisiana at the end of May 1860. By then Lillie was half a world apart, and
well down the path to becoming Madame Moulton, her marriage being in
1861 at age seventeen. For some time Lillie's mother appears to have had in
mind a much wealthier suitor than Charley, notwithstanding the friendly relationship between the Fay and Peirce families. Clearly the tremendous love
affair occurred before Charley left for duty with the Coast Survey in Maine
and Louisiana, during the months preceding August of 1859, for Lillie and
her mother journeyed to New York City where they boarded the *Commodore
Vanderbilt* on the seventeenth to arrive at Bremen late in that month. While in
New York, Lillie sang for George Bancroft, "the celebrated historian," and received from him a book of Bryant's poems inscribed to her "in souvenir of a
never-forgettable evening." They made their way without haste to London
for an appointment with Garcia—said to be the greatest singing master in the
world, who counted figures such as Jennie Lind among his pupils. After an
audition, she was accepted as a member of his studio. Lillie, it seems, made
a strong impression on almost everyone who met her in those days. Although she was described as "a great beauty," I confess that I didn't have that
impression when I saw the frontispiece portrait[†] in the first volume of her
memoirs.

Charley fulfilled his wish to return from Louisiana via New York City. He arrived by the nineteenth of May[†] 1860. According to his plan, he toured around, then met his father[†] at the Brevoort House on the twenty-third. Ben sailed for London on the *Amazon* at one P.M.[†] on the twenty-sixth. The Chief came down from Washington to see him off. Or was it because the evening prior to departure, Ben was the featured guest of "a most delightful symposium, at which some charming women were present, in honor of the departure[†] of your geometer." Charley probably missed that party, for he journeyed to Cambridge, reaching there[†] by the twenty-sixth. Upon arrival, as his journals show, he soon turned to writing philosophy.

New York City   *1860 May 19*
Prof. Alexander D. Bache
Superintendent. U.S. Coast Survey
Dear Sir:
    I am under the necessity[†] of requesting you to accept my resignation from the Coast Survey in which work I have had the honor of serving as aid. I would desire my resignation to date from to-day. I remain
      with the highest respect,   *Charles S. Peirce*

1860 May 20, 5th Ave. Hotel, N.Y.C
    Thursday before last[†] on the 10th of May, at Point Fortuna, La., we finished our work and set sail for Old Harbor Keys, La. on our way home. At about midnight however we shoaled our water and being on an unsurveyed course came to for the night. Next morning the 11th with a very light air & strong current dead ahead we made but little progress & did not reach the O.H. Keys til noon. Here we went ashore to look for an old station but didn't find it. The islands were covered with eggs of a kind which I believe are esteemed a luxury in these regions but we had too many of them & voted them a bore. We left this place about 4 P.M. and made a remarkably good run & got to Biloxi that night. Next morning the 12th I was dropped ashore & staid there till Sunday P.M. the 13th when I left for N.O. On arriving in New Orleans I found it so intensely hot that staying there almost a week till Saturday for the steamer was a thing not to be thought of; accordingly that evening I left by the Jackson road & reached New York Friday evening the 18th. I was just going up to bed when who should I see but Staunton Blake who told me father was going to sail next day. Accordingly we went down to the Brevoort where we were also told the same story—a wrong one, as he was delayed.
    Next morning the 19th after breakfast I walked out to find further news. I met Mr. Ruggles who took me round to Dr. Gibbs' where I met Dr. Gibbs' sister-in-law. Yesterday besides the above, I did nothing but look up Paine & Curtis—got a Roman Punch at Taylers—and in the evening called on the Miss Rus-

sel's & played a game of chess with Sophie whom I found as much absorbed in it as I am.

It's cold here.

(Cambridge, 1903 March). I grew up[†] in Cambridge and was about 21 when the Origin of Species *appeared. There was then living here a thinker who left no remains from which one could now gather what an educative influence his was upon the minds of all of us who enjoyed his intimacy, Mr. Chauncey Wright. He had at first been a Hamiltonian but had early passed over into the warmest advocacy of the nominalism of John Stuart Mill; and being a mathematician at a time when dynamics was regarded as the loftiest branch of mathematics, he was also inclined to regard nature from a strictly mechanical point of view. But his interests were wide and he was also a student of Asa Gray, the Harvard Darwinian. I was away surveying in the wilds of Louisiana when Darwin's great work appeared, and though I learned by letters of the immense sensation it had created, I did not return until early in the following summer when I found Wright all enthusiasm for Darwin, whose doctrines appeared to him as a sort of supplement to those of Mill. I remember well that I then made a remark to him which although he did not assent to it, evidently impressed him enough to perplex him:*

"Darwin's ideas of development have more vitality by far than any of your other favorite conceptions, and though they might at this moment be in your mind like a little vine clinging to the tree of Associationalism, yet after a time that vine would eventually kill the tree."

"Why do you say that?" he asked.

I replied, "Mill's doctrine is nothing but a metaphysical point of view to which Darwin's, which is nourished by positive observation, must be deadly."

All nature abounds in proofs of other influences than merely mechanical action, even in the physical world. They crowd in upon us at the rate of several every minute. And my observation of men has led me to this little generalization. Speaking only of those men who really think for themselves and not of mere reporters, I have not found that it is the men whose lives are mostly passed within the four walls of a physical laboratory who are most inclined to be satisfied with a purely mechanical metaphysics. On the contrary, the more clearly they understand how physical forces work the more incredible it seems to them that such mechanical action should explain what happens out of doors.

XXIII[†]
1860 June 11

The curse of civilization is Fashionableness; and one of the hundred ways of arriving at this conclusion here follows.

Consider the wretched condition of the working women. It must be owing to some injustice;

so that
>   *either that state of things in which the men do not support the women is a false one,*
>   *or the fact that women's modes of employment are so few depends on a universal disregard of women's rights.*

With regard, however, to the latter mode of accounting for the poverty of the working-women, it is obvious enough that women are in precisely that condition in which men could constantly be, if the latter always contented themselves with selecting an employment among those already existing and did not set themselves to work to <u>make</u> instead of to <u>find</u> a living.

This paucity of employment depends, therefore, upon the very nature of woman; and its existence that that nature is not the equivalent of man's and is not suited to making a living. Consequently the difficulty we should strive to remedy does not lie here, but in that state of society in which the women are not mostly supported by the men. But this exists because the men do not marry young, and this is because they cannot afford it, and this is because both they and the women spend too much—not on outward or inward necessities, surely—but on Fashion, and that is what I meant when I said that the curse of our civilization is Fashionableness.

There is an individual & a corporate & a national Fashionableness.

XXIV
1860 June 11
Errare est hominis

Observations may be wrong, but still it is not very likely they are quite the contrary of the fact, and as long as they are not, they are not essentially false; they only need additions and modifications.

So likewise, logical fallacies produce propositions, false, indeed, as they were intended, but yet with a modified meaning, true. This is obviously the case with the Illicit Process. In the cases of the Undistributed Middle, Negative Premises, and Ambiguous Middle, a modification of one of the premises will always make a conclusion possible.

This fact, that human errors are always those which addition or amendment will rectify, has given rise to the common saying that "genius never errs" and to the philosophers' boast "that science has never been in the wrong." The fact is, essential error can only arise from perversion, from wickedness, or from passion. Sincere & philosophic production have no other falsity than that which is inseparable from every human proposition.

This reflection should teach us the inhumanity of a polemic spirit & should teach us still to revere a great man notwithstanding his mistakes. In reading his books we can silently add & modify.

XXII
1860 June 23
The difference between Wisdom and Knowledge is this:
Knowledge is that which we get empirically but Wisdom is wrought by the unfolding of the mind.

THE RULES OF LOGIC†
LOGICALLY DEDUCED
1860 June 23
With no attempt at Originality however
but only at putting Old Ideas into a Suggestive Form:
With special reference to the Question whether
THE SYSTEM OF LOGIC is an ART and therefore
to be constructed only with reference to Convenience of Use
after the Older Logicians, or a SCIENCE and therefore
to be an erection consisting of all the known LAWS OF THOUGHT
after Hamilton & other smaller moderns.
By CHARLES S. PEIRCE

The terms of every proposition are presupposed to be comprehended; therefore no proposition can give us a new conception. What then does it do? It collates conceptions, collation is comparison, comparison is measurement, measurement is bounding; propositions therefore bound conceptions.

In an argument from two propositions, a third proposition is obtained as a product. Now to draw a third comparison from two comparisons, it is necessary that they should have a common term (Middle Term) while the resulting comparison will be between the other two terms. The relations of this middle term therefore will determine the different kinds of argument; while these relations themselves will depend upon the relation which the terms of a proposition bear to one another.

Now it will be seen that in all figures of the syllogism, the same term must at one time be subject and at another predicate; so that it follows that in Logic qualities must be regarded as things, for we cannot make the subjects qualities without leaving the qualities independent, which is regarding them as things. In Logic, therefore, instead of saying "A possesses the quality Z" we say "A is a thing possessing the quality Z" making the quality the mere vinculum† of a class of things, and substituting for "a thing possesses or does not possess or partially possesses this quality," the thing is <u>in</u> or <u>out</u> or partly in and partly out of such a class.

This view, also, enables us to apply Geometry both to illustrate and to prove the Doctrines of Logic. For since <u>in</u> & <u>out</u> are the only essential conceptions, a circle and a blot as fully expresses the essential form of a proposition as any other language could do. Thus,

$$A (*) \quad E *() \quad I *(**) \quad O **(*)$$

1860
Came back from Louisiana†
and took a Proctorship in Harvard.
Studied Natural History† and Natural Philosophy.

There was no school to attend over the summer, so Charley arranged to study biology privately† with Agassiz. But his journals continued to be full of philosophical and logical material.

Metaphysical Axioms and Syllogisms from Plato†
1860 June 30
THE APOLOGY OF SOCRATES

<u>Ax. 1.</u> *Conscience judges of actions by the quality of the character they proceed from.*

<u>Ax. 2.</u> *The summum bonum is the possession of truth & the perfection of the soul.*

CRITO

<u>Ax. 3.</u> *To do an injury is unjust.*

PHÆDO

<u>Ax. 4.</u> *One ought to keep just promises.*

<u>Ax. 5.</u> *Pleasure and Pain, in the Socratic use of the words, cannot be present at the same time.*

<u>Ax. 6.</u> *The Understanding only can give us the truth.*

<u>Ax. 7.</u> *The Ideas of Pure Reason are Real Objects. I should prefer to word this thus: Abstract qualities, or at least some of them, are real things.*

<u>Ax. 8.</u> *There cannot be a gap of time in the existence of a substance.*

<u>Ax. 9.</u> *Every event arises from its contrary.*

<u>Ax. 10.</u> *Our abstract ideas are suggested by outward objects, by empirical ideas.*

<u>Prop. 1.</u> *The only way in which we can have knowledge of a real thing not present to the faculties, is by memory.*

<u>Ax. 11.</u> *Qualities of empirical objects are not possessed infinitely.*

<u>Ax. 12.</u> *Opposite qualities cannot pertain to the same thing at the same time.*

<u>Def. 1.</u> *Knowledge is the conception of a real thing.*

<u>Ax. 13.</u> *We have ideas of abstract qualities.*

<u>Prop. 2.</u> *The knowledge of abstract qualities is not always present. (Drawn from Ax. 10 and the obvious empirical fact that there was a time when we didn't know these objects.)*

<u>Prop. 3.</u> *We did not learn our knowledge of abstract qualities from empirical objects. (From Ax. 11.)*

I. <u>The Argument that we existed before birth.</u> By Def. 1 and Ax. 7 it follows that to have a notion of abstract qualities is to know them.

Whence by Ax. 13 we know abstract qualities. Now by Ax. 10, Ax. 11, & Prop 1, when for the first time since birth this knowledge was suggested to us, we were reminded of it. But what we have been reminded of we must have known before; therefore this knowledge must either have been given to us at birth or else we possessed it before birth. On the former supposition, by Ax. 10 we must have forgotten it at the same instant, but as forgetting & learning are contraries this by Ax. 12 cannot be. Hence we must have possessed this knowledge before birth & of course must have existed before birth.

Ax. 14. Whatever is spiritual is simple & permanent.

II. The Argument that the Soul is not a quality of the Body arising from Composition. From I. it follows the soul existed before the body, but by Ax. 15 it cannot in that case be a quality.

Ax. 15. Qualities arising from composition do not exist independently of the thing to which they belong.

Remark. From this it is evident that Plato does not consider Qualities of things & Abstract Qualities as the same thing, otherwise this axiom would be contradicted by Ax. 7.

Ax. 16. All things possessing qualities, possess them by virtue of a partial manifestation of the abstract quality.

Ax. 17. Life is an essential quality of the soul.

Ax. 18. Equal contrary causes produce no effect.

GORGIAS

Ax. 19. There must be a passive object to every action.

Ax. 20. All desire is painful.

PROTAGORAS

Ax. 21. A man always acts as he thinks best.

PHÆDRUS

Ax. 22. A chain of causation never ceases of itself. (It may reasonably be doubted whether Plato meant this.)

Ax. 23. Matter cannot move itself.

Ax. 24. The Soul moves itself.

THEÆTETUS

Prop. 4. The conceptions which each faculty gives us are peculiar to itself.

Remark. This depends upon the following axiom.

Ax. 25. We only know our faculties by the conceptions or feelings they give us—by their results.

THE REPUBLIC

Ax. 26. To injure a thing is to lessen its excellence.

Ax. 27. Justice is a human virtue. That it is not just to injure one's enemies.

Ax. 26, Ax. 19, therefore To injure is not virtuous.

Ax. 27. therefore &c.

For Horatio Paine:
The Fundamental Distinction of Metaphysics†
1860 June 30

It is usually conceded or assumed that all metaphysics is based on some fundamental distinction. The fact is that every new system of metaphysics has some particular merit, which is based on some particular distinction. The distinction, for instance, upon which my system is based, obviously is between the thought and the thought-of. Above these partial views, however, it is obvious that the possibility & the utility of philosophy in general & of every science in particular must be based upon a metaphysical distinction. Thus, to take† a natural science, chemistry depends upon the quite metaphysical distinction of <u>Kind</u> & of <u>Quality</u>.

So, the possibility & the utility of philosophy in general, that is of the application of the understanding to experience, depends upon our having besides the facts of experience, certain universal <u>a priori</u> truths on objects of experience.

Metaphysics is the science of all that we are conscious of <u>a priori</u>. The fundamental distinction, then, is between <u>thought</u> & <u>unthought</u> which is to say between the

Thought & the Thought-of
The distinction on which All Philosophy is based is between
<u>Images of Reason</u> & <u>Images of Sense</u>
The distinction on which all Psychology is based is between
<u>Images of the Inner Sense</u> & <u>Images of the Outer Sense</u>
The distinction on which Metaphysics is based is between
<u>Images as Images</u> & <u>Images as Representations</u>

The foregoing is on a very abstruse subject, & was worded paradoxically so that it would either not be understood at all or be rightly understood. I think, however, some of the obscurities may be cleared up.

"We either think-of the unthought as thought." We certainly can think of the unthinkable as thought, we can think of the Infinite as thinkable, and in this case we have a positive conception of the thought INFINITE tho' we do not think the INFINITE.

"What is falsity & How can any representation possibly be false?" The fact is we call a judgement untrue when from its contradicting some other judgement, we conclude that in the framing of it our faculties did not act in the normal way. Now to whatever is thought-of there is a normal way of thinking-of; & that normal way gives a true thought of the thing; & that is an apprehension of the thing. And so even when the normal way of thinking of a thing gives an unintelligible result, it is either because it can't be thought of or because we have an unconscious idea of it. In the first case we have no thought† of it, it does not exist, hence we have a true thought of it. In the latter case, that unconscious idea accords with the definition of a true representation.

That will do† for one time. You can read it or not as you please. I write it because you said it interested you. If it continues to do so, you will ask me to go on. Then the real metaphysics will begin.

The Logical and the Psychological Treatment† of Metaphysics
1860 July 3
In speaking of the fundamental distinction of metaphysics I called it a branch of psychology & in speaking of the definition of it, I called Psychology applied metaphysics. These two modes of viewing metaphysics give rise to two methods of treating it. One starts by drawing the conceptions from logical relations and thence reasoning to their place in the mind; the other starts by drawing the conceptions from the systems of psychology & reasoning to their logical meaning.

The former seems to me, if less Psychologically exact, to be more metaphysically true, in its results, and it is the method I adopt.

XXV†
1860 July 12
The terms of every proposition are presupposed to be comprehended; therefore no proposition can give us a new conception, and Wisdom is not learnt from Books.

XXVI
1860 July 13
Metaphysics is the study of form. In the study of matter we have at least some idea of our subject & therefore are never wholly in the wrong, but a modified form is in no degree the same as the unmodified form, therefore in metaphysics we are never partly right.

XXVII
1860 July 13
Man's broad ideas are no nearer right than his narrow ones. Yet if they were corrected as soon, no system no thought could ever be worked out & despair might well result. This is the advantage of being taught by another & of having a genius here & there to teach us.

The Orders of Mathematical Infinity, 1860 July 13†
It is perfectly easy to remove any objection against my making Mathematical and Theological Infinity the same. The former, having <u>orders</u> would seem either not to be infinity at all or at least a very different kind of infinity from the latter. But it can be seen how this idea of order of infinity arises in mathematics without giving infinity any different definition from that which it has in Theology, both Natural & Rational.

XXVIII[†]
1860 July 15

The difference, as it strikes one, between a man who always wears a mask & one of your bluff, over-open natures, is the difference between a gentleman and a vulgar man. In fact, the same decency attaches to wearing some veil over the mind as to clothing on the body. I do not say a gentleman will parade his mask any more than he will parade his clothes; but he will wear it unostentatiously. It is no man's business what sort of an arm I have & no gentleman wishes to make it his business—and it isn't in the fitness of things that he should. And so with the mind. It is no man's business how my mind looks naked, no gentleman or lady desires to look at it, and it is not decent that they should. I tell no lies about it; I simply veil it,—showing more or less of its different parts on different occasions to different people, but never the whole to anybody. That is in no circumstances, modest.

XXX
1860 August

To be liked it is only necessary to be translucent.

XXXI
1860 August

Human Character, be it remembered cannot be specifically different. The remark is valuable in proportion to the clearness of our apprehension of a species.

Characters are generally purely individual though there are varieties in families.

XXXVII
1860 August

The essential of a thing—the character of it—is the unity of the manifold therein contained. Id est, the logical principle, from which as major premiss the facts thereof can be deduced.

What are called a man's principles however are only certain beliefs of his that he may or may not carry out. They therefore do not compose his character, but the general expression of the facts—the ACTS OF HIS SOUL—does.

What he does is important.

How he feels is incidental.

(Milford, Penn. 1898[†]). As early as 1860, when I knew nothing of any German philosopher except Kant, who had been my revered master for three or four years, I was much struck with a certain indication that Kant's list might be part of a larger system of conceptions. For instance, Kant points out[†] certain relations between the categories. I detected others; but these others, if they had any orderly relation to a system of conceptions, at all, belonged to a larger system than that of Kant's list. Here there was a problem to which I devoted three hours a day for the next two years, rising from it, at length, with the demonstrative certitude that there was something wrong with Kant's formal logic. Accordingly, I read every book I could lay hands upon on logic, and of course Kant's essay on the <u>falsche Spitzfindigkeit der vier syllogistischen Figuren</u>.

XXXII†
1860 September 15

Worship is the recognition of any being as him to whose will, as such, we ought to be entirely submissive.

Therefore, we cannot worship any but the one true god (to others we only pay honor), and the first commandment means we shall hold the truth which we do know in recognition.

XXXIII
1860 September 16

To sin is to act contrary to our higher motives. It is to have our lower impulses stronger than our higher ones. It is to not love what we recognize as most loveable. It is to follow after idols.

XXXIV
1860 September 16

The moral law says, not "thou ought" alone, but "thou must," for it needs only to be comprehended to be loved and followed.

XXXV
1860 September 16

It is not possible that a christian should have attained to the full stature of Christ. But all men, as they have heard Christ's doctrine and partially comprehended & therefore love it, are Christians.

XXXVIII
1860 September 16

It is on account of man's finite nature that he has a free will. His will is free only when he is in doubt—only therefore in certain critical moments. Hence the practical part of Ethics is the study of these critical moments.

XXXIX
1860 September 16
Entreateth of Witchcraft.

Everie soul is monarch of its own realme alone. Everiebody must be seduced by the temptings of his own heart. No free agent can be drawn but must be led astray.

When Psyche is beset and after a struggle overcome, the course of the storme hath three transitorie turnes and three progressive swaies, and the fourth carrieth the point. (Now the turnes are the critical moments when triumph hangs doubtfull.) And the swaies and the turnes are these:

The first assay is while Psyche is tickled with the allurements of the Devill and is pleasantly moved unto enjoyment. And in this charge she is drawn by fayre wordes to a place where the deed maie be done.

And the first turn is when she is overwhelmed with delight.

And the second sway is while she is provoked and impassioned.

And the second turn is when she strings her nerves to withstand his bland-ishment. And at this turn is the heat of the fray.

And the third sway is while the Devill holdes back her thoughts from dutie and assayles her most furiously with lust.

And now mayhap the delight will palle. And this will be a right criticall moment, for it is as though the hostes of the Devill were fagg'd. And then he must bring up his reserved force, and tempt the woman's mind by all manner of meanes, feeding her with milk and giving the passion sucke.

But the third regular turn is when the motion of the soul waxeth great, and her bloode does not leape in her harte but teares through her swelled veines and her breast heaves and her lappe fall downe and she gives herself over to the deliciousnesse of sensual pleasure. And this state of things is broken in upon by the Paen for the citadell hath yielded.

L

1860 September 20

Passion and Pleasure

We like persons and things but, I take it, it is only because they in some way cause events that we like. The _love_ we have toward people is a different thing, but the liking of events is lust.

Lust has various modes according to the modality of the event. Thus we wish for a possible event, we enjoy an actual one, we rejoice at a necessary one.

It is not a sensation, since we have no sensation of events; it is not a judge-ment, since desire is not; it is not a feeling, though it is accompanied by them. Lust is a force. Gratified, it is in equilibrium and all is quiet. But the friction be-tween the thought of possible future possession against that of actual absence, soon causes a polar disturbance and agitation incessantly waxing, till, with a burst of rapture, it rushes to the good which is its object.

Lust is a train of causality passing through the will.

A Secret Marriage

Charley's first wife[†] was Caroline Louise Badger—Carrie—of 13 Oxford Street, Boston, daughter of John L. Badger of the firm of Badger and Bailey, shipwrights and[†] calkers. He persuaded her to contract a secret marriage on the evening of 27 October[†] 1860, no doubt inspired by the example of Count Neipperg and Princess Maria Louisa as related in KINGS AND QUEENS; or Life in the Palace. The marriage contract began in verbal[†] form, but was later placed[†] in writing.

Naturally in the course of this project, I made friends with a number of persons who study Peirce's life and works. One of the earliest facts about Charley these folks mentioned to me years ago was that he had been married twice: first to Melusina (or Zina) Fay, and later to Juliette Pourtalais nee Froissy. I hate to be a revisionist, but the evidence is clear from a bundle of Carrie's letters sited in the appropriate place within Charley's autobiographical storage box. None of his messages to her survived, as far as Betsey and I can determine; because they were in Carrie's possession, it's likely that she destroyed them, for it's clear that toward the end of the affair, she pressed Charley to return her correspondence and their marriage contract. He did not return the letters; so, we have them, and they clearly establish the outline of the courtship, secret marriage, and separation. I've tried to track Carrie's later life in other sources, but the trail is cold.

Why did Charley retain the correspondence in his letterbook and, later, in his box of autobiographical papers? At home we discussed this at some length, then Betsey had an idea that originally shocked me. Suddenly— putting on her clinical face—she exclaimed,

"Have you noticed how at this time EVERYTHING in life seemed to ap- pear to him as an *inquiry*? This bundle of letters especially reminds me of a patient's record, like those kept by experimental psychologists or psychia- trists. Could it be that this was some kind of psychology experiment con- ducted by Charley to learn more about himself, especially about his devel- oping powers of manipulating and controlling women? It seems beyond doubt that it was at least a part of what he called his study of the physiology of marriage. This idea seems even more plausible because he placed the file next to those passages from his private journal on lust and on witchcraft. The paragraphs on witchcraft were surely copied from an old book in Cambridge, and those words are clearly advice about mastering the *science* of seduction. Those words may even provide us with an inside view of Charley as he began the seduction of Carrie, and that could be another reason her letters were collected and located just here in his box."

Betsey might be right about that. And if she is, Charley could be classi- fied—if that sort of thing appeals to you—alongside other men of genius who exhibited a similar trait, for example Ben[†] Franklin before Peirce's day and Richard Feynman[†] in recent times. On the other hand, maybe this episode simply represents nothing more than an intense case of post-adolescent sexual drive. Or, as we would say down on the farm in Oklahoma, "Charley spent several months as a sailor and came home horny as hell." Still, it's just a guess.

I've learned to respect Betsey's clinical instincts and intuitions. But I lack such powers. I plod along. Like the poor gumshoes in my novels, I'm addicted to the evidence. So here's the way I reconstructed it.

14. *Charles Sanders Peirce*

"She had received a copy of his class photo"
Tuttle Collection, Institute for Studies in Pragmaticism
By permission, Philosophy Department, Harvard University

Charley and Carrie had been friends for some years, at least as far back[†] as 1858, but probably longer. She had received a copy of his class photo, which was already kept in a special[†] place. He began a renewed correspondence with her while bored in Pascagoula on the mudstuck embarassed schooner[†] *Twilight*. He began in the role of an old friend early in 1860 by confiding[†] his plan to marry Lillie Greenough, "the fair lady who is to make the remainder of my life one bright dream of happiness." Carrie's second letter—like a loyal puppy dog—followed Charley back to Cambridge, finally reaching him on 30 May. She pressed to discover if he were really engaged, thinking that if so, it would not be proper to address candid letters[†] to him. It was signed: "Sincerely your friend Carrie." Miss Greenough, of course, was studying voice in London at this time, and would return to the United States in a few years as Mrs. Moulton.

The correspondence began in earnest between Charley in Cambridge and Carrie in Boston late in May as their relationship began to develop. At this point, she tried to contain it within gentle bounds:

It would give me[†] great pleasure to have you spend not only *one* evening with me but as many as please you. Do you know however that kisses are among the things that one never wishes to be thanked for? I hope Charley I do not need to warn you against passing the limit beyond which no woman, however free and easy she may be, if she is true to the name—woman—never permits a man to pass. I wish you to forget as far as possible the events of last evening and do not seek a repetition of them.

They continued now and then through the summer of 1860 to have "engagements"—today they would be called "dates"—arranging them by letter. For example, on the thirtieth of June, Carrie urged, "Come for old friendship's sake, to recall the evening before the Fourth two years ago. Yours as ever."

As I read these summer letters an impression unfolded. Charley was firmly in control of the developing courtship, yet against a background of subtle encouragement from Carrie: "Everiebody must be seduced by the temptings of his own heart; no free agent can be drawn but must be led astray." Then on the twenty-third of October Carrie's passion pushed free in unmistakable phrases: "I am more in love with you than ever, if that were possible. Come to me on Saturday evening next. I say Saturday because we will be less likely to be interrupted on that evening than any other. Come early—say half past seven. Believe me I shall count the very seconds until then."

So at half-past seven on Saturday the twenty-seventh of October, Charley arrived with a carriage to take Carrie[†] for a ride. Her parents were not home; they returned to retire without knowing that the flower of the family had been out at all. But her little sister Maggie observed the late return and asked, "Where have you been Carrie?"

She replied with a lie, "Out by Dorchester."

"Then you have been to ride. I think you must be in love† with him. I quite envy you such a splendid evening. I did not hear the carriage. It was imprudent to go out with nothing but that thin shawl on."

The remainder of the night was sleepless for Carrie as she privately considered the situation. Free of Charley's suasion, her mind was full of conflict. On the one side was her love for Charley and the fact that she had entered into a verbal agreement that evening, so that "Henceforth your commands, requests &c are to be obeyed† by me." On the other side stood forces of propriety and family loyalty, thus fear of recording their secret marriage in a private document, a step that was being pressed upon her:

> For mercy's sake, do not ask me to sign anything. The mere
> mention of it will set me crazy. I have thought until I can think no
> more—my poor head is almost bursting—cracked I may well
> believe—after showing so little will and determination as I did last
> evening. I confess now that I was very weak to yield to you so
> entirely. Oh Charley you cannot know the extent of the sacrifice
> you have asked† of me.

Her pain was removed during their next ride on Friday the first of November. The agent of its absence was his clear domination: "And then he must bring up his reserved force, and tempt the woman's mind by all manner of meanes, feeding her with milk and giving the passion sucke." Charley arrived "openly" at 13 Oxford Street—that is, while her family was at home. She dutifully reported in her letter the following day:

> Do you still wish† me to tell you what they said last night? Nothing
> at all, except—Did you have a pleasant ride? Of course it was. Did
> you not think so? You have my conscience or I might be troubled,
> as it is so I am perfectly calm and at peace. Charley I cannot write.
> When I feel the most I can say but very little. There is but one thing
> that could make me happier than I am now. Do you know what
> that is? Come to me as soon as you can even if you are not ready to
> take the fulfilment of my promise. How amazed every one will be
> when they know of it. Mercy I cannot write."

Her inner turmoil continued, the focus of agitation being his desire to place their agreement in writing. Having not seen Charley for about a week—probably the result of his suggestion of a "separation"—on the eleventh of November she did commit to writing a description of her boiling emotions:

> Oh Charley[†] dearest Charley is it well for us to separate in this way? Would it not be far best for us to be separated for a few years than forever if we love each other—and I *do* love you. I know you think me incapable of feeling any deep love, but I am hapless in love with you. I cannot take my own happiness and make miserable all my friends. I cannot grieve my mother as I should by contracting this secret marriage and yet be happy. Neither can I ever be happy without you. But whatever the future has in store for me whether it be happiness or otherwise, my remembrances of you will be the sweetest I have.
>
> You know that it takes very little from you to make me believe anything is right, but you will only make the sacrifice I make in giving you up the harder for me to endure. *Must* this be so? You request me to write to you occasionally. What can we write about? This subject is a dangerous one and we must avoid it. You say you cannot come to see me. I think perhaps it is best so. For you leave me in a state little fitted to endure the common realities of life.
>
> To think that I who believed myself so little liable to fall in love, should when I felt the most secure have become a victim to it. What useless beings the passion makes of us women. I have truly been good for nothing the past few weeks.
>
> Charley if you ever feel like coming to me, I pray you yield to it and come. You will only make me too happy by doing so. Please come to me. I cannot cannot live without you—but I *must.* I may as well accustom myself to living without you as soon as possible. But write to me, and Charley be kind.

The separation didn't last long. Carrie could not bear it, probably a fact Charley knew all along. He began to arrange more rides, sometimes to Cambridge. "Now you have made[†] yourself so *very* necessary to me you must come to me often. You will come on Monday or Tuesday—please—I *cannot cannot* wait until Friday."

The affair seemed to reach its blissful peak roughly during December of 1860. Their contract appears to have been placed in writing[†] by this time; it likely specified that they would join in public nuptials eventually, but without delay would secretly enjoy the benefice of marriage.

Carrie's letters during this period provide a useful insight into aspects of Charley's character and his impact upon at least some women, so it is important to extract them here.

It is all† right. Not a word was said, so I did not have to tell any more falsehoods. My mother never would suspect anything if my sisters did not first put it into her head. Why have you made yourself so very necessary to me that the time drags so heavily without you? Please Charley, *my* Charley, come to me as soon as it is possible, if—you want to. I tried with all my strength not to love you, but I could not help it. It is with me as I always feared it would be—when I once yielded and loved it would be with all my strength. I am happy—very happy—yet I would give all this great happiness to be as I was six months ago. I am perfectly disgusted with myself, and it would not surprise me if you had the same opinion of me. But how can I help allowing you the privilege you take? I confess I cannot. My only excuse must be my love for you. I do not think I ever realized the impropriety to its fullest extent I have been guilty of in visiting your room. Well I am very sorry that I have ever done so. But it has been done and cannot be undid. All we can do is to improve in the future. Regarding the request I made of you the other evening about the opium—would you do for me when my husband what you would not as a lover?

I am very angry† with you and I think I have reason to be so. I wonder if there is another case on record where a man was so much in love with a woman as you are or at least pretend to be with me—and let a whole week pass without going to see her or even writing to her. Last week I wanted, longed for you to come, but now since you are endeavoring to practise such great self-denial, I think I am perfectly indifferent whether you come or not. Do you not think yourself that you have been anything but loverlike this past week? What have you been doing? If you refuse to come I do not believe I shall ever give you the chance to refuse again. If you will not come, please let me know in time to make another engagement for the evening, for I should go distracted to stay at home alone with nothing to do but think.

Were you obliged to remain up all Friday night in order to do your work? It was very selfish in me to wish to detain you, but I could not help wanting you to stay. Why is it that I love you so passionately? I too, who fancied I could go through life calmly—coldly—never feeling more than lukewarm affection for anyone—certainly should never have love like this for anyone. I should be far happier if I could be indifferent. Then I should not feel so acutely the indifference you sometimes show. If what I fear should ever happen—your love for me changing—what would become of me? Charley darling, if you love me as I believe you do, how can you refuse to make me so perfectly happy, as supremely blessed as you

have it in your power to do? There is but one shadow on my love
for you. If that were only removed, how perfect a love it would be. I
wish I could talk to you when with you as I would like to, but I
cannot. Why I do not know unless it is because you kiss me and
hold me in your arms and then my happiness is so great I cannot
speak. What a fool I have been to let anyone attain such an
influence over me as you possess. Strive against it as I may, you
possess it still. Of course you know that you have this power. Now
dear Charley if it is not perfectly convenient for you to come this
week do not mind telling me so. I will wait patiently until you can,
but it will be very hard indeed. Only write to me and I will not
complain.

Her reference to opium most likely concerned Charley's frequent use of
it. His health had undergone some frightening episodes. He had experienced
serious attacks of neuralgia, as recently as his days on the old Schooner *Twilight* in Louisiana. Betsey looked it up in our copy of *Johnson's Universal Cyclopædia*, which we prefer[†] because it dates from Charley's day.

> [Gr. neuron, "nerve" and algos, "pain"].
> Pain in the course of a nerve is a symptom of many morbid condi-
> tions. The track and distribution of a cerebral, spinal, or visceral
> nerve may be the seat of the pain, which is sharp, occurs in parox-
> ysms repeated at intervals of a few seconds or a day, the pain be-
> tween the paroxysms disappearing or being replaced by soreness or
> dull pain. The suffering is often very intense. One curious feature of
> neuralgic pain is its occurrence on one side of the body only at any
> one time. Usually no redness or inflammation is visible in the af-
> fected region, though an exception to this rule is observed in neural-
> gia of the face, during attacks of which the eye is red and lachry-
> mose. The parts which are the seat of pain are usually over-sensitive
> during the paroxysms, and numb between them; there may even be
> loss of sensibility.

As in the case of his mother's erysipelas, there were few viable treatment
options at the time. Because his father's brother Charles was a Boston physician, and an expert pharmacologist, Charley probably understood from an
early time that opiates gave him some relief from neuralgic pain. Just when
he began using this treatment I couldn't say exactly. It seems clear that his
usage was well established by this summer. Betsey asks me to remind you
that derivative alkaloids of opium, especially morphia, were widely prescribed by health practitioners in Charley's day, for a host of ailments, and
especially for incurable painful diseases. A popular form was laudanum—

opium dissolved in alcohol. It was used by Ben Franklin for pain of his kidney stones; the poet Coleridge began using it in 1791 while a student and remained a lifelong addict. Opium in some form was about the only available effective medication for chronic pain, or for chronic depression, as Dr. Conan Doyle showed with the famous seven percent solution injected by Sherlock Holmes. That it was addictive meant that most people in the nineteenth century who had recurring serious pain problems *were* addicted. There was almost no other choice. Some, instead, inhaled the fumes of ether, but the downside in that approach was a hypnogogic stupor—the pain was reduced to nil, but so was one's consciousness. In our time we tend to think of anyone who takes opium on a regular basis as being a drug abuser. Automatically to attach that label to Charley through a kind of knee-jerk reaction, and by inference also to legions of his pain-wracked contemporaries, would be intolerant and anachronistic, an anti-historical mode of thought if ever there was[†] one. That Carrie knew Charley used the drug suggests that he made no attempt to hide it from friends and family; also it's a fair inference that his usage was known to some extent in the community, understood, and accepted (although perhaps reluctantly by some persons). Yet Carrie seems to have urged Charley to attempt giving up his addiction, apparently with no success.

The one shadow on her love was the fact, unpleasant as she sat and thought, that her marriage was not open. As she reviewed her position, awareness that she was being used began to grow, until eventually toward the end of the year she resolved to break up her relations with Charley:

> I shall be extremely[†] obliged to you if you can show me what means I could use to change the love I bear to you to simple *friendship*. It would be a mercy to us both, I still say, if by any process we could become *only friends*. For my part I must confess I think it impossible for me to have any medium feeling for you. I must *love* or *hate* you.

A move toward mere friendship—at Charley's[†] suggestion—seems to have been undertaken, and that entailed in Carrie's mind a dissolution of their written contract of secret marriage:

> You will no doubt[†] be very happy to hear that now instead of feeling about our new relations as I did at first I am, considering everything, glad of it. In fact I believe it to be a very wise arrangement and under the existing circumstances the very best that could have been made. I believe the best thing to be done when your love has been scorned by one, is to confer it as soon as possible on some one else who will value it. It is an excellent cure for the first love. You will surely come to see me this week. I shall expect

you. Bring with you that paper which we signed, and we will
destroy it. As you say it is perhaps of little importance, still I prefer
to have it destroyed. It has been the means of a great many
unhappy feelings, but we will have no more of them. It is too bad
we cannot be as we used to before all this happened. But cannot we
after all? I will forget we ever thought to be otherwise than friends.
Will you? By the way I am obliged to attend a wedding reception
on Thursday evening, so do not come then. I think weddings are
stupid affairs, but it is better than staying at home with nothing to
do but think. I must have a great deal of excitement for the next few
weeks to forget if possible what might have been were it not for so
many *ifs* being in the way.

As later writings[†] show, Charley maintained his power over her and
could still require her to yield in every regard, but for some reason he did not.
On the third of January 1861, Carrie returned some of Charley's letters:

Enclosed are the only letters I have remaining. I have not one of our
old correspondence and only those you wrote me last winter. Those
I may keep I suppose. Dearest Dearest Charley, do not make
yourself unhappy about me. Imagine I never existed—at least that
you never loved me. I cannot endure to have you unhappy. This
separation would not be so bad if I thought you did not care.
Thinking you will be unhappy makes me the more so. Was last
evening really *the last?* I cannot realize it. Never mind darling,
sometime you will find one everyway more worthy of your love
and yourself than I shall ever be. To belong to you for ever is a
happiness far too great to be mine.

Carrie continued to plead for her letters on at least six occasions, running into
June[†] of 1861, which request, of course, we know Charley did not honor, because we are eavesdropping into them from his letterbook. They did meet a
few more times, and Carrie tried every means—ranging from "Come and see
me and bring the letters, for I want you[†] to *so much*" to "You are making me
sick[†] by refusing my simple request."

Through this period Carrie most likely retained a love for Charley. But
even that was dashed, and the matter truly ended, as Carrie wrote on the
eighth of June 1861:

Perhaps you are such an experienced male-coquette you can give
me a few lessons in flirting. Just imagine my despair if I had been
foolish enough to believe all your flatteries sincere. Now that I have
seen how fearful you were that they had all been taken in earnest.

No indeed. I have a little too much wisdom, especially after seeing the heartless manner in which you endeavored to win the young love of my once very dear friend Annie Hall. I never can forget that. But I think this is about enough.

Those remarks ended the correspondence, at least as it has survived, and apparently concluded the affair.

Maybe Carrie did receive the secret marriage document, for it is nowhere to be found.

4

Let There Be Light

It has never been in my power to study anything, —mathematics,
ethics, metaphysics, gravitation, thermodynamics, optics, chemistry,
comparative anatomy, astronomy, psychology, phonetics,
economic, the history of science, whist, men and women, wine,
metrology, except as a study of semeiotic; and how rarely I have
been able to feel a thoroughly sympathetic interest in the studies of
other men of science (how far more than rarely have I met any who
care to understand my own studies), I need not tell you, though
fortunately I am of an ardently sympathetic nature,—I mean
fortunately for my scientific development, under chilling
circumstances.

Charles S. Peirce to Victoria Lady Welby, 23 December 1908

An Observer

"Ike, there's someone I want you to meet right now!" Betsey exclaimed
late Friday afternoon on the twenty-fourth of March 1985. She owns a community health clinic, where she is an independent nurse practitioner. It's located near our place. She had jogged home, dashed up four flights of stairs
into our Boston flat, and crashed into the easy chair, next to the writing desk
in my loft which overlooks 186 Tremont Street.

"One of my outpatients," puff "is incredible," puff "and can solve your
problem," huff, puff.

I hadn't worked on Charley's box for a few months. As Betsey landed, I
was struggling to finish the last chapter of my latest krimi, *The Sign of Adam.*

Six months earlier I had begun to dig into Charley's more challenging intellectual output and had promptly hit a brick wall. My problem was that I had no confidence in my grasp of Charley's scientific and philosophical language. As a bold amateur, I was willing to learn, and I *had* to learn if I was to explain parts of his manuscript for readers. But I needed a coach, a helper, a guide. Betsey and I had enrolled in only one philosophy course with Hilary Putnam, and while that was memorable, at the time he mentioned almost nothing about Peirce, and then only the obvious things—founder of pragmatism, great logician, controversial figure, and such. So I laid aside Charley's box and started writing a new detective novel about an ordinary guy—Jubal Adam—who had a strange birthmark, and how suddenly several people wanted to murder him for that fact alone. "What does my mark mean to these people?" he wondered, as he dodged and ducked. Circumstances were inexorably forcing him to learn how to become his own detective, you see. In the final chapter he almost reached the shocking self-revealing conclusion of his desperate and dangerous search for an answer . . . when Betsey's interruption broke up my concluding plot-work. I finished the novel later. As it turned out, the interruption was worth it.

"You'll never guess who came into my clinic today for treatment. He is the most unusual character I've ever met. His name is LeRoi Wyttynys."

Betsey was hopping up and down on both legs as women do when they get excited. Why does joy express itself in the exercise of our largest muscle group?

"He knew Charley!"

I dropped my fountainpen in genuine surprise. Where it fell, a big blob of ink terminated the half-blank page. Adam's penultimate birthmark crisis would have to remain in the purgatory that holds inactive muses.

"Such a piece of luck! He came into the clinic complaining of extreme cramps in his legs. I took a routine health history. When he gave his birthyear—which you gotta admit is unusual—my inner voice asked where he was born. Anyway, he said he was BORN IN 1885 to a working-class family. My little voice said, *Did he know anyone around Harvard?* so I blurted it out."

"*Why yes,* he replied, with a charmer's voice that's loaded with impeccable self-mastery. *I attended Harvard—philosophy Ph.D. in 1907. I knew many persons there.*"

"You know what my next question was, Ike, and he said, *Yes, I studied with Poiss and James and Royce, beginning in 1898!*"

Once again Betsey had solved a problem for me. Not only had Roy known Peirce well, he was a master in philosophy, particularly in Peirce's philosophy. By the way, he pronounced Peirce's name in an odd way, as Poiss, the same way he pronounced Nurse (noiss), Curse (coiss), Hearse (hoiss), and so on. Apparently this was just his way of vocalizing "purse." I later learned this was a North Carolinian accent. It seems some parts of his early life had been spent in that region.

His father was a Welsh sailor who married a ship's cook from Marseilles. They had struggled to give their extremely gifted only son a strong education. He had been a wunderkind, graduating in the Harvard class of '02, gaining a philosophy doctorate in '07, he accepted an assistant professorship at Central State Normal College in New York, and even published a famous but brief outline of American Philosophy: *From Plymouth Rock to Pragmatism.* In 1910 he earned one of the first federal radio amateur licenses—W1PRG—using an old spark-gap transmitter he had been operating for some time from his parents' home in Watertown on vacations. He claimed to enjoy teaching the few students he met who were devoted learners and to love study and writing. But he quickly came to hate the dead-headed lecture-and-sleep classroom environment or lock-step administrative thinking that permeates teaching universities.

He was a British subject—born on a Welsh vessel in Boston Harbor, thus having dual citizenship—so he abruptly resigned from the college in 1913, then joined the Royal Navy to get away and see the world. He easily earned a rating as wireless operator because, as an amateur with his own setup, he already knew more about the science of wireless than most persons in the military at that time. His educational background and operating skill eased his way into Admiralty staff—one of only a few sailors so to qualify, it turns out. In 1916 he was in Lord Jellicoe's flagship in the battle of Jutland, took some shrapnel in his legs one day when he saved Admiral Jellicoe's hide, got a medal, recovered fine, and after the armistice tried to continue radio work in the Royal Navy.

I say that he tried because shortly after the guns were silenced, a group of academics from Bryn Mawr College near Philadelphia contacted him, brought him out to their reform-minded campus, and persuaded him to become dean of liberal arts. They had read an article in *The Boston Globe,* the hook of which went something like this: "Welsh-American Volunteer in Royal Navy is Hero; Authority on American Philosophy Saved Admiral's Life." They could persuade Roy to take the job because Bryn Mawr had been organized from the start to foster excellence in interdisciplinary studies, and they were ready to try some new ideas, which he was to provide. He stayed through the 1930s becoming president in 1932. While pursuing educational reform, it was second nature for Roy to continue as an active researcher, and in 1938 he published a compactly reasoned little volume entitled *Graphical Logic: A Dialogue.* In that work he set out to confirm Charley's claim that logic and mathematics were empirical or observational sciences.

When Hitler invaded Poland, Roy called some political markers with influential friends in England to return to the Royal Navy. He always followed his heart without hesitation or care for consequences. Besides, going from a comfortable place into a war zone may have been just the excuse he needed to leave an old life and start a new one. He received a direct Royal commission as captain and served through the war as coordinator of Home Fleet Air Wireless Service with headquarters at Scapa Flow. In 1945 he mustered out, and because he had his fill of the academic life, re-entered the American Merchant Marine as a radio officer. At that time he bought an apartment near Boston Harbor where he lived when not at sea. The remainder of his life was a mixture of seafaring interspersed with study and writing in Boston and Cambridge or in foreign locales. He seemed to have traveled almost everywhere. Even his high political connections could not prevent his forced retirement from the sea in 1960. Since student days he had lived a spartan monastic life that reminded me of what I had read about Eric Hoffer or Ludwig Wittgenstein. The book on which he had been working for many years, he said, was almost done. He described it as an exposé of the vast dry rot deep in the center of the American university system. He never has let me see it, and I don't know what will become of it, or if he ever actually wrote it out. But I can testify that he had thought it through with passion and rigor.

To shorten this account, we have been fast friends since 1985. He agreed to guide as I learned my way through Charley's philosophy and logic and science discussions. As a matter of fact, one of the early questions I asked him concerned Charley's Kant-inspired juvenile writings on metaphysics initially written out for his Cambridge[†] friend, Horatio Paine. I quote from Roy's long letter to me.

You should not be particularly impressed by the intellectual gaudiness often exhibited by philosophers, and Kant was one of the gaudiest, notwithstanding his reputation as reclusive. Despite popular myth to the contrary, philosophy is rather basic. It is an attempt to answer a few fundamental and ultimately inescapable questions. The questions are easily stated, although gaining a capacity to take those questions seriously is a barrier for some persons; what is less capable of presentation is the nature of the attempt—the methods employed. Moreover, a typical philosopher's disease consists in falling in love with some aspect of these methods. Unfortunately today the public image of philosophy is often based upon such methodologically infatuated professional philosophers because that is now the condition of many prominent figures in the field (or at least that was the case until recently, when a sea-change for the better began to occur—I say *began*).

Back to those questions. Here is a partial list: What am I? Where am I? What is this place? How did I get here? What am I to do? What shall my conduct be, both privately and in regard to others? How should we live together? Why do bad things happen to me? What will become of me? Of course questions subsidiary to these are relevant as well, and this list could be expanded, but maybe you grasp the general thread.

Most people will take most of these questions seriously, at least at some time in life, although as I said, there is a constant supply of human beings who seem to think all such issues are frivolities. That aside, the factor wherein most persons encounter difficulty lies in the method for dealing with these powerful topics. As a matter of fact, the last question on the list should be: What method can I use to answer these questions?

Some persons deal with these issues by asking for answers from a person or institution they respect; or conversely, sometimes an institution attempts to enforce respect for, and obedience to, particular answers within a group or society. On occasion, persons simply psychologically overwhelm such questions—when they come to mind—by tenaciously enforcing the retention of a pre-existing or pre-conceived answer. Then there are people who deal with such questions according to the fashion of the times, even the academic fashion.

These general methodological tendencies have an interesting common feature: none of them makes a distinction between answers that correctly or incorrectly represent the real world. Instead each focuses upon some aspect of ego: What do *I* respect? What is the answer that is acceptable to my pre-conceptions? What is consistent with the fashion of *my* era, my group, my school, my party, my associates? On the basis of this property, they could be classified as egocentric or arbitrary methods. This factor is an important component of one of Peirce's favorite denunciatory concepts: "nominalist."

The Socratic tradition of philosophy, on the other hand, seeks a method that does distinguish between answers that correctly or incorrectly represent reality, and seeks to pursue these answers on the hypothesis that there is some reality which is accessible to us, which is independent of our arbitrary whims, which will gradually yield to our careful unselfish cooperative study. Now science is what we call this method when it is pursued for the objective results it can bring. Philosophy is what we call this method when the emphasis is upon the kind of being-in-the-world a person must possess successfully to conduct such a method. Science seeks results. Philosophy seeks a particular condition of personal being.

Now what does this have to do with Kant and Peirce? Of course you can look up Kant in any good encyclopedia: there is no substitute for hard work, Mr. Eisenstaat, so don't ask me to spoon feed you. First of all, Peirce came to be primarily a great methodologist. In this he also followed Kant who developed a new approach within philosophy, and promptly became profoundly infatuated by it: he called it the transcendental method—not to be confused with Emerson's transcendentalism which is a spiritual doctrine. Kant proceeded by noticing some aspect of normal experience, then asked "What background conditions would be required to make such a thing possible?" Answers about such conditions are sought by reasoning *privately* about the matter. This tends to make many of the answers Kant ultimately gave to fall within one of those egocentric methods I mentioned above. In the book Peirce particularly admired as a young man, *Critic of Pure Reason*, Kant asked "What background conditions would be required to make possible various kinds of knowledge that we take for granted?" One distinctive claim, which Kant took to be a major result of this method, was his notion that the human race universally has built into its perceptive abilities certain necessary features which enable us to construct our world in specified regular ways. Another interesting feature of Kant's work was his inventing a great many special terms for key notions, which you will also find in a good encyclopedia or dictionary. That is a habit Peirce learned from Kant: later he also invented a large terminological system for his own work.

Other factors he inherited from Kant can be enumerated. Peirce came to hold that logic should guide the efforts of philosophy to deal with the great questions. However, Peirce's mature logic, which he developed some years later, was much broader than that of Kant, as it is much broader than that of the contemporary analytic philosophical school, which shares the Kant/Peirce doctrine by the way. With Peirce's broad logic, this program has a chance of some progress; with a narrower logic (either the old narrow logic of Kant or the new narrow logic), the current program becomes yet another infatuation with a flashy method and a way of avoiding or side-stepping those grand questions in one's own life (a kind of self-deception via technique or method).

I was unaware of these early writings on metaphysics, Mr. Eisenstaat, and I am grateful you showed them to me, because I discovered that while Peirce was clearly at that time living within Kant's house, even from the start of his life as a scientist he was attempting to do interesting and original things with its resources. Later, Peirce came to see that to make progress, he would have to build a new house of his own. In particular (remember, *metaphysics* is but an alternate term for the pursuit of philosophy), he announced: "Everyman his own metaphysician," which is precisely the case in philosophy. The results of science are personally inter-transferable. I can discover how to make gunpowder from Salt-Peter, Sulphur, and Charcoal, then discover how to use such a compound to make a bomb. Not only can I make a bomb as often as I wish, I can teach you—who didn't discover the matter—how these bombs work, then you too can make them or even teach others, while you or the others know nothing of how to discover such things. The same is not true in philosophy. No one can do your philosophy then hand it over; you must do it yourself or it will not be done. Philosophy is not knowledge, nor is it memory learning obtained from lectures. Yes, if Everyman studies the great questions, necessarily he must be his own metaphysician; no one else can do it for him.

As the fall semester[†] of 1860 began, Charley moved into Massachusetts Hall number 5 where he took up duties as proctor. Apparently that arrangement lasted only a semester or so, for he seems to have moved back into a room at Function Hall in a few months. He undertook private study with Agassiz during the summer which he continued into the regular academic year.

Back to School

When I entered the Lawrence Scientific School[†] in the fall of 1860, Agassiz set me to sorting fossil brachiopods without knowing anything about them, and I understand that my work was preserved at the museum, as a most amazing monument of incapacity, to the high delection of all who entered as students for many years.

(March 1878). The conception of Continuous quantity[†] is the direct instrument of the finest generalizations. When a naturalist wishes to study a species, he collects a considerable number of specimens more or less similar. In contemplating them, he observes certain ones which are more or less alike in some particular respect. They all have, for instance, a certain S-shaped marking. He observes they are not precisely alike. In this respect, the S has not precisely the same shape, but the differences are such as to lead him to believe that forms could be found intermediate between any two of those he possesses. He, now, finds other forms apparently quite dissimilar—say a marking in the form of a C—and the question is, whether he can find intermediate ones which will connect these latter with the others. This he often succeeds in doing in cases where *it would at first be thought impossible; whereas, he sometimes finds those which differ, at first glance, much less, to be separated in Nature by the non-occurrence of intermediaries. In this way, he builds up from the study of Nature a new general conception of the character in question. He obtains, for example, an idea of a leaf which includes every part of the flower, and an idea of a vertebra which includes the skull. I surely need not say much to show what a logical engine is here. It is the essence of the method of the naturalist. How he applies it first to one character, and then to another, and finally obtains a notion of a species of animals, the differences between whose members, however great, are confined within limits, is a matter which does not here concern us. I only desire to point out that it is by taking advantage of the idea of continuity, or the passage of one form to another by insensible degrees, that the naturalist builds his conceptions. Now, the naturalists are the great builders of conceptions; there is no other branch of science where so much of this work is done as in theirs; and we must, in great measure, take them for our teachers in this important part of logic.*

LII†
1860 October 14
The use of every word is fixed in two ways.
lst By its meaning & the idea it is attached to.
2nd By its application & the thing it is attached to.
But now if it is found that the idea does not apply to the thing, which shall we loose & which hold? The answer to this question affords a very pretty test of a great difference in cast of intellect.

LIII
1860 October 24
We hear a great deal of the advantage, even of unsuccessful effort. But I do not believe that there is any good to be derived from scientific inquiries except so far as we pursue them right. The same would apply to gymnastics of the body.

(October 1913). In my twenties† I went to George Barker Windship (who graduated A.M. from Harvard in 1854 and M.D. in 1857), then conducting a gymnasium in 351 Washington Street, Boston, and after a few preliminary lessons and trials, began going twice a week and lifting 1000 lbs. a number of times. I was very decidedly below the average muscular strength. Later I had a proper platform of my own with a lot of old iron ballast round a cast iron disk suspended at its centre from a chain, and the chain, disk, and iron on the disk weighed just 1000 lbs. I had a couple of gigantic negroes to shift around the iron so that it should hold the disk exactly horizontal according to two carpenter's levels at right angles. This preliminary adjustment required me to lift the

weight so many times that at last I told the stronger negro to change places with me; but he couldn't lift it at all though he must have been ever so much stronger than I. When I did those liftings I was always substantially naked, and persons who looked said the way I changed color all over under the weight was striking. I was always wonderfully exhilarated and refreshed by it. "Felt like a fighting cock," as they say.

15. *Charles Sanders Peirce*
"Felt like a fighting cock"
Tuttle Collection, Institute for Studies in Pragmaticism
By permission, Philosophy Department, Harvard University

My notion of the second of my categories was gained when I decided that the best means to that end would be to note the state of consciousness while weightlifting when all my muscles were slowly contracting so very much & under such tension as almost to abolish all sensation.

In 1871 I noticed[†] the laboratory results of Prof. Austin Flint, Jr., which show that repeated contractions of the same muscles render the nerves unsteady and make the heart beat more rapidly but less efficiently. On the contrary, an exercise which systematically arouses a person's latent muscular strength, by overcoming successively increased weights or resistances, produces a definite increase of steadiness of the nerves. These observations lend decided support to Dr. Windship and his lifting cures.

LIV[†]
1860 November 25
Every man his own Metaphysician.

LV
1860 November 25
I have come to the conclusion that our primary conceptions are not simple but complex; that our elementary conceptions are not independent but linked complexedly together; that nevertheless properly speaking we have no a priori synthetical propositions, and that axioms are only definitions.

LV
The Thought of the Year 1860
Metaphysics has no practical bearing. Thus, the efficacy of prayer, a man's intellect, perhaps, would not endorse, but then when intellect has the ascendancy we do not wish to make use of that. When we feel no confidence in her, we pray.

It has long[†] been known, as well as any mathematical proposition so intricate can be said to be known by experience, that four colors suffice to color any map on an ordinary surface. About 1860, DeMorgan, in the Athenaeum, called attention to the fact that this theorem had never been demonstrated; and I soon after offered to a mathematical society in Harvard University[†] a proof of this proposition extending it to other surfaces for which the numbers of colors are greater. My proof was never printed, but Benjamin Peirce, J. M. Oliver, and Chauncey Wright, who were present, discovered no fallacy in it.

LVII
1860 December 30
When a man begins to be hard pressed with his own passion and power, he sees the nonsense of guiding his conduct by any rule of God or man and the necessity there is of excogitating a manner of life of his own.

1861
No longer wondered[†] what I would do in life
but defined my object.

(1902). I began the study of logic[†] in 1855, and it has been my principal occupation ever since[†] to work out a scientific system of logic, the first truly scientific study of logic that has ever been made in my opinion. Twice, I have made determined efforts to dismiss the subject from my thoughts, but the bent of my mind is such that I did not succeed in doing so for more than a few months each time. When I began I first spent almost all of my time reading the German philosophers and Aristotle. It was, however, not until 1861 that I ventured upon any serious original research, and not until 1866 that I was far enough advanced to offer anything for publication; so that subtracting distractions, forty years' work is about what my results have cost me.

1/19/61 Saturday. Called on Miss Zina Fay[†] for the 1st time.
1/21/61 Monday. Mr. William Wheelright Jr. wanted me to teach him mathematics.
1/22/61 Tuesday. Father's 3rd Lowell Lecture[†]
1/23/61 Wednesday. Called on Miss Zina Fay.

Apology to Miss <u>Fay</u> alias
<u>*Junks*</u>
for not writing some
Promised Verses
The temple of my heart[†] flows o'er
With ardent sentiment
Which does so crowd about the door
Of speech that none finds vent
To reach the audience hall of thine.
That door a charm must ope
The potent queen of Fays my lips
Inspire. Then would I hope
To sing a lay which should eclipse
E'en Codman's song divine.
While sweet Titania Junks my ditty should approve,
Who by the by is requested to reply to the above.

From <u>Autobiography and Letters of Orvill Dewey</u>,
edited by his daughter. Boston, 1884
The object of Benjamin Peirce's Lowell Lectures[†] on "the Mathematics of the Cosmos" is to show that the same ideas, principles, relations, which the mathematician has wrought out from his own mind, are found in the system of nature, indicating an identity of thought.

You see of what immense interest the discussion is. But Peirce's deliv-
ery of his thoughts is very lame and imperfect (extemporaneous). Two
lectures ago, as I sat by Agassiz, I said at the close, "Well, I feel obliged
to apologize to myself for being here."
"Why?"
"Because I don't understand half of it."
"No? I am surprised. I do.
"Well, that is because you are learned."
(Thinking with myself, however, why does he? For he knows no
more of the mathematics than I do. But I went on.)
"Well, my apology is this: Peirce is like nature,—vast, obscure,
mysterious,—great bowlders of thought, of which I can hardly get
hold; dark abysses, into which I cannot see; but, nevertheless, flashes
of light here and there, and for these I come."
"Why, yes, I understand him. Just now, when he drew that curi-
ous diagram to illustrate a certain principle, I saw it clearly, for I know
the same thing in organic nature."
"Aha! The Mathematics in the Cosmos!"
Was it not striking? Here are the Mathematics (Peirce), and Nat-
ural Science (Agassiz), and they easily understand each other, because
the lecturer's principle is true.

March 11, 1861

My Dear Mr. Peirce:

I was in town[†] yesterday. She has recovered her voice, though alas! not
the obliging disposition that once distinguished her! However, they *may* be
at home tomorrow evening, and if we go there she *may* condescend to sing. I
shall go in to Prof. Cooke's Lecture—& if you will meet me in the vestibule
we can walk down to 109 Beacon Street together and take our chance of
hearing the capricious nightingale.

As ever, Zina Fay

The lecturer in question was Josiah Parsons Cooke, Erving Professor of
Chemistry and Minerology in Harvard University, who was holding forth[†]
that winter at the Lowell Institute in Boston on religion and chemistry.
Cooke's line was rather a chemical version of Ben Peirce's approach concerning the divinity of geometry—in other words it was a presentation of
supposed chemical evidence for the argument from divine design. You will
appreciate the general thrust if I summarize a few lines from Cooke's opening lecture.

The time has been[†] when the Christian Church was an active antag-
onist of physical science; when the whole hierarchy of Rome united

to condemn its results and resist its progress; when the immediate reward of great discoveries was obloquy and persecution. But this has all passed. The age of dogmatism has gone, and an age of general skepticism has succeeded. The power of traditional authority has given place to the power of ideas, and physical science, which before hardly dared to assert its birthright, and could even be forced to recant on its knees, its demonstrated truths, has now become one of the rulers of society. By its rapid growth, by its conquests over brute matter, and by its wonderful revelations, it has deservedly gained the highest respect of man. But unfortunately elated by its success, the stripling has been at times proud and arrogant, usurping authority not its due. Forgetting his early faith, he has approached with irreverent thoughts the holy temple of our religion. No wonder the Church should become alarmed, that many of her best men should join in a general cry against the whole tendency of science and its results. But this is a great mistake: the phantom they fear is purely of their own creation, and, could they but know the whole truth, they themselves would see that to ignore the well-established results of science, and to denounce its legitimate tendency, is a policy as short-sighted as it is illiberal and unchristian.

It's important to note that Cooke was to become Charley's chemistry teacher at the Lawrence school, and a background associate of the Florentine Academy. I mentioned this to Betsey during an evening conversation. She wasn't interested in chemistry, but went directly to another aspect of Zina's remarks.

"Who was the capricious nightingale? Could that be Zina's cousin, Lillie Greenough, Charley's one true love? Was she back in Cambridge from Europe where her mother had taken her to remove her from Charley's influence?" Her interrogation provoked me to check.

Indeed, Lillie and her mother, Harriette Fay Greenough, had returned to Cambridge for a visit. I don't know the exact dates. But it can be confirmed: for instance Charley's aunt Lizzie wrote the following to relatives in Salem on 2 April 1861.

A wonderful singer[†] has come to Cambridge, Lillie Greenough— Her mother, Harriette Fay, was an old friend of mine. Mrs. G. took Lillie to Europe & had her instructed by the first masters. Lillie must have had many lovers & she has an offer from a very wealthy man, whom it is whispered she does not love—We hope she will not be tempted to sacrifice herself to him.

"My guess is that Charley had heard that Lillie might return to Cambridge for a visit, so he began cultivating a friendship with her cousin Zina to gain a convenient way to contact Lillie, in case the rumor was true."

Such were Betsey's musings on the topic. I wonder. Maybe Zina was just that—Charley's good friend. This letter from her dated a couple of months later, from the family home in St. Albans, Vermont, adds some plausibility to that view, and to the hypothesis that Charley had been hermetically sealed off from Lillie by her mother.

> Yes, Charley, my dear friend[†]—that was an awful sacrifice of Lillie! but when people worship the world and the pomps & vanities thereof—what else can be expected? Lillie's whole education has, as if on system, shut out from her contemplation every thing truly noble, generous and elevating. & she has been taught to be a trifler and a dilettante, and to live only for amusement. Therefore if she marries at all, she must marry some one who can give her all that pleasure, that for which she and her mother have so insatiable a craving—and what signifies[†] a roué provided he is elegant, amiable, and generous? It is true that there are some extraordinary individuals who look upon marriage as either a sacrament or a sacrilege—but I fear they are poor creatures who never make a sensation. Lillie was born to make thousands happy and herself famous—she will only make one insignificant man and herself wretched instead—and this is what women get by slavishly bowing down to Custom & Conventionality, and believing that they *must* marry, or be "failures," "missed destinies," and the like. How I detest the whole miserable Creed—the offspring of Paganism and of everything ignorant, narrow, selfish & vile, and now that you have seen one magnificent creature—whom nature meant to be the crown and glory of womanhood—*wasted*, I should think you would begin to reflect upon the system that makes Matrimony the only thing a woman has to look to for position and respectability. I've got a book I am going to make you read when you come up here. But, indeed, you do not know how entirely I sympathise with what I fear you feel on this subject.
>
> It was a great pleasure to get your letter, and if I can do anything for you in the shape of friendship I shall be most happy. I think you need a friend, poor child.

In May, after returning[†] to Paris, Lillie wrote to her aunt in Cambridge of her engagement to Charles Moulton. Her letter closed in a mood that seems to confirm Zina's conjecture: "I shall have a beautiful home, or rather homes, because they have not only a handsome hotel in Paris, but an ideal country place (Petit Val) and a villa in Dinard." From such surroundings her entrance into the court of Napoleon III was launched.

That Lillie was in France in May was her good fortune, for on the twelfth of April, the United States suffered a vast internal cultural explosion. As civil war began in earnest, both sides of the conflict were eager to join the rush to mass killing. The Queen's niece Emma—from The Queen's house in the sleepy college town of Columbia, South Carolina—recalled her family's reaction to the news that the "War for Southern Independence" had begun when Federal Fort Sumter in Charleston harbor was reduced by South Carolinian troops loyal to the rebellious Confederate[†] States.

> The joy—the excitement—how well I remember it. For weeks we had been in a fever of excitement. On the day the news came of the fall of Sumter we were all sitting in the library at Uncle John's. The bell commenced to ring. At the first tap we knew the joyful tidings had come. Father and Uncle John made a dash for their hats—Jule and Johnny followed. We women ran trembling to the veranda—to the front gate eagerly asking the news of passers-by. The whole town was in a joyful tumult.

Emma's father Joseph Le Conte and her uncle John, The Queen's spouse, dashed toward fairly high-level positions within the new government of the Confederate States of America. Earlier John Le Conte and The Queen, in the plainest language, had urged Ben[†] to join the emerging Confederate cause. There are plenty of reasons why an objective observer might conclude that Ben and The Chief had encouraged such persuasions because of their sympathy with some of the political and social convictions of the Le Contes, but when Confederate artillery began hostilities by firing on Sumter, Peirce and Bache and many other northern defenders of the Southern way of life became ardent in their devotion to the Union and to "the country." Indeed, in all of Cambridge "there was a passionate fire[†] of patriotism." This trend also appeared in the Peirce family as early as the sixteenth of April, in a note from The Chief to Ben.

> I wrote to Columbia[†] yesterday, tho' I had been greatly irritated by the tone of John Le Conte's letter to me, in which he indulges in politics & expresses sentiments with which he should have felt I could have no sympathy. After crying peccavi for not having written, & peccavisti for his writing on politics, I confined myself to affection & science. Just think how near that comes to realizing that we are no longer fellow citizens! Ohime! The actions of the seceders have crushed out my natural sympathies for them as peoples, only my heart is still right towards individuals.

Ben's response was impassioned and thorough.

> All Massachusetts[†] is ablaze for the war, and there is no resisting the current which is as deep as it is swift. All men are

ready to embark in the service of the government, lives and property and all which they hold most dear. There is a fullness and generosity of patriotism which is truly heroic, and the individual excitement is less noticeable than the calm and resolute determination to devote everything to the service of the country. No man withholds his hand and his heart from the cause—and the government need not fear to exhaust the heart of the state as long as it has one drop of blood or property which can be shed in the war. I am so bold as to enclose a mathematician's plan for prosecuting the war.

God save the Country! And we may be thankful that General Scott is in command and not some visionary civilian like the professor of Mathematics in Harvard College.

Goodbye—blessed Chief—If I can be of any service, I belong *wholly to the country*; and you may use me as you please.

Bache responded[†] that war requirements will put "a demand for our work," meaning the work of the Florentine Academy and the Coast Survey, "in all directions." Bache was a West Point man, and in a way, he was a casualty of the war, for in his wartime duties he literally worked himself to an early death in 1867.

Ben soon travelled to Washington with President Felton where for two weeks he conferred with Bache[†] and other leading figures. It's easy to understand why the services of an applied astronomer and geodicist such as Ben would be important to a nation lately thrown into battle. After all, an army and navy with more accurate maps would have a vital military resource, especially if its opponent lacked them. As Aunt Lizzie[†] noted, "The Coast Survey now proves to be of the greatest advantage to us—especially as the South cannot have the benefit of the unpublished papers."

I mention all this because it helps to understand an important juncture in Charley's career. Had he been caught up in the military mania that swept through Massachusetts in 1861, his life might have ended or have been much different. He had contacts and visits with some of his friends in their new military[†] circumstances, including his closest friend Horatio Paine[†] who entered service as a medical cadet. And he witnessed the street parades and other military rituals that quickly became prominent around Boston. Such scenes were no doubt behind his use of military examples in some of his later writing. For example, I found the following in some papers of 1907 when I was rummaging around seeking after another topic.

To understand the action of a sign[†] calls for close attention. Let me remind you of the distinction between dynamical, or dyadic, action; and intelligent, or triadic action. An event, A, may, by brute force, produce an event, B; and then the event, B, may in its turn produce a third event, C. The fact that the event,

C, is about to be produced by B has no influence at all upon the production of B by A. It is impossible that it should, since the action of B in producing C is a contingent future event at the time B is produced. Such is dyadic action, which is so called because each step of it concerns a pair of objects. But now when a microscopist is in doubt whether a motion of an animalicule is guided by intelligence, of however low an order, the test he always used to apply when I went to school is to ascertain whether event, A, produces a second event, B, as a means to the production of a third event, C, or not. That is, he asks whether B will be produced if it will produce or is likely to produce C in its turn, but will not be produced if it will not produce C in its turn nor is likely to do so. Suppose, for example, an officer of a squad or company of infantry gives the word of command, "Ground arms!" This order is, of course, a sign. That thing which causes a sign as such is called the object represented by the sign: the sign is determined to some species of correspondence with that object. In the present case, the object the command represents is the will of the officer that the butts of the muskets be brought down to the ground. Nevertheless, the action of his will upon the sign is not simply dyadic; for if he thought the soldiers were deaf mutes, or did not know a word of English, or were raw recruits utterly undrilled, or were indisposed to obedience, his will probably would not produce the word of command.

Despite the appearance of such military examples in his writing, and the fact that he certainly did not lack in courage, my guess is that he disliked the military life. Why? Again, my hunch is that, as the above example shows, he understood that part of the essence of such a life would require him to surrender his will to that of another or to live mechanically; he was too independent of mind to tolerate such a condition—"indisposed to obedience," having grown up in Ben Peirce's household where fiercely independent thought was a way of life.

"Don't forget that he suffered from a serious chronic and painful condition." Betsey wanted to be sure that I did not overlook relevant health considerations. "His neuralgia would have been a serious impediment to a military career."

Instead of volunteering as many of his friends did, he approached Ben about the possibility of employment as a computer within the project to determine longitudes that Ben had undertaken for the Coast[†] Survey, a wish which was promptly conveyed to The Chief.

Charley came to me today with an earnest request that I would get for him the vacant place in the computation of the Pleiades occultations. After trying, in vain, to head him off by telling him that he had better keep to his profession and wait until he could get money by his chemistry—to which he replied that he wants to get the means to buy books and apparatus and devote himself longer to the study of his profession—I finally consented to write you about it. But I told him that he must not expect to get it—for you may have reasons which would render it inexpedient to give the place to him. But if you can do it, I am ready to say that he is important to the work.

Bache promptly[†] replied that he had no objections, so Charley's formal application for the position was sent at once.

Cambridge   19 VI 1861
Dear Sir:
    As I hear[†] from my father that there is some work to be done upon the Pleiades which has not been assigned, I write to ask that I be appointed on the Survey to this work. I shall probably be in Cambridge for some years.
                                                                              Yr, Charles S. Peirce
Supt. A. D. Bache
The Coast Survey

An official letter dated July first from Bache to Ben[†] appointed Charley as computer to Ben's Pleiades longitude project, compensated initially at $35 per month. His position as aid to Ben continued officially until April[†] 1872. But in the summer of 1862, when the military draft began to bite deeply, Charley wrote to Bache:

St. Albans, Vermont   1862 Aug 11
Dear Sir:
    Does my appointment[†] in the C.S. service exempt me from draft or not? I have not had any letter of appointment so I am in doubt.
    This town has just raised a full company, tho' considerably above its quota. But I perfectly dread going. I should feel that I was ended & thrown away for nothing. Yours with much respect & love.
                                                                              Charles S. Peirce
Prof. A. D. Bache
Supt. U.S.C.S

The Chief replied on 16 August:

Yours of Aug. 11[†] is just rec'd. Certainly your employment in an executive department of the Gov't. viz: the Treasury exempts you from draft in the Militia. I have been within the week at Cambridge & left all well there.
                                                                              Yours truly, A.D.B.
Chas. S. Peirce, Esq.
U.S. Coast Survey

Thus—even though Ben, at the onset of war's rage, had declared he was ready to invest every drop of Massachusetts blood—it seems clear that Charley's resolve in regard to his personal stock of plasma had ever been to the contrary.

I am guided in this judgment by a letter from Francis Ellis, Charley's nephew:

I know that[†] my grandfather, Benjamin Peirce, had a great many close friends in the South, and corresponded before the war with Jefferson Davis. From what I have gathered from family conversation I strongly suspect that the war was not popular in my grandfather's family. The feeling was that the troubles between the North and South could have been settled without a war. In any event, none of my uncles, although of the right age, volunteered or enlisted in the army. This, I feel certain, must have created rather bitter feeling among some people in the Cambridge Community.

Just how early after the beginning of hostility had Charley planned to avoid military service? My guess is rather early. But he did have other things on his mind in the summer of 1861, which he began in July with an extended visit[†] to the Fay family in St. Albans, Vermont. There he began courting Zina Fay by way of chemistry[†] and metaphysics—an unusual strategy, you might agree. Zina and her sisters responded to Charley's chemistry lessons with a whimsical letter:

August 1861   St. Albans, Vermont
        Perfeser C. S. Peirce, Cambridge
Moon alias Kate Fay[†]
Noon alias Laura Fay
Night alias Zina Fay
Z. We shall have to depend on Kate for our wit this afternoon.
L. Kate got so "awful mad" over the hieroglyphics in the "Views of Chemistry[†] for Young Ladies" sketched by the perfesser (which she finds it absolutely impossible to understand).
K. You needn't talk, for you can't understand half the old thing yourself!
Z. My dears, since I flatter myself that the perfesser is not altogether enigmatical to my profounder (!) thought, I will try to enlighten you as to his meaning.
        P.S. Time, Sunday 10 p.m. Scene: Zina's room
L. Ah, Zie! what a pity Charley Peirce was not here today—such a day!—such music!—such sermons from Papa! How very original and satisfactory an arrangement it was to have Charles Hopkins play in the dim-lighted church on the organ for us this evening.

Z. Yes, our music today was supermagical. Charles is certainly wonderful on the organ. If he had only been playing for Mr. Peirce & me that night in the Music Hall we should have been lifted into the celestial spheres. By the way, I wonder where Mr. Peirce went to church today.

K. Probably he smoked all day long.

Z. Perhaps—but let us hope that something besides smoke ascended from him to Heaven.

August 1861
INTRODUCTORY TO METAPHYSICS[†]
   For Z.F.
   The analysis of conceptions is the synonym for metaphysics. And all reasoning is analysis. Metaphysics is then but another word for pure reasoning.
   Humanity always agrees upon truths when the conceptions have been perfectly grasped and analyzed; it is when this has not been done that these fruitless controversies have arisen. To learn how to analyze ideas, therefore, and to analyze them—in short to study metaphysics—is par excellence *education.*
   But I will go further than this and say that all wisdom is derived from the study of metaphysics. You cannot read metaphysics. It isn't in the books, but in the mind.
   The Logical and Psychological Treatment of Metaphysics. These two views of metaphysics give rise to two modes of treating it. One starts by drawing the conceptions from the system of psychology & reasoning to their logical relations & meaning; the other draws the conceptions from no system but from the thoughts as they present themselves in their Logical form. The latter seems to be the truly metaphysical course. It may be called the Logical Treatment of Metaphysics.
   I represent the fundamental distinction of metaphysics[†] thus:

Each chief step in science has been a lesson[†] in logic.
C. S. Peirce, 1877

In the Crucible

(1907). I remember[†] a blazing July noon in the early sixties when a fellow-student in the chemical laboratory, in whose company I was crossing the Harvard "College Yard," while the grass shone like emeralds, and the red-brick buildings, not red enough by nature for the taste of the curator, were blazing in a fresh coat of something like vermillion,—when this fellow-student casually remarked upon the pleasing harmony of color between the grass, the foliage, and the buildings. With eyes feeling as if they were balls being twisted by some inquisitor, I at first understood the remark as a sorry joke, like the gibes of some Indian captive at the want of skill of his tormentors. But I soon found that it was the utterance of a sincere feeling, and then, by a series of questions, soon discovered that my friend was blind to the red element of color. A man may have learned that he is color-blind; but it is impossible that he should be conscious of the stupendous gulf between his chromatic impressions and those of ordinary men; although it is needful to take account of this in all interpretations of what he may say about colors. In the course of my examination of that young gentleman, which occupied several days, I learned a more general lesson, worth multiples of the time it lost me from the laboratory.

Charley made arrangements through his father to study in the chemical laboratory of Professor[†] Josiah P. Cooke, Jr., at the Lawrence Scientific School. He was officially admitted in March[†] of 1861. William James began studies in the Lawrence School in fall of 1861. I think they met as a result of William's chemistry class, which was taught by the other chemist in the School, Professor Eliot, as shown in the correspondence of James from Cambridge to his family in Newport.

Cambridge   September 7, 1861
    Professor Eliot[†] is a fine fellow, I suspect, a man who, if he resolves to do a thing, will do it. I find analysis very interesting *so far.*
                                                         September 16, 1861
    This chemical analysis is so bewildering at first that I am entirely "muddled and beat" and have to employ most all my time reading up. Prof. Wyman's lectures on the comparative anatomy of vertebrates promise to be very good. Eliot I have not seen much of; I don't believe he is a *very* accomplished chemist, but can't tell yet. Young Atkinson is a very nice boy. The rest of this year's class is nothing wonderful. In last year's there is a son of Prof. Peirce, Charles, whom I suspect to be a very "smart" fellow with a great deal of character, pretty independent and violent though. In my

presence he attacked Herbert Spencer whose work I deeply admire; I felt spiritually wounded, as by the defacement of a sacred image or picture, though I could not verbally defend[†] it against his criticisms.

Willy

Professor Eliot in turn made an estimate[†] of his charge, William, which has survived: "James is a very interesting and agreeable pupil, but is not wholly devoted to the study of Chemistry; his work much interfered with by ill-health, or rather by something which I imagine to be a delicacy of nervous constitution."

Cambridge   December 25, 1861

Agassiz is[†] an admirable, earnest lecturer, clear as day, and his accent is most fascinating. He would rather take wholly uninstructed people, "for he has to unteach them all that they have learnt." He does not let them *look* into a book for a long while, what they learn they must learn for themselves, and be *masters* of it all. The consequence is that he makes *naturalists* of them, he does not merely cram them. One feels ready to go anywhere in the world with nothing but a notebook and study out anything quite alone. He must be a great teacher.

Chemistry comes on tolerably, but not as fast as I expected. I am pretty slow with my substances, having done but twelve since Thanksgiving and having thirty-eight more to do before the end of the term.

Willy

William also expressed a wish that his family could move to a home closer to Harvard, and in the spring of 1864, they did settle in a house in Boston at 13 Ashburton Place.

Betsey remarked, "It seems clear that William needed some help with his chemistry. Isn't it likely that he might have turned to Charley for assistance? After all, Charley had been a successful student in that field since age eight." Seems to me that Betsey might have a point there.

"Didn't we find earlier that he had been earning some extra money by doing some tutoring at that time?" He had indeed. He worked for awhile in 1861 teaching at Miss E. M. Hight's school for girls[†] in Kirkland Street, Cambridge.

While the United States Army did not fare well early in the war, the Navy had better fortunes, which gave Cambridge cause for joy. Captain Davis, Charley's uncle, began the War as second in command[†] to Commodore S. F. Dupont, United States Navy. An immense Union flotilla sortied to capture Port Royal, the finest harbor on the southern Atlantic coast, initially in Confederate hands. Davis was given considerable credit for his major role in the plan, which was imitated years later in Admiral Dewey's victory at Manila. The engagement was successful, and Uncle Davis's skill in military science and his personal courage were quietly celebrated by Ben's family. Later in the war, Davis assumed command of the Upper Mississippi gunboat flotilla, where he saw action throughout the great river, including the Memphis campaign and Farragut's effort at Vicksburg. But despite his considerable successful battle experience, he remained known principally as a Naval man of science. He was appointed admiral before his career ended. One of his three daughters married Henry Cabot Lodge, which is how that famous senator became a kinsman of Charley Peirce. Cabot Lodge was the husband of Charley's mother's sister's daughter. But in reality it was closer than that, for Admiral Davis in his status as Florentine Academician and close friend of Ben was an important scientific role model.

Charley: December 1, 1861
     This little thing† is not perfect enough for you to find it beautiful—but because it is true, perhaps you will not feel it alien.
                                                                    Zie

          To Charley

          A Heart was lying, dying.
          Unheard its sob & sighing,
          This world held no replying
               For its deep moan.
          From starry realms aloft
          A whispered word fell soft
          "O many a time and oft
               I am alone!"
          A Mind was shrinking, sinking
          From every hope of linking
          Its musings into Thinking
               Its dreams to Art.
          Low breathed the voice again
          "Nay, thou art not in vain.
          And who shall still my pain
               If thou depart?
          It woke the pulses' play
          the death-swoon passed away
          Black night broke into day,
               I knew not how.

Nor died the voice in air
I heard it everywhere,
In thought, in hope, in prayer.
Love, is it Thou?

Zina Fay

LVIII
Lesson of the Year[†] 1861
1861 Dec 27
*A man who makes a friend of a woman—however sympathetic, true &
good—is a nincumpoop.*

LIX
1861 Dec 27
*It would be an inexplicable paradox were the principles of Causation & of
Freedom both true & yet mutually explicable. For they are different simple conceptions. Now to be reconcilable they must not merely have a relation to each
other in experience but one thought in the very conception itself. Hence in the
one conception the other would be contained which would make them either
identical or possessed of a common element.*

LX
1861 December 27
*What Freedom is in terms of Causation so far as those terms can express it,
it is easy to say—a mere chimera. But what is it in its own terms? Let the
philosopher tell that and he has done his part.*

LXI
1861 December 27
*Freedom is the quality of acting normally notwithstanding disturbing influ-
ences.*
*The good man—he who does not his own will but God's—has then a free
will. But he who follows his own lead is the slave of external influences.*

St. Albans, Vt.   *1862 January*
*I arrived[†] at the Fay household at about 2 P.M. Tuesday. They profess not
to be recovered from this astonishment. The master of the house was gone. The
young ladies had already two visitors here in the shape of a young divine who
has been preaching for Mr. Fay & his pupil a boy alt. 17.*
Sleighing is fine—weather magnifique—Young ladies tolerable as usual.
*How we spend the day. We have breakfast at 5 1/2 AM. After breakfast
prayers, go to the village, compute Pleiades until dinner. After dinner, play the
fool—quite a pleasant amusement which I mean to introduce at home. After we*

get through playing the fool, we make ourselves mutually agreeable for a little while remembering how sleepy we shall all be after tea. At tea we have every night a new variety of preserves but I do wish they'd have some more of them quinces. After tea music. Meantime Zina goes to sleep & by occupying the sofa keeps the younger members of the family awake. When the rest go to bed Genl. Jackson & his wife smoke their pipes. Whenever I write in my journal all the young ladies look over my shoulder which isn't put down in that 'ere book of Etiquette.

St. Albans   *1862, Feb. 1*

I am having an excellent time[†] up here, & shall stay another week, at least. Miss Amy[†] the only member of the family whom I did not already know is a beautiful girl, very tall, of beautiful form, fine features, golden hair, & a very peculiar complexion. She is very animated and plays wonderfully. The weather is very mild and pleasant and the sleighing has been uninterruptedly good. I don't go to church quite so often as I did last summer having been but once so far. Very little happens to tell of—we go a sleigh-ride occasionally—we converse moderately. I have introduced the game of Authors—music is in abundance—that is about all. Mr. Fay tho' not very well is pleasant & I don't think they are tired of me yet.

(1898). There are several methods of mathematical computation[†] which present this peculiarity that if any mistakes are made, we have only to keep right on and they will correct themselves. Suppose for example that I wish to find the cube root of 2. I set down any three numbers one below another. I add the last two numbers of the column and to the tripled sum add in the number next above those two in the column and set down the result at the bottom of the column. I go on doing that the longer the better, and then the last number but one divided by the last will be one less than the cube root of two.

If anyone sits down to solve ten ordinary linear equations between ten unknown quantities, one will receive materials for a commentary upon the infallibility of mathematical processes, for you will almost infallibly get a wrong solution. I take it as a matter of course that you are not an expert professional computer. He will proceed according to a method which will correct his errors if he makes any.

This calls to mind one of the most wonderful features of reasoning, and one of the most important philosophemes in the doctrine of science, of which however you will search in vain for any mention in any book I can think of, namely, that reasoning tends to correct itself, and the more so the more wisely its plan is laid. Nay, it not only corrects its conclusions, it even corrects its premisses. The theory of Aristotle is, that necessary conclusion is just equally as certain as its premisses, while a probable conclusion somewhat less so. But were every probable inference less certain than its premisses, science, which piles inference upon inference, often quite deeply, would soon be in a bad way. Every astronomer is familiar with the fact that the catalogue place of a fundamental star, which is the result of elaborate reasoning, is far more accurate than any of the observations from which it was deduced.

That Induction tends to correct itself is obvious enough. That the same thing may be true of a Deductive inquiry our arithmetical example has shown. A celebrated error in the <u>Mécanique Céleste</u> concerning the amount of theoretical acceleration of the moon's mean motion deceived the whole world of astronomy for more than half a century. Errors of reasoning in the first book of Euclid's Elements only became known after the non-Euclidean geometry had been developed.

As for Retroductive (Abductive) Inquiries, or the Explanatory Sciences, such as Geology, Evolution, and the like, they always have been and always must be theatres of controversy. These controversies do get settled, after a time, in the minds of candid inquirers.

So it appears that this marvelous self-correcting property of Reason belongs to every sort of science.

I have[†] always, since early in the sixties, recognized three different types of reasoning, viz: 1st, <u>Deduction</u> which depends on our confidence in our ability to analyze the meanings of the signs in or by which we think; 2nd, <u>Induction</u>, which depends upon our confidence that a run of one kind of experience will not be changed or cease without some indication before it ceases; and 3rd, <u>Retroduction,</u> or Hypothetic Inference, which depends on our hope, sooner or later, to guess at the conditions under which a given kind of phenomenon will present itself.

LXII[†]

1862 April 7

The value of books is the amount of energy misdirected in writing them.

Senatus Universitatis Harvardiani Academicus
Omnibus ad quos hae litterae pervenerint Salutem:
Nos Praeses et socii Collegii Harvardiani
    Carolum Sanders Peirce,
alumnum ad gradum Magistri in Artibus admisimus eique dedimus omnia insignia et iura ad hunc honorem spectantia.
    Nos praeses et aerarii praefectus auctoritate nobis nomina subscripsimus.
vii-xvii-LXII

William James, Notebook V[†] 1862
Peirce:
    The Reductio ad absurdum can never be used in metaphysical discussion

& rarely in scientific, because it assumes that we know the sum of possibilities.
C. S. Peirce

Kant works critically until he finds it unsatisfactory—and then stops, at morality, freedom, God—Hume do & stops at cause. None succeed in leaving Faith entirely out. id.

The thou idea, as Peirce calls it, dominates an entire realm of mental phenomena, embracing poetry, all direct intuition of nature, scientific instincts, relations of man to man, morality, &c.

All analysis must be into a triad; me & it require the complement thou.

He makes a test of any man's right to write upon freedom that he explain the authority of a Father over his child. Unknown as yet—no one can even say what relation of father & child may be.

(1908). My late brother Jem once studied for the Unitarian ministry. I abominate[†] the Unitarians, because all through my boyhood I heard in our Unitarian family nothing but angry squabbles between Calvinists and Unitarians, and though the latter was less absurd than the former, I thought their church was based on mere denial & when I grew up I joined the Episcopal church, without believing anything but the general essence and spirit of it. That I did & do profoundly believe; but yet I look upon it as one of the species of that genus of religions of which Buddhism and Confucianism are others.

(1902). Forty years ago I read[†] La Logique of the Abbe Gratry, a writer of subtlety and exactitude of thought as well as elevation of reason. I remember that he considered every act of inductive reasoning in which one passes from the finite to the infinite—particularly every inference which from observation concludes that there is in certain objects of observation a true continuity which cannot be directly observed—to be due to a direct inspiration of the Holy Spirit.

(1903). Ever since Wundt[†] inaugurated the modern science of psychology in 1862 with the publication of his Beiträge zur Theorie der Sinneswahrnehmung I have pursued that study both experimentally and speculatively, and am thus better able than some physicists to appreciate the opinion of the psychologists.

LXIII[†]

1862 October 30

The applications of the results of the study of one subject to the science of another are suggestive but they are never exact. The reason of this is that they are loose generalizations, which always glitter.

Let not the man of science be proud of what science does for art.

The several methods[†] for fixation of belief,—tenacity, authority, conformity to rational tastes, and science,—do have their merits: a clear logical conscience *does cost something—just as any virtue, just as all we cherish, costs us dear. But we should not desire it to be otherwise. The genius of a man's logical method should be loved and reverenced as his bride, whom he has chosen from all the world. He need not contemn the others; on the contrary, he may honor them deeply, and in doing so he only honors her the more. But she is the one he has chosen, and he knows that he was right in making that choice. And having made it, he will work and fight for her, and will not complain that there are blows to take, hoping that there may be as many and as hard to give, and will strive to be the worthy knight and champion of her from the blaze of whose splendors he draws his inspiration and his courage.*

Married Again

Charley's several visits to the Fay home in St. Albans, Vermont, were augrim-signs of marriage with Harriet Melusina.

"And don't forget the exchange of love poems, not to mention inspiring his long letters to her on chemistry and metaphysics," Betsey urged.

Ben confided[†] the maturing tendency to The Chief in March 1862.

What do you say to Charley Peirce's having fallen in love with a young lady of Vermont, daughter of my old friend and chum in College, and grandaughter of Bishop Hopkins, Rev. Charles Fay of your church. Of course she is as poor as the crows and ravens, who fed the prophet in the wilderness. But she is very full of knowledge and really a person of great mind—and although far from a beauty, Charley is quite in love with her. She has begun by converting him to episcopacy and his mother thinks that her influence upon him has been in all respects of the best possible character, and that he is a greatly improved person. When they can be married, heaven only knows. But this thing is not to be spoken of, at present, and it is only the dear old chief and the chiefess who are permitted to know it, out of our immediate family in Cambridge. Even Agassiz does not know it—nor Gould.

The Chief responded to the news of Charley's pending engagement eight days[†] later.

I do not wonder that Charley should be captivated[†] by a Fay. He would not be his father's son if he were not susceptible to such influences. What a catholic creature you are old Functionary to take his conversion to Episcopacy so kindly & genially! That is one of the things that I love about you, never loving a friend the less for difference[†] of sign! Charley will make his way, & the engagement will be a stimulus to him nothing else could afford.

Ten days later, Ben confided further[†] in The Chief, as word of the engagement spread in Cambridge.

> A year ago this very Sunday I went to town with Charles Mills to ascertain if it were true that Sumter was taken.
>
> I have heard some very warm encomiums of Charley's Zina Fay from my friends the Washburns and Agassizs. They seem to regard her as a wonder of intellectual ability combined with the most sterling qualities which go to make up a good and useful woman and they also regard her as quite pretty. All I can say is that she seems to be exerting the best possible influence over the young gentleman and I think that we must also regard it as a great piece of good fortune for him to have secured such a prize. As to the religion question, my darling Chief, that is too sacred a question between a man and his maker for any human interference. It is even more a matter of heart, than the living woman herself, and who shall dare to choose the religion even for a son? Charley seems to me to be sincere in his course upon the subject, and I thank God that he feels the need of religion. He can only be on that account the dearer to me—and Zina is all the more acceptable that she has been the instrument of bringing him to a serious state of mind. He is working very well upon the Pleiades—and I am glad to be able to say that each new step upon these stars is a new confirmation of the accuracy of the method.
>
> PS: The matter[†] is now out. Can you see Zina Fay?

The Chief promised to call on "the Fay" later[†] that month.

Aunt Lizzie conveyed the dying secret to Salem relatives, and added her estimation[†] of Zina.

> Charley's engagement is a delightful one. Miss Fay is a very intelligent & highly educated & amiable girl. Her father was a class-mate and friend of Ben's. Her mother was a descendant of Bishop Hopkins. Miss Fay is as interested in the Episcopal Church as Sarah even could desire. Charles Peirce is also of the same mind as Miss Fay, as I understand from his mother.

"The Cantabrigians knew Vermont-born Zina because she was a Radcliffe girl—well, in spirit; yet in near fact as well. She attended the school of Mrs. Agassiz, the embryonic Radcliffe."

16. *Harriet Melusina Fay*
"Miss Fay is a very intelligent & amiable girl."
Tuttle Collection, Institute for Studies in Pragmaticism
By permission, Philosophy Department, Harvard University

Betsey insisted upon the honor of telling you about Zina whom she regards as her fellow[†] Radcliffe alumna:

"Although she was an Episcopalian, Zina was descended from a long
line of New England Puritans, including Anne Hutchinson. I mention that
because one of her lifelong personality traits was the typical Puritanical prin-

ciple of duty above all. Charley had this as well. Her mother was a brilliant person, but held down to childbearing and household duties by the reigning practices of the day. For example, her husband halted her education 'because she knew enough for a woman.' A great deal of Zina's life can be seen as an attempt to free herself from the fate that befell her mother. It is somewhat misleading to describe her as a feminist, because her ideas focused upon freeing women from drudgery so that they too could participate, if qualified, in a life of art or intellection. She felt that women could do some things well and some not so well. She only wanted a fair playing field for those things in which women could excel, but were prevented from taking up by the sort of duties and restraints imposed upon her mother. She became a friend of Waldo Emerson, and at his suggestion attended the Agassiz School for young ladies in Cambridge. She stayed with the Cambridge branch of the Fay family, who lived in what is now called Fay house at Radcliffe—just across the street from the house on Mason Street where Charley was born. The Fays were longstanding friends of Ben Peirce's family. Zina graduated in 1861 as the class orator. She was a wonderful conversationalist who had ideas on everything. She could be self-righteous and was intense and emotional, often rushing forward to a goal in a rash way. Her tremendous sense of duty could make her very bossy, for example, in the way she cared for her brothers and sisters after her mother's premature death in 1856. She was very much of a nativist who harbored an intense hatred for the Irish and indeed Roman Catholics. Quite some time before she met Charley, she had had some kind of affair with her uncle, Charles J. Hopkins, her mother's youngest brother. In the case of Charley, however, it apparently was he who pressed for marriage."

Ben and Sarah counseled Charley to delay the marriage, but as Ben informed The Chief in October, the groom had[†] other ideas:

> Charley has gone to be married, and I expect him home in a week
> or ten days. We thought that he and Zina had yielded to the evident
> reasonableness of the delay until spring. But Charley got into a very
> nervous state about his health, and last Friday we yielded to his
> wishes, and the irresponsible youth started at once for his bride. He
> understands, distinctly, that although we do not object, neither do
> we approve and that the responsibility of the affair must rest
> wholly upon him and Zina. With my present income, I can keep
> him along, until he gets something to do more than he has at
> present and which shall be a permanent means of living. But, I tell
> him that under this war, all things are so precarious, that my
> income may suddenly be cut into the least which I can live upon,
> and that the little money which I have laid by, is just about enough
> to complete the education of Ben, Nellie and Bertie, and that I shall

have no right to touch it for any other purpose. He will come and stay with us during the winter. It will make our quarters at home rather close. The day of the wedding is not fixed, but Charley will send me word when it is to be, and I shall go to it and take Sarah if her health can bear it.

The couple were married[†] in St. Albans, the "Maple Sugar Capital of the World," on 16 October 1862. The marriage license listed Charley's age as twenty-three and his profession as "Chemist"; Zina was twenty-six, no profession given. The bride's father, Rev. Charles Fay, officiated. After making a short visit to Bishop Hopkins in Vermont, they returned to winter[†] in Function Hall.

About this time Ben brought The Chief deeper into his confidence[†] by lamenting, "Only one of my sons is married, I am sorry to say, and I fear that the oldest is destined to be in the perpetual enjoyment of single cursedness."

"Was Ben disclosing to his best friend that he knew of Jem's homosexuality?" Betsey injected.

I can't confirm that, was my answer to her. But it is clear that such was[†] Jem's condition—Betsey and I had long since confirmed it. And I think it quite likely that Ben knew it full well.

"How did Charley's family regard the new bride?" Betsey's usual timely question. Aunt Lizzie (Ben's spinster sibling), who was something of a family chronicler, described her as "a very sensible & agreeable[†] young lady, quite learned and able to assist Charley in some of his occupations; she is not pretty—but she is lady-like[†] and unaffected, sensible & pleasant & we hope and trust the greatest of earthly blessings[†] to Charley."

The year ended well for Charley's occupations; a scientific essay—"The Chemical Theory[†] of Interpenetration"—was submitted from Cambridge during December. It appeared the following month in *The American Journal of Science and Arts*. The same issue carried news that the National Academy of Sciences had been founded[†] in Washington City by an act of Congress. This scheme of the Florentine Academy had suddenly come to fruition.

While only five pages, this article was Charley's first professional scientific publication. A few months after I had met Roy, I asked him what he thought about it and received a cryptic answer.

"It contained a good deal of the chemistry of that day, yet it also attempted to work with the logic of explanation, with Kant's chemical notions, and with some of the ideas relevant to the sort of considerations that lay beneath Mendeleef's Periodic Table of the Elements. Clearly he was engaged in logical and metaphysical inquiry within chemical notation and context. What is generally striking about the article is Peirce's complete placement within science, yet he is discussing what would today be described as philosophical or logical issues. This is the most distinctive aspect of Peirce's work. He is often today called a philosopher, but that is wrong;

he was a scientist whose scientific studies included philosophy or logic pursued in a scientific spirit, but always from within the most rigorous tradition of science.

"Perhaps the most noteworthy single feature of this essay is the last paragraph which contains a seminal version of a principle crucial for his later valency studies in logic. There he asserted that the addition of an odd radicle to another odd radicle will produce an even radicle, while the addition of an even radicle has no such effect."

I tried to pump Roy to explain all that valency talk. He would only say, "When the time is right."

Eliot

One evening Betsey and I were discussing Charley's graduate education as a chemist, and we were thinking about his teachers: Cooke and Eliot. Suddenly Betsey remarked, "Didn't Juliette Peirce mention someone named Eliot as bearing a lifetime grudge against Charley?" I found one such remark by Juliette[†] in 1914 that I had already noticed. But Betsey rummaged around and found a similar comment from 1921[†] I had not seen:

> When I married Mr. Peirce he had l'embarras des choix for the highest diplomatic[†] position abroad through the influence of my relations, since having passed out. But he refused in stating that he would not abandon his country, but his country did abandon him, more so Harvard. During Mr. Eliot's reign, he had a personal grudge against him, if ever a chance presented itself he would keep him out of Harvard, and he has scrupulously kept his nefarious promise, and having deprived students of such a learned man. If Pres. Lowell had been there all those years instead of Mr. Eliot, I am sure an opportunity would have been available, and would have spared fearful endless suffering.

She was right, of course. The Eliot whom Juliette mentioned in 1914 and 1921 was Charles W. Eliot, President of Harvard for forty years to the day, 1869–1909. As students we had been vaguely aware of President Eliot in the context of Harvard history but had no information on a person named Eliot who was a professor of chemistry in the Lawrence Scientific School in the early 1860s.

So I put my bloodhound techniques into gear and quickly discovered that these guys were one Eliot instead of two. Ah! now the clues begin to speak with a common voice. I take to heart the three pieces of advice from Sherlock[†] Holmes, which are most often violated by biographers, especially biographers of Peirce:

1. "How dangerous it always is[†] to reason from insufficient data" / *The Adventure of the Speckled Band*.
2. "I make a point[†] of never having any prejudices" / *The Reigate Puzzle*.
3. "It is a capital mistake[†] to theorize before one has data. Insensibly one begins to twist facts to suit theories, instead of theories to suit facts" / *A Scandal in Bohemia*.

It's hard to fool a detective novelist.

However, what I could find on Eliot, especially from the 1860s, was unsatisfying; it seemed rather laudatory and laundered and purified and empty: abstract sketch of a hollow character. The two-volume biography[†] by his close friend, Henry James, particularly struck me that way. There had to be more. Those bloodhound instincts.

Later that week, Betsey had gone off to heal the world for the day. Feeling adventuresome, I gathered up my briefcase carefully loaded with notes and four Anchor Steam beers, each carefully wrapped in a blue-and-yellow-makes-green plastic lock bag and each held at room temperature. Putting on some scruffy clothes and my meanest look, I walked over to the harbor on the chance I would find Roy in his apartment. He had been to our place several times, but I had never showed up at his doorstep unannounced. I knocked on his door and he let me enter.

He wasn't disturbed about my abrupt visit. Nothing seemed to unbalance him. Probably he was a guru for stoics. He placed me on a cane-bottom chair near his chrome and plastic motel-style dining table. There was only a kitchenette, a locked file cabinet, the table, two chairs, and a bed in the room. Everything was spotlessly clean. His floor was unusual. Deep black tiles alternated with pure white squares in a checkerboard pattern. The sides of each tile were 45° to the walls, except all four floor edges were tessellated[†] with triangular half squares. One black square on the east wall was inlaid with a white-letter motto: *Non nobis*. The blue walls were undecorated except for four certificates near his bed: an amateur radio license dated 1910 for callsign W1PRG signed by Hiram Percy Maxim (the "Old Man"), a Harvard Ph.D. diploma dated 1907 signed by President Charles W. Eliot, a certificate and medal for the Victoria Cross (which is the highest military honor of the United Kingdom) awarded to Chief Wireless Yeoman L. Wyttynys signed by King George V, and finally a master's license for the U.S. Merchant Marine dated 1946, issued to Captain Roy Wyttynys, the signature for which was indecipherable. The whole place was squared up and scrubbed down. It would have sailed through an Admiral's white glove inspection.

I opened my case, removed the notes and two of the longneck Steams. Roy would drink no more than two per day. He was temperate. There we were, comfortably seated, with true sippin' beer in hand and the small talk over. Then I played my trump card and asked Roy, who had been in Harvard while Eliot had been President, if he could help me through my present impasse. I'm glad I asked, and I think you will be too. Like Nero Wolfe's employee Archie Goodwin I have a photographic memory—or should it be called an audiographic memory? Here's a condensed version of our conversation, beginning with Roy's backgrounder on Eliot.

"He was only five years[†] older than Peirce; he graduated in the class of 1853. Like Peirce's father, his father Samuel Atkins Eliot[†] was associated with the university—as treasurer of Harvard College from 1842 to 1853. His boyhood was classically Boston Brahmin. He studied mathematics with Ben Peirce and from 1854 to 1858 he served as tutor in mathematics alongside his close friend and classmate, Jem[†] Peirce. He was promoted to assistant professor in mathematics from '58 to '61. He went over to chemistry in '61 and continued as assistant professor in the Lawrence School until 1863."

But was he the kind of man who bore grudges? I asked as I used my flat hand to wipe a circle of beer-bottle condensed water from the motel table. Keep it shipshape. Roy refused to talk without a supply of what he regarded as the best sippin' beer in the world, and he had made a long study. One doesn't drink such fine brew, one tastes it. With eyes gleaming, his imposing mind kicked into gear.

"Simply put, Yes. I shall always remember what Bill told me once in private."

Roy referred to William James as Bill, for he had been a close student and friend. Roy is somewhat unique in that he had studied logic with Peirce (unofficially, of course) and philosophical psychology (officially) with James. I can't think of anyone else who was a close student and friend of both men.

"He said Eliot had great personal defects, that he was a ruthless autocrat[†] who exhibited tactlessness, meddlesomeness, and a disposition to cherish petty grudges,—and he disliked Charles Peirce. When I heard those words in the late nineties, I wasn't satisfied, so I inquired of some of the senior professors who had started their careers in the sixties. I also did some research, for by then I had become quite interested in Peirce's work. As a freshman philosophy student I sat with awe during his Cambridge Conferences lectures at Mrs. Bull's home[†] on Brattle street in 1898. Bill had confided in me his regret that he had been unsuccessful in getting these lectures approved for delivery on Harvard Yard. I wondered then why an obviously distinguished and original intellect appeared to be barred from campus."

I mentioned that such actions seemed to involve more than a petty grudge. Roy took a long pull from his Steam, performed an almost imperceptible nod of affirmation, then said, "You are absolutely correct, Mr. Eisenstaat! It was far from trifling. It was a magnum. Benjamin Peirce had been nothing less than an instrument of the single greatest disappointment[†] and embarrassment of Eliot's life. Of course you also have to understand that in Eliot's mind Ben and Charles Peirce were politically inseparable because Charles was a junior member of the Bacheans—the closely-knit coterie of scientists who were headed by Dallas Bache you insist upon describing as the Florentine Academy. In other words, in later years Charles inherited some of Ben's rather potent enemies as well as some enemies of Bache and company. In my view, Peirce was extraordinarily brilliant intellectually, scientifically, and philosophically, but completely naive as an in-fighter in academic politics—a capacity in which his father was a master. Achieving mastery in such a field of endeavor entails acquisition of enemies. Peirce was an easy target, which his father's opponents were free to assault after Benjamin's death in 1880, were they so inclined, and some were.

"In school year 1862–63, Eliot was serving as acting dean[†] of the Lawrence Scientific School in view of the departure of Professor Eustis, a West Point man, to participate in the war. The previous year, he had prepared a plan for 'reforming' the School which was a square challenge to the existing order—which is to say, the Cambridge branch of the Bache group, chiefly Ben Peirce and Louie Agassiz. Eliot wanted to regularize courses in place of the individualistic style of instruction then prevailing in the school. This was a threat to Ben and Louie, who preferred a Socratic and personalized approach for pupils in science. Or maybe it would be better to say that those two old bears took offense at a young cub telling them how to conduct a scientific education for their pupils, especially a cub *who had very recently been their pupil.*"

I spoke silently to myself that Eliot seemed to be a major advocate of what I call the factory approach to education. Outwardly I remarked that what Ben and Agassiz favored was the same as my notion of the gentleman scholar. But actually I was imagining Betsey saying it to me with a wry smile and a quick glance in my direction. That little ironic grin of hers cuts right through my soul with a joyful blade, and she knows it, too.

THUNK!

Roy smacked the base of his beer bottle squarely onto the thin resonant table top. The full-bodied sound chased off my day dream.

"Indeed. You can see why this proposal from Eliot attracted the attention of Peirce and Agassiz. They handled the matter gently; with the aid of their friend and former student President Hill it was quietly dismissed. Eliot's idea, by the way, competed with the rather grand plan of the Bache group to remold Harvard[†] as conceived by Agassiz. Among other things they wanted to offer a set of "University Lectures" on top of the regular college course of study. This was the germ of an idea for a graduate school at Harvard.

"But a trend began to attract their attention. For instance, some years earlier Eliot had been an associate of Josiah P. Cooke, Jr., a professor of chemistry in the School; they had even coauthored a manual and shared a lab. But by 1859[†] the two had a serious falling out, and Eliot was forced to move his personal lab into a separate building. Cooke was associated with Ben and was identified with Ben's approach to religion through science, as evidenced in Cooke's 1864 book, *Religion and Chemistry.*

"Then an event Eliot regarded as a vivid professional opportunity appeared in 1861 when the Rumford Professor of Chemistry, Eben N. Horsford, gave up the School teaching lab or was forced out of it because of his mismanagement, it isn't clear which. Eliot took over the lab and made it an organizational success. There began to be talk—instigated by[†] C. W. E.—that he might someday succeed Horsford in all respects.

"In 1863 Horsford resigned entirely, so the Rumford chair was open. Eliot appeared to regard the chair as his due—after all, he had cleaned up the lab and was highly regarded for his administrative abilities. But the Bacheans, now forewarned about Eliot's dispositions and convinced that he lacked serious scientific credentials for such a distinguished position, began urging the candidacy of Wolcott Gibbs, a member of the Bache circle from New York who was regarded by many as the first chemist[†] of the nation. It was true that Eliot had only one article-length publication to his credit—even Charles Peirce had as good a record by 1863. Eliot's paper, which was coauthored by Francis Storer, had been reviewed by a solid chemist as a "pathetic and creditable[†] attempt at research by men without proper training and facilities." In the eyes of Bache's associates, Eliot was not a researcher, merely a plausible teacher and administrator. On the other hand, Gibbs had a distinguished preparation and was midway through a productive career. All of Bache's intimate scientific friends were exceptionally well qualified scientists; indeed that was one of the basic premisses of the group. In June 1863[†] Gibbs was appointed Rumford Professor and in September he was elected by the Lawrence Faculty as their new Dean. The term of Eliot's assistant professorship was to expire soon. President Hill offered him a professorship based upon income from the teaching laboratory he had reformed, but that was beneath Eliot's dignity. He had been humiliated by being passed over for the Rumford chair, but to be offered an under-salaried professorship, the income of which would be based upon his ability to draw students to the lab, he saw as[†] an outrage. Hill tried a second scheme[†] to secure a salary for Eliot by asking his wealthy relatives for donations. If such a thing were possible, this ill-considered move only deepened Eliot's profound nausea at the whole affair. Thus was Eliot in effect sacked from Harvard. It was the greatest[†] disappointment and embarrassment of his life. His close friend Storer wrote to a mutual acquaintance that Eliot had been "victimized by that damned Swiss[†] adventurer"—Agassiz. He should have added Ben Peirce's name as well, for Peirce and Agassiz were of one mind in such matters. Clearly the Cambridge Friends of Bache and their allies ruled Harvard in 1863."

I wondered aloud to Roy exactly how Eliot's candidacy had been blocked.

"Of course, there was the matter of Gibbs having much better qualifications, but our lock-step habit of first looking hard at qualifications when hiring an academic was not yet fully established in those days. As you know, hiring the scientifically best-qualified person was one of the articles of faith of the Bache group. Lacking anything of any significance as a scientific qualification, Eliot therefore undertook to bolster his candidacy on other more political foundations. And it is interesting that the Bacheans had an answer for that as well, a kind of response that Eliot eventually surely learned about and that in all likelihood deepened his hatred of Ben and of Charles.

"I don't have the exact words of the Agassiz/Peirce political counterattack on Eliot's supporters, but it involved Ben's apparent knowledge about some seriously negative aspect of Eliot's personal life. Otherwise how can one explain such comments as these from Ben dated one month before the appointment of Gibbs, which I copied out from his correspondence in Widener† Library: 'I had always associated Eliot with the portion of his family in Boston society and regarded him as a gentleman and a man of honour, but I grieve to write that he is far otherwise.'"

I mentioned that Betsey had once confided in me her guess that Jem's homosexuality was somehow connected with Eliot, who had been Jem's friend for many years. Roy raised his shoulders silently, as a way to say, "I don't know." Or maybe he meant, "No comment."

What then became† of Eliot immediately after losing his professorial status? That was my fully spoken question to Roy.

"He withdrew into his family, having decided upon a grand tour of the continent to study educational policies there. In a few years he returned to a professorial appointment at the newly created Massachusetts Institute of Technology. Of course, as you know, Harvard was to see him become its president for forty years beginning in 1869.

"It is interesting to reflect upon Peirce's banishment from Harvard during most of Eliot's presidency, to see it as but a token of the general type. I particularly have in mind, as another token, Emerson's banishment following the Harvard Divinity School Address he delivered in the spring of 1838. Although perhaps† not intended as such, the address was widely taken as an attack upon Massachusetts Unitarianism in its own academic stronghold. I have always read that masterpiece as an attack upon false religion of any stripe. To be sure, there was a huge outcry, and for a while the popular view was that Emerson was a dangerous man. He was blocked from speaking at Harvard for many years. And he did not. It is easy in the twentieth century to forget how closely Harvard and other universities were tied to church or other orthodoxies of the nineteenth century. And wherever there are orthodoxies, there also will be so-called dangerous men and women—*dangerous minds*—who are the unorthodox."

By this time we had consumed our quota of two Steam longnecks each per diem. As I got up to go, I told Roy how helpful his insights and comments were. I asked if he would come by my apartment the next day to see if there were any other points I was missing as I worked through Charley's box of manuscript. He didn't say anything. But he did give me a firm handshake as

I stood in his doorway. As I withdrew my hand, he closed the door ever so slowly while looking me straight in the eye. As I turned to stride home through the chilly dusk, I took that as a good sign.

The Chemist

Senatus Universitatis Cantabrigiensis[†]
Academicus In Republica Massachusettensi:
Quum CAROLUS SANDERS PEIRCE,
vir ingenio bono praeditus, moribusque probis ornatus, post usitatum tempus SCIENTIARUM studio impensum, examen rigidum publice subiisset in CHEMIA, et a PROFESSORIBUS esset pro more idoneus dictus ut ad Gradum in Scientia Baccalaureatei admitteretur, SUMMA CUM LAUDE. In cujus rei testimonium, literis hisce, Sigillo Academico munitis die Julii XV, anno Salutis nostrae MDCCLXIII, Reique Publicae Americanae LXXXVIII.
Benjamin Peirce Astron. et Math. Prof., Joseph Lovering Math. et Phil. Nat. Prof., Asa Gray Botan. Prof., Jeffries Wyman Anat. Prof., Josiah P. Cooke Jr. Chem. et Mineral. Prof., Thomas Hill, Prases.

(1893). My method[†] of investigation in philosophy has been condemned as contrary to that by which science has been advanced. An objector holds that a radically different, and thoroughly positivistic method is requisite—a method so intensely positivistic as to exclude all originality. I suppose he will not object to my forming an opinion concerning the methods of science. I was brought up in an atmosphere of scientific inquiry, and have all my life chiefly lived among scientific men. Since 1863 the study which has constantly been before my mind has been upon the nature, strength, and history of methods of scientific thought. In its logical aspect, I have partly considered it in various publications; and in its historical aspect I have long been engaged in a treatise about[†] it. My critic says that I am "very positivistic in my logic of science." This is a singular misapprehension. Few of the great scientific minds with whom I have come into personal contact, and from whom I endeavored to learn, were disposed to contemn originality or the ideal part of the mind's work in investigation; and those few, it was easy to see, really breathed an atmosphere of ideas which were so incessantly present that they were unconscious of them. Were I to name those of my teachers who were most positivistic in theory a smile would be excited. My own historical studies, which have been somewhat minutely critical, have, on the whole, confirmed the views of Whewell, the only man of philosophical power conjoined with scientific training who had made a comprehensive survey of the whole course of science, that progress in science depends upon the observation of the right facts by minds <u>furnished with appropriate ideas</u>. My long investigation of the logical process of scientific reasoning

led me many years ago to the conclusion that science is nothing but a development of our natural instincts. So much for my _theory_ of scientific logic. It is as totally opposed as anything can be to my critic's theory that originality is out of place in science.

But in my _practice_ of scientific reasoning I am accused of being a "constructionist"; that is, a theorizer unguided by indications from observation or accepted facts. To a mind upon whom that celebrated and splendid chapter of Kant upon the architectonical method failed to make a deep impression I may appear so; but _travesty_ is in truth hardly too strong a word to describe that account of my method.

Let me sum up the method my critic recommends. Eschew originality is its pious formula; do not think for yourself, nor countenance results obtained by original minds. Distrust them; they are not safe men. Leave originality to mathematicians and their breed, to poets, and to all those who seek the sad notoriety of having unsettled belief. Flee all philosophies which smack of this aberrant nineteenth century.

Kepler came very close to realizing my ideal of the scientific method; and, as my father remarked, he was one of the few thinkers who have taken their readers fully into their confidence as to what their method really has been.

I should not feel justified in inflicting upon my readers an autobiographical account of my own course of thought; but some things my critic's accusations force me to mention.

My method of attacking all problems has ever been to begin with an historical and rational inquiry into the special method adapted to the special problem. This is the essence of my architectonical proceeding. To look an inch before one's nose involves originality: therefore, it is wrong to have a conscious method says my critic. But further, in regard to philosophy, not only the methods, but the elementary ideas which are to enter into those methods, should be subjected to careful preliminary examination. This, especially, my critic finds very unscientific. It is, undoubtedly, the most characteristic feature of my procedure. Certainly it was not a notion hastily or irreflectively caught up; but is the maturest fruit of a lifetime of reflection upon the methods of science, including those of philosophy; and if it shall be found that one contribution to thought on my part has proved of permanent service, that, I expect, will be the one. This method in nowise teaches that the method and materials for thought are not to be modified in the course of the study of the subject-matter. But instead of taking ideas at haphazard, or being satisfied with those that have been handed down from the good old times, as a mind keenly alive to the dangers of originality would have done, I have undertaken to make a systematic survey of human knowledge in order to find what ideas have, as a fact, proved most fruitful, and to observe the special utilities they have severally fulfilled. A subsidiary object of this survey was to note what the great obstacles are today in the way of the further advance of the different branches of science.

(1893). Miss Maria[†] Fay, a very interesting and spiritual lady, presented me with <u>Substance and Shadow</u> by Henry James, the father. In particular, the obvious solution of the problem of evil is there pointed[†] out. James, the Swedenborgian, says: "It is no doubt very tolerable finite or creaturely love to love one's own in another, to love another for his conformity to one's self; but nothing can be in more flagrant contrast with the creative Love, all whose tenderness <u>ex vi termini</u> must be reserved only for what intrinsically is most bitterly hostile and negative to itself" (p. 442). It is a pity he had not filled his pages with things like this, as he was able easily to do, instead of scolding at his reader and at people generally, until the physics of creation was well-nigh forgot. I must deduct, however, from what I just wrote: obviously no genius could make his every sentence as sublime as one which discloses for the problem of evil its everlasting solution.

As his summa cum laude graduate degree from the Lawrence School shows, Charley dug deeply into his chemical studies in 1863 and earlier. Thus he had little time for philosophy, although we have seen that he learned the intellectual solution to the problem of evil—how a loving, merciful, omnipotent, and omniscient God could allow evil to be real in the world.

His father had been experiencing a version of natural evil, the uniquely intense pain of kidney stones, which was a problem he had struggled against[†] for several months. As he told The Chief, he did not seek relief in philosophy.

> God bless[†] you. I am stupider than ever—for I am just waking up from a blow which I have been having for the last three days—a most dissipated blow in which I have been in a regular state of intoxication from opium and ether for the whole time—and I am still so permeated with the direful forms of the intoxicating phials that I nearly hate myself. It was to save me from suffering during one of my ancient attacks from one of the seven devils who has taken up his abode in my kidneys. Poor fellow! He is more to be pitied than I am.
>
> Agassiz is again troubled with boils near and upon his head—and the doctor thinks he needs to be exceedingly careful of himself.
>
> Sarah has been making me anxious about herself on account of the very heavy fits of coughing which have shaken her almost to pieces, after going to bed, and the first half of the night—I hope that the Dr.'s cough mixture will do her good.

If this natural evil were not enough, Ben was struggling with a more human kind. Benjamin Mills had been rusticated from Harvard to Westford, Massachusetts, to resume his studies in a place free from distractions so he could reflect upon his conduct. His father encouraged him to make the most of it.

> My dear† Ben, you complain too much of your present lot. It is not
> manly to suffer yourself in such despondency. Were it punishment,
> you have brought it upon yourself and have no right to complain.
> But it was on the contrary the opportunity which was offered you
> to repair your own errors, and you ought to be thankful that it was
> granted you. It has been a very difficult effort upon the part of your
> parents to enable you to have this opportunity. God bless and
> preserve you.

Rustication† was a standard method for dealing with students whose high spirits interfered with the studies of their classmates. It featured exile to a country parsonage where the perpetrator's studies continued under ministerial supervision. It was a definite improvement over student flogging, common in Cotton Mather's time, or boxing, widely used as late as 1718. This latter form of punishment required the student to kneel; he was then slapped sharply on the ear. Ugh! The problem of evil, indeed!

President Hill did establish a part of the Florentine plan for improvement of Harvard when he instituted† the University Lectures. These featured campus professors—Agassiz and Ben were prominent in participation†—as well as distinguished off-campus figures.

Roy abruptly appeared at my place somewhat in the spirit of my showing up at his. After small talk, we began pursuing different chores. I continued working up the box materials while he started reading around the large library I have in my loft. We were growing closer, and to show my extreme good faith I told him he was to have free roaming rights in my office, including looking over my shoulder when I write—something I allow no one else to do, not even Betsey, although she does it sometimes to annoy me, to test if I am still alive. I made sure that he clearly understood the significance of the privilege.

As I began to write "and nothing else of interest happened to Charley in 1863," or words to that effect, Roy walked over, looked, and said, "A major event is missing. Peirce once told me that he found his adult scientific/philosophic public voice late in 1863. Isn't there anything in the box about that?"

There was nothing in Peirce's box about what Roy eventually explained as the topic of his remark: Charley's Cambridge High School Reunion Oration. So I did some library research. I was sceptical about finding anything, because an oration is a fleeting memorate. But I did promptly find an announcement in the *Cambridge Chronicle*.

bridge Chronicle

CAMBRIDGE HIGH SCHOOL
ASSOCIATION
ELEVENTH ANNUAL REUNION[†]

This Association will celebrate their
Eleventh Annual Reunion at the City Hall,
Cambridge, on Thursday evening, November 12. The exercise will consist of an Oration "The Place of Our Age in the History
of Civilization" by Charles S. Peirce, a
Poem by Mrs. Barrows, after which there
will be a Collation, a Special Business
Meeting, and reading of the Chronicles.

The same hometown newspaper on the fourteenth reported[†] that the "oration
by Mr. Charles S. Peirce, abounding in metaphysics and profoundity of
thought, was quite a scholarly production." Looks like he jumped back into
philosophizing soon after finishing up chemistry. After some more grubbing
around in Charley's non-box manuscripts, I found this.

*Earlier I had undertaken[†] a humble and passionate study of Kant's Critic of
the Pure Reason. With nobody to direct me to proper preparatory studies, I
worked over the book with the ardor of youth incessantly by day and by night
for long formative years. On lines laid down by that master, I began to think for
myself, setting out, as he did, from Formal Logic. That path inevitably led me
to an objective logic: and the first thing I printed was a Hegel-like paper on the
philosophy of history, with predictions as to the subsequent course of events. I
did not recognize the affinity of my thought to Hegel's, because in all details it
was entirely different, and because his weak logic and pretentiousness repelled
me then more than now. But my father's influence and the study of mathematics made me dissatisfied with the insecurity of my reasoning. I seemed to see
that methods of investigation ought to be the first object of study. So I assidu-
ously devoted three years to chemistry, which I had already studied as a boy,
and afterwards took up other natural sciences, always attending principally to
methods. I then began to read more widely in philosophy.*

My suspicion was that the Hegel-like paper on the philosophy of history
was Charley's Cambridge High School Reunion Oration, so I redoubled my
efforts to discover a record of it.

The next day I travelled to Harvard where I spent several difficult hours in Houghton Library looking at the microfilm of Peirce's manuscripts. I called Betsey about dark to tell her I planned to skip supper and stay late to search some more. She said, "You shouldn't do that because we are going to have chili and beans with *muy calliente* green peppers, your favorite. But you do sound depressed. Where have you been looking?"

I said I had looked through a big part of the Peirce manuscripts on microfilm and that my eyeballs felt like the inside of an Omnimax or Cinerama theater.

"What about the *Cambridge Chronicle* newspaper itself? Could they have printed the speech if they liked it so well?"

Sounded like a good abduction to me. (I'm accustomed to using Charley's term—abduction—for that part of the scientific method which is otherwise known as guessing.) So I looked, and doggone there it was. I made supper on time after all. Only extracts were printed, but even they belong here among the sequence of papers in Charley's box, because I think you will agree that Roy was correct. A few days later during a return trip to my library, Roy added this comment by way of evaluating Charley's first big scientific/philosophic public speech:

"While Peirce was to revise a number of ideas in it as his mature work began to flow, its singular aspect is a powerful voice of originality which his audience could not have missed. Furthermore, it is easy to discern threads reaching from his father, from Agassiz, from Cooke, from Emerson, and from his new wife, Harriett Melusina Fay—the Episcopalian minister's daughter."

I'm grateful for that clarification from Roy. It must have been a wonderful old-style elocution when delivered.

LADIES AND GENTLEMEN[†] OF THE HIGH SCHOOL ASSOCIATION:—In attempting to address you, I feel keenly the disadvantage of never having made any matter of general interest a special study. I am, therefore, forced to select a topic on which I have scarcely a right to an original opinion—certainly not to urge my opinion as entitled to much credit. I beg you, then, to regard whatever I say on THE PLACE OF OUR AGE IN THE HISTORY OF CIVILIZATION, as such a suggestion as might be put forth in conversation, and nothing more.

By our age I mean the 17th, 18th, and 19th centuries. There are those who, dazzled by the steam-engine and the telegraph, regard the nineteenth century as something sui generis. But this I think is doing injustice to ourselves.

Bring Bacon or Newton here, and display to him the wonders our century has to show, and he will tell you, "All this is remarkable and deeply interesting, but it is not surprising. I knew," he will say, "that all this or something very like it must come at this time, for it is nothing more than the certain consequences of the principles laid down by me and my contemporaries for your guidance." Either of them will say this. But now let us turn from the Century to the Age, (reckoning from the settlement of Jamestown.) Let us bring the sublimest intellect that ever shone before, and what would Dante say? Let him trace the rise of constitutional government, see a down-trodden people steadily bend a haughty dynasty to obedience, give it laws and bring it to trial and execution, and finally reduce it to a convenient cipher; let him see the human mind try its religion in a blazing fire, expose the falsity of its history, the impossibility of its miracles, the humanity of its revelations; and then let him see the restless boundary of man's power extending over the outward world, see him dashing through time, conversing through immense distances, doing violence to the lightning, and living in such a fire of activity as less salamandrine generations could have endured; and he who viewed Hell without dismay would fall to the earth quailing before the terrific might of intellect which God has scattered broadcast over this whole age. I equally disagree with those who think we are living in the age of the reformation. I do so on the ground that there was nothing rationalistic in the tendency of that age. In our time, if we wish to found a new government, religion, or art, we begin at first principles, consider the philosophy of our object and follow it out.

The Reformation was a struggle of humanity to regain its rightful master; in our day the aim is absolute liberty. From the moment when the ball of human progress received its first impetus from the mighty hands of Descartes, of Bacon, and of Galileo,—we hear, as the very sound of the stroke, the decisive protest against any authority, however venerable—against any arbiter of truth except our own reason. Descartes is the father of modern metaphysics, and you know it was he who introduced the term "philosophic doubt"; he, first, declaring that a man should begin every investigation entirely without doubt; and he followed a completely independent train of thought, as though, before him, nobody had ever thought anything correctly. Bacon, also, respects no philosophers except certain Greeks whose works are lost.

The human mind having been emancipated by these great skeptics, works of great originality were speedily produced, so that the same century saw the productions of Hobbes, Cudworth, Malebranche, Spinoza, Locke, Leibnitz, and Newton. The effects of these works was stupendous. Every question that the human mind had to ask seemed at once answered, and that too by works of such greatness of thought and power of logic, that the attention of every reasoning mind was engrossed by them. Their vastness, indeed, was overwhelming; so complete were they, so true, so profound, that, at first, they seemed to check originality. In the first half of the eighteenth century scarcely anything new seems to have been produced.

At last, however, the ball of progress was struck again. And by whom? By another, more powerful doubter, the immortal Hume. In his day, the philosophical world was divided between the doctrines of Leibnitz and Locke, the former of whom maintained the existence of innate ideas while the latter rejected them. Hume, accepting the latter doctrine, which was prevalent in England, asked

"How do we know that every change has a cause?" He demonstrated by invincible logic, that upon Locke's system, it was impossible to prove this, and that it ought not to be admitted as a principle at all. Of course, the doctrine of a first cause and the very idea of miracles, vanish with the notion of causality.

Immanuel Kant was reposing in a firm belief in the metaphysics of Leibnitz as theologized by Wolff when he first read the book of Hume. How many scholastics, nay how many theologians of our own day would have done otherwise than say, "Behold the fruit of our opponent's system of philosophy!" This mean, degraded spirit, which is eager to answer an opponent and still remain the slave of error, was far from being Kant's. He set about asking his own philosophy the question that Hume had asked of Locke's. "We say that this and the other are innate ideas," he said, "but how do we know that our innate ideas are true?"

The book in which he embodied the discussion of this question is, perhaps, the greatest work of the human intellect. All later philosophies are to be classified according to the ideas contained in it, for it is all the direct result of this production. And in these later philosophies, whether we consider their profundity or their number, our age ranges far above all others put together. This wonderful fecundity of thought, I say, is the direct result of Kant's Kritik; and it is to be explained by the fact that Kant presented a more insoluble doubt than all the rest, and one which has not been answered to this day, for while he showed that our innate ideas of space, time, quantity, cause, possibility, and so on are true, he found himself utterly unable to do this respecting the ideas of Immortality, Freedom, and God. Accordingly, all metaphysicians since his time have been endeavoring to remove this difficulty, but not altogether with success. Hegel's system seemed, at first, satisfactory, but its further development resulted in Strauss' Life of Jesus, against which the human soul, the datum upon which he proceeded, itself cried out; the sense of mankind, which he had elevated into a God, itself repudiated the claim. We thus see, however, that all the progress we have made in philosophy, that is, all that has been made since the Greeks, is the result of that methodical scepticism which is the first element of human freedom.

If, then, all the glory of our age has sprung from a spirit of Scepticism and Irreverence, it is easy to say where its faults are to be found.

Modern progress having been detached from its ancient mother by the dark ages, that fearful parturition, has since now lived a self-sustaining life. Its growth, its outline, its strength are all its own; influenced to some degree, by its parent, but only through an exterior medium. The only cord which ever bound them, and which belonged to either, is Christianity. Since the beginning of Christianity the growth of civilization has had six stages.

The 1st is the Age of the Rise of Christianity, the 2d is the Age of the Migrations of the Barbarians, the 3d is the Age of the Establishment of Modern Nations, the 4th is the Age of the Crusades, the 5th is the Age of the Reformation, and the 6th is our own age, or as we are fond of calling it, the Age of Reason.

It seems to me apparent that all this civilization is the work of Christianity. If it is not so clear respecting the progress of our own age, it is because we have not seen the termination of it, and do not understand the philosophy of it.

Christianity is not a doctrine, or possible law; it is an actual law—a kingdom. And a kingdom over what? "All things shall be put under his feet." What then does it not include? Do you assert that liberty is of any value? "His service is perfect freedom." If we are Christians it seems to me we must believe that Christ is now directing the course of history and presiding over the destinies of kings, and that there is no branch of the public weal which does not come within the bounds of his realm. And civilization is nothing but Christianity on the grand scale.

Now let us see if Christianity, the plot of History, does not follow determinate laws in its development, so that from a consideration of them we can gather where we are and whither we are tending.

Religion ought not to be regarded either as a subjective or an objective phenomenon. That is to say, it is neither something within us nor yet altogether without us—but bears rather a third relation to us, namely, that of existing in our communion with another being. Nevertheless, religion may be revealed in either of the three ways—by an inward self-development, or by seeing it about us, or by a personal communication from the Most High.

Every object is obliged to appear under a certain set of forms. The most familiar exemplification of these is found in a proposition*. Every statement may be regarded as an object, that is it is something outside of us which we can know. The first condition of a statement is that it shall state something,—that it shall have a predicate. But this implies a whole series of conditions previously to the statement of the proposition, which shall enable you to comprehend the notion which I wish to convey as well as the language in which I convey it. Before a man can read a book, he must understand the meaning of terms, that is, he must already have the elements of the thought which the book propounds. In the same way, before a man can hear the voice of God or even comprehend an example of religion he must have a notion of what religion is, and that implies that he must previously have had an inward revelation of religion. In compliance with this condition, both heathen and Jews, before the birth of Christ, had attained to the idea of an intimate union of humanity with Deity, such that they should be brought into ordinated harmony, in which the creature should be so completely in unison with the creator that all his motions should be brought under law, as much as inanimate natures are, and yet that man should in this very subjection and passivity find his highest freedom, activity, and rounded completion. This, then, is the predicate of the formula by which I propose to express Christianity—and I will call it the Kingdom of heaven.*

After the inward revelation, comes the objective revelation, and the latter must itself be the culmination of the former, for bearing as it must a higher message it must itself act suggestively in order that its meaning may be perceived. This culminating point will be the phenomenon of perfection in such a form that man can see and know it; that is, it must be perfection in human form. The first condition, therefore, the enunciation of the predicate, was fulfilled in the birth of Christ.

The most striking tendency of our age is our materialistic tendency. We see it in the development of the material arts and the material sciences; in the desire to see all our theories, philosophical or moral, exemplified in the material world, and the tendency to value the system only for the practice. This tendency seems to be opposed to another great movement of our age, the idealistic movement. The idealist regards abstractions as having a real existence.— Hence, he places as much value on them as on things. Moreover, by his wide and deep study of the human mind he has proved that the knowledge of things can only be attained by the knowledge of ideas. This truth is very distasteful to the materialist. His object being the ideas contained in things, there is nothing that he would more carefully eradicate than any admixture of ideas from our own minds; so that it seems like overturning natural science altogether to tell him that all truth is attained by such an admixture. He thinks at least that nothing more than common sense should be admitted from the mind. This amounts to admitting the loose ideas of the untrained intellect into his science, but to refuse admission to such as have been exercised, strengthened and developed. He retorts that the conjunction of speculation with science has constantly led to error. Be it so; but then it is only by means of idealism that truth is possible in science. Human learning must fail somewhere. Materialism fails on the side of incompleteness. Idealism always presents a systematic totality, but it must always have some vagueness and thus lead to error.—Materialism is destitute of a philosophy. Thus it is necessarily one-sided. It misunderstands its relations to idealism; it misunderstands the nature of its own logic. But if materialism without idealism is blind, idealism without materialism is void. Look through the wonderful philosophies of this age and you will find in every one of them evidences that their novel conceptions have been to a very large extent suggested by physical sciences. In one point of view indeed, pure a priori reasoning is a misnomer; it is as much as to say analysis with nothing to analyze. Analysis of what? I ask. Of those ideas which no man is without. Of common sense. But why common *sense? Metaphysics stands in need of all the phases of thought of that uncommon sense which results from the physical sciences in order to comprehend perfectly the conceptions of the mind. So much so that I think that a due recognition of the obligations of the idealists to natural science will show that even their claims will receive a just award if we interpret the whole greatness of our age according to this materialistic tendency.*

See too, what truth, and what peculiarly Christian truth there is in this tendency. There are two fields of human learning, the science of outward things and the science of the mind itself. Now materialism opposes itself to this latter; not as an ornamental study, a regulative study, or an educative study, but as having any value or truth in itself. It is the assertion that man was not made to turn his eye inward, was not made for himself alone, but for the sake of what he should do in the outward world. And I will now ask how Christianity will appear if we look upon it from a materialistic point of view? There is one aspect which it certainly will not present; there will be no German refining away of Christ into a class or into self. It will be inclined to slight the subtleties of dogmas and look upon dogmas in a common sense way. True religion, it will think, consists in more than a mere dogma, in visiting the fatherless and the widows and in keeping ourselves unspotted from the world. It will say that Christianity reaches beyond even that, reaches beyond the good conscience, beyond the individual life; must transfuse itself through all human law— through the social organization, the nation, the relationships of the peoples and races.

The fulcrum has yet to be found that shall enable the lever of love to move the world. Is our age never to end? As man cannot do two things at once, so mankind cannot do two things at once. Now Lord Bacon, our great master, has said, that the _end_ of science is the glory of God, and the use of man. If then, this is so, action is higher than reason, for it is its purpose; and to say that it is not, is the essence of selfishness and atheism. So then our age shall end; and, indeed, the question is not so much why should it not, as why should it continue. What sufficient motive is there for man, a being in whom the natural impulse is—first to sensation, then reasoning, then imagination, then desire, then action—to stop at reasoning, as he has been doing for the last 250 years. It is unnatural, and cannot last. Man must go on to use those powers and energies that have been given him, in order that he may impress nature with his own intellect, converse and not merely listen.

First there was the egoistical state when man arbitrarily imagined perfection, now is the idistical stage when he observes it. Hereafter must be the more glorious tuistical stage when he shall be in communion with her. And this is exactly what, step by step, we are coming to. For if you will recur a moment to my dry analysis of the formula of Christianity, you will perceive that the conclusions of the preceeding ages have answered three kinds of questions concerning that proposition. Two were metaphysical, what is its predicate and what is its subject? two were dynamical; is it hypothetical or actual, and is it categorical or conditional? two were mathematical; what is its quality and what is its quantity?

And now there are questions of but one kind more that remain to be asked, and they are physical. And they are two. The first is, is Christianity a fact of consciousness merely, or one of the external world? And this shall be answered by the conclusion of our own age. The second is, is this predicate true to the understanding merely, or also to the sense? And this, if we may look forward so far, will be answered by Christ's coming to rule his kingdom in person. And when that occurs, religion will no longer be presented objectively, but we shall receive it by direct communication with him.

When the conclusion of our age comes, and scepticism and materialism have done their perfect work, we shall have a far greater faith than ever before. For then man will see God's wisdom and mercy, not only in every event of his own life, but in that of the gorilla, the lion, the fish, the polyp, the tree, the crystal, the grain of dust, the atom. He will see that each one of these has an inward existence of its own, for which God loves it, and that He has given to it a nature of endless perfectibility. He will see the folly of saying that nature was created for his use.—He will see that God has no other creation than his children. So the poet in our days,—and the true poet is the true prophet—personifies everything, not rhetorically but in his own feeling.—He tells us that he feels an affinity for nature, and loves the stone or the drop of water. But the time is coming when there shall be no more poetry, for that which was poetically divined shall be scientifically known. It is true that the progress of science may die away, but then its essence will have been extracted. This cessation itself will give us time to see that cosmos, that aesthetic view of science which Humboldt prematurely conceived. Physics will have made us familiar with the body of all things, and the unity of the body of all; natural history will have shown us the soul of all things in their infinite and amiable idiosyncrasies. Philosophy will have taught us that it is this all which constitutes the church. Ah! what a heavenly harmony will that be when all the sciences, one as viol, another as flute, another as trump, shall peal forth in that majestic symphony of which the noble organ of astronomy forever sounds the theme.

Teacher

(1910). I came substantially† to my mature views on probability in the year 1864, by long and deep reflexion on the chapters about it in Boole's _Laws of Thought_, although I regarded Boole's own views as insufficiently considered. I have found mathematicians to be, by far, the best reasoners of any social class that excludes them; and yet it seems that an exclusive absorption in their studies, which more than any others demand exclusive devotion, tends to blind them to other kinds of reasoning.

1865, January 1
My book on the Natural History of Words† was begun just six years ago. Since that time my ideas of classification are greatly developed; still I think that this is a good beginning. Words belong (as it now seems to me) to the Kingdom of Representations and the Type of _Symbols_. They constitute I suppose—at least, any one language no more than constitutes—a particular _class_ of that Branch.

They are divisible into orders on the ground of comprehensibility. Thus words denoting elements of phenomena will be the highest order. Then words denoting artificial objects. Third words denoting natural objects. Abstract words *will come under the highest order that it can come under. Thus Nastiness must come into the 1st order. Handiness into the second, &c. Emotional words generally belong to the 1st order, Ah! being a term for emotion in general.*

The words of any order denote entirely different things as Sensation & Thought will constitute families, the larger differences as Sight & Hearing genera, the smaller differences as Blue & Red, species.

Word reached Charley[†] that in the spring of 1865 he was to give a set of University Lectures on the Logic of Science, his debut at Harvard. In view of this, a question was nagging at me: Why would he want to go into university teaching and lecturing? Clearly he could have had the support of his politically influential father. But I doubt Charley would have used that connection to push himself forward as a teacher unless he had qualifications and inclinations in that direction.

Not knowing how to resolve this puzzle, I asked Roy. I had invited him to spend several days of concentrated study and conversation in our apartment, going through the sequence of Charley's box in this interesting period surrounding 1865. The temptation was all the Steam he wanted and several meals featuring Betsey's scones. Somehow she had learned her grammarrie (the magical art of which scone-making is a part) in the way of the auld countrie, and Roy admired them just as much as Nero Wolfe liked peanut-fed yearling pork. Besides, we had a comfortable guest room that we had helped Roy set up in the Spartan style that he favored.

"The answer is simple, Mr. Eisenstaat. He *was* a teacher, a great one. If one worked *seriously* with Peirce for a while as a student, eventually one was sure to be transformed—'born again' in a secular sense. He had a startling natural capacity for connecting to a student on the learner's own terms, then aiding that person to develop toward becoming self-sustaining. He didn't spoon-feed, nor force-feed, nor indoctrinate, nor participate in factory-like schooling. That is to say, he didn't do all the unfortunate things that today—in the era after the so-called reforms of *iste damnatus* Eliot—are regarded as routine and appropriate in what is known as higher education. In various subtle ways Peirce helped his wards to become independent inquirers, which is to say, self-controlled humble students of the cosmos. By the way, that often misunderstood phrase means 'the egotistic self under control,' or I suppose one could also translate it as 'scientific disinterest,' or even as 'impersonal.' Lacking that quality, one cannot really be a man or woman of science. Without it, one is merely a technician, a plumber for hire.

"His pedagogical abilities certainly were manifest in face-to-face exchanges and lectures, but they still make contact with attentive readers of even his most abstract writings, even today after his death. He was a natural and gifted practitioner of Socratic[†] Maieutic. Indeed, Peirce defined 'maieutic' for *The Century Dictionary*. Reflect upon this, Eisenstaat."

Maybe I was no longer a midshipman in his eyes. Before today he had always addressed me as *Mister* Eisenstaat.

"Compare 'You must be born again,' which seems to say that Jesus was a maieute or therapeute. Maieusis is the method of 'teaching' of persons like Weil, Buber, Jesus, Wittgenstein, or Peirce. Watching a student begin to learn *independently* is in itself an extremely satisfying event.

"WAIT!"

Roy whacked the conference table in my study with an open fist. I hadn't seen him this agitated since I met him. I thought he was a cool Puritan. Maybe this was his French side.

"That isn't the right language. Satisfaction is the wrong concept because it implies that such a 'teacher' somehow deserves credit. It would be better to say that a Woman of Calling who had been considered a teacher genuflects toward the intelligence of the Kosmos embodied perhaps for the first time in a nearby so-called student who has just shed the rituals of sham education and has begun to engage in true self-motivated learning. I insist upon a strong distinction between genuine attentive learning versus effort directed merely at achieving high grades or academic honors. Academic distinction is too frequently based on something like muscular effort, whereas the onset of genuine learning[†] is an act of the spirit. In such moments there is no teacher and no student. Those roles are discarded as mere expediencies, no longer required. Both creatures simply stand as equals before the problem, in the same sense as we say in the United States that citizens stand equal before the law. I know all this from my own experience with Peirce. And I know it from conversation with other students whom he taught—James of course, plus Ladd, Jastrow, Franklin, Royce, Mitchell, indirectly Dewey, Marquand, Judge Russell, Lathrop."

I remarked in a know-it-all tone, *Those others may have been, but James wasn't Peirce's student.*

"Yes, I know that is the usual picture." Roy stood up so he could look down at me. This gave him a peculiar authority of posture compared to my couch-potato slump. "You may be surprised to learn how Bill James felt in this respect which I will convey to you in a roundabout way.

"I often visited Mrs. Peirce at the Peirce home in Milford during the '20s and early '30s when I was in Bryn Mawr."

You visited Juliette Peirce!!!?

Somehow I was now standing, no doubt with every body sign registering eager surprise. Damn. I was ashamed to have lost my Choctaw cool. Betsey, who was bringing in another load of scones, grimaced at my impolite outburst then whacked me on the upper arm so hard that I fell back into my chair. I regained some composure, and looking up into Roy's passive face, I sputtered, "I'm sorry; I hope you understand we've been struggling to learn something about Juliette Peirce and her origins, and we've come up with a big, fat zero. In particular we have never spoken with anyone who had met her."

"You should feel no shame, because probably no one else now alive knows the answers to those questions." Roy's tone was businesslike, signifying that I could again rest confidently in his good graces.

"Do you know anything about her past, Roy?"

"Yes, I do."

Pause.

"No such person as the one you call Juliette existed. But that is another story separate from the present topic. I will be glad to explain my thoughts to you on that subject, but first let me finish the current account."

We had no choice, so Betsey and I steeled ourselves to wait while hearing about the present topic.

"As I was about to say, I considered it necessary occasionally to drive to Milford, only four counties up the right bank of the Delaware, to check on her welfare, to care for the widow of my friend and teacher. One has a moral duty to care for the widows and orphans of fallen brethren. It was uplifting to see how she was invigorated to converse with anybody who had been one of Peirce's students. We also corresponded a bit. I can remember one of her letters to me received shortly before she died in 1934—you are welcome to put it in your book. It states the matter more succinctly than even I could do based upon my personal contacts with James, who told me for his part of it much the same thing. You no doubt recall that the first Harvard University Press volume of Peirce's papers had appeared at last in 1931—the so-called *Collected Papers*—and that four of the final eight volumes were in the bookstores by 1933. I think you also know Mrs. Peirce's command of English was none too good."

"I can remember every word of her letter."

I asked Roy to write it down so we could add it to the box. He picked up the lap board from Charley's box looking for all the world as if he knew exactly how to use it—indeed—*had* used it many times. He sat down on my straight-backed Harvard chair, expertly adjusted the board to his lap. Betsey handed him a few sheets of typing paper, which he laid on. With his black, extra-fine Pilot rolling-ball pen and no effort at all, he wrote out the following from his prodigious memory:

> When my husband and I[†] met with financial losses Prof. James promoted a small pension to enable my husband to finish his book. I absolutely refused my share and stated that when one is brought up to give, one cannot take. He was much disappointed but he insisted upon me managing the money for my husband on account

of his broken down health and that there was no charity in it and that he was under great obligation to my husband.

When they entered college, James studied for Dr. of Medicine. They were great chums since childhood and my husband remarked to James, "You are not qualified to carve people. I am going to produce the finest psychologist out of you." He certainly succeeded and James gave me the same version of it, hence his gratitude to my husband. Harry James is most anxious to acquire from me the early correspondence and lessons between the two men and he offered to buy them, but he will never get them for instead of trying to assist me in urging Harvard to compel them to give me my entitled royalty he is blocking my claim in standing by that scoundrel Woods, who had claimed he had bought it but former President Lowell has eliminated that in assuring me that by my written proofs I had not sold it, but that I must wait until the $18,000.00 donation and subscription was recovered. They have had that amount for twenty years and the interest thereon. My answer was "In waiting for such a length of time, one could have rattled the nuts from the tree with my bones." I ascertained from the Century Company that on such a manuscript they advance money to the writer and the royalty on such book would yield, at least, twenty to thirty per cent. Their offer is now the magnificent sum of $25.00 per month and knowing I am not for long, but refused me the royalty.

As he handed it over, he continued the story.

"Charles Hartshorne, a fellow Harvard Ph.D. and one of the editors of Peirce's papers in the six-volume Harvard edition, once told me at an American Philosophical Association meeting that when he was working with the papers in the twenties, the James family had asked him to destroy some of Peirce's correspondence[†] to them. As he remembered: he took it from them, destroyed some, and kept the rest.

"The sequence of events goes like this. Bill James first met Peirce[†] in 1861 when Charles assisted Bill with Chemistry during Bill's first year at Lawrence Scientific School. They talked philosophy to some extent[†] then, but James had resolved to go on into Harvard Medical[†] School, so it was only an avocation for him at that time. He did next enter Harvard Medical, which was quite the academic joke[†] in those days. His Cambridge studies were interrupted when he joined Louie Agassiz on a biological expedition[†] to Brazil in 1865. Bill became ill in South America and was forced to leave for home before the main party. As he returned to the U.S., he reflected that he wanted to resume active discussion[†] of philosophy. It just happened that Charles and Zina Peirce were planning to start their own private school[†] at this time. So Peirce took on Bill as a private student which began the process of Bill's move from Med-

17. William James, 1858
"Bill James first met Peirce in 1861."
James Collection, Houghton Library, Harvard University
By permission, Houghton Library and Mr. Bay James

icine to Psychology and Philosophy, just as Mrs. Peirce described. All this co-incided with Bill's family moving into 20 Quincy[†] Street, next door to Ben Peirce's house, and only a few blocks from the house of Charles and Zina at tiny little Arrow Street. After the Jameses moved to Quincy Street, Charles became an intimate[†] of the family, with familiar access to their home. Charles particularly revelled in the philosophic company of Henry James Senior, the

Swedenborgian. So while Charles was tutoring Bill in psychology and philosophy, Charles was absorbing from the mind of Henry Senior.

"This is the debt that Bill had toward Peirce. Through Peirce's efforts, which I will deign naming teaching, he nurtured Bill's growing philosophical abilities and helped him to move out of medicine into the endeavors in psychology and philosophy that would later constitute his distinguished career. Thus it is that you can see that Mrs. Peirce was exactly right about the debt which Bill owed Charles. It was much more than compassion for a penurious friend, which is a form of pity. I describe it as the feeling a successful student has toward the person who successfully taught, these terms of course being understood in their deeper senses, all of which is a feeling of great admiration and gratitude and has little directly to do with pity or compassion. As Mrs. Peirce said, it was not charity but repayment of a debt."

Roy turned his darkly gleaming eyes upon Betsey.

"Do you know the Hippocratic Oath, Darbey?"

She nodded yes, as a little girl would do.

"Recite it!"

It was a sharp order, barked out by a ship's captain. She surprised me. She had it. She spoke automatically, that is, without considering. The words came as they come to an oracle. I had never seen her speak with this power.

"I swear by Apollo the physician, by Aesculapius, Hygeia, and Panacea, and I take to witness all the gods, all the goddesses, to keep according to my ability and my judgment the following Oath: To consider dear to me as my parents him who taught me this art; to live in common with him and if necessary to share my goods with him. . . ."

Roy held up his hand to stop her. It was shaking ever so slightly. Betsey's visage lost its shine. The oracle-spell ended as sharply as it had appeared.

"Of course he did not teach medicine to Bill, but he did bring him out of medicine; he did teach him philosophy and psychology. The principle is the same."

Betsey's clinical radar picked up the tiny atypical palsy. No doubt she interpreted that Roy had shown at least one sign of tiring.

"All persons intimate to *this* household are now required to take an afternoon siesta by order of the ship's medical officer." Betsey pointed to a nearby wall that contained her diplomas and certificate as Fellow of the American Academy of Nurse Practitioners. Obediently we adjourned each to an easy chair in our sitting room.

It is an excellent Latino tradition I learned as a youngster working in the Johnson grass hay fields of Oklahoma. I never turned it down. Besides I don't contradict Betsey's nursing judgment.

I only dozed for a half hour. I snuck past the other two reclining-chair snorers to get back at Charley's box in my lofted study. There I found this which seemed to confirm all that Roy had told us, but from Peirce's perspective:

In the sixties[†] I started a little club called the Metaphysical Club. It seldom if ever had more than half a dozen present. Wright was the strongest member and probably I was next. Nicholas St. John Green was a marvelously strong intelligence. Then there was Frank Abbot, William James, and others. It was there that the name and the doctrine of pragmatism saw the light. There was in particular one paper of mine that was much admired and the ms. went around to different members who wished to go over it more closely than they could do in hearing it read.

Days later Betsey and I tried to gain an overview of this matter. My mind went back to some of Charley's obituaries and other remarks from that period and remarks even common today, most of which suggest that the relation between James and Peirce was that of a philanthropist toward a supposed psychically crippled charity case. Now I wondered silently if Roy was right, that Peirce was James's teacher, who brought him out of medicine into psychology and philosophy. It is certainly clear that by the mid-sixties Charley had been a devotee of the latter two disciplines for almost two decades. I decided to keep an open mind and hope that something more would turn up later. A detective has to be patient, not to mention cautious.

Santiago

I had been wonderfully patient. I was proud to have regained my usual stoic restraint. So after we had eaten and rested, I decided to show off my refurbished self-control. In an unbelievably swave and de-BONE-ur manner that even the legendary Nattily Attired would envy, I asked Roy if he knew the origin or background of Juliette Peirce. He scratched his chin while wrinkling his brow and puffing out his lower lip. Quite an exercise in facial gymnastics. I guess he was deciding whether to trust me. Or maybe it was mild punishment for my previous outburst. After that microexpression of hesitation, he began to speak in a professorial tone.

"To talk of knowing is perhaps too strong. I have an extensive set of thoughts based on a fair amount of information which I obtained from Peirce or from Mrs. Peirce—whom you call Juliette—or from other persons here and in Europe. You could say this problem has been a modest hobby of mine for many decades, since I first met her in Cambridge when she accompanied Peirce on one of his lecturing trips near the turn of the century. She had a charismatic appearance, and it was clear to any but the cruelest critic that Peirce loved her completely. I can only give you my conjecture. Perhaps in the future you can confirm or disconfirm the hypothesis."

Betsey and I passed none too secret glances between us, for we had experienced nothing but collisions with brick walls on this issue, despite repeated attempts. Apparently there were no records about her in France, and precious little in the United States. Juliette seems to have dropped into Charley's life around 1876 as if fallen freshly from heaven with no passport, no birth certificate, no documentation of any kind—possessing no past, having only a present and a future; she seemed to be a woman without a country. Roy noticed our silent exchange, speared a bite of scone, and while munching he began deploying his proposal.

"I leave aside chronological order, starting instead with what was for me the logical opening of the issue. After I had met Peirce at Mrs. Bull's[†] during his lecture series in 1898, at his suggestion I began reading Schröder's[†] *Vorlesungen über die Algebra der Logik,* a three-volume work which was published in Leipzig. I was routinely looking out a reference to one of Peirce's papers in the bibliography of the first volume, which appeared in 1890, when I noticed an exceedingly curious thing. The heading for the eleven published papers cited there was *Peirce, Charles[†] S(antiago)."*

With a feeling of disappointment that Roy's big hypothesis was a fizzle, I remarked in a routine tone that it was well known that Peirce had taken an additional informal name—Santiago, Saint James—as a tribute to William James, who had organized a pension for him. Roy responded sharply, with the precision and force of a navy captain maneuvering a large vessel into home dock after a long and troublesome voyage.

"Yes, that is what everyone *believes,* thanks to the early unchecked *speculations* of disciples of James such as Bart Perry, expressed only after both James and Peirce were dead. But surely it is not true. For one thing, Peirce and James were going their separate ways for the most part in 1890, and James had raised no pension for Peirce at that time because he didn't require one, since he was still in the employ of the Coast Survey. The matter of a pension came much later, after 1898 anyway. So there was no reason for Peirce to give tribute to *Saint Bill James* in this way in 1890. No, it was for another reason entirely.

"What that other reason might be didn't occur to me until the early twenties while visiting Mrs. Peirce in Milford during the years I was in residence at Bryn Mawr. On a pleasant spring afternoon we were chatting in French on the south veranda of Arisbe when a horse-drawn caravan of Gypsies came up the stage road that ran from Port Jervis to Milford immediately in front of the house, not more than twenty metres from where we sat. Over the years in my travels I have learned quite a bit about Gypsies. Indeed, it was Peirce himself who introduced me to the fascination of Gypsy words; they call themselves *Rom,* hence their name for their language is *Romany.* I wondered at the time why he had become a student[†] of the subject, apparently having gone out of his way to read some rather esoteric nineteenth century books[†] in the field. Also, I had the good fortune in England, during the second war, of knowing and working with Professor Walter Starkie[†] who was at that time perhaps the greatest expert on the subject, especially Spanish Gypsies. Walter was ostensibly a cultural officer in the British embassy in Spain, but he and his Spanish Gypsy friends cooperated in a few covert operations with which I had been involved as supervising wireless coordinator. We became good friends and continued our discussions over the years.

"Walter told me that there had been Gypsy groups in America since the early nineteenth century, but I had never encountered one before that day. The leader of this band was the only mounted person—the rest walked or rode in one of the brightly decorated carts. His handsome mount fitted with beautiful tack paced directly toward Mrs. Peirce, and to my amazement they exchanged familiar and enthusiastic greetings in the Spanish dialect of Romany, which I understand perfectly well. As the conversation unfolded he addressed her as Fabiola de Lopez. Gypsies have several names, but among themselves they use a special 'real' name known only to others conversant[†] with 'the affairs of Egypt,' another slang-like self reference to internal Gypsy matters. Their special language is the principal means they use to enforce this strong ingroup sense. A non-Gypsy person who knows their language immediately gains their respect, and after a while if the outsider proves trustworthy, he or she will soon be treated like a Rom, like an insider. The word for such a trusted Romany-speaker is *Rai*, which would be pronounced as in *rye whiskey*.

"So you see Romany functions as a common international language among Gypsies. Yet each country has a noticeable dialect with ties to the basic ancient language which has been traced by historical linguists to a Hindi language source in northwest India from which place scholars suppose the original Gypsy band began its migration[†] toward Europe around 1000 AD. Gypsies anywhere can usually understand one another through the commonalities of basic international Romany. However, these two were conversing fluently[†] in Calo, that is to say, the Spanish dialect of Romany.

"Unaware that I comprehended Gypsy ways (which I decided to keep to myself for the moment), Mrs. Peirce explained in French that these people camped on her homestead during their normal travels. Then she invited me to follow as she directed the band to one of her pastures, where they set up camp. I surprised them when, noticing their tents were not yet unlimbered, I turned to the duke, speaking very slowly and distinctly in Calo, *Laches chibeses[†] plaloros?*: Where are the tents? Both were very surprised. Ultimately we enjoyed a wonderful evening around their campfire.

"As I participated in their conversation and good company, I found myself reflecting on my earlier puzzlement about Peirce's added name in 1890.

"I see you are perplexed. Perhaps you don't know that Saint James is the patron saint of Spain, who in Spanish is titled *Santiago*. You may recall that this word was the war cry of those Spaniards who conquered vast portions of the new world. The bones of Saint James are said to lie in Spain at Santiago de Compostella, which was one of the three great pilgrimage sites in late medieval times. The others were Rome, as you know, and Canterbury of Chaucerian fame. In those days every loyal believer was under an obligation to travel to one of the pilgrimage sites if at all possible, and every believer not travelling was obliged to help such pilgrims along their way. It was this latter obligation that enabled the first band of Gypsies to find support from noble houses as they allegedly made their way to Santiago de Compostella, supposedly in order to do a penance they told everyone the Pope had placed[†] upon them. Some authorities think such forged Gypsy *safe conducts* were the prototypes[†] of our modern passport system. In particular one can trace the progress of bands under Duke Andrew and Duke Thomas as they entered Europe[†] around 1400 AD. Among the Rom today, this episode from their legendary history is known as *Jonjano Baro*, the great[†] trick.

My thought then, and now, is that when in 1890 Peirce added this name informally he was paying tribute to his wife, whom he dearly loved, and to her cultural origin as a Spanish woman who was a Gitana, or Spanish Gypsy of Andalusia. An additional point that is relevant here lies in the fact that in 1890 Mrs. Peirce was travelling by ship[†] to Gibraltar. The addition of *Santiago*, then, was a tribute by Peirce to his beloved Gitano wife who would be in Spain when Schröder's book appeared. He might also have been saying from the perspective of the new world that 'she conquered me' just as the conquistadores had gained dominion over new lands in the Americas."

I *was* perplexed. I finally stammered that everyone I had spoken with around Harvard and Milford or elsewhere told me that Juliette grew up in France and was French.

"She spent time in France as a child, and as a child she learned to speak ordinary French fluently, and other languages too, but that doesn't mean that she was a Frenchwoman in the usual sense, or that her family were French. Indeed she had strong ties to France. However, consider that Peirce himself confided in me several things about her past during the days I studied with him in Cambridge, after I had become very close to him as a student in the particular special sense of logic that he pursued. As a matter of fact, I was probably the only student anywhere at that time who enjoyed both a close philosophical and personal relationship with him. One never felt, by the way, that he taught anything; he was simply an agile and devoted fellow scientist. We worked together to solve problems, in other words. In any case, he told me[†] that his wife arrived in the U.S. with no name and that all her names after that time were assumed. The names you have no doubt encountered—alleged names from a supposed previous marriage, such as Madame de Pourtales or Pourtalais or Pourtalai, or her purported maiden name Juliette Annette Froissy[†]—were in all likelihood[†] made up. Perhaps you know that Peirce was a frankophile. Indeed, through personal instruction he had developed his wife's command of literary[†] French. So I think it is quite likely that after meeting her, Peirce and others helped her construct a complete new French identity in order to conceal her true background. I suspect you might be asking, 'Why would they want to conceal her background?'

"Probably she had arrived in the U.S. without benefit of passport. Furthermore, were her status as an illegitimate child or her origins in a Gypsy family known, she would have been subject to some common prejudices and irrational hatreds of the era. But there is an additional possibility. Gypsies do not easily take to the women of their bands[†] marrying a busno, a non-Gypsy—a gentile, in other words. So first of all, she was the child of a Gitana/Busno union. Then she compounded the matter by associating with Peirce. Hence, once she and Peirce became irreversibly emotionally attached, and until her family and band in Europe could be placated, it would be best were she to have another identity that would keep her whereabouts unknown. And by 1883 when she had become Mrs. Juliette Peirce, there was no reason to reverse field and explain everything. A few family members knew the details. In particular Peirce's brother Herbert was aware of the matter, principally through his contacts as a high-ranking U.S. diplomat."

Betsey interrupted with an important observation: "That might explain the strange letter Herbert wrote to his sister Helen shortly after Charley's death. He referred to Juliette as a vile creature. He also said that Charley's great ability had been wasted. . . . Let me look it up in your draft, Ike. Here it is . . . 'Charley's native sweetness and great ability which has been wasted by the alliance he formed with that vampire[†] who has finally sucked his last drop of life's blood.' How would Berts have known more about her? You say his diplomatic service. Does that mean Juliette had some special connection with the diplomatic community?"

"As a matter of fact she did. And Herbert was well informed about her origin I am sure."

Roy wished to appear to be preoccupied with sipping from his Steam. But I sensed he was still upset with our pushy questions and our general excitement. The only excuses we had were all those futile nonproductive efforts to discover something about Juliette Peirce. Now that we seemed to be getting somewhere with the problem, we shouldn't be blamed for the thrill of the chase.

"I wish to return to my train of thought. I remember very clearly the last time I saw Peirce. It was Tuesday the sixth of January 1914, not long before he died. I was going to war and didn't know if I would survive. I could see from his emaciated appearance that he probably didn't have long to live. I think you told me he had cancer. I noticed he ate reasonably well, but despite that, he was quite thin and fragile. He was exceedingly glad I had come to visit but was apprehensive of my entry into the Royal Navy. Peirce said with a grin that if I became a sailor, I would be only the second Navy man he had ever met in whom he had complete confidence, the first having been his late uncle, Admiral Charles Henry Davis[†], who was a Civil War hero and a great scientist. He urged me to be mindful of my personal safety using a phrase I shall always cherish: 'Take special care Wyttynys because the logic of relatives must survive through you and a few others.' We had a long and wonderful conversation. At one moment when Mrs. Peirce absented herself to refill the tea pot, Peirce suddenly said in absent-minded Latin, knowing I comprehended the language but his wife did not at all, as if offhandedly conveying a great secret to me perhaps contrary to his wife's wish: 'Hodie Uxor[†] L annos nata est': Today is my wife's fiftieth birthday. Often in warfare when one assumes death is near, a strange intimacy is created between men. Peirce and I knew each was close to death, yet our prospective deaths had different frames."

I did some quick arithmetic. I could see the abacus inside Betsey's head was working too. She said: "Then if Peirce met her in 1876 as you said, she would have been twelve years old?"

"Yes, that is correct. Let me tell you the whole story of her trip to the U.S. and Peirce's meeting her. That will be the most efficient manner to calm all your questions.

"She travelled with a duenna, a chaperone or governess, the Marquise de Chambrun; they arrived in New York from Havre on 23 November 1876, the Marquis having proceeded them[†] the previous July. They took up residence somewhere around Washington Square, and their social headquarters was the Brevoort House—Fifth Avenue at Washington Square. Peirce had just returned from a long stay in Europe in order to familiarize himself with pendulum work there and to arrange to connect United States gravity stations with the international network. He stayed for a while at the Brevoort House in October while locating quarters nearer to his pendulum[†] station; Peirce had been coming to that hotel for years. He told me that he was known to every staff member and that he found himself at home[†] there. Zina had left him, despite his trying one more time to persuade her to accompany him to New York where he had been ordered by the Survey to establish a gravity station at Stevens Institute[†] in Hoboken.

I remarked that I had found a letter of January 1978 by Peirce to President Gilman of Johns Hopkins University describing the end of his marriage to Zina. Roy wanted to see[†] it.

I have been for a number of years in disagreement with my wife. Not having lived with her for a long time, and having not even seen her for over a year; and the reasons for this on the one side and on the other will, I hope, never be known. It is however certain that we shall never live together again.

Why had Charley and Zina split up? I knew better than to overload the communication channel. So I stayed mum on that issue. But I wanted to know why Juliette, or I should say Fabiola de Lopez, had come to New York City.

"Her father was Adolphe Fourier[†] de Bacourt, a distinguished French monarchist[†] diplomat, and . . . How can I say it politely? . . . Bacourt and his associates worshipped the idea that aristocrats should govern. Democracy disgusted them. This attitude, shall we say, resembled that of the Peirce family. George Bancroft, the former master at Round Hill School, met him when Bacourt was the French ambassador to Washington during 1840–42. They became close friends in London after President Polk appointed Bancroft[†] as our ambassador—or *minister* as the post was called in those days—to the Court of St. James in England. Bacourt was born in Nancy in 1801 and died there in 1865. He was a diplomat of wide experience, especially in French and German circles. Another of his posts had been minister to the court of the Duke of Parma in 1847, then allied with the French crown. He was a great favorite in the French court and had been practically adopted by the German Kaiser and his household.

"Mrs. Peirce's mother was a widely-known well-to-do Gypsy dancer and entertainer who specialized in Flamenco dance and Cante Jondo, or deep song, which is an exceptionally emotional and spontaneous manner of singing unique to the Gitanos of Andulusia. She accompanied herself on a small harp. Indeed, within Spain the musical type[†] is also well known as Cante Gitano. Once one has heard a true master or mistress of cante jondo, one is a committed afficionado[†] for life."

A pause.

Why?

"Would you care to see her photograph?"

"Agatha Christie's underwear! Would we!" Excuse my language, but I can't help it. I was raised by a bunch of cowboys. Instinctively I start to swear when I get excited. I really have to watch myself.

So saying, Roy reached inside his coat pocket to retrieve a small cardboard protective folder from which he carefully withdrew a small photograph. He handed it first to Betsey. She stared, then slapped her forehead with her free hand. Roy didn't move a single muscle. The old dude had set us up and was surely enjoying the show deep in his soul.

"Oh my word! Look, it's Grandpa Darbey's little box!" Betsey leaned over so I could see the photo but with her loose finger indicated the left side of the scene where on an ornate table sat an elaborate container. The woman's right hand touched it as if in a caress. It was the same casket we had

18. *Madame de Lopez*
"Would you care to see her photograph?"
Victor Lenzen Papers, Bancroft Library, University of California
By permission, Bancroft Library

removed from the secret compartment in Charley's box, the one my expert said was manufactured in Cordova. When we found it there was no jewelry, but it contained a special set of playing cards and a crest with the name Bacourt. Somehow neither of us had recalled this small box when Roy had mentioned Bacourt earlier in his account. But now the significance of it all settled upon us like Granny Hannah's heavy feather coverlet on a cold winter night in Love County. The crest in the small casket had to be Bacourt's coat of arms, the crest of Juliette's father. And this was Juliette's mother's jewel box, probably given to her as a special gift by Bacourt.

We returned the photo to Roy who carefully replaced it. Having had his fun, he continued, knowing full well what was in our minds.

"Mrs. Peirce gave the photograph to me the last time I visited her in late 1933. She asked me to preserve it according to my best judgment. She told me a number of other things about her history which I am conveying to you. I shall never forget the conversation, for we spoke in French heavily sprinkled with Calo, or Spanish Romany, which she delighted in using with me since it reminded her of childhood days and her mother, who had died when she was six."

The fact Roy had let us see the portrait meant, therefore, that he regarded us as worthy and well qualified.

Roy turned to face Betsey. Now he was addressing a daughter instead of giving a professor's speech. The change in his manner was an enchantment.

"The small casket which your grandfather gave to you, which Mrs. Peirce had given to him, which her mother had given to her, originally held Madame Lopez's jewelry. Mrs. Peirce sold that jewelry over the years to support Peirce's logic book project. But it also held a special pack of cards. It was a tradition that came down through Madame Lopez's family that the cards had been used to foretell Napoleon's downfall. They were used by her mother to tell fortunes. Mrs. Peirce also used them in like manner. All Gypsy women[†] are trained in penar bahi: fortune telling. Mrs. Peirce was well-known around Milford for telling fortunes somewhat frivolously at fairs in support of the Red Cross[†] and other charities, but she also had a private group of followers for whom she gave readings[†] which they took seriously. You should understand, Darbey, that this box and its contents have a high meaning for the female descendants of Madame de Lopez. By strange good fortune, you have the honor to be the legitimate current female owner."

Betsey was quiet, as if she had received a benediction. Roy leaned back, then turned toward me. His gaze hardened. The professor had returned.

"Mrs. Peirce's mother was attached to the Duke of Parma's household. Her name was Agustina de Lopez, a Gitana who was the widow of a Gypsy Duke from Andalusia. The chieftain of a band was known both on the inside and the outside as duke[†] or count. Often the public image of Gypsies is one of poverty and squalor, but in those days and still today there were and are many wealthy, talented, and highly-placed Gypsies. In the nineteenth century Gypsies were especially valued among nobility and gentry as entertainers and as confidants or fortune-tellers particularly within the courts of France, Germany, Austro-Hungary, and Russia. The Russian instance is noteworthy, because there the large Gypsy choral groups[†] lived almost as royalty.

And because the Rom were widely dispersed in Europe and possess their private and secretive Romany language, they were valued in the diplomatic service as conduits for information within the various European courts in which many were employed.

"Mrs. Peirce, or Fabiola, was the illegitimate daughter of Agustina de Lopez and Adolphe de Bacourt. They had been acquainted for some time. I can't be sure about it, but it seems quite likely that Bacourt initially became intimate with Señora de Lopez through matters involving diplomatic intelligence. This could further explain the devotion of Bacourt's friends toward the young Fabiola. Bacourt died a year after Fabiola was born, and her mother died in 1870. Fabiola received a basic schooling in France around Bacourt's home in Nancy, but because of her status outside the direct family line, social pressures eventually built to the point that it was wise for Fabiola to leave. Remember that Gypsies were routinely persecuted off and on throughout European history, depending upon which regime was in power. Perhaps the Nazi persecution was the most hateful and vicious, but there have been many other persecutions. These have left the Rom with an inbred suspicion[†] of all governments. Also, Fabiola's health was not good. At the onset of menstruation, she became weak and incapacitated for several days each month and sometimes suffered from what was described[†] as hysteria. It was considered that physicians in the U.S. might be able to help her. All these factors brought her to New York with an adequate financial allowance under the supervision of high-ranking and influential friends and admirers of Bacourt, of whom there were a great many among European aristocracy.

"As I have mentioned, George Bancroft[†] was in this group—not because he was a monarchist; he was a convinced Jacksonian Democrat, but he had to be on intimate terms with monarchists and aristocrats in his diplomatic career, for they still ruled in Europe. He had particularly come to know Bacourt well as part of the inner Royal circle in the French Court in 1847. Bancroft arranged with Ben Peirce and other well-placed friends and old hands in Washington to look after the young Fabiola and her duenna first in the aristocratic Brevoort House, then later at their Washington Square apartment nearby. She was initially known to this group of mentors under the code name of 'Madame Pourtalais,' a good choice for respectable anonymity since that surname was about as common among well-to-do Europeans as 'Smith' is among Americans. Addressing the child as a married woman, as 'Madame,' was another bit of useful cover indulged by her group of mentors as a further means to ensure her privacy.

"Peirce told me once that Bancroft 'in his old age'—which is to say between 1874 and 1891 after returning from serving as our minister in Berlin to take up residence at 1623 H Street in Washington—had been a great friend[†] to his wife. He also mentioned that his father—as a close friend of Bancroft—

had been among the original mentor group[†] for 'Madame Pourtalais' and that indeed Peirce himself had been drafted, due to his fluent French, as yet another chaperone and mentor of the young Fabiola."

I was reminded of an odd note among Charley's papers, so I showed it to Roy. Across the top, in Peirce's late scrawl, is but one word—"Juliette."

6 January 1877
Would Mademoiselle consent[†] to look over and correct something written in French, today?

"Peirce was preparing a scientific paper in French at that time which he would soon present to the International Geodetic Association meeting in Stuttgart. By the way, this note appears to confirm two points of my hypothesis. 'Madame Pourtalais' was indeed not a married woman nor a widow but a young never-married lady or mademoiselle. Peirce's strong knowledge of French culture would have prevented him using an inappropriate form of social address. The 'Widow Pourtalais' would *not* have been addressed as Mademoiselle but as Madame. And it supports my view that he was part of her chaperone group for a few years, along with other members of the Peirce[†] family.

"But you take me from discussing Bancroft. Such a high-level diplomatic connection with him also shows how Fabiola could have entered the country undetected and unrecorded, especially so if some diplomatic favors were being settled, or if the principle of assistance for widows and orphans was involved. Her chronic health problems, of course, only support the thesis. Moreover, all this explains for me what I had always regarded as a curious but definite truth: namely that Mrs. Peirce had a life-long capacity for easy access to governmental and social leaders.

"Actually, I think that Bancroft was more than a friend—*godfather* would be a much better description. It is difficult to convey just how impressively significant close friendship with Bancroft was in post–Civil War Washington. For instance, he was one of the few noncongressmen who had been admitted to the floor of the U.S. Senate—a great honor. His advice and effective assistance was sought by powerful figures around the world. Perhaps his status in those days could be compared to that of Henry Kissinger today. He was truly a lion in retirement, but one that was still quite active intellectually and socially. His house on H Street became a salon for cosmopolitan scholars and diplomats[†] of Washington. At that time his strong relation to Benjamin Peirce, also a legendary figure in the political aspect of national[†] science, is clear. Couple his charisma and friends with the equally strong charisma of Bacourt and his friends here and in Europe, and one has quite a force at hand. And one should not forget that she was receiving about 18,000[†] francs per annum for support."

I walked over to Charley's box and removed a sheet dated 1890 and showed it to Roy. On it these words[†] were written:

When I first saw this dear young lady, she had on a very thick brown veil. It hid her face from me but it did not hide the delicacy, the nobility, the truth, and the strength of her heart. That shone out; not with all the clearness and radiance it did later, but still enough for me to feel the charm of it.

"That records his impression when he first met the young Fabiola; he said it was at a costume party in the Brevoort near Christmas time in 1876. My guess is that Ben Peirce introduced them as he inducted Charles into the mentoring group.

"But the period of his acquaintance at that time was relatively short. He was very busy[†] with establishing the pendulum station in Hoboken, and he was working hard to arrange to be sent to Stuttgart to the International Geodetic Convention where he wanted to defend his controversial critique of the standard pendulum support system then in use at international gravity measurement stations. Peirce had discovered that the support was flexing a microscopic amount, but still in a manner that would alter results significantly. He was able to defend his findings, which then became the new international standard. Peirce saw little of Fabiola until some years[†] later."

I commented that indeed, there was a note among his papers stating that Charley had taken passage on the Steamship Suevia of the Hamburg Mail Line which sailed from New York the thirteenth of September[†] 1877. According to those records, he returned to New York from Hamburg on the Steamship Herder to arrive on 18 November 1877[†] and returned to quarters at 42 Seventh Street,[†] where he plunged into an intensive period of scientific work.

Roy added, "Meanwhile Fabiola had been moved from the initial apartment off Washington Square with the Marquise de Chambrun to the home of another group of friends, the Dudleys."

Betsey spoke up. "This explains an odd sheet of paper from one of Charley's calendars. It was simply labelled *Juliette*, and had a list of years[†] and names."

> *arrived*
> *76 Washington Square NY*
> *77 Dudleys NY*
> *78 28th Street NY*
> *79 30th Street NY*
> *80 Warfields NY*
> *81 Hales NY*
> *82 1324 Riggs Street DC*

After examining the list, Roy said, "This coincides with the results of my studies. Mrs. Peirce essentially lived in New York prior to 1882 in the company of first one and then another of her supervising group. I am convinced that Peirce's relationship with her until their marriage in 1883 was entirely chaste[†] and proper. One consideration consistent with that view lies in the fact that she had chronic female troubles. Peirce told me that prior to and after their marriage, on doctor's orders she kept to her bed[†] several days each month due to what was known as a fallen womb.

"My assumption of their chaste relationship also is entirely consistent with Gypsy culture wherein nothing is valued more than premarital chastity. Yet at the same time, Gypsy women are extremely companionate with men, a factor which often leads to misunderstandings with non-Gypsies who mistake the close companionship for sexual license. This has led to a disproportionate number of Busno deaths in Spanish cafes that feature Gitana singing and dancing. Gypsy men often criticize busno men for mistaking Gitana companionship for sexual invitation.

"Sometime very early in 1882 I think Mrs. Peirce moved[†] to Washington, D.C., where initially she was quite ill and could hardly walk. She recovered by the end of the month, because Peirce told me that he and she had attended the trial of Charles Guiteau, the assassin of President Garfield. Seats were ordinarily impossible to get, but Peirce said that Walter Cox, the presiding judge in the trial, had provided Madame[†] Pourtalais with two reserved places."

I don't know how Roy continued his entirely calm presentation, because this whole revelation, especially the last remark about rare tickets arranged for by the presiding judge, was causing my jaw to bounce off of the floor.

"Peirce continued to be one of the group nursing her. She apparently desired her own home, so one was obtained for her at 1324 Riggs Street[†] which she occupied by March[†] of '82. Peirce's divorce from Harriet Melusina Fay was granted in a final decree from the Baltimore Circuit Court[†] in April 1883. He then proposed marriage to 'Madame Pourtalais.' He told me that she did not at first consent and that his mother finally convinced her to accept in a very affectionate letter urging the marriage upon her and welcoming her[†] into the Peirce family. They were married in New York City in a civil ceremony[†] on the twenty-sixth of April. She was nineteen, he was forty-four. They left for France in May where Peirce had been ordered[†] on Coast Survey business."

Betsey took an item from my desk. "Do you think this might have been taken just after their marriage, during their trip to Europe, on their honeymoon?"

He exchanged his empty Steam bottle for the photograph in Betsey's hand.

19. *Fabiola de Lopez, Mrs. Juliette Peirce, 1883*
"The ring is transferred to the right hand when she is married"
Tuttle Collection, Institute for Studies in Pragmaticism
By permission, Philosophy Department, Harvard University

"Indeed, you are correct Darbey. Notice the brand new wedding ring on her right ring finger. It is the custom in Europe for an engaged woman to wear a gold band on her left hand. The ring is transferred to the right hand when she is married."

Lecturer

I planned to continue working ahead on material by Charley from the box. But I heard Roy puttering in our guest room. I had loaned him a Zenith Robodial console radio from 1937, which, under his knowledgeable hand, is repaired and working better than anything one can buy nowadays. Roy enjoys surfing the shortwave bands with the great old machine. He has converted the guest room according to the school of interior design practiced in the new recruit bays at West Point or Annapolis. The Zenith is his only concession to luxury. I asked him why he preferred this approach to room decoration and furnishing. His reply was interesting.

"My mind—your mind—is inside of you[†] *and* outside of you. This loft apartment is your mind and Darbey's mind. It is implicit in my status as a guest that I be allowed to arrange my room here as my mind."

I grasped that but risked arousing his cranky side by pressing for the reason for the choice of styles. I could see his desire to redecorate, but why so sparse?

"That is a way to put my mind in focus." He uttered these words from his perch in a hard-bottom, chrome-steel chair. From an end table he took up a well-thumbed copy of *The Simone Weil Reader*. Instantly his attention was with the book in his hands.

I could see this was the end of the conversation. (I smiled internally. It reminded me of *The Shadow*: the old radio show, the one with a hero who "knows what evil lurks in the hearts of men.")

I gave Roy a thumbs-up (which he didn't notice), then returned to my cluttered study where I plunged back into a big pile of papers from Charley's box.

1865 February 5

As I am going[†] to make a slight reference to Kant's theory of Apprehension in Intuition in some lectures next term, I have been led to reexamine Frank Abbot's objections to his doctrine.

It seems to me, however, that both his refutations of Kant are defective and if I am mistaken, I earnestly desire to be set right. I shall ask Abbot to do it if he thinks he can do it in a small time.

The question Kant has in view may be stated thus. The present instant is felt, the past is remembered, the future is expected with certainty. How can the phenomena of memory & feeling be connected into one continuum seeing that there is feeling in each instant of time though in this instant is no continuum? How can pre-remembered time & future time be known; if they can be known? The same with reference to Space. Here are some prerogative instances of space-perception. The eye can easily see objects which make smaller images on the retina than the distances of the nerve-points. The fin-

ger can feel finer texture by moving than when still. The retina is not a field for a picture but a bundle of tubes each containing a nerve point.

Scientific men when they adopt hypotheses excuse themselves by saying that it is only by doing so that the facts can be comprehended (that is, brought to a logical unity) and they say they do not believe these hypotheses as facts in themselves but only so far as they do bring the facts to a unity. In the same way Kant admits universals on the ground they are indispensable for bringing to the unity of consciousness, not facts merely, but the very impressions of sense.

I observe Abbot complains of the technicality of Kant's terminology. He did not invent all these terms or give them their modern meanings at one jump. For many years the truly scientific spirit of Germany had been producing and developing this philosophic language. Every science in a vigorous state must have a scientific language of its own: it is pedantry to confine oneself to classical language when one ought to have post-classical ideas.

Very likely Abbot will sweep away some of my objections: though I cannot say I hope so since I have a personal enthusiasm for Kant.

The division of the elementary kinds of reasoning[†] into three heads was made by me in my first lectures entitled the Logic of Science, University Lectures, second term of the Harvard school year 1864-65, specifically February through[†] May.

(1907). Deduction: not _necessary_[†] but _compulsive_ reasoning.
Abduction: persuasive, seductive.
Induction: appeals to you as a reasonable being.

Deduction points to the premises & to their relation & then shakes its fist in your face and tells you by the eternal powers, you have _got_ to admit the conclusion. _Effort required_ distinguishes deduction. Compulsive means you are forced to admit the conclusion.

Now, resume the division of reasoning. You begin with _perception_ which brings _surprise_. To make that reasonable you resort to Abduction. This resembles perception in bringing the _new_, and after this no new idea enters into reasoning.

Now comes Deduction by which this new forces you to join with it a _transformation_,—no new _matter_ but only a new _form_. And Deduction is defined as including all that.

Finally, Induction, or the Experimental Method, tests its truth.

Observe _Regular Gradation_ from the incoming of the new, first in Perception, then in Abduction, then _formally only_ in Deduction, while the reasonableness quite absent in perception begins to appear in Abduction, still more forcibly in Deduction, and in its highest development in Induction.

PM 11:00 1865 March 17
My lectures fell through[†] for want of an audience. Rather mortifying, but I

was not sorry. I study for my own satisfaction and am bored with my own thought if I have to explain it & don't wonder others are.

I wasn't sure if Charley meant that his first lecture or two fell through, or if the whole series fell through. So I tried to do some verifying. In the Harvard administration Reports to Overseers[†] one finds that "during the Second Term of the year 1864-65 lectures were delivered as follows under the title of University Lectures: A course on the Logic of Science, by Charles S. Peirce, S.B." So I conclude that the series was given. Maybe one of those Cambridge blizzards delayed its start. President Hill would not have lied to the Overseers in a formal report, especially since he was[†] a Reverend. The evidence also shows[†] that Hill had assigned Ben a role in arranging the current sequence of University Lectures.

Roy walked into my study at that point with a cup of the strong chicory coffee he preferred. When I explained what I was pondering, he remarked, "Don't forget another aspect of these lectures that is significant. Peirce was being presented to his audience as a recently qualified and now practicing scientist, in his scientific specialty which was the logic of science. It was his debut, if you will. To my mind he was not conceived, at that time, nor for a long time, as a philosopher. He began and continued as a scientist working on topics relevant to scientific methods."

Roy didn't have to convince me of that way of regarding Charley. I had previously confirmed[†] that guess.

UNIVERSITY LECTURES: THE LOGIC OF SCIENCE
Second-Term 1864–65, February through May
By Chas. S. Peirce, S.B.

Though I ask your attention[†] to one of the studies of the ancient Trivium— a study therefore according both to etymology and long prejudice, trivial—I trust I need not at this day defend it from the charge of piddling. It is now pretty plain that although modern science has scorned the scholastic terminology it has either continued to employ or has been forced to relearn the ideas that terminology conveyed, having simply thrown away the advantage of exact expressions. Logic in itself, however, has never been contemned by profound minds. It was a particular scheme of logic and not the science itself against which Bacon protested (see Aphorism XI); hence, he proceeds at once to substitute for that scheme another of his own,—and that intended to be a strictly logical one as I shall hereafter show. In the same way the reform of Ramus, the reform of Kant and all the reforms of sciences have been logical reforms. The Ramists sneered at the scholastics, the modern natural theorists sneer at both, and certain persons are now beginning to sneer at the natural theorists. Another reform seems to be coming: it is in the air. Several logical questions are already under discussion by scientific men. Naturalists are divided into two classes, more according to Lyell upon a logical question than anything else. An eminent mathematician has proposed a reform of the most important part of the theory of probabilities on logical grounds. And physicists ought not to feel too secure of the logical character of the hypothesis of impenetrability and its consequences which has already been attacked by men of high standing. On this account, I believe that there are not _now_ many thoughtful men of science who will think that the investigation of the logical character of scientific reasoning is a needless or unimportant inquiry.

These lectures will take up two points in order,

1st The degree and character of the certainty of scientific ratiocination.

2nd The degree and character of the certainty of scientific primitive principles.

The first point will be considered in this order.

1st The conception of logic.

2nd A theory of induction developed out of Aristotle's, which I prefer.

3rd The study of the modern theories of Boole, Apelt, Herschel, Gratry, Whewell, and Mill.

4th The theory of Bacon.

The second will be considered in this order.

1st The full presentation of Kant's theory of this subject.

2nd Consideration of the effect of modern researches in modifying this theory.

The one great source of error in all attempts to make a Logic of Science has been utter misconception of the nature and definition of logic. All the pure and formal logicians agree upon that. What then is logic? Of course, the definitions of a subject which has been pursued with ability for two thousand years and more have been very various. They may however be divided into two classes; those which do not and those which do give to logic a psychological or human character.

Of the unpsychological views there are several that occur to me as interesting. In the first place, there is the definition attributed rather doubtfully to Aristotle that Logic is the science of Demonstration. St. Augustine calls it the science of truth. There is great merit in the view, but it is too broad; for logic does not consider how an object or idea may be presented but only how it may be represented; _eyesight_, that is to say, and _inspiration_ are both beyond the province of logic. Another curious definition is that of Hobbes. "Ratiocination is Computation." A very remarkable and profound conception.

Of the psychological definitions, the commonest is that of Cicero which was adopted by Ramus. "Dialectica est ars se tradere bene disserendi." The Hindoo definition agrees with this. This identification of logic with the art of discussion, is at once the narrowest and lowest view of the subject which has ever been taken. Mr. Mill says "Logic is the science of the operations of the understanding which are subservient to the estimation of evidence."

All statements as these are worse than erroneous, in the extreme. Logic has nothing at all to do with the operations of the understanding, acts of the mind, or facts of the intellect. This has been repeatedly shown by the Kantians. But I will go a step further and say that we ought to adopt a thoroughly unpsycho-

logical view of logic, and that we may do so without entirely overturning established ideas.

Perhaps the most[†] extraordinary view of logic which has ever been developed with success is that of the late Professor Boole of Dublin. His book is entitled An Investigation of the Laws of Thought, on which are founded the Mathematical theories of Logic and Probabilities. It is destined to mark a great epoch
in logic; for it contains a conception which in point of fruitfulness will rival that
of Aristotle's Organon.

I shall establish[†]

1st The distinction of thing, form, and representation; together with the subsidiary one of object, logos, and image

2nd The distinction of sign, symbol, copy

3rd The definition of logic as the general conditions of the reference of symbols
to objects

4th The difference between deduction, induction, and hypothesis

5th The fact that every mental representation is a symbol in a loose sense and
every conception is so strictly

6th The fact that hypothesis gives terms or problematic propositions; inductions
propositions strictly speaking—assertory propositions; and deduction apodictic
propositions or syllogisms proper. That thus every elementary conception implies hypothesis and every judgment induction

7th The relations of denotation, connotation, and information and

8th The peculiarities of simple, enumerative, and conjunctive terms.

Thus we find ourselves in a condition to solve the question of the grounds of
inference by putting together these materials.

I fear I have wearied you[†] in these lectures by dwelling so much upon
merely logical forms. But to the pupil of Kant as to the pupil of Aristotle the Analytic of Logic is the foundation of Metaphysics. We find ourselves in all our
discourse taking certain points for granted which we cannot have observed.
The question therefore is what may we take for granted independent of all experience. The answer to this is metaphysics. But it is plain that we can thus take
for granted only what is involved in logical forms. Hence the necessity of studying these forms. In these lectures, one set of Logical forms has been pretty thoroughly studied; that of Hypothesis, Deduction, Induction. Another set has been
partly studied, that of Denotation, Information, Connotation.

Corresponding to these there are evidently certain conceptions of objects
in general. To denotation corresponds the conception of an object, to information the conception of a real kind, and to connotation the conception of a logos
or quality. So to Induction corresponds the conception of a Law, to Hypothesis
the conception of a Case under a Law, and to Deduction the conception of a
Result.

There are also principles of the Judgment corresponding to these conceptions of which we have instances in the laws that all things, forms, symbols are
symbolizable.

All the principles that can be so derived from the forms of logic must be valid for all experience. For experience has used logic. Everything else admits of speculative doubt.
I thank you, gentlemen, for your kind attention.

When Mill's[†] <u>Examination of Hamilton</u> came out in the spring of 1865, I put the volume into my portmanteau and betook myself alone to a sea-side hotel, long before the season had begun to open, in order that I might study it in solitude; and it influenced me decidedly, and helped me to clear up my opinions. Chauncey Wright, on the contrary, regarded the doctrine as the most certain truth in the world; and the effect upon him of the <u>Examination of Hamilton</u> was to complete the demolition of what little remained of his early Hamiltonianism. As to that, he and I agreed pretty well: but we must have fought out nearly a thousand close disputations, regular set-to's concerning the philosophy of Mill, perfectly dispassionate of course, before the Metaphysical Club had been started. These discussions had been of the greatest service to me. In the course of those years, my Kantism got whittled down to small dimensions. It was little more than a wire,—an iron wire, however.

LXIX[†]
1865 May 2

It is a corollary from no. lxiv that there is a truth of emotions which is essentially the same as the truth of conceptions. The truths of religion are inconceivable. How then is a religious truth to be stated? Only in propositions; but in propositions absolutely inconceivable. But that which is absolutely inconceivable is impossible. In propositions therefore which though absurd present an absurdity which is virtually solved by an emotion which is true.
Anthropomorphology held as inadequate is then the only true creed.

"Eisenstaat, seeing this particular important remark on religion from Peirce's private journal dated in May 1865 reminds me to tell you that for a long time I have been convinced that something dramatic happened to his inner life approximately at that time. Between his 1865 University Lectures on the Logic of Science and his Lowell Institute lectures of 1866 on the same subject, he came upon his own thought, or perhaps better, it came upon him. From that point in his life as a lover of wisdom, this embryo grew, sometimes steadily, sometimes sporting noncontinuously, but always as something developing, not a series of intellectual revolutions as some have argued. And history shows that his pragmatism was the first original philosophical approach arising in the United States to achieve worldwide acclaim. So here we have an important event, which cannot be passed over without notice.

"He told me about it thirty-eight years later. He was in Cambridge delivering lectures on pragmatism in Sever Hall. I had been studying his work since 1898, often aided by long personal conversations with him. We were engaged in one such conversation in 1903 as we walked across the Yard at a vigorous pace. I was just becoming intellectually independent myself. I wanted advice. When our conversation turned to that topic, I recollect he brusquely halted, so abruptly and resolutely that I bumped into him. His tweedy coat, the one with a little buttoning strap in front, scratched me. Whereupon immediately he gave the following statement in a solemn tone, which was difficult considering he had a high-pitched voice. By the way, Peirce always addressed his friends and close students by their family name. That meant he had a special affection for you. Normally he addressed acquaintances and lesser friends as *Mr.* Story or *Miss* Crowninshield or *Mrs.* Holmes. There was no occasion, in our many dialogues, when he addressed me as LeRoi or Roy; and you know my memory has never failed me. We two when alone always conversed in French, for both of us were fluent and at home in that tongue, which we admired. By the way, Peirce was garrulous in his old age, as perhaps you have discovered. For myself, I loved to hear him and considered his remarks almost always to be profound."

Certes, Wyttynys, la première manifestation[†] de notre indépendance scientifique est un événement que l'on peut à bon droit définir comme un phénomène distinct, voire remarquable, peut-être même un don du ciel. Habituellement elle est précédée d'une période de recherches particulièrement intenses, ce qui a été mon cas durant les deux années qui viennent de s'écouler. En vérité, à partir du moment où j'ai été tant soit peu capable de penser, et jusqu'à ce jour, j'ai été avec diligence et assiduité occupé par l'étude des méthodes de la recherche, aussi bien celles qui ont été et sont encore mises en oeuvre que celles que l'on devrait poursuivre. J'avais une excellente connaissance non seulement de tout ce qui, à l'époque, était connu dans le domaine de la physique et de la chimie, <u>mais aussi de la façon dont procédaient ceux qui réussissaient à faire avancer la connaissance</u>. J'ai prêté la plus grande attention aux méthodes des sciences les plus exactes et me suis intimement entretenu avec certains des plus grands esprits de notre temps dans le domaine de la physique et, pour ma part, j'y ai contribué de façon positive. Je suis totalement imprégné de l'esprit des sciences physiques. J'ai étudié à fond la logique, ayant lu tout ce qu'il y avait d'important dans ce domaine, consacrant beaucoup de temps à la pensée médiévale , sans négliger pour autant les oeuvres des Grecs, des Anglais, des Allemands, des Français, etc., et j'ai élaboré mes propres systèmes en logique déductive et inductive. Mes études ont été moins systématiquement poussées dans le domaine de la métaphysique; cependant j'ai lu et profondément médité tous les grands systèmes, sans jamais me satisfaire jusqu'à ce que je fusse capable de les concevoir comme les concevaient leurs propres défenseurs. Ma philosophie peut être décrite comme la tentative d'un physicien pour faire des conjectures quant à la constitution de l'univers, *pour autant que peuvent le permettre les méthodes de la science, avec l'aide de tout ce qui a été fait par les philosophes précédents. Je justifie mes propositions par les seuls arguments en mon pouvoir. On ne peut envisiger de preuve démonstrative. Les démonstrations des métaphysiciens sont toutes des balivernes. Ce qu'on peut faire de mieux, c'est d'avancer une hypothèse non dénuée de toute vraisemblance, dans la ligne générale du développement des idées scientifiques, et capable d'être confirmée ou infirmée par des observateurs futurs.*

Je me souviens d'une agréable flânerie tout en fumant, le long du Charles, à la mi-mai 1865 vers la fin de l'atroce guerre, promenade agréable à l'époque qui conduisait de mon logement au 2 de la rue Arrow. J'avais l'habitude, au cours de ces excursions, d'avoir sur moi un carnet de notes pour le cas où une idée me frapperait l'esprit et tout un réseau de pensées de ce genre jaillit effectivement en moi vers la fin de cet après-midi-là, qu'il fallait à tout prix noter. Ce sentiment fut si soudain et si discontinu que je me rappelle avoir marqué le début de mes notes d'un seul mot écrit en grosses lettres

C O M M E N C É

Ce mot était destiné à noter ce sentiment assez particulier que <u>mes propres pensées</u> avaient jailli pour la première fois. Mon crayon, de sa propre volonté, volait littéralement à travers les pages de mon petit carnet, le remplissant frénétiquement et totalement en quelques minutes: <u>Cum saccus rumpitur aqua fluit.</u> Les quelques années qui suivirent, à mesure que je commençais à élaborer des résultats particuliers dans la logique de la science pour les publier par la suite vers la fin des années soixante, je revenais à ces notes élémentaires sommaires mais fécondes sur ce que j'appelais alors la logique téléologique.

N'oublie jamais, Wyttynys, que mon travail est destiné à des <u>gens qui veulent découvrir</u>; les gens qui veulent que la philosophie leur soit prodiguée à la louche peuvent aller ailleurs. A chaque coin de rue il y a, Dieu merci, des marchands de soupe philosophique.

J'ai travaillé durant de nombreuses années à développer mes idées. Au cours de ce processus de maturation, j'avais l'habitude, quant à moi, de rassembler mes idées sous l'étiquette de <u>fallibilisme</u>; et de fait le premier pas vers <u>la découverte</u> consiste à reconnaître que notre savoir n'est pas encore satisfaisant.

En vérité, il m'a toujours semblé que toute ma philosophie découlait d'un fallibilisme confessé, combiné à une grande foi en la réalité de la connaissance et à un vif désir de découvrir les choses.

As Roy concluded, he turned to me and said, "Eisenstaat, I don't recall anything like that soliloquy in French from Peirce's autobiographical box. Could something of this sort exist elsewhere in Peirce's effects? It would be important as a record of the beginning of his life as a philosopher in science, the beginning of pragmatism."

Good thought, LeRoi! Later, after a search here, there, and elsewhere, Betsey and I did have a chance to copy a small notebook entitled *Teleological Logic,* which the descendants of Charley's brother Herbert Henry Davis (known within the family as Berts) had found in an attic and kindly showed us. We added it to the material in Charley's box.

B E G U N

1865 May 14†

   Logic is objective symbolistic.

   Symbolistic is the semeiotic of symbols.

   Objective symbolistic is that branch of symbolistic which considers relations to objects.

   Semeiotic is the science of representations.

   Representation is anything which is or is represented to stand for another and by which that other may be stood for by something which may stand for the representation.

   Thing is that for which a representation stands prescinded from all that can serve to establish a relation with any possible relation.

   Form is that respect in which a representation stands for a thing prescinded from all that can serve as the basis of a representation & therefore from its connection with the thing.

   Thus *Science* is divided into

      1 Positive Science. Or the science of things.

      2 Semeiotic. Or the science of representations.

      3 Formal Science. Or the science of forms.

                      Representations

are of three kinds according to their truth or coincidence with their objects. These are

      1 Signs. Representations by virtue of a convention.

      2 Symbols. Representations by virtue of original or acquired nature.

      3 Copies. Representations by virtue of a sameness of predicates.

   By a symbol is meant such a representation as is regarded as a representation in another system of representations. A word for instance upon being presented to the mind, immediately calls up a conception of the object without resembling it, and without any reference to the convention, which has however existed. Concepts are a species of symbols.

   A symbol is created by a *logos,* equivalent to another symbol in the system in which it is regarded as a symbol, and stands for an object.

   A *Logos* is an embodied form.

   An *object* is an informed thing.

   The science of the general conditions to which every symbol is subjected in so far as it is related

$$\text{to} \begin{cases} \text{a } logos \text{ is } \underline{\textit{General Grammar}} \\ \text{a language is } \underline{\textit{General Rhetoric}} \\ \text{an Object is } \underline{\textit{General Logic.}} \end{cases}$$

Hence we have

Science

Formal   Science Semeiotic   Positive Science

Science of Copies   Symbolistic   Science of Signs

Grammar   Rhetoric   Logic

But the word *pragmatism* was not in the notebook, so I asked Roy how he (and apparently Peirce) could claim that this was the onset of Charley's invention of pragmatism. I thought pragmatism was inaugurated by his articles for the *Popular Science Monthly* in 1878, some thirteen years later. Of course he drafted those ideas earlier, and discussed them even earlier, but— I had been taught—certainly nowhere near as early as 1865.

"You are being mesmerized by a single word; *pragmatism* is not merely a term, but a maxim embedded within a wider set of doctrines about the logic of science—which is to say, the semeiotic of science. To be sure, you will search in vain for that word in the 1877-78 articles[†] that are usually taken as the introduction of the pragmatic approach.

"Much of the received account of Peirce's life and work is wrong, including the part concerning how pragmatism came to be. To get clear on this we have to distinguish two senses of the notion. *Pragmatism* in the narrow sense is a maxim for determining the meaning of scientific terms. Peirce invented the maxim as a corollary within methodology; in turn, it is one of the three branches of semeiotic. In a second broader sense, pragmatism is a general system of science—a "philosophy" of science if you will—which Peirce obtained by constantly employing that maxim and related principles he developed. And don't confuse Peirce's pragmatism in either sense with those espoused by James or Dewey or Schiller or whomever today. They are all later than Peirce and derivative from his efforts and differing in various ways. To distinguish between these unauthorized copies and distortions of his original invention, after the turn of the century Peirce came to insist upon identifying his old approach as *pragmaticism*, which, he said, was a word ugly enough[†] to be safe from kidnappers. But I can see in your eyes that all this is opaque to you. You need a road map. Have you seen Peirce's posthumously published autobiography?"

He read faces well enough; college presidents and poker players and sea-hardened captains can do that. Roy was all of the above. I *was* stuck and confused, showing an open mouth. Furthermore I thought Betsey and I—with Roy's help—*were preparing Charley's autobiography*, from the box, for posthumous publication. What was this talk of another?

I closed my mouth, relaxed my face, popped a longneck Steam from the little reservoir in my study, handed it to Roy:

"Is there another autobiography?" (I would never ask a man to work, or travel in foreign lands, without wages, if aught be due him.)

"Yes," he grasped the bottle with authority, "a rather brief one finally published in 1983, although Peirce composed it in 1904. I remember because he asked me to read a draft shortly after he wrote it."

Roy surprised me by walking over to *my* bookcase, rummaging for a second, then pulling down a journal volume I had not read. (Many amateur bibliophiles read only a small percentage of their collection, a syndrome from which I suffer.) His gleaming eye always takes in every nuance of a room or a person. Probably he noted long ago that I had the journal and had filed that datum for future use. Roy thumbed a page, handed the journal to me, then began to speak in what I instantly recognized as his "college president lecturing Rotary club" mode.

"In 1904 Mattoon Curtis at Western Reserve University in Cleveland had been put in charge of the American portion of the tenth edition revision of Überweg's *Geschichte der Philosophie*, then the greatest international reference work on the history of philosophy. He applied directly to Peirce for an account suitable to that purpose. Peirce penned a splendid short autobiography, comprising ten pages as finally published[†] in this journal. One of Peirce's many significant remarks in this piece is the following," so said Roy, pointing at it while looking over my shoulder.

Although I am much given[†] to raising doubts about my own philosophy, yet the alterations it has undergone since 1866, except for the introduction of the problematical tychism and a few minor corrections, and an increasing insistence on the exclusion of psychological premises from logic, consist in the extension of my inquiries to new problems and the greater fullness of my positions.

"From this we learn that his philosophy—*his*, mind you, H I S philosophy—which everyone including himself called pragmatism, began in 1866, although at that time he used the name in conversation but not in print. Bill James—as I recall, without as much as a 'by your leave' from Peirce, first introduced the term *pragmatism* in print, and also what he *thought* was Peirce's maxim, in a speech[†] in California in 1898. This was hardly the act of a friend, especially since Bill got Peirce's maxim seriously wrong. Moreover, 1866 was the year of Peirce's second set of lectures on the Logic of Science in which he deployed the insights of his epiphanatic notebook about teleological logic, recorded in May of 1865. The War of Southern Rebellion ended the same year that Pragmatism began! And Bill had nothing to do with the advent of pragmatism in Peirce's thinking and lecturing at this time, particularly in view of James's travel abroad with Louie Agassiz's expedition in Brazil[†] during April 1865 through March 1866.

"The very next sentence[†] gives an even more important disclosure about his way of thinking: "In order to understand my doctrine, which has little in common with those of modern schools, it is necessary to know, first of all, how I classify the sciences." This hierarchy of the sciences gives an outline of Peirce's system, which was not a system of philosophy in the contemporary sense, but was instead a system of science. He went on to describe it in this manner:

> I divide[†] all science into Science of Research, Science of Review (comprising such works as those of Comte and Spencer, and the doctrine of the classification of the sciences itself), and Practical science. That of the third branch, though elaborately worked out, need not detain us; and that of the second has not engaged my attention. The classification of Science of Research is shown in outline in the following scheme.

> MATHEMATICS
> PHILOSOPHY
>   Phenomenology (or Ideoscopy or Phaneroscopy or Phanerochemy)
>   Normative Science
>   Esthetics
>   Ethics
>   Logic
>   Speculative Grammar
>   Critic
>   Methodeutic or Methodology
>   Metaphysics
> IDIOSCOPY (Bentham), or SPECIAL SCIENCE
>   Physics
>   Psychics

> This classification is to be regarded as Comte's classification, corrected. That is to say, the endeavor has been so to arrange the scheme that each science ought to make appeal, for its general principles, exclusively to the sciences placed above it, while for instances and special facts, it will find the sciences below it more serviceable.

> That which embodies[†] an idea is a sign, and it is best to make logic the science of the general properties[†] of signs; logic is by me made synonymous with semeiotic, the pure theory of signs in general, comprising speculative grammar, critic or logic in a narrow sense, and methodeutic.

There was a new tone, or a new attitude, coming from Roy. I don't know how it had happened. I was no longer a supplicant or subordinate. Usually he was leading, but sometimes I had the point. But it didn't matter who was in charge, who was presenting. I became aware that we were sharing a tough-minded yet friendly regard for one another.

"I spare you Peirce's long lists under *physics*—basically the physical sciences of today—and *psychics*, which we now call the social sciences and humanities. Several things can be noticed about this listing. For one, philosophy is within science (contrary to the inverse typically presupposed today). Another: his statement of an equivalence relation between logic in a broad sense and semeiotic (or theory of signs, or one could call it the theory of interpreting). The logic of today, roughly formal logic, is certainly logic in a narrow sense and corresponds to Peirce's critic, which means that in Peirce's mind the contemporary science of logic presupposes and indeed requires what he called semeiotic."

I asked Roy if there wasn't a problem in using a classification scheme of 1904 to understand what he regarded as Charley's development of pragmatism in 1865.

"Not at all. It is but an instance of a typical presupposition in biographical work. Typically a person will accomplish something in later life, and a good biographer takes that to be basic while an exploration is conducted about the subject's earlier life. A biographer of John Rusworth Jellicoe, Earl Scapa, for example, would be motivated in his task by the great accomplishments of the Admiral's later life, which he would use as a guide while exploring the early years. The great later feats are a finding tool for what might be significant about early events and experiences. In the Admiral's case, one is led forthwith to his early work in gunnery as one explanation of his battle success in the Great War."

"I don't understand, Roy; what is the great event in Charley's life that you are comparing with Jellicoe's victory at Jutland? I concede, of course, that Jutland assured the supremacy of the Royal Navy for decades, which in turn contributed to the triumph of the United Kingdom in World War II."

"Clearly it is the late development of his well worked out—although to be sure not in every detail fully completed—system of science. And of course we should take that as a finding tool to examine his early life. It is the content of that system of science that constitutes Peirce's greatness.

"Today Peirce is associated with pragmatism. But that was not his major discovery. Within his system of science the major discovery and accomplishment was semeiotic, his general science of sign action. Contrary to what you will hear, it was well worked out in his late manuscript writings, the relevant parts of which, however, are not yet properly published. Pragmatism in the narrow sense is but one corollary among many such corollaries of semeiotic. And pragmatism in the general sense is the kind of scientific philosophy one obtains if one applies the insights and techniques found in semeiotic. This was clear to Peirce from the beginning of pragmatism and semeiotic in 1865–66, as he wrestled them out from his deep interest in the logic of science, from his reading† of Kant, Boole, Berkeley, and, a few years later, of the medieval logicians."

"I still don't see it. Why should a general science of signs be important?"

"It is the master science, the glue that will re-cement the broken soul of Western civilization. It will reunite the split that has been created between matter and mind, between nature and spirit, physics and psychics, which is to say, natural science and the humanities. Why would this be important? Lacking a long disquisition, I can only answer with a comparison. It has a status similar to that of another question, to wit: What would be important today about being a corporation that owned and controlled the operating system that every computer in the world used?

"You see, if semeiotic is the basic science that holds together the sciences of body and mind, its master or owner would be in a supremely dominant position. Peirce's late system of semeiotic/logic was and is a chamber of marvels with applications and consequences in every imaginable direction. It is no amazement that the few who understood what he had accomplished late in life, while in a state of poverty and hardship, also wanted his ideas and eventually his manuscripts to be nearby so they could be conveniently appropriated, often without credit or acknowledgment. You don't have to cast far to obtain examples of that process. And we can see the year 1865 as the marker from which this marvelous system first clearly began to emerge from his philosophically and logically inclined scientific mind."

The emotional force of this sudden speech danced around my body like high-frequency current from one of Tesla's coils. I could smell spark-born ozone. Yet my rational voice whispered, "Beware." The old boy caught that somehow. He's a mind reader. A few noticeable seconds passed. The silence confused my train of thought. He addressed me again.

"This will help to clear up the matter." So saying he reached inside his lightweight deck jacket to pull forth a neatly folded packet of sheets tied four ways with a linen ribbon of the kind libraries use. Taking the bundle he had opened, I immediately recognized it as Crane's Superfine linen laid paper bearing Charley's original and unmistakable hand in strong black ink. Why did Roy just happen to have it with him? I have an intuition that he anticipates my needs before I am aware of them. Without reflecting, and with a sudden anger which surprised me as soon as it appeared, I almost shouted, "That's one of Peirce's manuscripts; How did you come across it?" Why was I angry with my fellow creature? Roy paused, then replied with near saintly calm.

"It is an early draft of an article on Pragmatism the editor of *The Nation* asked him to prepare. Peirce handed it to me in 1907 asking my evaluation of its effectiveness as a popular account of his approach. He added that he wanted me to keep it, for he had already prepared at least one later version. It should help you see that the pragmatic maxim is a methodological principle of scientific laboratories, which—within Peirce's system—arises out of semeiotic, which in turn arose out of phaneroscopy and mathematics."

Roy handed it to me, and I began to read, feeling a little sick with myself. It was helpful indeed, and I reproduce it for you here, with Roy's permission.

Topics of the Nation Article on Pragmatism[†]
G. Papini, Italy; New Zealand:
Mr. Editor: The philosophical[†] *journals, the world over, are just now brimming, as you know, with pragmatism and anti-pragmatism. The number of* Leonardo *that reaches me this morning has an admirable piece on the subject by a writer of genius and of literary skill, Giovanni Papini. Yesterday brought news of discussions along the same line in New Zealand.*
Misunderstandings:
Often, however, one hears glib utterances that betray complete misunderstanding of this new ingredient of the thought of our time; so that I gladly accept your invitation to explain what pragmatism really is, how it came into being, and whither it is tending.
Any quite new idea in philosophy will be false:
Any philosophical doctrine that should be completely new could hardly fail to prove completely false; but the rivulets at the head of the river of pragmatism are easily traced back to almost any desired antiquity.
Socrates:
Socrates bathed in these waters.
Aristotle:
Aristotle rejoices when he can find them. They run, where least one would suspect them, beneath the dry rubbish-heaps of Spinoza.
The illuminating definitions of Locke:
Those clean definitions that strew the pages of the "Essay concerning Humane Understanding" (I refuse to reform the spelling) had been washed out in these same pure springs.
Berkeley the great pragmatist:
It was this medium, and not tar-water, that gave health and strength to Berkeley's earlier works, his "Theory of Vision" and what remains of his "Principles."
Pragmatic tendencies (rather occasional essays) in Kant:
From it the general views of Kant derive such clearness as they have. Auguste Comte made still more,—much more,—use of this element; as much as he saw his way to using.
The violent conflict of Cartesianism with common sense:
The monstrous[†] *errors of Descartes and all his star-multitudinous progeny mark his, and all their, blindness to light of this color. But this particular new recognition of the light, this flinging open of the curtains which agnosticism and John*

Mill's individualistic nominalism had needlessly drawn was originally the act of very humble hands. It was in the early seventies that a knot of us young men, calling ourselves semi-ironically, semi-defiantly, the "Metaphysical Club," used to meet in Old Cambridge, sometimes in my study, sometimes in William James's.

My first articles:

Our proceedings had all been in winged words (and swift ones, at that, for the most part) until at length, lest the club should be dissolved without leaving any material souvenir behind. I drew up a little paper expressing some of the opinions that I had been urging all along under the name of pragmatism. This paper was received with such unlooked for kindness, that I was encouraged on the invitation of the great publisher, Mr. W. H. Appleton, to insert it somewhat expanded, in the Popular Science Monthly in a six-part series entitled "Illustrations of the Logic[†] of Science."

Terminology:

In those medieval times, I dared not in type use an English word to express an idea unrelated to its received meaning. The authority of Mr. Principal Campbell weighed too heavily upon my conscience. I had not yet come to perceive, what is so plain today, that if philosophy is ever to stand in the ranks of the sciences, literary elegance must be sacrificed,—like the soldier's old brilliant uniforms,— to the stern requirements of efficiency, and the philosophist must be encouraged,—yea, and required,—to coin new terms to express such new scientific concepts as he may discover, just as his chemical and biological brethren are expected to do. As late as 1893, when I might have procured the insertion of the word pragmatism in the Century Dictionary, it did not seem to me that its vogue was sufficient to warrant that step.

Pragmatism is not a doctrine of the truth of things, but only of the meanings of signs:

It is now high time to explain what pragmatism is. Pragmatism is, in itself, no doctrine of metaphysics, no attempt to determine any truth of things. It is merely a method of ascertaining the meanings of hard words and of abstract concepts. Pragmatism is[†] plainly, in the main, a part of methodeutic which is in turn part of general semeiotic; and therefore it should be kept free from all metaphysical admixture, in order that such metaphysical propositions should be criticized and investigated with all the resources of methodeutic. If pragmatism is taken to assume any doctrine of metaphysics, pragmatism cannot be used in ascertaining the truth of that doctrine.

All pragmatists agree 1st that pragmatism is only a method for ascertaining meanings; 2d that it is the experimental method[†] of science:

All pragmatists of whatsoever stripe will cordially assent to that statement. As to the ulterior and indirect effects of practising the pragmatistic method, that is quite another affair. All pragmatists will further agree that their method of ascertaining the meanings of words and concepts is no other than that experi-

mental method by which all the successful sciences (in which number nobody in his senses would include metaphysics) have reached the degrees of certainty that are severally proper to them today. Thomas Beddoes[†] showed, as early as 1792, that it is the procedure[†] even of mathematics. To you, at[†] least, this theory is quite unproved; yet it does not present itself without certain credentials. For the method is but a special application of the sole method by which physical science has achieved its successes during the last three hundred and odd years, having previously to the adoption of this method been universally looked upon as the most uncertain and intractable of all branches of science. It is the experimental or correctly inductive method; itself an amplification, or fuller development, of a wider method, exemplified in the maxim, or logical rule, "By their fruits[†] ye shall know them."

<u>Slightness of divergence between James and Peirce especially in practice:</u>
I understand pragmatism to be a method of ascertaining the meanings, not of all ideas, but only of what I call "intellectual concepts," that is to say, of those upon the structure of which arguments concerning objective fact may hinge.

<u>Intellectual concepts, how different from differences of feeling:</u>
Had the light which, as things are, excites in us the sensation of blue, always excited the sensation of red, and <u>vice versa,</u> however great a difference that might have made in our feelings, it could have made none in the force of any argument. In this respect the qualities of hard and soft strikingly contrast with those of red and blue; because while red and blue name mere subjective feelings, only, hard and soft express the factual behavior of the thing under the pressure of a knife-edge. More singularly stated, the whole meaning of an intellectual predicate is that certain kinds of events would happen, once in so often, in the course of experience, under certain kinds of existential circumstances. A most pregnant principle will this "kernel of pragmatism" prove to be,—provided it can be proved to be true. But how is this to be done?

I might offer[†] half a dozen different demonstrations of the pragmatist principle, but the very simplest of them would be technical and lengthy. It would not be such as a reader of this journal, a student of current literature, could be expected to undertake critically to examine. Such a reader would like to know the color of the thought that supports the positive assertion of pragmatism, without entering too minutely into details.

<u>A Sign mediates between its Object and its Meaning:</u>
To begin with, every concept and every thought beyond immediate perception is a sign. So much was well made out by Leibniz, Berkeley, and others about two centuries ago. The use of the word λόγος shows that the Greeks, before the development of the science of grammar, were hardly able to think of thought from any other point of view. Let anybody who may desire evidence of the truth of what I am saying just recall the course of what passed in his mind during some recent and sincere and fervid self-deliberation. If he is a good introspecter, he will remark that his deliberations took a dialogic form, the arguer

of any moment appealing to the reasonableness of the _ego_ of the succeeding moment for his critical assent. Now, it is needless to say that conversation is composed of signs. Oh, I am confident the reader will grant that every thought is a sign.

Now how would you define a _sign?_ I do not ask how the word is ordinarily used. I want such a definition as a zoologist would give of a fish, or a chemist of a fatty body, or of an aromatic body,—an analysis of the essential nature of a sign, if the word is to be used as applicable to everything which the most general science of semeiotic must regard as its business to study.

Everybody recognizes that it is no inconsiderable art, this business of "phaneroscopic" analysis by which one forms a scientific definition. As I practice it, in those cases like the present, in which I am debarred from a direct appeal to the principle of pragmatism, I begin by seizing upon that predicate which appears to be most characteristic of the definition, even if it does not quite apply to the entire extension of the definition. If the predicate be too narrow, I afterward seek for some ingredient of it which shall be broad enough for an emended definition, and, at the same time, be still more scientifically characteristic of it.

Proceeding in that way with our definition, "sign," we note as highly characteristic, that signs mostly function as such between two minds, or theatres of consciousness, of which the one is the agent that _utters_ the sign (whether acoustically, optically, or otherwise), while the other is the _patient_ mind that _interprets_ the sign. Without taking the least account of exceptional cases, I remark that, before the sign was uttered, it already was virtually present to the consciousness of the utterer, in the form of a thought. But, as already remarked, a thought is itself a sign, and should itself have an utterer, namely the ego of a previous moment to whose consciousness it must have been already virtually present, and so back. Likewise, after a sign has been interpreted, it will virtually remain in the consciousness of its interpreter, where it will be a sign,—perhaps a resolution to apply the burden of the communicated sign,—and, as a sign would in its turn have an interpreter, and so on forward. Now it is undeniably conceivable that a beginning series of successive utterers should all do their work in a brief interval of time, and that so should an endless series of interpreters. Still, it is not likely to be denied that, in some cases, neither the series of utterers nor that of interpreters forms an infinite collection. When this is the case, there must be a sign without an utterer and a sign without an interpreter. Indeed, there are two pretty conclusive arguments on these points that are likely to occur to the reader. But why argue, when signs without utterers are often employed? I mean such signs as symptoms of disease, signs of the weather, groups of experiences serving as premises, etc. Signs without interpreters less manifestly, but perhaps not less certainly exist. Let the cards of a Jacquard loom be prepared and inserted, so that the loom shall weave a picture. Are not these cards signs? They convey intelligence,—intelligence that, considering its spirit and pictorial effect, cannot otherwise be conveyed. Yet the woven pictures may take fire and be consumed before anybody sees them. A set of those models that the designers of sea-going vessels drag through the water may have been prepared and with the set a complete series of experiments may have been made; and their conditions and results may have been automatically recorded. There, then, is a perfect representation of the behaviour of a certain range of forms. Yet if anybody takes the trouble to study the record, there will be no interpreter. So the books of a bank may furnish a complete account of the state of the bank. It remains only to draw up a balance sheet. But if this is not done, while the sign is complete, the human interpreter is wanting.

Having found, then, that neither an utterer, nor even, perhaps, an interpreter is essential to a sign, characteristic of signs as they both are, I am led to inquire whether there be not some ingredient of the utterer and some ingredient of the interpreter which not only are so essential, but are even more characteristic of signs than the utterer and the interpreter themselves. We begin with seeking the essential ingredient of the utterer.

By calling this quaesitum an _ingredient_ of the utterer, I mean that where this quaesitum is absent, the utterer cannot be present; and further that where there is no utterer, it cannot be that this quaesitum together with all the others of a certain body of "ingredients" should all be present. A fact concerning our quaesitum, which we can know in advance of all study, is that, because this quaesitum will function as a sort of substitute for an utterer, in case there be no utterer, or at any rate fulfills nearly the same, but a more essential function, it follows that since it is not the sign that constructs or voices or represents the utterer, but, on the contrary, the utterer that constructs voices, and sets forth the sign, therefore, although _ex hypothesi_ the quaesitum is something quite indispensible to the functioning of the sign, yet it cannot be fully revealed or brought to light by any study of the sign alone, as such. Knowledge of it must come from some previous or collated source.

Since the most acute[†] minds, in dealing with conceptions unfamiliar to them, will blunder in ways that astonish those who are habituated to such dealings, I will propose an example, that of a weather-cock. Now a weather-cock is one of those natural signs, like a sign of the weather, which depend upon a physical connection between the sign and that of which it is the sign. But a weather-cock having been devised, as everyone knows, to show which way the wind blows, itself signifies to what it refers; and consequently it may be argued that no collateral observation is called for to complete its significance. But this reasoning commits two faults. In the first place, it confuses two incompatible ways of conceiving a weather-cock; as a natural sign, and therefore as having no utterer; and as a human contrivance to show the direction of the wind, and as such, uttered by its original inventor—for I speak of The Weather-Cock, the type, not the single instance. In the second place, the reasoning overlooks the *obvious truth that when thoughts are determined or revealed by a sign, the sign exists first (virtually, at any rate) and those thoughts subsequently. Hence, thoughts applied to devise a weather-cock cannot be revealed by the weather-cock but come under the head of "previous or collateral" information.*

It is now easy to see that the "requaesitum," which we have been seeking is simply that which the sign "stands for," or the idea of that which it is calcu-lated to awaken. We now have a clearer idea of the requaesitum than we had, at first, of the "object of the sign."

Marine fossils found on a mountain, considered as a sign of the sea-level having been higher than the levels of deposit of those fossils, refer to a distant but indefinite state. Here, there is no utterer, but this is what might have re-mained unexpressed in the mind of the utterer, though essential to the signifi-cance of the sign, if that sign had been devised and constructed to give the human race a first lesson in geology.

This requaesitum[†] I term the Object of the sign; or the immediate object, if it be the idea which the sign is built upon, the real object, if it be that real thing or circumstance upon which that idea is founded, as on bed-rock. The Object of a Sign, then, is necessarily unexpressed in the sign, taken by itself.

So much[†] for the object, or that by which the sign is essentially awakened or otherwise[†] determined in its significant characters in the mind of its utterer. Corresponding to it there is something which the sign in its significant function essentially awakens or otherwise determines in its interpreter. I term it the "in-terpretant" of the sign.

For instance, the meaning of the command[†] "Ground arms" is the act of slamming down the muskets, and through the action of the sign, it becomes the effect of the commanding officer's state of mind; while the meaning of a piece of music is that play of feeling that it awakens or otherwise determines, of which the original cause was a simpler play of feelings in the heart of the com-poser. In all cases, the interpretant includes feelings; for there must, at least, be a sense of comprehending the meaning of the sign. If it includes more than mere feeling, it must evoke some kind of effort. It may include something be-sides, which, for the present, may be vaguely called "thought." I term these three kinds of interpretant the "emotional," the "energetic," and the "logical" interpretant.

I am now[†] prepared to risk an attempt at defining a sign,—since in scien-tific inquiry, as in other enterprises, the maxim holds, Nothing hazard, nothing gain. I will say that a sign is anything, of whatsoever mode of being, which me-diates between an object and an interpretant; since it is both determined by the object relatively to the interpretant, and determining the interpretant in refer-ence to the object, in such wise as to cause the interpretant to be determined by the object through the mediation of this "sign."

To summarize[†] these distinctions have to be drawn. I have separated the immediate object, or the object as it is represented in the sign, from the real ob-

ject, or the object as it really is. In like manner we must distinguish three "meanings," the "interpretants." There are first the meaning as it is expressed in the sign; second, the meaning, as it is, in fact, produced by the sign; and thirdly, the meaning, as the ultimate logical result that deliberate reason ought to draw from the sign. Finer distinctions than these will, I can plainly see, be required when logic gets to be more closely studied. Meantime, the effect of a general sign upon conduct must itself be general. As it is expressed in the sign, it obviously is so; and as it results in conduct, it is a habit; and a habit is a general mode of action. In its ultimate logical form, it will be a general principle, or law. An experience, on the other hand, is a single event, as is also the actual expectation of the experience. Now no aggregate of single objects can ever make up a general.

The day was ebbing away. I was drained and empty of thought. Roy took the last pull from his longneck and placed it on my coffee table.

"I have an engagement. I am grateful to you and Darbey for these pleasant few days." He didn't offer any details or say with what or where he was engaged. He pulled on his P-jacket and grabbed his small knapsack.

"Don't be depressed. Persons who read quick accounts of Peirce aren't exposed to his real system. Moreover, almost no one understands his system when they first hear of it. Remember he said it had little in common with the modern schools. That means his system is in direct opposition to the philosophical underpinnings of this era—mostly materialism, Cartesianism, mechanicalism, physicalism. I mean it is opposed to the unconscious philosophical principles youngsters in our civilization learn by osmosis, virtually through their mother's milk. So keep trying[†] and give it some time."

The next day, I continued to marinate in all of Roy's tidings. His comments had resurrected an old problem that had troubled Betsey and me when we first began this project: Why did it seem that the live Peirce was so unwelcome in academia and in other forms of civilized company, while the voluminous papers of the dead Peirce were passionately sought? Here was a genius with something of significance to produce for the good of humanity, but it appears he was hindered in many ways. When I began to grasp the drift of Roy's conversation yesterday, and the critique of human nature it seemed to entail, it was too much for me. I felt shocked and a little sick to stomach.

"You look green, Ike." Betsey had just come in from her clinic. It's difficult to hide a corporeal reaction from a good nurse. I rehearsed my musings induced by yesterday's conversation with Roy to see what she thought.

"But Ike, this gives a possible motive for the way in which Charley was treated in later life. That would help solve the problem, wouldn't it? Having the papers and therefore his important ideas conveniently at hand would make it easy to mine them. Moreover, if an aura of whackiness had been encouraged and placed—either consciously or unconsciously—around Charley, the author of those thoughts, well then the better to pick his brains, or his manuscripts if you will."

Somehow this moves too fast for me—too grand a leap. I'm just a plodder. I'm going to have to stagger further into this maze. But I have to admit I'm aroused when Betsey starts talking about motives. It probably comes from reading too much pulp fiction.

The year 1865 ended well for the Peirce family, with Ben beginning a series of University Lectures in the fall, finishing on the eighteenth of January 1866. Charley put a paragraph[†] of his notes of Ben's first lecture in the box at this point.

Beginning of first lecture: With infinite powers of ratiocination & logic we could deduce the created universe from the intelligent creative mind & conversely we could deduce the creative mind from the created universe. Now compare the mind—the mind of man which is a type of the divine mind—with the universe around. In the first place, what would the mind be without the universe? The mind would thus be deprived of all intellectual food. The body when deprived of food, after a few miserable hours of agony is resolved into its primitive elements. But the mind, being immortal, when deprived of food would be condemned to suffer forever the pangs of intellectual starvation. In the second place what would the universe be without the mind? A waste of power which we dare not attribute to the Almighty.

A New List

Betsey had arrived home looking pretty beat up. Nursing is such emotional work. So I asked her if there had been some difficulty in her practice.

"Not in my practice, but in me. It's just that I can't stop thinking about a beautiful homeless lady that I treated early this morning for congestive heart failure. As I worked with her, she eventually told me how she came to be on the street. It is a common cycle that goes something like this: she was in a relationship with an abusive man, she developed a congestive heart, couldn't work, so couldn't afford the medication, abuser left which was good, but no more income which was bad, lost her apartment, wants to work but can't without medication; without treatment her circulation is shot and unless she stands up all day her legs swell up, can't sleep, on the surface doesn't look sick, but is really a wreck. All day, every time I thought of her, I would think of The Queen, who became a tragic figure for me. Sherman's army burned Columbia, South Carolina, the city where she lived. What was her ultimate fate after the Civil War? Had she been reduced to a miserable state like my patient? I've been feeding a sadness all day with thoughts about morbid possibilities for women."

We went out for supper.

You may think it odd that this would upset Betsey, but her own personal history is involved. You would have to know it to appreciate how a distressed yet noble female, whether living or historical, can put her into this kind of depression. Maybe the two notions in conjunction—living and historical—somehow increased the effect. We said little during our meal, but I was furiously thinking. Finally something occurred to me.

Upon returning home I led her into my study. Some volumes on the Le Conte family and the Civil War had recently arrived. I thought they might be relevant to Charley's affairs, so I had ordered them from John Gach Books, an out-of-print house with which I do business. I also suspected they might contain some information on The Queen. I urged Betsey to help me dig into them; I kept quiet, but I guessed that just knowing about The Queen's fate might be one way to ease the grip this feeling had on her spirit. I also needed to know so I could complete the exorcism of my obsession with Charley's box. So we took up the books, and from what we found I constructed this account which I read to Betsey later that evening.

Following the war, the Le Contes were[†] alive but in a sad state. Ben Peirce had tried to send aid to The Queen and her family by way of a friend of his who was a Union general officer detailed to Columbia. In a fit of pride and undying fervor for the lost Confederate cause, they refused aid from that source. Contact with the Peirce family seems to have been severed from that day forward. In 1867, The Chief died from overwork in the war. Ben succeeded to his position as Superintendent of the U.S. Coast and Geodetic Survey, and to nominal head of the remaining Florentine Academy. Many expatriot Confederates turned their eyes to the west coast and California, and so did the Le Conte clan. At Oakland, the new University of California was being opened. John had applied for a professorship in physics, for which he was well qualified. Joseph Henry, who was still in charge[†] at the Smithsonian Institution, backed him vigorously, and on 17 November 1868 John received word from the University of California that he had been hired as the first faculty member of the newly founded institution and was instructed to report to Oakland in the spring of 1869. The Queen followed soon. Ben Peirce, Louis Agassiz, and George Holmes had also written strong letters in support of his candidacy. John went on to become the first president of the new university. This institution was founded rather along the lines of the kind of national research university that the Florentine Academy had urged for years. Now the Confederacy Florentines—for Joe Le Conte was hired soon afterwards—became part of its first faculty. And Joe became one of the chief mentors for the young Josiah Royce during his undergraduate career at the University of California. Here is another secret influence of the Florentine Academy.

In late April of 1891 John Le Conte took sick with severe bronchitis. Josie had been ill the year before. He died on the twenty-ninth, just four months past his seventy-third birthday and two months short of his golden wedding anniversary. The Queen was prostrated by John's death. She never recovered from it, enduring a melancholy life under the care of the Le Conte clan. Her end came while dozing in her rocking chair. A newspaper fell from her lap into the fireplace. Her gown caught fire, and she eventually succumbed to the burns near the end of 1894, fourteen years after Ben Peirce had died. A California newspaper obituary described her as "a seventy-year old lady who was one of the most magnificent appearing women in the state." After discovering all this, I happened to speak with some of her descendants. Because of the depressing mode of her death, within the family she is affectionately known as "Aunt Dozie," as well as by her earlier title, "Aunt Josie." I prefer to think she died as the once and still reigning Queen of Science.

Betsey was quietly and calmly weeping. Saying nothing, I stared at a hole in my left shoe. Eventually she swiped her cheeks with the back of one hand, stood up from her chair, walked over and sat in my lap, leaned against me, whispered softly in my ear, "You're a better nurse than some Nurses I know."

Betsey is tall yet slightly built. It was easy to pick her up, to carry her to bed. She was already asleep as I loosened her clothing and covered her with a beautiful pattern quilt my grandmother had patiently sewn with arthritic hands when she was seventy-one and living alone in the family farmhouse in Oklahoma.

It was quite late, but I was still wide awake, still possessed with Charley's affairs after the last intense session with Roy. So I returned to my study to continue the slow process of reading through the manuscripts, working deeper into the yielding night, trying to burn their fascination out of my own soul.

Private Thoughts LXX[†]
1866 November 20
What is not a question of a possible experience is not a question of fact.

My Dear Captain:

I can hardly[†] let you know how delighted we all are at your magnificent success with the undersea cable. Would that the peak of commerce bring you again to our shores.

My son James, who is going to make a tour of a year[†] in Europe, will tell you all about us. We are all, indeed, quite well.

My son Charles has been delivering a course of Lowell lectures upon the logic of science, in which he has quite astonished me by the the breadth, and depth and strength of his arguments, and his powers of research.

Benj. Peirce

THE LOGIC OF SCIENCE
By
Charles Sanders Peirce

<u>I</u>: September 1866

Ladies and Gentlemen, I address you[†] upon an exceedingly dry subject which I cannot hope to make entertaining; but the great importance of which to everyone who is to use his mind at all ought to render it interesting. I shall be obliged to call upon you for an exertion of intellect which is unnecessary in a popular lecture upon any subject which presents less unity or depends less upon long trains of thought; but I think that for the sake of the object to be gained you will be willing to make the effort, and I refuse to believe that a people as subtile as any under the sun and who promise to eclipse every nation since the Greeks in their genius for abstract studies should be generally unable to follow the necessarily complicated arguments of the Logician.

Logic is a much abused science. Like Medicine, Law, and in short any branch of knowledge which has important practical bearings, it is brought by its applications to an ordeal which is sure to make its shortcomings manifest. It is no more perfect than any other product of humanity and we have the same right to be dissatisfied with its present state than we have with everything else that <u>we are in a condition to improve</u>.

What is logic? It is the science by which we are enabled to test reasons. Now to test anything there is a particular sort of facts which it is necessary to know. The bank-note detector contains the science by which we test bank-notes, and that consists in a classification of all bank-notes with an accurate description of each species. So with analytical chemistry; it is nothing but a system of classification of bodies; and the whole subject of chemical physics—the reason <u>why</u> in chemistry—is totally out of the analyst's line. And so you will find that it is a universal rule that to have a <u>testing art</u> we need no other knowledge than a <u>classifying science</u>. And accordingly, if we wish to be able to test arguments, what we have to do, is to take all the arguments we can find, scrutinize them and put those which are alike in a class by themselves and then examine all these different kinds and learn their properties. Now the classificatory science of reasons so produced is the science of Logic. And it is so obvious, that the research I have described, however difficult presents nothing transcending human power altogether; and that the possession of the resulting knowledge— so long as men are constantly erring in reasoning and so long as the scientific world is divided upon a question which it must call in logic to solve—would be very useful, that those who sneer not merely at this or that antiquated yet once valuable logic but at all logical studies whatever display an ignorance not only of what logicians have already accomplished but also of the very nature of the science itself.

But, indeed, few persons who have not had some special interest in the subject are at all aware of the immense progress which has been made in the science during the present century.

Logic is a very ancient science; it is 2300 years of age. It has been more constantly studied than any except Law, Medicine, and Divinity. It has always been pursued by men of learning principally. And it found its Newton, almost at its birth. The subject has gradually become encumbered with a great mass of useless subtileties.

Another thing which brought logic into disrepute was the fierce Medieval dispute of the nominalists and realists. No definite notion of the nature of the disagreement can be afforded by a brief statement. Suffice it to say that the Realists believed that there is really humanity in man, animality in animals, and so forth; while the Nominalists held that humanity, animality, and such terms, are merely words indicating the applicability to men, animals, _et cetera_, of their class appellations. The discussions of the learned doctors sometimes ended with black eyes and bloody noses; and even monarchs patronized one party or the other and protected it by the power of the state.

We have, at present, Formal logicians and Anthropological logicians. Anthropological logicians think that Logic must be founded upon a knowledge of human nature and requires a constant reference to the facts of human nature. Formal logicians believe that logic can be learned merely by the comparison of the products of thinking. For my part, while admitting that the greater array of talent is upon the side of anthropologists, I agree myself with the formal logicians.

Let us suppose, for example, that the opinion of James Mill be adopted that all inference arises merely from the association of ideas. Here is one of those psychological or anthropological facts which Stuart Mill thinks has a great bearing upon logic. But would such a fact make any argument good which we had hitherto supposed to be bad? Not at all. Does it make any argument bad which we had hitherto supposed to be good? Not at all. Then I say that however true and important the discovery may be, it has nothing to do with logic whatsoever.

_II_: September 1866

Zeno, we are repeatedly[†] informed, was considered by Aristotle as the originator of Logic. If so, it was the mere germ of the science which he originated: our gratitude is chiefly due to Aristotle himself. In order to understand Zeno's curious arguments we should observe his historic standpoint. For three hundred years after the Homeric poems, the Greeks were satisfied with such an account of the _all_ of things as their mythology afforded. Then first appeared the Ionian *wise men who thought that all the world was made out of <u>water</u> or some other element. The necessity for a unity in all things had begun to be recognized and at first they sought it in its crudest form as the one material of the universe. A century later, the Eleatic philosophers seized upon this unity in all its abstractness. "All that is, is one," said Xenophanes; and herein he enunciated the first postulate of Philosophy. To explain is to show the unity at the heart of the manifold. To explain the conduct of Hamlet is to show how one character gave rise to his most contradictory actions. To explain the polarization of light is to show how all the varied phenomena arise from a single property. In the same way, to explain the totality of things, which is the business of philosophy, we must show that one essence is at the bottom of it all. What we call the Absolute, is what the Greeks more philosophically termed the <u>One</u>. In saying that all things are one, Xenophanes laid the corner-stone of Metaphysics. But Parmenides added: The <u>Many</u> is a mere illusion, he carried out the conception one-sidedly. However such came to be the opinion of the only real school of philosophers at that time; that the <u>one</u> alone was real, the <u>many</u> false and illusive. Zeno was the pupil and defender of Parmenides; and Protagoras, the greatest of the Sophists, was his contemporary. These two men, Zeno and Protagoras, were antipodes, for they rested their several philosophies upon two contrary propositions. In this way, they are a commentary upon one another. Protagoras said, there is no absolute, every man is the measure of things, of what is that it is, and of what is not that it is not. Both philosophers, therefore, identified <u>being</u> and <u>thinking</u>, but in different ways. Zeno made the unity of thought the real being. Protagoras made the manifold of experience the only reality. He adopted from Heraclitus the opinion that all things are in a state of flow—never are but only are <u>becoming</u>—and so his central conception was that of <u>CONTINUITY</u>. On the other hand, it was an axiom with Zeno that continuity is incomprehensible, and therefore false. And it is upon that axiom that his four famous arguments against the possibility of motion, or rather against the reality of space owing to certain characters of motion, were founded.*

<u>III</u>: September 1866

Those capitalists who[†] laid out so many millions in laying the Atlantic telegraph—not because they were improvident and overweening madcaps for they were solid Englishmen, intrepid, unflinching, and cool; upon what did they rest their hopes of success? Why, upon just such an argument as this. If a telegraph can work across the Channel, they said, it can work across the Atlantic. Every argument by which we get to any new truth is also of such a kind as this. The faculty for this sort of reasoning makes up shrewdness, and is the essence of genius. The alliance of man with the divinity is more plainly seen here than anywhere. He observes the regularities of the animal kingdom now, and he knows from that how it was in some geological era—a million ages ago. He observes that a thousand, or a million or a billion men have died, and he leaps to the fact that all men <u>will</u> die;—he has not <u>observed</u> it of those who now live but he <u>knows</u> it of them and all other men who ever shall be, though they be so numerous that a billion will be to them but as the number of grains of sand in ten thousand cartloads to all that lie upon the sea-shore. In short, he observes the finite and he seems to know the possible infinite. For my part, I could not imagine a more sublime manifestation of the Deity, than that which thus appears in the nature of inference itself.

Nevertheless I must say that these theological conclusions are no part of Logic. Man requires to comprehend his own arguments; and unless he can comprehend them he is dashed from this lofty pinnacle to the level of an irrational machine. If he is impelled, he knows not upon what principle, without any conscious principle from one belief to another, he has no more reason than the pen with which he writes. The lofty speculations of the theological logicians are not needed in logic, for the mere faculty of colligating facts and drawing general conclusions from them—a faculty however which appears to be as divine as any other—is quite sufficient to show the rational nature of logic.

The same logicians who take this view of scientific presumption, also sometimes tell us that logic rests upon the goodness of God. But of all logical improvidence, it seems to me that the greatest is that of those men who would deprive themselves of the advantage of using Logic and Scientific reasoning generally, as an evidence of the goodness of God. If this most goodly frame the earth, and this most excellent canopy the air, look you, this brave o'erhanging firmament, this majestical roof fretted with golden fire, will not prove that God is good, think you that any syllogism which is at best but a barren turning about of what we already know is going to do it? <u>FIE</u>! There is no sense in such a thought. And yet this is the logical consequence of resting Logic upon Theology.

<u>VI</u>: October 1866
Practical Maxims of Logic
1. Beware of a† syllogism.
2. Remember that a <u>hypothesis</u> must have more antecedent probability than the facts which it explains. Extent of predicate greatest possible.
3. In reasoning from individuals to a whole class, the class should be the one, including those individuals, whose content is the greatest possible.
4. There is no valid inference from parts to whole if the parts have not been taken at random.
5. Everything can be explained.

<u>VII</u>: October 1866
Ladies and Gentlemen, in entering the second half† of the course, I cannot refrain from expressing my appreciation of the attentive hearing which you have accorded to me thus far. The subject, though of extreme importance, is al-

*together shunned by unreflecting minds; it is of a kind which requires a real ex-
ertion for a trained mind to follow, and when delivered orally this difficulty is
much increased. That a hundred gentlemen and ladies, engrossed in their daily
business or avocations, should be found to listen to six lectures upon the forms
of syllogism was something which, I confess, was not to be anticipated, and
which it seems to me puts in a very clear light the superior cultivation and
greater intellectual taste of the people of this city. I am confident that such a dry
course of lectures would have been impossible anywhere else in the country
than in the hall of this celebrated and extraordinary institution. I said in my first
lecture that it seemed to me the New Englanders had a peculiar genius for philosophy; it is not only because they have Edwards, Channing, Parker, Bushnell,
Emerson, James, Bowen, Abbot, and many other philosophical writers, although we have here a list of names very creditable both individually and for
the variety of mind they show. But what more than this makes me hope that
New England will shed a light upon these subjects is the subtlety and ideality
of the Yankee mind as seen in its uncultivated state. But though the Yankee is
thus fitted to do so much good service in philosophy, let us by no means forget
that he has not done it hitherto. Let us not mistake promise for performance. No
American Philosophy has as yet been produced; and we may perhaps never
live to see our country take the place which she ought to do before the world
in this particular. I, for one, as an humble student of the works of philosophers
am ready to stand by the first Yankee who can do something better. I do not say
that I am ready to adopt his philosophy, but I am ready to do what little I can
to encourage the developement and presentation of his thought.*

*Now, ladies and gentlemen, I here announce[†] the great and fundamental
secret of the logic of science. There is no term, properly so called, which is entirely destitute of information, of equivalent terms. The moment an expression
acquires sufficient comprehension to determine its extension, it already has
more than enough to do so.*

*Consider what a word or symbol is; it is a sort of representation. Now a rep-
resentation is something which stands for something. I will not undertake to analyze, this evening, this conception of standing for something—but it is sufficiently plain that it involves the standing to something for something. A thing
cannot stand for something without standing to something for that something.
Now what is this that a word stands to? Is it a person? We usually say that the
word homme stands to a Frenchman for man. It would be a little more precise
to say that it stands to the Frenchman's mind—to his memory. It is still more accurate to say that it addresses a particular remembrance or image in that memory. And what image, what remembrance? Plainly, the one which is the mental
equivalent of the word homme—in short, its interpretant or identified symbol.
Conversely, every interpretant is addressed by the word; for were it not so, did
it not as it were overhear what the word says, how could it interpret what it says?
There are doubtless some who cannot understand this metaphorical argument.*

I wish to show that the relation of a word to that which it addresses is the same as its relation to its equivalent or identified terms. For that purpose, I first show that whatever a word addresses is an equivalent term,—its mental equivalent. I next show that, since the intelligent reception of a term is the being addressed by that term, and since the explication of a term's implication is the intelligent reception of that term, that the interpretant or equivalent of a term, which as we have already seen explicates the implication of a term, is addressed by the term. The interpretant of a sign, then, and that which it stands to are identical. Hence, since it is of the very essence of a symbol that it should stand to something, every symbol—every word and every conception—must have an interpretant— or what is the same thing, must have information or implication.

IX: November 1866

 Ladies and gentlemen, at the last[†] lecture, we made some reflections upon the proper mode of conceiving the progress of truth from the outward things to the full understanding. We found that the first impressions upon our senses are not representations of certain unknown things in themselves but are themselves those very unknown things in themselves. Our first impressions are entirely unknown in themselves and the matter of cognition is the matter of fact and what is not a question of a possible experience is not a question of fact. These impressions are grasped into the unity which the mind requires, the unity of the I think—the unity of consistency, by conceptions and sensations. These are nothing else than predicates which the mind affixes by virtue of a hypothetical inference in order to understand the data presented to it. A hypothetical predicate is one which is affixed to a thing which has not been experienced as possessing it in order to bring the manifold in the experienced thing to unity. Now this is just the character of a conception or sensation. Take the sense of beauty as an example; when we hear a sonata of Beethoven's the predicate of beautiful is affixed to it as a single representation of the complicated phenomena presented to the ear. The beauty does not belong to each note or chord but to the whole. We have not therefore heard the beauty for we have heard only the single chords successively. What we have heard is therefore only the occasion of the feeling that is beautiful, only the data to reduce which to unity the sense of beauty serves. Beautiful is therefore a hypothetically adjoined predicate. This illustrates how the logical function of sensations is that of a hypothetical predicate.

 The same thing is still more obvious in the case of a conception. I make five dots on the chalkboard. Now a person in a drowsy state might see those dots and not reflect that they were five. The conception of five is, therefore, not in the eye, is not seen, since that drowsy person would see all that we do, but is introduced by the mind in order to comprehend (or reduce to a consistent whole) what is seen. Thus both sensations and conceptions are hypothetic predicates. They are, however, hypotheses of widely different kinds. A sensation is a sort of mental name. To assign a name to a thing is to make a hypoth-

esis. It is plainly a predicate which is not in the <u>data</u>. But it is given on account of a logical necessity; namely the necessity of reducing the manifold of the predicates given to unity.

Sensation is, as it were, the writing on the page of consciousness. Conception is the meaning of the sensation. A conception, therefore, is not in the mind in the sense in which a sensation is; it requires to be embodied in a sensation, as much as it requires to be embodied in matter in order to be carried out into the external world.

Of the numerous conceptions of the mind, some apply only to certain special collections of impressions and are called <u>particular</u>. Others apply to all collections of impressions and are called <u>universal</u>. Of universal conceptions, the most outward, the first that is reached as truth enters the mind, is <u>Substance</u>— or the <u>very thing</u>—that is the conception of the immediately present in general. In another point of view it is that which can only be subject never predicate. The last conception, the most inward, which lies at the centre of consciousness and completes the act of understanding is <u>being</u>—or that which whatever is intelligible possesses in itself.

Between <u>substance</u> and <u>being</u> we found that there intervene three universal conceptions:—

Reference to a Ground
Reference to a Correlate
Reference to an Interpretant.

The manner in which we made sure that these three conceptions and these only intervene between the manifold of substance and the unity of being is sufficiently simple when you once take it in. We began by distinguishing three kinds of mental separation: 1st <u>dissociation</u>, 2nd <u>abstraction</u> or <u>prescission</u>, and 3rd <u>discrimination</u>. We dissociate one object from another when we think of it without thinking of that other at the same time. We can for example dissociate a <u>colour</u> from a <u>sound</u>; but we cannot dissociate space from colour. We <u>prescind</u> one object from another, when we suppose it to be without that other. For example, we can <u>prescind</u> space from colour because we can suppose a space to be uncoloured. We discriminate one thing from another when we can recognize that they are not the same—thus we can discriminate colour from space though we cannot prescind colour from space.

Quality is the 1st conception before <u>being</u>.

<u>Relation</u>, or reference to a correlate is the next conception in order.

The next conception in order is reference of things to a mediating representation or <u>interpretant</u>.

A Representation is either a Likeness, an Index, or a Symbol. A likeness or icon represents its object by agreeing with it in some particular. An index represents its object by a real correspondence with it—as a tally does quarts of milk, and a vane the wind. A symbol is a general representation like a word or conception.

XI: November 1866

Ladies and Gentlemen, philosophy is[t] the attempt—for as the word itself implies it is and must be imperfect—is the attempt to form a general informed conception of the <u>All</u>. All men philosophize; and as Aristotle says we must do so if only to prove the futility of philosophy. Those who neglect philosophy have metaphysical theories as much as others—only they are rude, false, and wordy theories. Some think to avoid the influence of metaphysical errors, by paying no attention to metaphysics; but experience shows that these men beyond all others are held in an iron vise of metaphysical theory, because by theories that they have never called in question. No man is so enthralled by metaphysics as the totally uneducated; no man is so free from its dominion as the metaphysician himself. Since, then, everyone must have conceptions of things in general, it is most important that they should be carefully constructed.

I shall enter into no criticism of the different methods of metaphysical research, but shall merely say that in the opinion of several great thinkers, the only successful mode yet lighted upon is that of adopting our logic as our metaphysics. In the last lecture I endeavored to show how logic furnishes us with a classification of the elements of consciousness. We found that all modifications of consciousness are inferences and that all inferences are valid inferences. At the same time we found that there were 3 kinds of inference: 1st Intellectual inference with its three varieties—Hypothesis, Induction, and Deduction; 2nd Judgments of sensation, emotions, and instinctive motions which are hypotheses whose predicates are unanalyzed in comprehension; and 3rd Habits which are Inductions whose subjects are unanalyzed in extension. This division leads us to three elements of consciousness: 1st <u>Feelings</u> or Elements of comprehension, 2nd <u>Efforts</u> or Elements of extension, and 3rd <u>Notions</u> or Elements of Information, which is the union of extension and comprehension. I regret that the time does not permit me to dwell further upon this theory but I wish to pass to a loftier and more practical question of metaphysics in order to put in a still stronger light the advantages of the study of logic. The question which I shall select is "what is man?" I think I may state the prevalent conception thus: Man is essentially a soul, that is, a thing occupying a mathematical point of space, not thought itself but the subject of inhesion of thought, without parts, and exerting a certain material force called volition. I presume that most people consider this belief as <u>intuitive</u>, or, at least, as planted in man's nature and more or less distinctly held by all men, always and everywhere.

We have already seen[t] that every state of consciousness is an inference; so that life is but a sequence of inferences or a train of thought. At any instant then man is a thought, and as thought is a species of symbol, the general answer to the question What is man? is that he is a symbol. To find a more specific answer we should compare man with some other symbol.

I write here the word <u>six</u>. Let us ask ourselves in what respects a <u>man</u> differs from that word. A man has a consciousness; a word has not. We attribute it to animals but not to words, because we have reason to believe that it depends upon the possession of an animal body. In the second place, consciousness is used to mean the knowledge which we have of what is in our minds; the fact that our thought is an index for itself of itself on the ground of a complete identity with itself. But so is any word or indeed any thing, so that this constitutes no difference between the word and the man. In the third place, consciousness is used to denote the <u>I think</u>, the unity of thought; but the unity of thought is nothing but the unity of symbolization—consistency, in a word (the implication of <u>being</u>) and belongs to every word whatever. It is very easy to think we have a <u>clear</u> notion of what we mean by consciousness, and yet it may be that the word excites no thought but only a sensation, a mental word within us; and then because we are not accustomed to allow the word written on the board to excite that sensation, we may think we distinguish between the man and the word when we do not.

> Most ignorant of what we're most assured
> Our glassy essence!

How much more the word <u>electricity</u> means[†] now than it did in the days of Franklin. These words have acquired information; just as a man's thought does by further perception.

You see that remote and dissimilar as the word and the man appear, it is exceedingly difficult to state any essential difference between them except a physiological one.

Enough has now been said, I think, to show a true analogy between a man and a word. I dare say this seems very paradoxical to you; I remember it did to me, at first. But having thought it over repeatedly, it has come to seem the merest truism.

The necessary and true[†] symbol is immortal, and man must also be so, provided he is vivified by the truth. If instead of <u>six</u> we had written <u>Jove</u>, we should have had a symbol which has but a contingent existence; it has no everlasting witness in the nature of things and will pass away or remain only in men's memories without exciting any response in their hearts.

Gentlemen and ladies, I announce to you[†] this theory of immortality for the first time. It is poorly said, poorly thought; but its foundation is the rock of truth. And at least it will serve to illustrate what use might be made by mightier hands of this reviled science, logic, <u>nec ad melius[†] vivendum, nec ad commodius disserendum.</u>

There is another important corollary which may be drawn from the law of symbols. The interpretant is evidently the Divine <u>Logos</u> or word; and if our former guess that a Reference to an interpretant is Paternity be right, this would be also the <u>Son of God</u>. The <u>ground</u>, being that partaking of which is requisite to any communication with the Symbol, corresponds in its function to the Holy Spirit.

(1905). It must have been in 1866[†] that Professor De Morgan honored the unknown beginner in philosophy that I then was by sending me a copy of his memoir, "On the Logic[†] of Relations." I at once fell to upon it, and before many weeks had come to see it, as De Morgan had already done, a brilliant and astonishing illumination of every corner and every vista of logic. Let me pause to say that no decent semblance of justice has ever been done to De Morgan, owing to his not having brought anything to its final shape. Even his personal students, reverent as they perforce were, never sufficiently understood that his was the work of an exploring expedition, which every day comes upon new forms for the study of which leisure is, at the moment, lacking, because additional novelties are coming in and requiring note. He stood indeed like Aladdin gazing upon the overwhelming riches of Ali Baba's cave, scarce capable of making a rough inventory of them. It was quite twenty-five years before my studies of it all reached what might be called a near approach toward a provisionally final result (absolute finality never being presumable in any universal science); but a short time sufficed to furnish me with mathematical demonstration that indecomposable predicates are of three classes: first, those which, like neuter verbs, apply but to a single object; secondly, those which like simple transitive verbs have two subjects each; and thirdly, those predicates which have three such subjects, or correlates. These last never express mere brute fact, but always some relation of an intellectual nature, being either constituted by action of a mental kind or implying some general law.

THREE PAPERS[†]
ON
LOGIC.
READ BEFORE
THE AMERICAN ACADEMY OF ARTS
AND SCIENCES. 1867
By C. S. Peirce.

Students of logic (and persons who will study it) will be supplied, upon application to the author by letter, with copies of these papers and of others which are to follow. The latter will be sent only to those who express a wish to make use of them.

CHARLES S. PEIRCE
2 Arrow Street
Cambridge, Massachusetts

It is true[†] that I have not received much credit either for pragmatism or any other part of my work. However, as it was not done for the sake of anything of that kind, I have no reason to complain. What I expected to gain when I did it,

I have gained. I began on the scale of printing a logical research every month. My motive then was a mixed one. I wanted the statement of my results in print for my own convenience in referring to them, and I thought it would be a gain to civilization to have my entire logical system. But after a very few months, I found that nobody took any notice of my papers, and I lost all interest in their publication, and simply filed away my mss. for my own use.

When I was in the twenties[†] I devoted more than two years with all the passion of that age to the study of phanerochemy (phaneroscopy), in almost every waking hour and dreaming of nothing else. But I was not to be content with less than solid truth; and at the end of two years and a half (reduce it to that by deducting intervals) my situation was this. In regard to the qualitative differences between the different elements of thought, I had made out some relations with certainty, much as one can make out some relations between the different colors. Three pages of letter paper recorded all that I regarded as relatively certain, together with some things that did not seem certain. On the whole, I concluded to abandon the research to some greater genius. But there was a triad of mere differences of quantitative complexity that did not seem to me to be open to any doubt at all. This was recorded in a paper printed in the Proc. Am. Acad. Arts & Sci. for May 14, 1867,—"On a New List of Categories." During the third of a century and more that has since elapsed, I have done all that man could to guard myself against self deception. I have given up years to the operation of instilling pooh-poohs of it into my soul. I have earnestly striven against the conviction. But for a long time the game has been quite up. It is too evidently true.

1910, Sep 2 PM 2:00

Phaneroscopy, or the science[†] of what might appear or seem. I do not pretend to have a definite conception of this study as a whole; but I think this must be something like, or taking the place of, a corrected version of Hegel's Phänomenologie des Geistes. It is what a boy of ideal intelligence would say to himself on first waking up to the fact that he _is_;—that he is a thinking _being_ that can measurably control his thoughts. That begins his development as a philosopher; and the first Question, perhaps, that he opens, having just discovered his own personal reality as an inference from his mistakes and from his ignorance, may be, "What could direct effort, i.e. _attention_ accomplish, and how?" At any rate it will be granted that before he could be led to ask himself any _normative_ questions, he must have asked other questions, and must have thought out answers to them, and must have entertained doubts of those answers. If he were less vigorous than we have supposed him, Thou and I, Reader,—his suffering might have led him to discover his own soul earlier, and have thrown himself into the error of believing he knows outward reality through inward reality, instead of recognizing the truth that he only knows his own existence as a plausible theory to account for outward experience,—outward, I mean, to himself whether outward to his person or not.

HOW TO DEFINE

I

1909 Dec 22 PM 2.30
DEFINITION 3rd DRAUGHT 1†
   Three studies are needlessly and very unhappily confounded: Phaneroscopy (as I call it, or Phenomenology), Logic, and Psychology Proper. One of the three is a Science, though youthful and immature; that is Psychology Proper. One is an Embrio-science; so I rate Logic, because it still lacks that considerable body of well-drilled workers pursuing methods acknowledged by all, taking advantage of one another's discoveries to push research still on and on, and turning out new discoveries at a healthy rate; all of which I take to be essential to a developed science. The third is Phaneroscopy, still in the condition of a science-egg, hardly any details of it being as yet distinguishable, though enough to assure the student of it that, under the fostering care that it is sure to enjoy, if the human culture continues long, it surely will in the future become a strong and beneficient science.
   By Psychology Proper I mean the Empirical Science of the workings and growths of Minds and their relations to the animal or other organisms in which Psychical phenomena can be detected. In short, it is a sort of Physiology of the Soul. By Logic I mean the study of the distinction between Truth and Falsity, and the theory of how to attain the former together with all that the investigator of that theory must make it his business to probe. It comes, in my opinion, in the present state of science, to a study of the general nature of Signs and the leading kinds of Signs. By Phaneroscopy I mean the study of whatever consciousness puts into one's Immediate and Complete possession, or in other words, the study of whatever one becomes directly aware of in itself. For such Direct objects of Consciousness I venture to coin the term "Prebits." Some may think this word would idly cumber the dictionary in the unlikely contingency of its ever coming into use. They will regard it as a superfluous synonym of "appearances," or "phenomena," "data," etc., etc. I admit that "datum" might do. But then many other things are called "data"; as for the word "phenomenon," I think that is better reserved to express those more special meanings to which it is usually restricted; as, for example, to denote any fact that consists in the uniformity with which something peculiar and perceptible to the senses (without or with instrumental aid) will result from the fulfillment of certain definite conditions, especially if it can be repeated indefinitely. Thus, the fact that small bits of paper or anything else that is light enough will be attracted to a rod of shellac, glass, vulcanite, etc. provided this has just before been briskly rubbed upon a soft surface of suitable material with a harder backing is one single phenomenon, while the fact that a rod of steel or of one of a few other substances will attract small filings or other bits of iron, as magnetite, etc. is a different single phenomenon. By a "Prebit" I do not mean anything of that nature, but a single Object of immediate consciousness, though usually indefinitely denoted. As for

the word "Appearance," it would be stretched in an inconvenient and quite un-expected way if it would be applied to some of the objects I call Prebits. Before he has read many pages the Reader will come upon an example that will bring the truth of this home to him. In the above Definition of "Prebit," the adjective "Immediate" is not to be understood in a Properly Psychological sense, as if it were intended to exclude the case of my becoming aware of a Prebit in conse-quence of becoming aware of another thing, whether Prebit or not; but what I do mean is that once I do become aware of the Prebit, I am aware not merely before of a Sign Substitute for it, or any sort of proxy, vicar, attorney, succeda-neum, dummy, or representative of it, but am put _facie ad faciem_ before the very Prebit itself.

The importance of distinguishing between the three studies is due in the first place to the diversity of their general aims. Phaneroscopy asks what are the possibilities of consciousness. Psychology deals with questions of what we are directly conscious of, and involves very little or no reasoning. Logic involves no more observation than Pure Mathematics itself, and is entirely occupied with necessary reasoning. Logic inquires into the theory of what must follow or is likely, or a warrantable assumption in hypothetical cases. Psychology reunites in itself all the methods and all the difficulties of the other Empirical Sciences; it endeavors to make known the positive facts of the workings of the mind.

In the Second place, the methods of the three inquiries are as divergent as their aims. In Phaneroscopy there is little reasoning. Its questions are only set-tled by the finest of keen observations. Logic on the other hand involves no more observation than does Pure Mathematics itself, that is to say only the ob-servation of our own diagrams. It is a science of reasoning and subtle distinc-tions. Psychology Proper again uses all the methods and involves all the diffi-culties of all the other Empirical Sciences.

For the purposes of the present essay, however, the most urgent reason for distinguishing these studies from one another, and more especially the two that are most apt to be confounded,—Phaneroscopy and Psychology Proper,—is that, on the one hand, Logic must be founded on the results of Phaneroscopy, so that the _Phaneroscopist has no right to appeal to the science of logic;_ while on the other hand, Psychology Proper, more than any other study, excepting only metaphysics, depends for its support upon the science of Logic, in conse-quence of which the _Logician is forbidden to appeal for support to Psychology Proper_. Moreover, Psychology Proper, thus mediately rests on Phaneroscopy and _can furnish no support to the latter._ Still less can it question the latter's re-sults, which would be not more nor less than sawing off the bough on which it is astride.

II

I have often heard psychologists speak with contempt, pity, or disdain of that division of the functions of the mind or ("Parts of the Soul") into Feeling, Volition, and Thought, which has recommended itself to so many and many *thinkers, since Kant gave it his sanction. For my part I cannot believe that an Idea of that sort that has recommended itself to so great a variety of powerful minds to express a truth, should have no ingredient whatever of Truth in it; and it seems to my own self-observation that Feelings, Volitions, and Thoughts are Prebits, that there are in truth in those three Prebits three utterly different Phaneroscopic elements that appear as so many kinds of Awareness, and no more, that are severally contained in those three kinds of Prebits mentioned. Beginning with Feeling, in order to show what qualifications I have for describing it, I may mention that for more than twenty years, from before 1865 to after 1885, I was almost daily training myself to recognize and analyze by immediate consciousness the different elements and respects of difference of colors, odours, flavours, and other sensations. I also paid a good deal of attention to phonetics. I desire not to exaggerate the degree of success which I attained. It was considerable, yet by no means extraordinary. In regard to each sense, I have met a number of persons whose powers surpassed my own, though my powers of distinction and recognition were much above the average. For instance, though I am so far from being a musician that if I attempt to sing a tune I make my auditors laugh. They tell me I skip from one octave to another; I nevertheless have no difficulty in picking out three or four harmonics in a note struck on a piano-forte. Perhaps everybody can do the same: I do not know. I also seem to have a somewhat unusual faculty of catching the accent of a foreign tongue. For example, I once desired to remain for a fortnight or so in a certain rural vicinity, and inquiring who thereabouts took boarders was informed that a French farmer and his wife not far away received a few in summer. It was then autumn, but their being French recommended their table to me, and so I went toward their house. As I strolled along the husband overtook me. He was evidently a Belgian but he said his wife was a Parisian and no doubt would be glad to take me in. I went and was presented and we were on the point of closing the agreement when I happened to speak of myself as an American. Instantly her manner changed; she raised various objections, and at last said flatly she would not take me. I persisted without being able for a long time to penetrate her objection, until finally I took the husband aside and asked him what the real objection was.*

"Why, you see," he said, "she distrusts you because of your sailing under false colors."

"What do you mean," I asked.

"Why do you pretend to be an American?"

"Why! Because I am."

"Oh come! You know that isn't so."

"What do you think?"

"Well, I might take your word, but my wife says it is nonsense. He is a Parisian. No American ever spoke like him."

This seemed to me as sincere a tribute to my French as I could easily find.

As to Feeling, by which I mean Qualities of Sensation and other Passions, I remark that most persons, David Hume, for example, reckon as one kind of ingredient of it a certain Prebit which seems to me to form no part of Feeling. I mean the <u>Vividness</u> of a Feeling. For Feeling is a Quality and though it certainly has two Quantities connected with it, its total intensity and the relative intensity of its leading ingredient, both being Quantities of Quality, I do not recognize Vividness as the Quantity of any Quality or predicate at all, but simply as a non-relative or non-predicative Quantity. Now what is non-predicative Quantity that is a Prebit? It is a <u>force</u>. On the other hand, Quality is entirely Passive, and is no force. Vividness, therefore, is no part or essential attribute of a Feeling: it is something of an utterly different nature. I have doubted whether I was not led into an error in saying this by a psychological action. I have asked myself whether Vividness is not Intensity of Feeling to which a psychological correction or allowance has subconsciously been applied. But this theory distinctly does not fit the facts. For such allowances are always insufficient when they are very large. A dime, for example, may seem to be of the same size at a distance of ten inches and of three feet. But it certainly looks smaller thirty feet or a hundred feet away. To an eye not accustomed to recognize what it sees, snow in ordinary shade and snow in the light of bright clouds may be supposed to look equally white, although in fact, the former is deep violet blue and the latter bright yellow. But let the case be sufficiently exaggerated by contrasting snow almost in darkness with snow in the glare of a very blazing noon, and any eye will see the difference of color once it is pointed out. Now it makes no difference at all how dim my memory of a certain stick of sealing wax is. If I recollect its color at all, I remember it correctly as a brilliant vermillion or as a dull one.

Hume, then, gave evidence of his being but a poor psychological observer when he based his Philosophy, in considerable part, on a confusion of Vividness with the Objective Intensity of Sensation. An experimental research of my own has convinced me that Vividness is no element of a Sense-Quality. It is the pervasive Reaction from the waking-up force of the Vivid Experience. It therefore neither is, nor is an ingredient of, any Feeling-Quality whatever. It is a pure sense of Force and not an ingredient of the peculiar characteristic of Feeling. It is something else admixed to that; and in order to cognize the peculiar characteristic of Feeling we must get rid of this admixture,—this adulteration,—by an operation of <u>Discrimination.</u>

You will, I suppose,—and I hope,—inquire what I mean by Discrimination, thus showing yourself to be a reader who cares for precision of Thought. In the <u>Proceedings of the American Academy[†] of Arts and Sciences</u> for 1867 May 14, in my article entitled "On a New List of Categories," you will find that I have explained that there are three Modes of separability of elements of a Thought-Object, which I called, <u>Precision</u> (a corruption of speech for which I now substitute "Prescission"), <u>Dissociation,</u> and <u>Discrimination.</u> Let there be two ele-

ments of an Object of Thought, A and B. If I can <u>imagine</u> A to be present without B, I say I can <u>Dissociate</u> A from B; and I can then generally Dissociate B from A, too. If I can definitely <u>suppose</u> A to be present without any supposition at all about the presence or absence of B (and, of course, without self-contradiction), I say that I can <u>Prescind</u> A from B, and that I can <u>Abstract</u> B from A. If I can suppose one of the two to be equally present or absent in two cases, while in the other respect the cases differ, I say that I can <u>Discriminate</u> each from the other.

I quite acknowledge that this bit of analysis of forty-odd years ago now sadly needs an overhauling; but in the mean time it will serve our turn for the present juncture. I cannot imagine a Feeling-Quality without some degree of Vividness, however small, in the Experience I so imagine; but I can imagine the Vividness to vary while the Quality itself remains quite unchanged. If I experience a Quality, say a certain rose color, having previously dreamed of a perfect match to it (which will render the experience more vivid), and some years after call up a reminiscence of that experience, the three Feelings may be closely alike as to the Quality of the red,—its luminosity, its chroma (or saturation), and its hue,—but they will surely differ widely, almost enormously, in their Vividness. But now if I think of the color of the rose, as it would be if nobody were looking at it, or dreaming or recollecting it, that Thought will not attribute much or little Vividness to it but only a Capacity for every degree of Vividness. That pure Quality, in its hue, its chroma, and its luminosity, or Feeling <u>minus</u> Vividness, will be an example of the characteristic ingredient of the mode of Awareness that we call Feeling. I will call it Feeling-Quality. It is a Prebit-category.

A feeling is the only true <u>Ding an sich</u>. Everything else is relative, and has its Being in something else. But the color of Vermillion is just what it is without reference to blue or green. It is what it is, and there is nothing that can describe it but itself. Everything (as it seems, at least) has its own flavor, Shakespeare, Bernard Shaw, Rudder Grange, The Autocrat, Bach, Chopin, all have Qualities absolutely their own. Every lapse of time in one's life whether it be a lifetime, a season, a waking day, a quarter of an hour, ten seconds, a fraction of a second, makes as a whole an impression of a quality absolutely simple and entirely without ingredients, and peculiar to itself. But the universality of these statements may be delusive. I have no right to say more than that so it seems. It is true that if two qualities or more be compared, their similarities will be felt. But since everything seems to have its Feeling-Quality, so has the comparison; and those similarities are the Qualities of the comparison, not of the Feeling compared. For the Feeling-Quality resides in itself. In saying this I am not conveying information, nor setting up a doctrine to be approved or rejected: I am only explaining what I mean by a Feeling-Quality. It is that which is immediately sensible as absolutely simple and <u>sui generis</u> in every whole to which my feeling is directed; and you have only to feel in order to know what I mean.

But Feeling-Quality cannot be known in a state of purity. For *in itself* it does not exist, but only *may be.* Existence is conferred upon it by so much Vividness as it has; and Vividness is an example of the Second kind of Awareness, which we find in Volition. However, it is with Volition as we found it to be with Feeling: I mean that its characteristic essence is only Experience mixed with something else. That something else in the case of Volition is Purpose. We never do exert our Wills without Purpose. Yet the characteristic of Volition is Volition *sans* Purpose: it is just brute exertion, which I call *Molition*. Molition is a Mode of Awareness entirely different from Feeling. One does not Feel it at all, as anybody can convince himself by repetitions of the simplest experiments. For example, hold a dumbbell out at arm's length and tell yourself at the outset not to do anything whatever with that arm,—neither pulling it up nor putting it down,—until you give yourself the word. After a while gravity will catch the arm in such a state that it will take a little step down, which is not surprising, since gravity is pulling at it unceasingly, while the state of the arm is not one of ceaseless inertia. But what is a little surprising is that after each of these little descents the arm springs up a little, although you did not tell it to. For you, I am supposing, have given the arm no orders of any kind since you told it not to move until you gave the word. It comes up with what appears like an elastic rebound. All this time, you have made no exertion whatever. You have been perfectly quiet, but you have felt a certain pain. Now that you are about to give the mental word for your arm to come down, be on the alert to see whether you have any Feeling of that giving of the word. Now, actually give the word, and the arm comes down so instantly that you cannot tell which reached your brain first, the report that your order had been received, or the report that the arm was falling. You even suspect the latter report came first. But the significant circumstance is that there was nothing like a *Feeling* connected with giving the mental word. You were aware of doing so, as quite distinct from being aware of purposing to do so; but there was not a trace of Feeling now of your willing the arm should drop. You may vary the experiment in a hundred ways, but such will always be the result. In saying this, I am supposing that you are expert in performing these experiments. You may lay your hand, palm upon a table with a kilo upon it or whatever weight will be sufficient to make you quite aware of the effort of lifting it by bending your elbow, without the effort being so great as sensibly to prevent your noticing any Feelings. It will be well to have your hand so cold that there is hardly any feeling in it. It will also be well for your arm to be unclothed. Let your hand lie quiet and gather all your attention. When this is accomplished, and while your attention is at its best (for it will have its pretty rapid ebbs and flows), or just coming to its best, hold your breath, so as the better to hold your attention, give the word (mentally) for the weight to be lifted, and watch for anything like Feeling,—that is, for anything as much of the nature of color, or odour, or the sense of beauty or sublimity, as these Feelings are like one another. Of course you will have what is called "kinesthetic sensation," but to my power of discrimination that sort of consciousness has no trace of Feeling in it, though there will be skin sensations from which you must abstract your attention. I expect that such experimentation, repeated and verified until you find no more room for doubt, will bring you to the same conviction to which it has brought me. But, of course, if your mind is of the wordy sort, and you think that reading about an experiment, or imagining it, or performing a slouchy imitation is just as good as a sincere course of earnest and candid experimentation, you had better consult a book, or toss a penny in order to decide upon your verdict. Even if you do go through the experimentation and come to my Belief, it will be well to remember that you and I may both be in the wrong, and to hold yourself, as I shall myself, open to conviction upon this delicate question.

But in the meantime I can only go upon my own experiment-formed conviction, mistaken though it may be. Having reached a result that seems to me indubitable, my own practice is to let that department of my mind lie fallow for a year or more, and then to review my former reasoning and endeavour to find flaws in it by prying into every corner of my argument that seems to be the least suspicious, as well as by pursuing, if I can, an entirely different inquiry or fresh inquisition from a different point of view, and this process I repeat at least once more, but oftener several times.

There are several drawbacks to this method. I must confess that it has fostered in me an exaggerated self-distrust; so that I have several times abandoned perfect demonstrations, moved by unsound objections, sometimes put forth by others, but oftener by myself. It has also caused me to be blamed unjustly in two ways. Some of my friends lament my unproductiveness,—a complaint due to my diffidence. But I think that considering how many more ideas and theories are yearly put forward in my line than any one could satisfactorily appraise, it ought to be regarded as a merit that I do not ask a hearing until I have something pretty thoroughly well-considered to say. On the other hand, that class of persons who think the highest merit a book or memoir or theory can possess is that of not occasioning the slightest surprise in any mind look upon me as a lover of original opinions, as such. If they were to come to know me better, they might learn to think me ultra-conservative. I am, for example, an old-fashioned christian, a believer in the efficacy of prayer, an opponent of female suffrage and of universal male suffrage, in favor of letting business-methods develope without the interference of law, a disbeliever in democracy, etc. etc. The newness of no theory is a recommendation of it to me, and no theory that I have ever put forward was novel to my own mind. On the contrary in so far as a belief's being widespread and familiar goes to show it to be instinctive, I regard its being so as very strong reason indeed for holding it to be approximately true. At the same time, I must confess that I do not hold this opinion, or any other broad philosophical opinion, on authority _alone;_ and that is just my point of difference with the good souls who admire as such writings put forth to support commonplace opinions. They argue from authority pure and simple, as a habit of life. In order to judge of the merits of this habit, to which so many passionately cling, I have carefully and calmly studied the history of science; and I must say that my friends the haters of novelty do not figure in that history in a way to compel my assent to their method.

Although I have endeavoured above to give a preliminary description of that Element which I discern, or think I discern in all Feelings, and although I have been careful to add that no reader can interpret my description unless he experiments for himself upon watching his Feelings and comparing them with other Modes of Awareness, yet I feel sure that a few words more are needed from me in order that my Idea may be rightly conveyed to the Reader.

Without doubt, some will make the following objection to my doctrine:

"You say," some readers will object, "that every Feeling-Quality is perfectly simple, or, at least, irresoluble (for we do not see that you can have any right to say more than that, and that it is also, in itself, _sui generis_). That being the case, it certainly follows that no true Feeling-Qualities can resemble each other in any respect. But this is plainly impossible; for such resemblance would consist in their both partaking of a common ingredient. It is impossible that so obvious a difficulty should have escaped you. Please say, then, how you hold that you escape it?"

To this very pertinent question, I reply by first pointing out that multitudes of pairs of Feeling-Qualities are so much alike that they are distinguished with difficulty. Such, for example, are orange-colour bordering upon red and a scarlet verging toward yellow; or a turquoise blue and a very bluish green, or a cool violet and a very violet blue. These phenomena are indisputable; and psychophysically they are due to the mixtures of the same excitations in different proportions. But my experiments and ponderings have led me to believe, whether rightly or wrongly, that the resemblances do not reside in the separate Feelings compared, but in _secondary_ Feelings excited by comparing two Primary Feelings, and in the interpretation of these secondary Feelings in Judgments, whose Awareness is of an utterly different kind from Feeling, and is only confounded with Feeling because it is, so to speak, of so transparent a kind that the secondary Feeling behind it is more perceptible than the Awareness of the Judgment, itself. But whether one thinks me right or wrong in my notions of the Phaneroscopy of Feeling, I cannot conceive that anybody should think that all the infinite varieties of Feeling (no one of which occurs twice), have any Quality-ingredient in common, that there is, for example, any Feeling in common excited by the sight of Mont Blanc from the Hotel des Bergues, in its early evening flush, and the taste of a strong old-fashioned Gin cocktail made with Hagerty's! At any rate, such is not my opinion. But I think that the general reminiscence of Feeling has a character, as far as possible from being a Feeling-Quality, which distinguishes it sharply from the other Modes of Awareness of which I shall speak. This character is of the nature of a Concept of a highly Abstract kind, and purely Phaneroscopic, that is, relating to the Awareness as Awareness simply. Namely, I think that all Feeling is distinguished by its Unity in the sense of Simplicity, and by its being of what Quale it is in Itself purely;

and though I use two clauses to describe this character, I do not conceive it as two characters but as One only. In other words there is only One thing present in Feeling; it has but one Aspect. The other Modes of Awareness we shall find to have essentially two or more Aspects presenting themselves together, though one may be accented by the Interpreter more than the other.

I come now to[†] Thirdness. To me, who have for forty years considered the matter from every point of view that I could discover, the inadequacy of Secondness to cover all that is in our minds is so evident that I scarce know how to begin to persuade any person of it who is not already convinced of it. Yet I see a great many thinkers who are trying to construct a system without putting any thirdness into it. Among them are some of my best friends who acknowledge themselves indebted to me for ideas but have never learned the principal lesson. Very well. It is highly proper that Secondness should be searched to its very bottom. Thus only can the indispensableness and irreducibility of thirdness be made out, although for him who has the mind to grasp it, it is sufficient to say that no branching of a line can result from putting one line on the end of another. Even in the most degenerate form of Thirdness something may be detected which is not mere Secondness. If you take any ordinary triadic relation, you will always find a mental element in it. Brute action is secondness, any mentality involves thirdness. Analyze for instance the relation involved in 'A gives B to C.' Now what is giving? It does not consist in A's putting B away from him and C's subsequently taking B up. It is not necessary that any material transfer should take place. It consists in A's making C the possessor according to Law. There must be some kind of law before there can be any kind of giving,—be it but the law of the strongest.

(1892). Though a life-long student[†] of reasonings, I know no way of giving the reader the benefit of what I ought to have learned, without asking him to go through with some irksome preliminary thinking about relations.

For this subject, although always recognized as an integral part of logic, has been left untouched on account of its intricacy. It is as though a geographer, finding the whole United States too vast for convenient treatment, were to content himself with a description of Nantucket. This comparison hardly, if at all, exaggerates the inadequacy of a theory of reasoning that takes no account of relative terms.

A relation is a fact about a number of things. Thus the fact that a locomotive blows off steam constitutes a relation, or more accurately a relationship (the Century Dictionary, under relation, 3, gives the terminology. See also relativity, etc.) between the locomotive and the steam. In reality, every fact is a relation. Thus, that an object is blue consists of the peculiar regular action of that object on human eyes. This is what should be understood by the "relativity of knowledge."

Now consider any argument concerning the validity of which a person might conceivably entertain for a moment some doubt. In order to show that this inference is (or that it is not) absolutely necessary, it is requisite to have something analogous to a diagram with different series of parts, the parts of each series being evidently related as the parts of the actual argument are said to be; and this diagram must be so contrived that it is easy to examine it and find out whether the course of the argument in question is in every case such as it is here proposed to be inferred. Such a diagram has got to be either auditory or visual, the parts being separated in the one case in time, in the other in space. But in order completely to exhibit the analogue of the conditions of the argument under examination, it will be necessary to use signs or symbols repeated in different places and in different juxtapositions, these signs being subject to certain "rules," that is, certain general relations associated with them by the mind. Such a method of forming a diagram is called <u>algebra</u>. All speech is but such an algebra, the repeated signs being the words, which have relations by virtue of the meanings associated with them. I may mention that unpublished studies have shown me that a far more powerful method of diagrammatisation than algebra is possible, being an extension at once of algebra and of Clifford's method of graphs; but I am not in a situation to draw up a statement of my researches.

If upon a diagram we mark two or more points to be indentified at some future time with objects in nature, so as to give the diagram at that future time its meaning; or if in any written statement we put dashes in place of two or more demonstratives or pro-demonstratives, the professedly incomplete representation resulting may be termed a <u>relative rhema</u>. It differs from a relative <u>term</u> in retaining the "copula," or signal of assertion. If only one demonstrative or pro-demonstrative is erased, the result is a <u>non-relative rhema</u>. For example, "— buys — from — for the price —," is a relative rhema. On the other hand, "— is mortal" is a non-relative rhema.

A rhema is somewhat closely analogous to a chemical atom or radicle with unsaturated bonds. A non-relative rhema is like a univalent radicle; it has but one unsaturated bond. A relative rhema is like a multivalent radicle. The blanks of a rhema can only be filled by terms, or, what is the same thing, by "something which" (or the like) followed by a rhema; or, two can be filled together by means of "itself" or the like. So, in chemistry, unsaturated bonds can only be saturated by joining two of them, which will usually, though not necessarily, belong to different radicles. If two univalent radicles are united, the result is a saturated compound. So, two non-relative rhemas being joined give a complete proposition. Thus, to join "— is mortal" and "— is a man," we have "X is mortal and X is a man," or "Some man is mortal." So likewise, a saturated compound may result from joining two bonds of a bivalent radicle; and, in the same way, the two blanks of a dual rhema may be joined to make a complete proposition. Thus, "— loves —," "X loves X," or "Something loves itself." A univalent radicle united to a bivalent radicle gives a univalent radicle (as H-O-); and, in like manner, a non-relative rhema, joined to a dual rhema, gives a non-relative rhema. Thus, "— is mortal" joined to "— loves —" gives "— loves something that is mortal," which is a non-relative rhema, since it has only one blank. Two, or any number of bivalent radicles united, gives a bivalent radicle (as -O-O-S-O-O-), and so two or more dual rhemata give a dual rhema; as "— loves somebody that loves somebody that serves somebody that loves —." Non-relative and dual rhemata only produce rhemata of the same kind, so long as the junctions are by twos; but junctions of triple rhemata (or junctions of dual rhemata by threes), will produce all higher orders. Thus, "— gives — to —" and "— takes — from —," give "— gives — to somebody who takes — from —," a quadruple rhema. This joined to another quadruple rhema, as "— sells — to — for —," gives the sextuple rhema "— gives — to somebody who takes — from somebody who sells — to — for —." Accordingly, all rhemata higher than the dual may be considered as belonging to one and the same order; and we may say that all rhemata are either singular, dual, or plural. It is also[†] quite easy to show that no triple rhema can be composed from any number of dual rhemata.

Such, at least, is the doctrine I have been teaching for twenty-five years since 1867, and which, if deeply pondered, will be found to enwrap an entire philosophy. Kant taught that our fundamental conceptions are merely the ineluctable ideas of a system of logical forms; nor is any occult transcendentalism requisite to show that this is so, and must be so. Nature only appears intelligible so far as it appears rational, that is, so far as its processes are seen to be like processes of thought. I must take this for granted, for I have no space here to argue it. It follows that if we find three distinct and irreducible forms of rhemata, the ideas of these should be the three elementary conceptions or categories of metaphysics. That there are three elementary forms of categories is the conclusion of Kant, to which Hegel subscribes; and Kant seeks to establish this from the analysis of formal logic. Unfortunately, his study of that subject was so excessively superficial that his argument is destitute of the slightest value. Nevertheless, his conclusion is correct; for the three elements permeate not only the truths of logic, but even to a great extent the very errors of the profounder logicians. The ideas which belong to the three forms of rhemata are firstness, secondness, thirdness; firstness, or spontaneity, secondness, or dependence; thirdness, or mediation.

> Let us maintain a half-smile on our faces.
> Thich Nhat Hahn

I Think I Might Be a Cenopythagorean

With a sense of living inside a great and beneficent school which had been called to recess, I let fall from my grip the sheet on which was hand-scribed Charley's comments duplicated above—because a pure feeling of familiarity had flashed through me. Something about this discussion of his categories demanded my attention, yet put me a bit off balance or disaligned gravity vertical. Betsey couldn't help me; she didn't share the feeling and couldn't acquire it from my attempts to describe it. After some palpitation all she could say is that I'm medically correct.

The unalloyed sensation nagged at me and wouldn't let me loose, as if it would not cease from begging for interpretation that I did not have. So I walked from our apartment next to 186 Tremont Street over to Boston Harbor, hoping to run into Roy. He didn't believe in telephones or television, but I knew he loved thinking and writing in his flat and strolling around the harbor, where he had many old seafaring friends. And I had drop-in privileges by now.

I found him out at the end of a pier, leaning on a baluster, smoking a clipped churchwarden pipe, looking out toward sea. I couldn't help thinking: Here is an admirable old salt whose body is stuck on shore but whose mind and spirit still roam as they will. He spoke no words but welcomed me in some way I could not describe. On my battered clipboard I had a xerograph of Charley's sheets, which he examined after I greeted him. I described as well as I could the odd feeling that was gnawing at me.

He tapped the ashes from his pipe and secured it in a shirt pocket. It was impossible to miss his attitude, an air of someone who had emerged from a waiting room. Pulling a stubby lead pencil from his pocket, he sharpened the tip with a razor-keen cord knife carried in his P-jacket, then ever so slowly but ably wrote these equation-like lines on the back of the sheet:

$$1 + 1 = 0$$
$$1 + 2 = 1$$
$$2 + 2 = 2$$
$$3 + 1 = 2$$
$$3 + 2 = 3$$
$$3 + 3 = 4$$
$$3 + 3 + 3 = 5$$

For N equal to or greater than 4, $(N - 2)3 = N$

"Does this look like sound arithmetic, Eisenstaat?"

Shocked that he had uttered sounds, I could only innocently say, "No—none of the sums adds up correctly."

"Good for you. You are right; it isn't arithmetic, but it is sound."

He chuckled at his minor-league trick question. I had never seen him chuckle. (Was there something to be happy about today?)

A square-foot scrap piece of damaged cord netting lay on the dock where a mender had discarded it. Roy sat down crosslegged next to it. Me being part Choctaw, I instinctively sat down the same way. He picked it up and with his knife trimmed several knots from the net so that various knots had different numbers of loose strings dangling from them, some with 1 or 2 or 3 or 4 loose strings. As I sat on the dock looking at these little models Roy had made, he held up a knot having one loose string.

"In those expressions I wrote, the symbol 1 on the left side stands for an object or a function such as this having one loose string or connecting point; the symbol 2 stands for one such object with two loose strings, and so forth. Now the symbol + in my expressions stands for the action of composing or joining the ends of two loose strings together."

With his knife he scraped a bit of day-old chewing gum from a nearby plank, then applied a dab of it to each of the ends of two of the single-string knots. With hands that struggled to grasp the little objects, he pressed the two sticky-ended loose strings together.

"The right side in each of the expressions is a symbol telling how many loose strings one has left after completing the joining operations or compositions described by the symbols on the left side. So, you *see,* $1 + 1 = 0$!"

In his left palm he held forward triumphantly two singly-loose-ended knots with the tips of the two loose strings joined by tiny gumballs. Obviously there weren't any free ends anymore. (I couldn't stifle an internal smile while silently speaking to myself the phrase "gumball math." Was I telling jokes to me?)

"Now consider that you and I have only two extremities, our arms. That means we are imagining ourselves as functionally similar to knots each with two loose strings, namely our arms—with hands as connecting agents in place of gum. By the way, the knot is no longer a knot, but merely a symbol for whatever thing it is that has those particular loose ends or connectable termini. In chemistry these are substances with free ions, the means by which they combine or compose or compound with other materials with free ions to make a new chemical."

I began to withdraw my right hand from examining the model in his left palm.

Violently he grabbed my right with his right in a surprise handshake while barking like a drill sergeant, "$2 + 2 = 2$!" He waved his free left hand, so I did too. (Monkey see, monkey do.)

You might think I would have reacted to the amazing speed of his predatory movement by drawing back. I didn't: that must mean that my body trusts Roy at a fundamental level. (What was he hunting? If I was game, shouldn't I run?) Instead I began to smile. I don't know why; I didn't intend it. He saw my unplanned response and released me. Without willing it, playfully, for our mutual inspection, I held up three fingers with my left hand and three fingers with my right hand. I joined the two index fingers end to end, wiggled the four fingers of each hand that remained free while merrily babbling, "$3 + 3 = 4$!"

"See—The Mathematics in The Cosmos!"

So said Roy with one gleaming eye and the other grim, probably the same expression all university presidents bear after the board of regents has just voted their way on some crucial and hard-fought issue. (That look on his face always reminded me of the *Beauseant*, the battle flag of the Knights Templar—*pauperes commilitones Christi Templique Salomonici*—with its black-white tiled squares representing human nature as a mixture of good and evil.)

20. *Doctor LeRoi Wyttynys*
"One gleaming eye and the other grim"
Photograph by Curt Richter ©
By permission, Mary Bernice Townsend

We played with Roy's knot models until I had satisfied myself that I understood all his equations, and also understood that no quantity or combination of models with two loose ends could combine to make a model with three loose ends, while models with four or more loose ends could be made with the right number of triadic units.

"In his later years, Peirce liked to refer to his categorial hypothesis—perhaps with tongue partly in cheek—as Cenopythagoreanism. You recall that the ancient scientist Pythagoras regarded the universe as somehow constructed from number, a notion probably too extreme for Peirce, hence his qualifier 'Recent' in the form of the Greek 'Kainos' brought forward in its Latinate form 'Ceno' which, by the way, is pronounced just like 'sin,' as in 'original sin': Sin-o-pie-thag-o-*re*-an-ism."

Roy teased out the long word in a measured mock drawl. Usually he wore a serious face, but now he was playful in a serious way. He tilted his head, looked at me from the corner of his eye and slowly half grinned. Crowfoot eye wrinkles blossomed on each temple. I had never seen this expression on him.

"I like to think of that long word as Peirce's little terminological joke."

Instinctively, in a way I didn't understand, I half grinned too.

"Joke or not, Peirce had contributed thousands of definitions for the *Century* for its first edition in 1889, and when he was asked to submit new words for the post-1900 *Century Dictionary Supplements,* he added a definition of that word, followed by definitions of each of the three categories. You should get those."

I did, and here they are:

Cenopythagoreanism: Of or pertaining[†] to a modern doctrine which resembles Pythagoreanism in accepting universal categories that are related to and are named after numbers.

Firstness: In the phenomenology[†] of C. S. Peirce, the mode of being of that which is whatever it is regardless of anything else. This is true only of qualities of feeling, such as red or scarlet, and of such qualities of a similar nature as we suppose things to possess. Thus, although hardness consists in resistance to being scratched by a second thing, yet our ordinary common-sense conception is that a hard body possesses in itself a quality which it retains although it never comes into contact with another, and that this quality, which it possesses regardless of anything else and would possess though all the rest of the universe never existed, is the cause of the difficulty of scratching it. The mode of being of such an internal quality is first-ness. That which has firstness can have no parts, because the being of an object which has parts consists in the being of the parts, which are none of them the whole. Any analysis of the constituents of a quality is a description of something found to be true of whatever possesses that quality. But a quality of feeling, as it is in its mode of being as a quality, has no parts.

Secondness: (a) The mode of being[†] of an object which is such as it is by virtue of being connected with or related to another object or objects, regardless of any triadic relation. (b) The mode of connection or relation of such an object with such other. (c) In a looser sense, the secundal, or relative, character which belongs to an individual object, as having such a mode of being.

Thirdness: The mode of being[†] of that which is such as it is by virtue of a triadic relation which is incapable of being defined in terms of dyadic relations.

"Relational forms which cannot be subdivided into simpler forms are, of course, indecomposables. Peirce discovered that there are three indecomposable external relational forms: monovalents, bivalents, and trivalents. All other external relational forms are decomposable into patterns of combinations of those basic three forms.

"This whole thing is another instance of how Peirce brought forth lessons for logic from his knowledge of laboratory practice and the history of science."

Roy pulled out his well-worn copy of Cohen's *Chance, Love, and Logic* from inside his equally well-worn P-jacket, thumbed to page nine, and read aloud in a triumphant tone:

Each chief step in science has been a lesson in logic.

He handed the book to me, but I know by heart that passage from Charley's series of six articles, really a book, published in the *Popular Science Monthly* as "Illustrations of the Logic of Science." (Why had he brought it along?) The volume made its way back to Roy's storage pocket.

"These lessons were scattered everywhere for Peirce to learn as he came to manhood among the Bacheans, both inside and outside Cambridge.

"Pragmatism, you see, is but an abstract of general laboratory procedures in science generally; one such lesson science gave to logic.

"You may have wondered why he wanted to study with Agassiz upon his return to Cambridge from Louisiana. Louie was an expert on scientific classification: another lesson for logic waiting for Peirce's harvest. Classification was an important topic at that time in biology; much the same could be said in that day for chemistry, from which Peirce early acquired similar notions and inspirations. I remember a comment he made in 1906 when he explained the connection to me."

In classification[†] generally, it may fairly be said to be established, if it ever was doubted, that Form, in the sense of structure, is of far higher significance than Material. Valency is the basis of all external structure; and where indecomposibility precludes internal structure, as in the classification of elementary concepts—valency ought to be made the first consideration. I term this the doctrine of <u>cenopythagoreanism.</u>

"You see, this odd word refers to a principle that is even more basic than the categories: it alludes to one of the principles underlying the formation of Peirce's categorial system, which is the heart and engine of his entire philosophy, which is to say, his logic of science. The other thing he learned from Louie is the doctrine of real definition. That principle means that scientists strive to set up their concepts to divide where nature divides, to repeat one of the slogans one hears."

Yet something bothered me. Wasn't there a contradiction lurking in Peirce's long discussion from 1909 that distinguished between psychology, phaneroscopy, and logic? It described the method he used in 1867 to develop the categories by using the procedures[†] of prescission, abstraction, dissociation, and discrimination. A few days ago I had pulled out his '67 article[†] and read it again to refresh my memory. It bothered me that prescission and the other procedures sounded like old-fashioned introspective psychology. And if these procedures eventually provided the supports for logic, wasn't Charley violating his own dictum that logic could not be based upon psychology?

"That has been debated among scholars, to be sure. Furthermore, in his 1867 article, Peirce was in the process of breaking free from the influence of Kant. Don't forget that in 1867 he had to earn a living, and the logic of the universities was infantile, so almost no one appreciated what he was doing: maybe only his father and a few others. Indeed, throughout his life he had difficulties finding persons who grasped his ideas. This was but one of the components contributing to his loneliness. Such factors tend to retard progress. But recall that in that 1909 discussion you are concerned about, he acknowledged that 'this bit of analysis of forty-odd years ago now sadly needs an overhauling; but in the mean time it will serve our turn for the present juncture.' I think this implies that even in his mature thinking, he recognized the techniques of the 1867 article as useful teaching devices to allow readers to gain a first approximation of what he was proposing. The mature categorial hypothesis, however, takes account of your doubt by developing the categories without any aid from prescission *et cetera*, or from any psychological method. You will be able to track through it. Here I give you only an outline.

"Peirce's whole system presupposes common sense. Using only common sense reasoning abilities, mathematics develops. Mathematics, of course, is the science of diagrammatic thought directed at what is deducible from hypothetical situations. As Peirce said, it requires no positive facts. Phaneroscopy, the next science in the list, is guided by mathematics applied to common facts, sensations, appearances. These common facts are such as any normal human person experiences without the aid of equipment of any kind—without telescopes, microscopes, meters, transducers, other such apparatus. Valency analysis and other findings from mathematics applied to the commonalities faced within phaneroscopy yielded his categorial theory, which is the grand outcome of phaneroscopy. This move was, I think, inspired by Boole[†] who had interpreted algebra onto logic. Peirce, following Boole's general spirit but not his content, applied topology to our common sense experiences—the phaneron, literally 'that which appears'—to get his categories. These categories are the key to pragmatism and the rest of his system. They are his guess at Emerson's Riddle[†] of the Sphynx.

"Oh, and by the way, it was thought for years that Peirce's categorial results were either suspect or downright mistaken. His hypothesis or guess can be summarized in this way: 'What there is' is relations, and (a) there are only three kinds of elemental relation forms: monads, dyads, and triads; (b) triadic relations are not reducible to, or decomposable into, dyadic relations; whereas (c) relations having equal or greater complexity than quadratic relations are reducible to sets of triadic relations joined in particular ways. This means we can divide concepts and experiences where nature divides them, according to their external relational form. However, recently the mathematics in Peirce's conjecture[†] in relation theory has been confirmed at the highest level of rigor. So we should now follow sound mathematical practice and describe it as Peirce's Principle. It has any number of important applications within all kinds of science, and especially in computing, which of course Peirce helped to found[†] although he has not been widely acknowledged for that feat. Peirce's nonrelational logic is now routinely used in computing. Once these scientists begin to take seriously and use the now verified results of Peirce's Cenopythagoreanism, who can say what great progress can be made? As a matter of fact, that fellow Percy you admire has written a lot about the significance of Peirce's results and, I believe, even claimed[†] to be a cenopythagorean.

"Of course, my reference to logic in this context is a ready invitation to misunderstanding, because the current meaning of that term has become very narrow, virtually restricted to formal logic, which is the part of Peirce's system he called Critic. I give you a lamenting remark on this topic he made to me when I was about at the stage you are now, as I began to study with him. It is a personal favorite of mine."

Roy pulled out his copy of *Chance, Love, and Logic* and grabbed a sheet he appeared to be using as a bookmark. It was in Peirce's hand. Roy read it out loud:

It is my fate[†] to be supposed an extreme partisan of formal logic, and so I began. But the study of the logic of relations has converted me from that error. Formal logic centers its whole attention on the least important part of reasoning, a part so mechanical that it may be performed by a machine, and fancies that is all there is in the mental process. For my part, I hold that reasoning is the observation of relations, mainly by means of diagrams and the like. It is a living process. This is the point of view from which I am conducting my instruction in the art of reasoning. I find out and correct all the pupil's bad habits in thinking: I teach him that reasoning is not done by the unaided brain, but needs the cooperation of the eyes and hands. Reasoning, as I make him see, is a kind of experimentation, in which, instead of relying upon the intelligible laws of outward nature to bring out the result, we depend upon the equally hidden laws of inward association. I initiate him into the art of this experimentation. I familiarize him with the use of all kinds of diagrams and devices for aiding the imagination.

"Keep some humility."

(Was I exhibiting an overconfident aura?)

"You have progressed in Peirce's system only to the point of comprehending phaneroscopy. There is a great deal more to pass through before your work is complete, before you will understand this system as well as those who advocate it. But you have made an important beginning. Well done."

(I knew the significance of those two words within the heart of a seaman and received them gratefully, but I still had this strange feeling.)

"Your feeling, Mr. Eisenstaat, is one of recognition."

(Hey, I had merely thought that sentence. How did he know?)

"I like to call these relational principles we have rehearsed by the name Valency Analysis. It is a title I made up for my own use. What your unconscious creative engine is trying to get the rational outer shell of your soul to interpret is that the relational patterns which Valency Analysis summarizes were found seminally in Peirce's first paper on chemistry, at the end, in that passage[†] you thought odd, which you begged me to explain to you, but which action I refused, to your chagrin. You had no ears to hear it at the time."

I'll be gloop-slathered. The instant Roy uttered those words, the eureka feeling swept over me and that demanding pressure for interpretation I had felt for days evaporated; my balance returned, gravity realigned vertical. I hadn't grasped the valency aspects of Charley's early chemistry paper at the time because the principles I had learned today were not available to me then, yet something in me must have sensed the similarity. It made clear sense now. Another lesson for logic from science: the living feel of hypothesizing, an emotional[†] interpretant.

Now I thought: Peirce was a rather common-sensical guy in many ways, more down-to-earth than I had been led to believe; only his terminology is foreboding.

Looking at my watch for the first time, I realized we had been talking into the end of the day. While the discussion was alive, I had no sense of time.

Now that I could look back upon it as an object of thought I could compute its place on the twenty-four inch gauge of hours.

The long discussion on the end of a wharf in Boston Harbor came to an end just as the day ended. We fell silent. My mind was full of many things which I would have to reconsider before assimilating, before making them fully part of my world. But already down in the basic parts of my being some vaguely sensed dry and rusty crankshaft had just been oiled and had rotated a semi-cycle. And my obsession with Charley's writing box was receding, as over the past few years I had become aware—piece by piece—of the basics of his way of thinking. But now the components were starting to connect systematically in ways I wasn't controlling. This wasn't just a lecture. I hadn't merely memorized some stuff as I did in college. Intellectually finished products weren't being transferred to me. I was *doing* my *own!* Sure, I had a guide, but only I lived this process.

And the process has—what can I call it?—uh . . . existential results. (I automatically recalled the words of Benjamin Peirce Senior[†] on the effect of science.) The world is new. Even the air feels different now. I am oddly relaxed or maybe satisfied. No, it is as if somebody else here within me is relaxed again, having been chronically tense since late childhood. Something happened to me today—an occurrence not a listening. I was now real in a way I had not been when the day began. It was good. It was beautiful. It was some kind of truth of internal reconfiguration—earned, not inherited, not received in a transfer.

Yet a nagging thought appeared: "As significant as this is, I can't even communicate it to myself; how could I tell Betsey or anyone at all what it is? No one will believe me."

In receding light I watched Roy reload his Churchwarden with strong Louisiana Perique tobacco, the kind he said Peirce had taught him to smoke. I have to admit I was getting accustomed to its offbeat aroma. (Was I learning to march to the beat of a different smell? Lordie, I'm starting to babble nonrationally.)

He put a match to his bowl. Little singularities of tobacco strings danced and metamorphosed in the heat of that tiny refining fire. (Why did I notice that?) The flame quickened his face as well. With that same sideways look, he half grinned at me again. Twice in one day!

Without warning, a twilight dream of young Betsey, years ago in our flat in Somerville, filled[†] the firmament, which is to say, filled the phaneron. The temple forelocks of her long Irish red hair were drawn back in a graceful Y to be joined just above her collar with an exquisite clutch bearing the Celtic mark of St. Brigid—she was saying as I sat on the floor viewing Charley's box for the first time: "When he gave it to me, Grandpa said in an odd tone of voice, 'Take care, it has transforming powers.'"

While this vision captured me, something like Betsey's voice whispered words, which I took to be verse.

Maybe.
I recorded them.

Everything is a Poem

And a true poet knows in the bones,
not merely in words.
We usually don't think everything is a poem
(it does sound crazy)
we say, "Oh here is a nice poem—theyre rare, you know."

We think everything is mostly not a poem and
a poet makes poetry up
in a unnatural fashion
against the grain of basic cosmic meanness.

We think a poem is the result of a poet's skill
and hard work
in the face of
no cooperation
from many
factors.

But remember Ion[†]
said,
"I didn't do it."

Literary critics would probably say that this
is a metaphysical poem.

* * *

Didn't you laugh, even just a little?
I knew you would, for you are
genuine (poet).

I shuddered. (Surprising.) Adiabatic process of cooling air, or some other?

Roy was regarding the sea. Infinity curtained his eyes. Perfectly calm. He blew a consummate smoke ring, then muttered,
"The Mathematics in Nature."

END
Book the First

Epilogue

Abbreviations

Notes

Bibliography

Index

Epilogue

On Method

I hope that readers will find the format and method of this book to be both informative and pleasant. Many books have been written about Peirce, and many more will be written. The challenge I set for myself was to make his *Life* available to any reader interested enough to take up the book. Also, I wanted to accomplish that in such a way that his voice would be prominent as the story unfolded. Often biographies tell us more about their authors than about their subjects; I hoped to push that factor near to its logical minimum.

It is time to confess and set the record straight. As far as I know, Charles Sanders Peirce never wrote an autobiography of this length. Yet he did constantly wax autobiographical, even in his more technical or abstract writings and certainly in his correspondence. What has been presented here as his autobiography are Peirce's words almost totally. Indeed, one cannot labor for long in his manuscripts without noticing the wealth of autobiographical information to be found there.

For many years, while working on other tasks, I found it pleasant to imagine the broad contours that such an autobiography would possess. This innocent pastime remained a figment until fate brought me to encounter Walker Percy.

How odd! I had never even heard of Percy nor met him until my colleague Fran Scott mentioned in 1984 that he had some interesting things to say about Peirce and that I should read his work. That was wonderful advice. Reading his essays and novels was a pleasure, even a transforming experience. I was fortunate to make contact with him to share our mutual interest in Peirce. In 1995 this episode was placed in the public record by Percy's biographer, Father Patrick Samway, S.J., in a book called *A Thief of Peirce: The Letters of Kenneth Laine Ketner and Walker Percy*. To make the story short, an idea precipitated in Percy's mind, whence he persuaded me that I should undertake a life of Peirce. By then I respected the gentleman so much that I could not refuse him. I knew, perhaps as well as almost any other earthling, the vast quantities of materials available to a biographer of Peirce. I also knew that Peirce was like Leonardo da Vinci: he attained expert status and made original contributions in a large number of fields. To write a standard academic book covering all these areas of endeavor would require a single author with powers equal to those of Peirce, or one would have to appoint a committee. I knew I was not that person, and although I tried, I was unable to convene a committee.

Encountering Percy had enabled me to learn more—in a direct, nontheoretical way—about the power of literature, about its flexibility, about the way in which truths can be expressed within proper fictional settings, in some cases better than in scientific prose. One might even say that something like a science is appropriate to novels.

Percy, the good physician, helped me to learn that one has to have nerve as a writer, as a thinker, and as a crafter of words. And in all seriousness, he declared, "If you can't have fun at it, don't write."

These themes merged as I sat down to face the empty page's great white eye: well, actually the blank cathode ray tube. I began to see that it would be possible to reproduce quite a significant stream of autobiographical jottings from Peirce. But I found early in the game that such a straight record had gaps and loose ends and discontinuities. At first I supplied standard scientific prose for such spots. But then my friends and colleagues, Nancy Ridenour and Darlene Norton from the Texas Tech University Health Sciences Center School of Nursing, read an early chapter draft and remarked, "This commentator ought to be a character with a personality in a world." That was all the excuse I needed to develop my method.

The speeches of Peirce and other historical figures given herein are sometimes lightly (and innocently, I think) modified or conflated so that they might fit into the flow of the story; in many cases, there are no modifications. There is an extensive endnote system providing sources and showing any significant changes or the rare cases in which I have created complete speeches "by Peirce." For readers who don't care to chase endnotes constantly, I can say that all the autobiographical passages or letters or articles quoted are historically genuine except for minor editing.

The conversations of Ike Eisenstaat, Betsey Darbey, and LeRoi Wyttynys about Peirce are also based upon historical and philosophical research: mine and that of many other persons as indicated. However, the adventures of those three characters, and their life histories, are fictional creations.

No footnotes or other scholarly apparatus appear directly on the pages of the text. That is because I wanted to make it possible to read unimpeded—as a good historical novel should be read—the story of Peirce's life for its own sake as an interesting and enlightening piece of our national cultural heritage. Instead, a superscript † is placed against the end of a word signifying to readers that a note is provided for that location. Within the section on notes, each note is keyed to a page number, line number, and a few words in the main text. Thereby, any interested person can determine the source or check whether the small changes introduced for the sake of the story are modifications that significantly alter the ideas in the unedited sources; or one may dig further into the fascinating essays scholars have written about Peirce.

Those persons who are even vaguely familiar with Peirce's writings will find it no surprise to learn that this project is planned to appear in three volumes, of which this is the first. With recent advances in publishing technology, it makes no sense to withhold the first part while the other two parts are in preparation. And that same technology will make possible a thorough revision of the entire effort once the third part is completed. The fact that this is a work about a fallibilist by a fallibilist also adds to the rationale behind that strategy. All of this of course assumes that the Grand Architect will want to keep me on the job for a suitable length of time.

The method used here also has the advantage of giving Peirce a voice he has not had, plus supplying at least one viable interpretation of his life and work to educated persons in all areas of endeavor and interest who might want to know something about him without having to become a specialist in his work. The goal has been to show forth the best single guide to the life and work of Peirce—Peirce himself—and to do that in a way that is both respectful and honest and fallible.

I hope the fictional threads holding the work together will be understood as a tentative conversation about the nature and importance of Peirce's life. Perhaps this conversation will become part of a long dialogue on that topic within our civilization, a dialogue in which many minds from diverse backgrounds will participate. There is no cosmic law that requires us to maintain a flat mood while considering the life of a great man. It is no disrespect, no failure of scholarly responsibility, both to grin and to weep. So kick back. Have an Anchor Steam with Roy. Accept a bandaid from Betsey. Like Ike, savor the amateur's distinctive pleasure of maintaining an open mind.

The fact that the present work is fundamentally and ontologically fiction does not remove it from the category of scholarship. And by adopting this fictional technique, I do not intend to show disapproval of other more standard approaches to Peirce scholarship. Indeed, to do so would be to scold myself, because I have passed a long apprenticeship there, principally under the eye of my friends Carolyn Eisele and the late Max Harold Fisch. During my junior year (1959) at Oklahoma State University, I became interested in Peirce through the influence of Professors Millard Everett, Neil Leubke, Thomas Mayberry, Walter Scott, John Susky, and especially John Bosworth (who had been a student with Fisch at the University of Illinois). Later I had the pleasure of working directly with both Eisele and Fisch on a number of projects involving Peirce.

I have been continually aware of my immense debt to Max, the great intellectual biographer of Peirce. It is true that he never succeeded in bringing his long awaited book to press, but he left us an unsurpassed biographical resource in his thousands of notes and files, as well as in his published articles on Peirce's life, many of which have been gathered in *Peirce, Semeiotic, and Pragmatism: Essays by Max H. Fisch* (Indiana University Press). These valuable essays go a long way toward showing the kind of biography Max hoped to develop. It would have been a spectacular work. His voluminous files represent the achievement of more than forty years of first-rate scholarly labor by himself, his wife Ruth Bales Fisch, and their many correspondents and collaborators. These records constitute a monument to his remarkable success as an intellectual detective, and I was fortunate to have been granted access to this extraordinary collection. And I am deeply grateful to have received permission and encouragement from Max Fisch, my mentor and friend, to carry out this project using his resources. This came during a memorable conversation with him at the 1989 International Peirce Congress at Harvard. (This permission was later confirmed by Indiana University — Purdue University at Indianapolis, the designated custodian of the Fisch Papers.) I like to think that Max might have found this project to be a sign true to the real man it humbly strives to represent.

My indebtedness extends to many other persons as well: Lee Auspitz, John Barlow, Ann Boggs, Ronnie Broadfoot, Robert Burch, Peder Christiansen, William Conroy, Frederic H. Cowart III, Gerard Deledalle, Hermann Deuser, Eddie Dupuy, Edward George, Robert Georges, the late Joe Goodin, Lawrence Graves, Donald Haragan, Charles and Sue Hardwick, Anjali Haryana, Clyde and Susan Hendrick, Nathan Houser, Menno Hulswit, Teddy Jones, William O. Kearse, M.D., the late Berti Gabriella Zehetmeier Ketner and my dear son Kenny, Christian Kloesel, John Lachs, Ivan Little, Margaret and Lorenz Lutherer, Sara P. McLaughlin, Thomas McLaughlin, Robert G. Meyers, E. T. Nozawa, Harley Oberhelman, Jay O'Brien, Klaus Oehler, Sharon Kathie O'Reilly, Lisa Palafox, Mrs. Walker Percy, Janet Perez, David Pfeifer, the late Vincent Potter, S.J., Hilary and Ruth Anna Putnam, Joseph Ransdell, T. J. Reilley, Curt Richter, Jane Robertson, Patrick Samway, S.J., Fran and O. V. Scott, Kate Schmit, Arthur Stewart, P. Thibaud, Gordon Treadaway, Patricia Turrisi, the late Preston A. Tuttle, Mark O. Webb, William Westney, John R. Wilson III, and Jane Winer.

The project was initially sponsored by a three-year fellowship from the National Endowment for the Humanities (RO-22240-91). Additional matching funds under that grant were provided by the President's Council at Texas Tech University, Friends of the Texas Tech University Library, Mr.W. B. Rushing of Lubbock, and an anonymous donor.

Special gratitude goes to the many persons who have supported the Institute for Studies in Pragmaticism at Texas Tech University, especially as embodied in the Claude Ventry Bridges Memorial Fund (the Institute endowment).

I am grateful to the following agencies and persons who allowed me to use materials: Department of Philosophy and Houghton Library at Harvard University for permission to publish extracts from the Peirce Papers and related material; Harvard University Archives for permission to use photographs and manuscripts; photographs and other materials from the Preston A. Tuttle Collection in the Institute for Studies in Pragmaticism; Mrs. Walker Percy for permission to use a Curt Richter photograph of Walker as my image of Roy Wyttynys (Walker was one hell of a witness); Archives of the National Academy of Sciences for permission to use a photograph of the Founders Painting by Albert Herter; Cambridge Historical Commission for permission to publish the Roger Gilman photograph of 31 Quincy Street (Ben Peirce's house); Nancy Hopkins for permission to use the photographs of The Queen (Josephine Le Conte) in the collection of Carolyn S. McMillan; the Bancroft Library for permission to use the photograph of Madame Lopez from the Victor F. Lenzen papers, as well as other items; Mr. Bay James and the Houghton Library at Harvard for permission to use the photograph of young William James and other materials; Indiana University Press for permission to extract from *W*; and Harvard University Press for permission to extract from *CP*.

Professor Hershel Womack (Texas Tech University) deserves special mention for his outstanding work in rescuing and preparing the photographic images used here.

I will close with a final word of caution: Take care. Contrary to received opinion, available materials by Peirce (and those written about him) are indeed vast in quantity, and no doubt more will surface in the future. To make this a manageable and readable book, I have included *far* less than everything available to me. Occasionally that has been a painful policy to enforce. As Ike discovered, obsession really does lurk in this huge and fascinating body of evidence, and hubris constantly tempts one toward achieving a God's-eye view of the material.

Kenneth Laine Ketner
Institute for Studies in Pragmaticism
Texas Tech University

Abbreviations

STANDARD EDITIONS OF PEIRCE'S WORKS

CB

A Comprehensive Bibliography of the Published Works of Charles Sanders Peirce. By Kenneth Laine Ketner, with the assistance of Claude Ventry Bridges and Arthur Franklin Stewart, second edition, revised. Bowling Green: Philosophy Documentation Center, 1986. A microfiche edition of Peirce's lifetime publications is available from the same source. Items published by Peirce during his lifetime are catalogued chronologically in this work; for instance, "On the Algebra of Logic" of 1880 is *P* 167. Important works by persons other than Peirce, which appeared during his lifetime, are often referenced in this bibliography. Such works are cited by *O* followed by a bibliographic identification number. For instance, *O* 1248 is Jastrow's obituary of Juliette Peirce.

CD

The Century Dictionary: An Encyclopedic Lexicon of the English Language. Edited by William Dwight Whitney. New York: The Century Company, various editions beginning 1889. Peirce wrote thousands of definitions for this work (many of these identified in *CB*). References will appear as *CD* followed by a page number. Two additional supplementary volumes appeared in 1909 as *The Century Dictionary Supplement*, edited by Benjamin E. Smith (New York: The Century Company, 1909). In these volumes Peirce supplied several definitions characteristic of pragmatism, which by then had become widely known. These additional volumes will be cited as *CD Supplement* followed by volume and page number.

CP

Collected Papers of Charles Sanders Peirce. Edited by C. Hartshorne, P. Weiss (volumes 1–6), and A. Burks (volumes 7–8). Cambridge: Harvard University Press, 1931–1958. An electronic edition of these books is available from Intelex Corporation, P.O. Box 859, Charlottesville, Virginia 22902-0859. References appear as *CP* followed by volume and paragraph numbers.

HP

Historical Perspectives on Peirce's Logic of Science: A History of Science. Edited by Carolyn Eisele, 2 volumes. New York and Berlin: Mouton-DeGruyter, 1985. References appear as *HP* followed by volume and page numbers.

MS

Charles Sanders Peirce manuscripts in Houghton Library at Harvard University—usually followed by catalogue number and sheet number (according to the sheet numbering system established at the Institute for Studies in Pragmaticism, Texas Tech University). Catalogue numbers are assigned in *Annotated Catalogue of the Papers of Charles S. Peirce,* by Richard R. Robin (Amherst: University of Massachusetts Press, 1967), or in "The Peirce Papers: A Supplementary Catalogue," by Richard R. Robin, in *Transactions of the Charles S. Peirce Society,* 7 (1971): 37–57.

Some references to the Harvard Peirce Papers will employ the earlier numbering system developed by Knight W. McMahan in his "Catalogue of the C. S. Peirce Manuscripts" (a typescript at Houghton Library, Harvard University). One may find a cross reference from McMahan to Robin numbers in *Annotated Catalogue* pages 233–244. 'VB1a(2)' is an example entry in the numbering system McMahan developed.

A few items from Peirce's manuscripts are uncatalogued. References to these will employ descriptions that present available information (especially locations in the Fisch papers).

N

Charles Sanders Peirce: Contributions to The Nation. Edited by Kenneth Laine Ketner and James Edward Cook, 4 volumes. Lubbock: Texas Tech University Press, 1975–1987. (A digital edition of these volumes will soon be available from Intelex.) References are shown as N followed by volume and page numbers.

NEM

The New Elements of Mathematics by Charles S. Peirce. Edited by Carolyn Eisele, 4 volumes in 5 books. The Hague: Mouton, 1976. References appear as *NEM* followed by volume and page numbers.

PPM

Pragmatism as a Principle and Method of Right Thinking: The 1903 Harvard Lectures on Pragmatism. Edited by Patricia Ann Turrisi. Albany: State University of New York Press, 1997. These appear as *PPM* followed by page numbers.

PW

Semiotic and Significs: The Correspondence between Charles S. Peirce and Victoria Lady Welby. Edited by Charles S. Hardwick. Bloomington: Indiana University Press, 1977. These, too, are cited as *PW* followed by page numbers.

RLT

Reasoning and the Logic of Things: The Cambridge Conferences Lectures of 1898 by Charles Sanders Peirce. Edited by Kenneth Laine Ketner, with an introduction by Kenneth Laine Ketner and Hilary Putnam. Cambridge: Harvard University Press, 1992. References appear as *RLT* followed by page numbers.

W

Writings of Charles S. Peirce: A Chronological Edition. Edited by Max H. Fisch and others. Bloomington: Indiana University Press, 1982–. References use volume and page numbers after *W:*.

OTHER SOURCES

BPH
The Benjamin Peirce, Junior, Papers at Houghton Library, Harvard University, are cited as *BPH* followed by dating information.

CLL
Chance, Love, and Logic: Philosophical Essays by Charles Sanders Peirce. Edited and introduced by Morris R. Cohen, with an essay by John Dewey. Bison Books introduction by Kenneth Laine Ketner. Lincoln: Bison Books of the University of Nebraska Press, 1998.

F
The Max H. Fisch Papers—at the Peirce Edition Project, Indiana University–Purdue University at Indianapolis—are cited according to the following scheme (sheet numbers are based upon the authorized copy at the Institute for Studies in Pragmaticism, Texas Tech University).

For Fisch's chronological file, F followed by a two digit number plus other information. For instance, "F65:34, BP2 to CSP 3/24/1865" refers to Fisch's chronological file for the year 1865, sheet number 34, BP2's letter to CSP [Benjamin Peirce, Jr., to Charles Sanders Peirce], March 24, 1865. For the nineteenth and early twentieth century, the first two digits are dropped: for example, 1865 will be cited as F65. Additional information may appear if required.

References to Fisch's alphabetic files are cited as Falpha:'word' where 'word' is the alphabetic item, for example, Falpha:opium.

HUA
The Harvard University Archives, cited as *HUA* followed by pertinent information.

HUP
Philosophy Department, Harvard University, cited as *HUP* plus dating information.

NARG
National Archives Record Group, followed by a number, indicates a location in the National Archives.

INITIALS USED IN THESE NOTES

ADB	Alexander Dallas Bache
AHJ	Alice (Mrs. William) James
AWB	Arthur W. Burks
BES	Benjamin E. Smith
BMP	Benjamin Mills Peirce, CSP's brother
BP1	Benjamin Peirce, paternal grandfather of Charles Sanders Peirce
BP2	Benjamin Peirce, Jr., father of Charles Sanders Peirce
CEP	Charlotte Elizabeth Peirce, sister of BP2
CH	Charles Hartshorne

CHD	Charles Henry Davis
CHP	Charles Henry Peirce, brother of BP2.
CLB	Caroline Louise Badger
CLF	Christine Ladd-Franklin, Mrs. Fabian Franklin
CPH	Charles Phelps Huntington
CSP	Charles Sanders Peirce
EL	Elias Loomis
FAW	Frederick Adams Woods
FBE	Francis B. Ellis
FCR	Francis C. Russell
FCSS	Ferdinand Canning Scott Schiller
FEA	Francis Ellingwood Abbot
GP	Gifford Pinchot
HHDP	Herbert Henry Davis Peirce, CSP's brother
HMF	Harriet Melusina Fay, Zina, Mrs. CSP
HMP	Helen Mills Peirce, CSP's sister; later HPE Mrs. Helen Mills Peirce Ellis
HP	Hilary Putnam
HPE	Mrs. Helen Huntington Peirce Ellis, CSP's sister, earlier Helen Huntington Peirce
ISP	Institute for Studies in Pragmaticism at Texas Tech University
JHW	James Houghton Woods
JJ	Joseph Jastrow
JMP	James Mills Peirce, CSP's brother
JnLeC	John Le Conte
JoLeC	Eleanor Josephine Graham Le Conte (Mrs. John Le Conte)
JP	Juliette Peirce, Mrs. CSP
JR	Josiah Royce
JraP	Jerathmeel Peirce, father of BP1
JsLeC	Joseph Le Conte
KLK	Kenneth Laine Ketner
LRP	Lydia Ropes Nichols Peirce, mother of BP2
MEH	Mary E. Huntington
MHF	Max Harold Fisch
PC	Paul Carus
SMP	Sarah Hunt Mills Peirce, CSP's mother
SP	Sarah (Sally) Peirce, sister of BP1
VFL	Victor F. Lenzen
VW	Victoria Lady Welby (previously Victoria Stuart-Wortley)
WCL	William C. Lane
WHD	Reverend William H. Darbie
WPG	Wendell Phillips Garrison
ZF	Zina Fay (later Mrs. CSP)
ZFP	Zina, or Harriet Melusina Fay Peirce, Mrs. CSP

Notes

All notes are introduced by phrases repeated from the text, and each note's location is indicated by the page and line numbers in the left margin. For example, 7:11 signifies page 7 of this book, line 11. The reader should be aware that line numbering has been based on a standard text page of forty-three lines and that all pages, regardless of illustrations or other design components, are treated as if line one is at the top of the page. Thus, line numbers signify consistent relative position: for example, line twenty-two always approximates the middle of the page.

Chapter 1

7:11   like a *Vargueno* : CD 6698.

10:2   It's an allusion to: *The Complete Illustrated Shakespeare*, ed. Howard Staunton (New York: Park Lane, 1979), 2:605.

10:24   taken from Whetstone's: *The Complete Illustrated Shakespeare*, ed. Staunton, 2:598.

10:40   nineteenth-century critic described: Staunton, ed., *Complete Illustrated Shakespeare*, 2:639, signed "Drake."

10:40   as a devolved: Percy's notion of a devolved sign may be found in *Lost in the Cosmos* (New York: Washington Square Press, 1984), 105, where it forms part of that wonderful forty-page intermezzo devoted to the theory of signs.

Chapter 2

13:28   last Will and Testament: Register of Wills, vol. J, April 1913–, Court House, Pike County, Pennsylvania.

14:16   Charley dear: F14:37, HPE diary, several entries for April 1914.

14:27   Dearest little: *MS* VB1a(2), HHDP to HPE 4/21/1914.

16:1   By 1914: F14:88, *NARG* 59, HHDP to Phillips 1/4/1915; *National Cyclopædia of American Biography* (New York: James T. White & Company, 1900), 27:273.

16:21   provided by: F14:60, JP's notes of 5/14/1914.

16:24   NOTED LOGICIAN AND PHILOSOPHER, DIES: *New York Herald*, 4/21/1914.

17:4   Helen's son, remembered: F14:41, BPE scrapbook.

18:19   his body: *MS* VB1b, JP to AHJ 4/1914.

18:22   she confided: The cremation was on Tuesday afternoon 4/28/1914 at the chapel in New Jersey. F14:52, JP to AHJ 4/25/1914.

18:34   Carus promptly requested: F14:43, PC to FCR 4/22/1914. For further information about Carus, see also Harold Henderson, *Catalyst for Controversy: Paul Carus of Open Court* (Carbondale: Southern Illinois University Press, 1993), a fine biography of his significant life.

19:1   Concerning: *O* 1232.

19:35   our great American: Actually, William James said, "An American philosopher of eminent originality," *Varieties of Religious Experience* (Cambridge: Harvard University Press, 1985), 350.

19:44 on the fundamental problem: Here Russell referred to a brisk exchange in *The Monist* between Carus and Peirce concerning determinism. See *P* 474, which was answered by Carus at *O* 475; *O* 478; and *O* 481. Peirce responded at *P* 525, but as editor of *The Monist* Carus got the last word at *O* 526.

20:9 I am trying to be patient: *MS* VB1a(3), HPE to JP 4/23/1914.

20:25 conveyed to Helen: *MS* VB1b, Mrs. Henry Cabot Lodge to HPE 4/23/1914.

20:31 Mrs. William: F14:52, JP to AHJ 4/25/1914.

21:1 I don't think: *MS* VB1b, BPE to HPE 4/27/1914.

21:39 Helen noted: F14:54, HPE diary entries for April 1914.

22:4 I could hardly bear: F14:55, Sally B. Rice to HPE April 1914.

22:19 It is terribly hard: F14:56, MEH to JP 4/28/1914.

22:29 in a column in *The Nation*: *O* 1234.

23:34 Herbert contacted: *MS* VB1a(2), HHDP to HPE April or May 1914.

24:17 in the issue for: *MS* VB1a(3), HPE to JP 5/19/1914.

24:20 It would be difficult: *O* 1230

25:24 Herbert and Helen collaborated: F14:54, HPE diary Saturday 5/16/1914; F14:58, HHDP to HPE 5/2/1914.

25:26 its perspective: *O* 1229.

27:38 I desire to record: *O* 1235.

28:32 over our joint: "On Small Differences of Sensation" *P* 303.

30:6 My uncle James M. Peirce: Fcorrespondence (Burks) FBE to AWB 1/26/1954.

30:18 I have seen: changing to Fcorrespondence (Burks) FBE to AWB 3/11/1949.

30:22 He was a fine figure: returning to FBE to AWB 1/26/1954.

31:32 a plan for proper care: F14:92, CH packet in *MS* JP to AHJ 10/6/1914.

31:34 seventh of May: F14:59, CH packet in *MS* JP to AHJ 5/7/1914.

31:35 recently visited Arisbe: F14:65, JJ to JP 5/22/1914. On the origin of Arisbe as a name for Peirce's homestead, see MHF's "Peirce's Arisbe," in *Peirce, Semeiotic, and Pragmatism: Essays by Max H. Fisch*, ed. Kenneth Laine Ketner, and Christian J. W. Kloesel (Bloomington: Indiana University Press, 1986).

32:15 Grandpa William: F14:67, JJ to WHD 6/10/1914. The Reverend William H. Darbie was the historical minister of the Episcopal Church in Milford that JP and CSP attended. In this book William Darbey is the fictional grandfather of the fictional Betsey Darbey.

32:28 responded to him: F14:73–74, JJ to WHD 7/6/1914.

33:4 its magisterial overview: *HUA*, library files JR to WCL 7/8/1914.

35:7 Royce dispatched the following: *HUP*, JR to WHD 7/8/1914.

35:40 Argument for the Existence: JR's misquotation here is a serious one. The title of CSP's essay in *The Hibbert Journal* (*P* 1166) was "A Neglected Argument for the Reality of God." In CSP's approach, the distinction between 'real' and 'exist' is basic and important.

38:16 issues of broad: See JR's two books *War and Insurance* and *The Problem of Christianity*.

38:20 in typical histories: See two articles by Thomas C. Cadwallader, "Charles S. Peirce (1839–1914): The First American Experimental Psychologist," *Journal of the History of the Behavioral Sciences* 10 (1974): 291–298; "Peirce as an Experimental Psychologist," *Transactions of the Charles S. Peirce Society* 11 (1975): 167–186.

38:29 deal with such matters: See Hilary Putnam, "Peirce the Logician." *Historia Mathematica* 9 (1982): 290–301, and his comments on CSP's 1898 lectures in *RLT*. See W. V. Quine, "Peirce's Logic" and Randall R. Dipert, "Peirce's Underestimated Place in the History of Logic: A Response to Quine," in *Peirce and Contemporary Thought: Philosophical Inquiries*, ed. Kenneth Laine Ketner (New York: Fordham University Press, 1995).

38:32 sometimes minimized: Perhaps nowadays the leading misrepresenter of Peirce's approach is Richard Rorty.

38:35 principles or results: These are too numerous to mention in a brief space. For a start, see the list of eleven volumes that arose from the 1989 International Congress on Peirce, organized by Harvard University and Texas Tech University (the list is in Ketner, ed., *Peirce and Contemporary Thought*, xiv n.1). See also Robert W. Burch, *A Peircean Reduction Thesis: The Foundations of Topological Logic* (Lubbock: Texas Tech University Press, 1991); Kenneth Laine Ketner, "Peirce and Turing: Comparisons and Conjectures," *Semiotica* 68 (1988): 33–61; and *CP* 3:vi-ix.

39:3 I could kick: WP to KLK 10/8/1984 in *A Thief of Peirce: The Letters of Kenneth Laine Ketner and Walker Percy*, ed. Patrick H. Samway, S.J. (Jackson: University Press of Mississippi, 1995), 4.

39:8 There he: Walker Percy, "The Divided Creature," the 1989 Jefferson Lecture sponsored by the National Endowment for the Humanities. Alternate versions of the lecture may be found in Samway, ed., *Thief of Peirce* and Percy, *Signposts in a Strange Land*, ed. Patrick H. Samway, S.J. (New York: Farrar, Straus & Giroux, 1991).

39:26 My belief: Whitehead to CH 1/2/1936 in Victor Lowe, *Alfred North Whitehead: The Man and His Work* (Baltimore: The Johns Hopkins University Press, 1985, 1990), 2:345.

39:43 monumental contribution: HP to KLK letter 1/9/1991.

41:17 false myth: See introduction of *CB*; also John J. Stuhr, *Classical American Philosophy* (New York: Oxford University Press, 1987), 23n.5, which debunks another common claim, namely that Peirce himself said he couldn't finish his work. He can be made to "say" that by way of some selective quoting, but when the full context is supplied, it is clear he was stating that a *particular* book could not be finished if financial assistance were not available.

41:19 The Harvard Peirce papers alone: See *Annotated Catalogue of the Papers of Charles S. Peirce*, by Richard R. Robin as described under the abbreviation *MS*.

41:25 microfiche edition: See the large microfiche edition (published by Philosophy Documentation Center) of Peirce's published works, catalogued in *CB*.

41:39 Bruce Kuklick: *The Rise of American Philosophy: Cambridge, Massachusetts 1860–1930* (New Haven): Yale University Press, 1977.

41:43 wrote to Royce: *HUP*, WHD to JR 7/17/1914.

42:37 she confided: F14:85, CH packet in *MS* JP to AHJ 8/24/1914.

43:9 the last: *University of California Calendar* 7/20, 22, 27, 29,31/1914.

43:17 in the published form: Royce, *War and Insurance* (New York: Macmillan, 1914), iii.

43:21 a recent book: Royce, *The Problem of Christianity*.

44:2 the pragmatic school: James, *Practical Results*.

44:9 fearful forest: F14:103, CH packet in *MS* JP to AHJ 10/29/1914.

44:19 letter to Juliette: *MS* Vdelta Mrs. William Darbie to JP 11/4/1914. The books were Sabatier, *Outlines of a Philosophy of Religion*; Royce, *The Problem of Christianity* and *The World and the Individual*; *The Works of George Berkeley*, 3 volumes; Fiske, *Outlines of Cosmic Philosophy* and *The Idea of God*; Munsterberg, *The Eternal Life*; Sneath, *The*

Ethics of Hobbes; Sterrett, *The Ethics of Hegel*; Muirhead, *Elements of Ethics*; James, *Psychology*, 2 volumes, and *The Will to Believe*; Joseph, *An Introduction to Logic*; *Rubáiyát of Omar Khayyám*; O'Rell, *Joraltiam and His Continent*; Browne, *Religio Medici*; Denison, *Astronomy without Mathematics*; Andrews and Howland, *Elements of Physics*; Waldstein, *The Subconscious Self*; Coe, *The Spiritual Life*.

44:23   The gears in Cambridge: *HUP*, JR to JHW 12/13/1914; F14:113, CH packet in *MS JP* to AHJ 12/18/1914; *HUP*, JR to JP 12/13/1914; *HUP*, JHW to WCL 12/16/1914.

44:27   Juliette informed Royce: *HUP*, JP to JR 12/9/1914.

44:28   sage guidance to Woods: *HUP*, JR to JHW 12/13/1914.

44:38   Royce penned: *HUP*, JR to JP 12/13/1914.

45:19   a fateful letter: *HUP*, JHW to JP 12/18/1914.

46:4   two days later to Woods: *HUP*, JP to JHW 12/20/1914.

46:17   by this time contained: F14:118, list 12/20/1914.

46:21   another department: *HUP*, JHW to Julian L. Coolidge 12/21/1914.

46:30   another prospective donor: *HUP*, Richard H. Dana to JHW 12/21/1914.

47:7   He later wrote: Lenzen "Reminiscences," 5–6.

47:39   Lenzen's impressions: Lenzen "Reminiscences," 6–7.

48:36   a sense of desperation: *HUP*, VFL to JHW 12/28/1914.

50:38   Woods telegraphed instructions: F14:124, JR to VFL 51:40 12/20/1914.

51:40   and will be kept: F14:124, JR to VFL 12/20/1914. A case can be made that this promise for careful keeping was soon violated after Royce's death. See Nathan Houser, "The Fortunes and Misfortunes of the Peirce Papers," in *Signs of Humanity*. 3 vols, ed. Michel Balat and Janice Deledalle-Rhodes (New York: Mouton de Gruyter, 1992), 3:1259–1268

52:1   enormous pile of manuscripts: VFL's postcard announcing shipment of Peirce's manuscripts is in *HUP*, VFL to JHW 12/31/1914. FAW's reminiscence of JR's remark is at *MS* VB3b#4, FAW to Albert Edward Wiggam 2/12/1923.

52:35   Peirce's methods and results: Lenzen, "Reminiscences"; *MS* VB3b#4, FAW to Albert Edward Wiggam 2/12/1923. The latter contains the following:

> Royce had a weekly evening seminar on logic and scientific methodology. At this there were four or five advanced students. Southard and I used to go to it with great eagerness and regularity about 1910 to 1912.
>
> Royce was always quoting Charles Peirce. I have no doubt he mentioned his name ten times as often as that of any other.
>
> One time I loaned him that long letter that Peirce wrote to me [*MS* L477, CSP to FAW drafts]. Royce wished to read it to the seminar, and I was of course very pleased to have him do so.

53:3   the day she died: During the years between CSP's death and her own, JP fussed with various persons at Harvard about lack of publication and about her view that she had been deprived of intellectual property rights CSP had conveyed to her in his last will. This struggle is well documented in Fisch's chronological files after 1914. The following (*HUP*, JP to FHW 1/15/1921) represents the tone of the discussion (compare F1926, JP to HUP 10/9/1926; *MS* Valpha, JP to GP 11/1926):

> Dear Professor Woods: Six years have elapsed—no publication of my husband's works. When Mr. Lenzen gathered my husband's last works here written in his great suffering you wrote me at the time: "Last night about a

dozen of us gathered [JP is quoting from *HUP*, FHW to JP 12/1914 to 1/1915] to welcome the first installments of the precious manuscripts which you had entrusted to Mr. Lenzen's care. Prof. Royce delighted us by pointing out how many sciences have been illuminated by Mr. Peirce's genius and we began on the spot to plan for the publication of at least three volumes of essays. I shall [JP shifted to quote from *HUP*, JHW to JP 2/4/1915] take it upon myself to see that there is as little delay as possible in arranging for publication." My dear husband's library I was glad to present to Harvard. My husband and I was always very fond of Pres. Lowell. But not the manuscript. My husband in his last month always remarked, on publication of my works, life would not be so hard for me.

The books were donated but not the M.S.

53:6   statute of limitation: JP's claim was that she had entrusted the papers to Harvard (see her lawyer's letter to JHW at *HUP*, Alfred Marvin to JHW 5/22/1929 and JHW's reply at *HUP*, JHW to Alfred Marvin 6/10/1929), which meant that she thought she retained intellectual property ownership and should receive a royalty from the publication of *CP*. At the time of publication of the last two volumes of *CP*, officials at Harvard appear to have assumed that JP had either given or sold the papers to Harvard. JP's claim that "the M.S. was not donated" and her repeated demands for royalty income present a third option that no one appears to have taken seriously: a scenario in which an owner of a famous author's *nachlass* arranges with a press and its editors to bring out an edition. *Entrust* seems an appropriate word for this process. Surely the widow of a famous author today would be treated differently. A legal opinion was sought and received in 1956 as volumes 7 and 8 of *CP* were in final stages of production (see F1956, AWB to attorney Oscar M. Shaw 14/1/1956, and F1956, AWB to Professor Morton White 1/30/1956). The attorney advised Harvard University Press to proceed with copyright and copyright renewal.

As late as 1927, in regard to publication of *CP*, JHW wrote to CH (*HUA*, 10/21/1927): "We should take the risk and the profit. If we make anything it could go to a publication fund." This appears to leave no room for royalties to JP. JHW also argued that as a publishing venture *CP* had lost money, so nothing should be paid to JP. But the flaw in that approach, from the standpoint of a typical publishing contract of today, is that royalty fees are normally based on sales of individual books; under such a plan, therefore, JP's royalties, if there were losses, would be part of such loss. In some theatrical circles nowadays JHW's approach is known as "Hollywood accounting." Had JR lived longer, the story might have been different, but as it was, JP had no powerful son of a widow to step forward and defend her rights.

53:10   the draft: F1955, VFL to AWB 11/23/55: "Professor Woods told me that Mrs. Peirce had held out on some of the manuscripts. . . . ." See also *HUP*, JP to CH 7/13/1928; *HUP*, JP to JHW 9/1928; *HUP*, Alfred Marvin (JP's lawyer) to JHW 5/22/1929. Clearly JP owned CSP's papers and the associated intellectual property rights. Is it cheeky for someone to say, in such a situation, that "She held out"?

53:32   Peirce was a profound thinker: F1927, *HUA*, CH to JHW 10/16/1927.

53:36   magnificent prayer: The prayer of 1859, see p. 161.

53:41   I call him: Changing to F1927, *HUA*, CH to JHW 10/28/1927.

54:1   a whole new: Probably Hartshorne was referring to Peirce's Semeiotic, see p. 301f.

54:10   Every volume: Changing to F1927, *HUA*, CH to JHW 12/18/1927.

54:12   Some of: Skipping to a later page only for this sentence (same CH letter).
54:15   after all he: Returning to an earlier paragraph (same CH letter).
54:26   tried to dissuade him: *HUA*, JHW to CH 10/21/1927.
54:44   It is a rather profound study: Hammett, *The Maltese Falcon* (New York: Vintage Crime, 1992)—the interlude is chapter 7. One may find discussion by literary critics on the connection between Peirce and Hammett in Richard Layman, *Shadow Man: The Life of Dashiell Hammett* (New York: Harcourt Brace Jovanovich, 1981), 112; William Marling, *Dashiell Hammett* (Boston: Twayne, 1983), 76; Julian Symons, *Dashiell Hammett* (San Diego: Harcourt Brace Jovanovich, 1985), 71.
55:13   Charley had any other effect: See, for example, Umberto Eco, *The Name of the Rose* [*Il nome della rosa*] (New York: Warner, 1984), Sebeok and Umiker-Sebeok, *"You Know my Method": A Juxtaposition of Charles S. Peirce and Sherlock Holmes* (Bloomington: Gaslight, 1980); *The Sign of Three: Dupin, Holmes, Peirce*, ed. Eco and Sebeok (Bloomington: Indiana University Press, 1983).
55:34   important popular lectures: In addition to the works mentioned, here are other recommended introductory readings: Joseph Esposito, *Evolutionary Metaphysics* (Athens: Ohio University Press, 1980); Kenneth Ketner and C. J. W. Kloesel, eds., *Peirce, Semeiotic, and Pragmatism; Studies in the Scientific and Mathematical Philosophy of Charles S. Peirce; Essays by Carolyn Eisele*, ed. Richard M. Martin, (The Hague: Mouton, 1979); Walker Percy, *The Message in the Bottle: How Queer Man Is, How Queer Language Is, and What One Has to Do with the Other* (New York: Farrar, Straus & Giroux, 1975); Samway, ed., *Thief of Peirce*; Stuhr, *Classical American Philosophy*; *CLL*; *W.*
56:9   *Private Thoughts*: MS 891.
56:27   to borrow and mangle: Sartre's maxim, as discussed in Ketner, "Pragmaticism Is an Existentialism?" in *Frontiers in American Philosophy*, ed. Robert W. Burch and Herman J. Saatkamp, Jr., volume 2 (College Station: Texas A&M University Press, 1991), 105–111.

Chapter 3

61:34   I am going to write: *MS* 339:332v 10/28/1908.
62:6   heart to heart: *CD: confabulation*, "easy, unrestrained conversation."
62:9   For these twenty years: *MS* L390, CSP to FCSS 5/12/1905.
62:15   But logic is a science: *MS* 339D:304r, 9/1/1908.
62:15   quite without: *myoterizing* is not in *CD*, but probably is "flinching" or "blinking"; in *CD*, *vulgar* is "common, in general use, ordinary."
63:6   Born: *MS* 1634.
63:8   An extraordinary thing: *MS* 1602:02.
63:16   sufficiently proved: *MS* 703:12f.
63:28   loved as a jovial man: This sentence has been added; also two other sentences below: "And to his mother . . ." plus "I was named. . . ."
63:31   Elizabeth Peirce: *BPH*, BP2 to CEP 9/10/1839.
64:8   Good news! Dearest: *BPH*, BP2 to LRP 9/10/1839.
64:35   My ancestors: *MS* 1606:02.
66:1   PEIRCE, Charles: *MS* 1603:02.
66:7   numerous researches: See *CB* for a complete listing of CSP's truly vast lifetime publications.
66:40   Cambridge in 1839: Gardiner Mumford Day, *The Biography of a Church* (Cambridge: Riverside Press, 1951).

67:39   Essex County: James Duncan Phillips, *Salem and the Indies: The Story of the Great Commercial Era of the City* (Boston: Houghton Mifflin, 1947); and Phillips's *Salem in the Eighteenth Century* (Salem: Essex Institute, 1969).

68:1   *The Century:* and see *CD* 9:798 (proper names), "Peter."

68:7   few miles east: *National Cyclopædia of American Biography* (New York: James T. White & Company, 1900), 27:273.

68:18   Revolutionary War: F1800: 5, JraP to BP1 6/16/1800; see also Phillips's histories of Salem.

68:23   Benjamin (1778–1831): *Dictionary of American Biography* (New York: Charles Scribner's Sons, 1930), 14:394 (BP2); *National Cyclopædia of American Biography*, 10:180–181 (BP1).

68:33   settled into room one: F1797:7, BP1 to JraP 8/27/1797.

68:40   wear his drawers: F1798:10, SP to BP1 6/1/1798.

69:4   The field of science: F1797:9, BP1 to SP September 1798.

69:11   think of himself as a philosopher: F1799:5, BP1 to LRP 3/30/1799.

69:16   his maternal cousin: F1798:3 (BP1 to SP 2/26/1798) and 4 (BP1 to SP 4/7/1798); F1797:11, LRN to BP1 9/18/1797.

69:18   school for young women: F1799–1801, several letters from LRP, especially early in 1801, concerning a "newspaper war" about the controversial school for women in Salem.

69:19   also indications: F01:4 (LRP to BP1 2/21/1801) and 10 (Dudley L. Pickman to LRP February 1801).

69:21   was the mother: See Moira Ferguson, and Janet Todd, *Mary Wollstonecraft* (Boston: Twayne), 1984.

69:23   high among: F01:18, BP1 to JraP 5/?/1801.

69:24   approval of President: F04:1, President Joseph Willard to BP1 6/16/1804.

69:24   a merchant's life: F10:3, BP1 receives conveyance of a church pew in Salem, where he is a merchant.

69:25   the firm of Wait: F25:8–10, contract 10/1/1825.

69:26   their engagement: F03:19 (BP1 to Captain Ichabod Nichols, father of LRP 10/29/1803) and 20 (Captain Ichabod Nichols to BP1 11/2/1803).

69:28   fourth of April: *Dictionary of American Biography*, 14:393–397.

69:29   was elected: F11:2, Commonwealth of Massachusetts to BP1 5/13/1811, official notice of election to the Senate of Massachusetts; *National Cyclopædia of Biography*, 10:180–181.

69:30   Federal Republican: F12:1 (BP1 speech at the Federal caucus 4/3/1812) and 1 (Nath'l Bowditch and others to BP1 7/4/1812).

69:31   served for several: *Dictionary of American Biography*, 14:393.

69:32   Young Ben: *Dictionary of American Biography*, 14:394.

69:41   fierce logical gaze: *BPH*, BP2 to LRP 10/22/1825.

70:35   began to anticipate: F26:10, 7/14/1826.

70:36   Porter's Tavern: F26:15, BP1 to LRP 8/20/1826.

70:37   boarding house: F26:2 (CEP to her aunt Betsy Peirce 1826) and 11 (BP1 to Reverend President Kirkland 8/15/1826).

70:37   talented and scholarly: F26:14, LRP to BP1 8/19/1826.

70:40   through the office: F26:10 (LRP to BP1 8/3/1826) and 13 (BP1 to LRP 8/16/1826).

70:40   position of head librarian: F26:2 (CEP to Aunt Betsey 1826), 11 (BP1 to President Kirkland 8/15/1826), 13 (BP1 to LRP 8/16/1826), and 15 (BP1 to LRP 8/20/1826).

70:42   writing from Cambridge: F26:2, CEP to Aunt Betsey 1826.
71:13   confirmed by the Overseers: *HUA*, Records of Overseers 8/24/1826.
71:14   economic depression descended: F26:23, John Pickering to BP1 9/23/1826.
71:17   his splendid Salem mansion: F26:18, Henry Peirce to BP1 9/12/1826.
71:23   Christened: *MS* 1634.
71:27   which I distinctly: *MS* 1634.
71:29   I remember nothing: *MS* 1602:02–3.
71:33   I remember early visits: *MS* 1602:05.
71:34   Miss Margaret Fuller: CSP also mentioned riding with Fuller in *MS* 1606:02.
71:39   I remember a gentleman: *MS* 1602:03.
71:41   And I remember: *MS* 1602:03.
71:42   It is not: *MS* 292.
72:12   Went to church: *MS* 1634.
72:14   That the idiosyncrasy: *MS* 359:15–16 Lowell Lectures of 1866—the voice is adjust-
         ed to first person.
73:14   Attended a: *MS* 1634.
73:16   I remember well: *MS* 1602.
73:27   I can recall my father: *CP* 1.366.
74:33   I cannot recall it: *CP* 1.583.
75:11   widely known attack: F28:2.
75:15   roundly understood: F29:1.
75:17   who was born: F29:1.
75:31   was of course: F28:7; see also F29:1.
75:35   argued the affirmative: F29:3–4.
75:35   he went immediately: *BPH*, BP2 to BP1 11/19/1829.
75:40   he proudly declared: *BPH*, BP2 to BP1 1/12/1830.
76:5   A letter to home: *BPH*, BP2 to BP1 11/19/1829.
76:8   how grand I feel: *BPH*, BP2 to LRP 5/17/1830.
76:10   Mr. Bancroft and Mr. Cogswell: *BPH*, BP2 to BP1 11/19/1829.
76:13   a spectacular temper: *BPH*, BP2 to BP1 11/19/1829.
76:23   Round Hill School: Russel B. Nye, *George Bancroft: Brahmin Rebel* (New York:
         Knopf, 1945), 68–69. The following account of Round Hill School is adapted from
         Nye.
76:26   ultimately through: *BPH*, BP2 to BP1 1830.
76:29   the company of Sarah: *BPH*, BP2 to LRP 5/17/1830.
76:33   teaching mathematics to young ladies: *BPH*, BP1 to BP2 2/20/1830. Concerning
         BP2 visiting around Northampton, see *BPH*, BP2 to BP1 8/1/1830.
76:33   I should much rather: *BPH*, BP2 to BP1 2/20/1830.
77:11   Bancroft proudly: Nye, *Bancroft*, 69.
77:12   The great object with us: Nye, *Bancroft*, 69.
77:18   diligent but playful: *BPH*, BP2 to LRP 12/23/1830 signed "Son Ben Purse."
77:34   Benjamin Peirce: F31:7, CHP on the death of BP1 7/26/1831.
78:2   probably easily hidden: William O. Kearse, M.D., personal communication. See
         CD under *meninges* and *meningitis*.
78:12   the best librarian of Harvard College: F31:2, CEP 4/18/1831.
78:13   received strong praise: *BPH*, BP2 to BP1 8/1/1830, in F. Parkman, Review of
         *Catalogue of the Library of Harvard University in Cambridge, Massachusetts. Christian
         Examiner* 8 (1830): 321–325.

78:15   edited by John Pickering: BP1, *A History of Harvard University* (Cambridge: Brown, Shattuck & Co., 1833). There is a good obituary of BP1 in the book; see also *Dictionary of American Biography*, 14:393.

78:20   he was prepared: *BPH*, BP2 to Uncle Benjamin R. Nichols 7/27/1831; Benjamin R. Nichols to BP2 7/30/1831.

78:27   I was delighted, my Dear: *MS* Vgamma, BP2 to CHP 8/3/1831.

79:8   mathematics and natural philosophy: *MS* Vgamma, BP2 to CHP 8/3/1831. Ex-President Eliot's memory of Ben's position and title was different (Eliot in Raymond Claire Archibald, *Benjamin Peirce 1809–1880* (Chicago: Open Court, 1925); he stated that Ben was first tutor and afterwards University Professor, then finally Perkins Professor. Edward Everett Hale in *A New England Boyhood* (New York: Cassell, 1893), 175, stated that BP2 was initially appointed Hollis Professor of Mathematics. But a letter of 2/17/1832 (at F32:4) from CEP to LRP mentioned "Benjamin Peirce, Tutor, Cambridge." A letter from LRP to BP2 dated 5/6/1832 (*BPH*) was addressed to "Mr. Benjamin Peirce, Tutor Harvard College."

79:13   I felt true: *BPH*, BP2 to SMP 1831.

80:36   closed by betrothal: F32:1, diary of CPH 1/4/1832.

80:37   she one year younger: Falpha: Peirce.

80:38   Cambridge for a while: *BPH*, CPH to BP2 11/9/1831; F32:1, LRP to CEP 1/5/1832.

80:40   made a diary: F32:5, diary of CPH 4/17/1832.

81:19   family of Judge: F34:4, Judge Samuel Jones to LRP 2/8/1834.

81:20   widower of New York: *BPH*, LRP to BP2 11/16/1832, LRP to her parents 11/19/1832, LRP to CEP 1/16/1833.

81:20   Judge's farm: F34:4, Judge Samuel Jones to LRP 2/8/1834.

81:27   Ben is well established: F33:9, LRNP to parents 4/19/1833.

81:33   morning of 23 July 1833: F33:12; F33:24, diary of CPH 12/29/1833; see also Eisele "Benjamin Peirce."

81:36   Dana House in Cambridge: *BPH*, Harriet Mills to Helen Huntington 5/1/1834; F34:13.

81:39   New England Mutual Life: F35:1.

81:44   These ultimately ranged: This information may be found on the outer back cover of number 1; a copy is located at ISP catalogued as PRAG QA 5345 P3.

82:38   appearing in 1835: F35:1.

83:2   One of his students: The account given is a composite from the following three sources: Edward Everett Hale, "My College Days," *Atlantic Monthly* volume 71 (1893): 355–363; *A New England Boyhood*; "'Tis 60 years Since' at Harvard," *Atlantic Monthly* volume 78 (1896): 496–505.

84:38   intimate member: James Taft Hatfield, *New Light on Longfellow* (Boston: Houghton Mifflin, 1933).

85:9   Fell violently in love: *MS* 1634.

85:12   School to Ma'am Sessions: *MS* 1609:02.

85:15   I forgot to mention: *MS* 1602:04.

85:26   I well remember: *MS* 1602:04–5.

85:35   One of my earliest recollections: *MS* 1606:02.

85:40   Emerson's Nature of 1836: An extract from Emerson's "Nature" in *The Portable Emerson*, ed. C. Bode (New York: Penguin, 1981), 7–8.

86:31   When I was about five: *MS* 753.

87:26   and commenced my researches: *MS* 1634.

87:29   When I was about six: F45:30, CSP to WJ 4/24/1910.
87:31   I remember driving: *MS* 1602:05.
87:42   I remember many: *MS* 1602:04.
88:1   Even in my old: The first two sentences are from F45:31, CSP to MEH 1/27/1910.
88:4   It was in the summer: The remainder of this paragraph and the displayed quotation are from F45:21, MEH to HPE date unknown (late, probably after CSP's death); the voice has been changed from MEH to CSP.
88:32   I must count it: *MS* 325:04-5.
88:36   Reflective activity: Composite from *MS* 296:41ff.; *PW*:113ff.; *MS* 619:03ff.
89:17   the Italian Antonio: *Encyclopedia Britannica*, 13th edition, vols. 11-12:417.
89:33   Also near to the heart: Falpha: Greenough, Horatio.
89:36   sculptor who designed: *CP* 5.75.
89:40   I was educated: *MS* 1608:02.
90:6   I was brought up: *PW*:114.
90:7   My father: *MS* 619:05-7.
90:10   rapid games of double-dummy: This is said to be similar to the game "War."
90:34   first Perkins Professor: F42:13, Josiah Quincy to Thomas H. Perkins 6/4/1842: "At the request of Benjamin Peirce, Perkins Professor of Astronomy, in Harvard University, I take the liberty of introducing him to your acquaintance. I need not inform you that he is one of the most distinguished mathematicians in our country, and he is entering upon his new professorship with a spirit & ardor, which promises, in time, important results."
90:35   Quincy Street: F42:13, CHD to BP2 5/23/1842; F46:8.
90:40   Ben made his debut: F43:8, ADB & John Ludlow to BP2 4/26/1843.
90:42   Bache had amassed: This paragraph is summarized from "Bache" in *Dictionary of Scientific Biography*, 1:363.
91:15   they quickly became: F43:14 (ADB to BP2 11/28/1843), 15 (ADB to BP2 12/4/1843), 16 (BP2 to ADB 12/8/1843).
91:19   Ben promised: F43:14, BP2 to ADB 11/28/1843.
91:26   Bache learned in December: F43:15, ADB to BP2 12/4/1843.
91:38   constructed for them: Hamilton Vaughan Bail, *Views of Harvard* (Cambridge: Harvard University Press, 1949), 10, and Plate II (the Wadsworth Survey of Harvard Yard on which BP2's house is item 20); also log of the Cambridge Historical Commission (Peirce-Lane House at 31 Quincy Street).
92:28   it was a great: Edward Lurie, *Louis Agassiz: A Life in Science* (Chicago: University of Chicago Press, 1960), 146.
92:34   compute latitudes: F45:12 (ADB to BP2 4/21/1845), 16 (ADB to BP 4/25/1845).
92:41   daughter was born: *BPH*, CPH to BP2 12/12/1845, BP2 to EL 12/24/1845.
93:2   slow in recovering: F46:12 (BP2 to EL 1/22/46), 13 (BP2 to ADB, 1/29/46), 18 (BP2 to Loomis 1/30/46).
93:5   parents feared: *BPH*, SMP to BP2 8/?/1846, SMP to BP2 8/21/46, SMP to BP2 8/23/1846.
93:9   The great naturalist: This paragraph is summarized from Lurie, *Agassiz*, around p. 120.
93:36   passing behind: *CD* 4073.
94:2   His biographer captured: Lurie, *Agassiz*, 127.
94:27   Agassiz had been introduced: Lurie, *Agassiz*, 126.
94:33   also known: The Lazzaroni (or the "Laz" or "LL," as they described themselves in

epistolary shorthand) begged for money for science. For an introduction to the Lazzaroni (the "Florentine Academy" will be the preferred name here), see Robert V. Bruce, *The Launching of Modern American Science, 1846–1876* (New York: Knopf, 1987); George H. Daniels, *American Science in the Age of Jackson* (New York: Columbia, 1968); A. Hunter Dupree, *Asa Gray* (Cambridge: Belknap Press of Harvard University Press, 1959); Mary Ann James, *Elites in Conflict* (New Brunswick: Rutgers University Press, 1987; Kenneth Laine Ketner, "Peirce and Turing: Comparisons and Conjectures," *Semiotica* 68 (1988): 33–61; Lurie, *Agassiz*; Merle M. Odgers, *Alexander Dallas Bache* (Philadelphia: University of Pennsylvania Press, 1947).

95:30   founders of American science: Bruce, *Launching*.

95:40   scornful epithets: Bruce, *Launching*.

96:41   I will designate: *MS* 1634.

96:43   1846. Discovery: *MS* 1609:02.

97:1   The sum total: *MS* 450:09.

97:11   enables me to recommend: *MS* 1634.

97:13   1847. California: *MS* 1609:02.

97:16   Although I was not: *MS* 1606:02–3.

97:25   When I was first: *CP* 3.470.

97:31   How many times: *CP* 6.316.

97:39   my first lesson: *MS* 1634.

97:41   1848. French: *MS* 1609:02.

97:43   dry goods business: F48:37; see *Boston Directory* 1848–49.

97:44   moved to 1 Park Street: F49:21, see *Boston Directory* July 1849.

98:1   Reverend Sullivan's school: Adapted from Robert Means Lawrence, *Old Park Street and Its Vicinity* (Boston: Houghton Mifflin, 1922), 111–113.

98:8   ambiance around the Church: Lawrence, *Old Park Street*, 113.

98:23   I remember in 1848: *MS* 205:15.

98:31   My aunt: F49:16, memorandum of MEH to HPE put into CSP's voice.

98:43   admitted as a member: *MS* 1634.

99:1   1849. Macready: *MS* 1609:02.

99:3   Whoever has any practical: *MS* 649.

99:20   young Victoria: *Wanderers: Episodes from the Travels of Lady Emmeline Stuart-Wortley and Her Daughter Victoria, 1849–1855.* ed. Nina Cust (London: J. Cape, 1928), entry for 12 August 1849; also see Lady Emmeline Stuart-Wortley, *Travels in the United States, etc. During 1849 and 1850* (New York: Harper & Brothers, 1851), 47.

99:39   Mademoiselle Anne: speech of VW and her mother edited into VW's voice from Stuart-Wortley, *Travels*, 343.

99:42   A History: *MS* 1634.

99:44   1850. Coup: *MS* 1609:02.

100:17   John S. C. Abbot: *Kings and Queens; or, Life in the Palace* (New York: Harper & Brothers, 1855), title page.

100:30   A secret: Abbot, *Kings and Queens*, 61.

101:1   When I was: *MS* 1139:15–16.

101:17   My original: *MS* 1139:16.

101:24   I shall: *MS* 1139:16.

101:29   Somewhat later: *MS* 1606:02.

101:30   is a book: *CP* 7.256.

102:2 Established: *MS* 1634.

102:4 1851. Kossuth. Lane: *MS* 1609:02. George Martin Lane was made University Professor of Latin at Harvard in 1851 (Samuel Eliot Morison, *Three Centuries of Harvard: 1636–1936* [Cambridge: Belknap Press of Harvard University Press, 1936], 298).

102:8 I hope that you: *MS* VB1a(4)#1.

102:30 The third annual Exhibition: *Cambridge Chronicle*, 9 August 1851.

103:17 early became interested: *MS* 619:07. See Fisch's excellent discussion of CSP's early work in chemistry in *Peirce, Semeiotic, and Pragmatism: Essays by Max H. Fisch*, ed. Kenneth Laine Ketner, and Christian J. W. Kloesel (Bloomington: Indiana University Press, 1986), 380.

103:23 in its chemical: *MS* 1041.

103:34 in the year 1851: combining three sources—*MS* 842:07–8, *MS* 619:07, and *MS* L477, CSP to FAW 10/14/1913.

103:38 as subsequent tests: starting *MS* L477, CSP to FAW 10/14/1913.

103:40 From that day: back to *MS* 842:08.

103:41 although my training: *MS* 842:06–8.

104:5 How successful: *MS* 842:09–11.

104:17 It seems strange: *MS* L477, CSP to FAW 10/14/1913.

104:29 By the time: momentary change to *MS* L169, CSP to Ginn and Company 3/11/95.

104:33 was one: back to *MS* L477, CSP to FAW 10/14/1913.

104:37 I use the word: *MS* L477, CSP to FAW 10/14/1913.

105:4 The reader: *MS* 684:05.

105:35 where he met Ben: Joseph Le Conte, *The Autobiography of Joseph Le Conte*, ed. D. Armes (New York: D. Appleton & Company, 1903), 128.

105:38 Lawrence Scientific School: *Dictionary of American Biography*, 11:90ff.; see also Joseph Le Conte's memory of his studies with Agassiz and acquaintance with the Florentine Academy during 1851 in his *Autobiography*, 141–143.

106:16 Mrs. Le Conte: W. Le Conte Stevens, "Sketch of Prof. John Le Conte," *Popular Science Monthly* 36 (1889): 114.

106:27 AAAS meeting of 1851: Subsequent correspondence shows that Benjamin and Josephine met for the first time at this Albany conference.

106:28 speech by The Chief: Odgers, *Bache*, 167–169; for more background on the Florentines and the AAAS, see Bruce, *Launching*.

106:39 visionary board of trustees: Stevens, "Sketch," 115.

107:16 give you this collection: The opening line of this section—"Charley's note"—has been added. The correspondence is in F (Benjamin Peirce Junior to Le Conte) as transcriptions of originals held in the Bancroft Library at The University of California at Berkeley. Publication of the letters and photographs of The Queen is by permission of Nancy Hopkins. Dates in this form "18 I 52" (BP2's dating method, meaning the 18th day of the first month of the year 1852) or in more standard forms in the letters of other persons, identify the letters. Hence no additional identifying notation is required. This correspondence has been heavily edited to condense the file a great deal while preserving the tone and historical content. In some cases, material was moved out of strict chronological sequence; such cases will be annotated using letter dates.

112:2 Omnium professorum: To the most learned Fraser. Of all professors the most learned. To you I wish to submit a question which is very difficult. Philosophers who are dolts in experimentation speak of a male devil and a female devil—that there are devils dramatic, lyric, politic, scientific, humorific and fearful. To you I propose to investigate on behalf of the academy of sciences what would be the form of a female devil—a form clothed in female shape, Le Conte, little known among humans. Ignorant but loving. The Penetrator.

113:2   you in heart: these sentences were erased in the original but can be read via impressions in the paper.

120:3   with you singing: previous sentence from BP2 to JoLeC 19 XII 58.

121:9   Its author: Oliver Wendell Holmes, Senior.

121:10   The boys desire: last sentence is from BP2 to JnLeC 18 I 59.

121:25   for the day must: BP2's joke about April Fool's day—his birthday was 4 April.

122:2   that the world: BP2 to JnLeC 8 IV 59 documents all Ben's troubles with the Nautical Almanac office—his not being appointed director of the Harvard Observatory and other difficulties.

122:42   joy is in store: These two sentences from BP2 to JoLeC 25 VII 59.

122:43   as a reporter: This sentence has been added.

123:24   Last night, a son: BP2 to JoLeC 7 IX 59.

123:29   have been delighted: BP2 to JoLeC 11 IX 59.

126:19   do for a black: More on BP2's racism and this lecture is given in BP2 to JoLeC 21 I 60.

128:13   Joined a debating: *MS* 1634.

128:15   1852. Death: *MS* 1609:02.

128:17   composition of the class: *MS* 200.

128:21   you recall: *MS* Vdelta, MEH to HPE 1919. First sentence has been added.

128:36   THE BEAUTIES OF EBRATUM: *MS* 1247.

129:19   EXHIBITION OF THE HIGH SCHOOL: *Cambridge Chronicle, 129:33* 8/7/1852.

129:33   a fast man: *MS* 1634.

129:35   1853. My first visit: *MS* 1609:02.

129:38   Private Thoughts: *MS* 891.

129:43   Procul, o procul: "Stand far away, far away, profane souls!"—Publius Vergilius Maro, *Aeneid*, 6:258.
         Spoken by the Sybil as she invokes aid from the goddess to open the underworld to Aeneas. After extensive sacrifices the goddess approaches and the Sybil cries: "Here comes our lady! Fall back unhallowed souls!" This religious formula excluding the uninitiated is similar to the cry of the herald prior to the beginning of the Eleusinian Mysteries, "Depart, all ye profane!" See Virgil, *The Æneid*, trans. Frank O. Copley (Indianapolis: Bobbs-Merrill Co., 1965), and Virgil, *The Æneid of Vergil*, ed. R. D. Williams (New York: Macmillan Education Limited, 1972).

131:20   Order of Exercises: F53:39, 8/6/1853.

131:37   August 13, 1853: *Cambridge Chronicle*, 8/6/1853.

132:1   In 1853: F53:51, JMP to T. S. Perry transferred to CSP's voice, with additions from SMP to BP2 (at F53:53) October 1853.

132:20   joined Dixwell's school: *MS* 1634.

132:22   1854. Crimean: *MS* 1609:02.

132:25   Theories of C. S. Peirce's: F54:5, ZFP's bible; compare *MS* 891.

132:35   XI: *MS* 891.

134:3   I was first entering: *MS* Vdelta, MEH to HPE 1919.

135:9   ANNUAL EXHIBITION: *Cambridge Chronicle*, 8/5/1854.

135:38 I recall my father: Thomas Wentworth Higginson, "How I was Educated, "*The Forum* 1 (1866): 176.

136:6 and began the study: *MS* 1634.

136:8 The first year: *MS* 310:07. For a recent translation of the book CSP mentioned, see Schiller, *On the Æsthetic Education of Man, in a Series of Letters*, trans. with an introduction by Reginald Snell (New Haven: Yale University Press, 1954).

136:9 Mrs. Anna Cabot: The inner phrase about Mrs. Lowell has been added. That the good angel was Mrs. Lowell is identified at F55:94 (from a scrap in *MS*).

136:30 Having been bred: *CP* 4.2 from a draft of *RLT* (lecture two); the final draft may be seen at *RLT* 124 (some of which has been intermingled here).

136:39 a book by Vera: Augusto Vera, *Introduction a la philosophie de Hegel*, Paris 1855.

136:40 I spent two: *MS* 231:05 6/22/1911.

137:1 XV: *MS* 891.

137:27 1855 June 16: Falpha:opium.

138:10 Father's brother Charles: F55:140, BP2 to ADB 6/20/1855, but changed to CSP's voice.

138:14 six days of creation: Thomas Hill, review of three books on creation, *Christian Examiner* 59 (1855): 375–398.

138:18 The first account: Hill, 391.

138:27 If mathematical analysis: Hill, 392.

138:32 This first chapter of Genesis: Hill, 395.

138:38 Everything which is obscure: F55:59, BP2 to ADB 3/11/1855 elaborating on his views as mentioned in the Hill review.

139:1 At sixteen: F55:85, *MS* scrap; see also *MS* 1609:02. It was common for students to enter Harvard at this age, or earlier. For instance, Edward Everett Hale and Thomas Wentworth Higginson (both students of mathematics with BP2) entered at age thirteen.

139:1 I entered: adding some lines from *CP* 5.111.

139:3 wooden treatise by Whewell: F55:85, from here to "When I got to be. . . ."

139:5 lent me a translation: F55:94. Perhaps the version CSP read was Schiller, *The Æsthetic Letters, Essays, and The Philosophical Letters of Schiller*, trans. J. Weiss (Boston: Charles C. Little & James Brown), 1845.

139:9 When I got to be: This combines elements of F55:85–86 and *MS* 619:08.

139:9 a college: Switching to *MS* 619:08.

139:17 Schiller's letters: *MS* 619:10.

139:27 I read very carefully: F55:85–86, *MS* scrap.

140:23 I began the study: F55:95.

140:26 Harvard in 1850: Morison, *Three Centuries*, 287.

140:30 quit the discussion club: From about 1855, BP2 was a member of the Saturday Club, a dining and discussion group that was loyally frequented by Emerson, Agassiz, O. W. Holmes, Senior, Richard Henry Dana, Junior, and others (see F56:85; Gay Wilson Allen, *Waldo Emerson: A Biography* [New York: Viking, 1981]). In 1859, BP2 quit the Saturday Club, a step he reported to The Queen (BP2 to JoLeC 21 XII 1859): "I have left a club in which some of the most accomplished scholars of Boston were accustomed to meet and have a good dinner once a month—because as I honestly told them, they had become such desperate abolitionists."

140:37 Lawrence Scientific School: Morison, *Three Centuries*, 306–307, a few slight changes have been made.

141:37   privately admonished: F56:4.
141:37   of Latin and for: F56:94.
141:38   a private admonishment: F57a:163.
141:39   he was assigned: F57a:169.
141:40   on December 7 1857: F57b:145.
141:41   admonition for 7: F57b:146.
141:41   he was privately: At F55:137–138, but these two entries are for the year 1859 (4/25 and 5/2).
142:1   in the Faculty Reports: F57a:17.
142:7   Ben urged his son: *BPH,* BP2 to SMP 1/22/1857.
142:14   various Florentine: F57a, various letters in January and February from BP2.
142:16   in the Faculty Reports: F57a:82.
142:23   undertook the pursuit: *MS* 1634.
142:25   in my college days: *CP* 8.378.
142:27   early and late: *MS* L 159, CSP to WPG 1906 (see F56:30).
142:29   going up Monadnock: Katharine M. Abbott, *Old Paths and Legends of New England* (New York: G. P. Putnam's Sons, 1909), 103. A mountain-climbing expedition.
142:31   I remember when: *CP* 7.396.
142:36   remember about 1856: F56:42, CSP family record.
143:1   Glen House, New Hampshire: *MS* VB1a(4)#1, CSP to SMP 1856.
143:38   XVII: *MS* 891.
144:17   That the attention: Charley's discussion of "soul" and "attention" here is remarkably similar to the way those words appear in the works of Simone Weil (for example, pp. 44–52 and 313–340, in *The Simone Weil Reader,* ed. George A. Panichas [New York: David McKay, 1977]). At least, that's my opinion.
144:23   been reading Kant: *MS* VB1a(4)#1, CSP to SMP 8/21/1856.
144:37   Cambridge is awaking: *MS* VB1a(4)#1, CSP to SMP 8/26/1856.
145:1   XLII: *MS* 891.
145:14   Fall 1856: *MS* 1633.
146:30   Mrs. Anna Lowell's: Anna C. Lowell, *Seed-Grain for Thought and Discussion,* 2 vols (Boston: Ticknor & Fields, 1856).
146:31   The foundation stone: Lowell, *Seed-Grain,* 2:70.
146:33   Hence it is: Lowell, *Seed-Grain,* 2:71.
146:35   Would'st with thyself: Lowell, *Seed-Grain,* 2:94.
146:37   Rank exists: Lowell, *Seed-Grain,* 2:279.
146:43   undertook to enjoy: *MS* 1634.
147:7   XVIII: *MS* 891
148:7   concomitants in Audience: *MS* 891:07
149:6   XIX: *MS* 891:08.
150:1   Emerson's Over-Soul: in *Portable Emerson,* 215.
150:9   Swedenborg's Treatise on Influx: Swedenborg, *A Treatise on the Nature of Influx: or, of the Intercourse between the SOUL and BODY Which is supposed to be either by PHYSICAL INFLUX, or by SPIRITUAL INFLUX, or by PRESTABLISHED HARMONY,* trans. Rev. Thomas Hartley (Boston: I. Thomas & E. T. Andrews, 1794), 29.
150:18   Swedenborg's Divine Love & Wisdom: Swedenborg, *Angelic Wisdom Concerning the Divine Love and the Divine Wisdom* (New York: Swedenborg Foundation, 1971), 191. First U.S. edition and English translation was 1851.
150:24   It must have been: *O* 1243, CSP to CLF in 1905, as cited by CLF in her article.
150:36   One of the books: *MS* L80:38, CSP to BES (of The Century Company).

151:5   The Synonyms: *MS* 1140–42.
154:17   Gave up enjoying life: *MS* 1634.
154:20   Harvard Orthoepy Klub: F58:175, OK Catalogue; see C. J. W. Kloesel, "Charles Peirce and the Secret of the Harvard O.K.," *The New England Quarterly* 52 (1979): 58. CSP's voice on this topic has been supplied based upon Kloesel's article.
154:25   I provided: *MS* 1636.
154:38   Orthoepy is the art: *CD* 4161.
155:5   My piece: *P* 13.
155:8   XXIX: *MS* 891.
155:27   My essay: *P* 1.
157:1   THE CLASS OF 1859: F58:46; *MS* 1635. The list is much longer than the selections provided here.
158:34   Father's letter: F58:58, BP2 to BMP 2/22/1858. The voice has been changed from that of BP2 as if written to CSP and copied by CSP. While the letter was written to Benjie (Benjamin Mills, Charley's younger brother), it represents viewpoints and sentiments Benjamin displayed toward his entire family. Compare *The Letters and Journals of General Nicholas Longworth Anderson: Harvard, Civil War, Washington, 1854–1892*, ed. Isabel Anderson (New York: F. H. Revell, 1942), General Nicholas Longworth Anderson to his mother 9/27/1856: "At Albany I met Jimmy Peirce [James Mills Peirce] and we journeyed together all day, at one time gravely speaking upon scientific subjects, at another time running off upon some lighter theme. Of course we discussed politics. Now open your eyes with astonishment. Jimmy is the most radical, ultra, out and out pro–slavery man. These sentiments he imbibed from his father, who thinks slavery a blessing rather than a bane."
159:17   When I was in: F55:87, *MS* scrap on Procedure of science.
159:38   During my college years: F55:85, *MS* scrap.
160:1   Kant's Deduction of the Categories: F58:2, *MS* scrap.
160:35   insouciant student: *CP* 5.585.
161:33   Went to Maine: *MS* 1634.
161:35   XXXVI: *MS* 891.
162:30   Lillie Greenough: *MS* 1629b:184–185, 1859.
164:14   I am of a meditative: *MS* VB1a(4)#1, CSP to SMP 5/11/1859, revised as solo speech.
165:27   class photograph: See p. 214.
165:29   letter to his mother: F59b:24, BMP to SMP 5/17/1859; see also F59b:42, BP2 to SMP 5/24/1859.
165:38   a collaborator: *P* 13.
166:1   George Rapall Noyes: *National Cyclopædia of American Biography*, 18:307; *Dictionary of American Biography*, 13:587.
166:22   In the past: *MS* VB1a(4)#1, CSP to SMP 5/19/1859.
166:38   There are several: *MS* VB1a(4)#1, CSP to SMP5/21/1859; the name "Lillie" has been substituted here for "Julia" in the original, where it probably served as a mere placemarker in Charley's example letter.
167:38   VALENTINE: *MS* 1629b:187. On same sheet of paper as "Anacreontic Valentine." Probably written for Lillie Greenough. Wonder what LG's eye color was?
168:13   ANACREONTIC VALENTINE: *MS* 1629b:186–187. *Anacreontic* means "in the style of Anacreon, in praise of love, amatory" (see *CD*).
169:11   Domain of Metaphysics: F59:32 *MS* 921.
169:24   Charley became seriously ill: BP2 to JoLeC 6 VI 1859.

169:29 was confined: BP2 to JoLeC 6 VI 1859.
169:30 Ben and The Chief: *BPH*, ADB to BP 6/18/1859; ADB wrote to Ben on the same subject again on 6/27 and 6/29.
169:32 Ben noted: BP2 to JoLeC 27 VI 1859.
169:38 Ben informed The Chief: Inferred from *BPH*, ADB to BP2 6/27/1859.
169:40 he was catheterized: This can be inferred from *BPH*, ADB to BP2 6/29/1859.
170:2   Metaphysics as a Study: *MS* 921:17ff. There is a later version at *MS* 921:15.
170:31 salt junk: *CD* 3254, *junk* 1, 2: "Naut., old or condemned cable and cordage; 4: Salt beef or pork supplied to vessels for long voyages: so-called from its resemblance in toughness to old ropes' ends."
170:43 But I will: Adding on a paragraph written later at *MS* 921:16.
171:8   Definition of Metaphysics: *MS* 921.
171:16 The philosopher as such: CSP obviously changed his mind on this point a few years later.
171:40 of other Substances: *MS* 921.
172:15 I attend: *P* 2–7; CSP's reportage upon the meeting is much more detailed than what is presented here, the present purpose being, of course, to display Life.
172:15 thirteenth annual meeting: *P* 2.
172:43 meeting of the Association: *P* 3.
173:43 gave a levee: *CD* 3425, "a morning reception held by a prince or great personage."
174:8   The members assembled: *P* 4.
174:28 partake of a collation: *CD* 1100, *collation* 8, "A repast; a meal; a term originally applied to the refection partaken of by monks in monasteries after the reading of the lives of the saints."
175:8   In accordance: *P* 5.
176:17 The Association met: *P* 6.
177:40 The general meeting: *P* 7.
178:20 Camp life: *MS* VB1a(4)#1, CSP to SMP 8/19/1859 revised into CSP's solo voice. In *NARG* 23 OGS Personnel Records 1844–1863, p. 302, one finds this note: "Chas. S. Peirce joined the Survey as Aid Sept. 21, 1859. 1859 $15 pr mo Aid Sec I. Supt's Party. From Sept. 1859 to June 1, 1860: Aid in Superintendent and Asst. C. O. Boutelle at station 'Mahomet' making obs'ns for Time, Latitude and Magnetic Constants."
179:21 1859, August 21: *MS* VB1a(4)#1, CSP to HHDP 8/21/1859, revised into CSP's solo voice.
180:10 1859, August: *MS* VB1a(4), CSP to JMP 9/25/1859, revised into CSP's solo voice.
180:27 Station Western: *MS* VB1a(4)#1, CSP to SMP 8/30/1859.
181:5   Thursday, September 1: *MS* VB1a(4), CSP to JMP 9/25/1859, CSP's diary within his letter to JMP.
181:38 I leave here: *BPH*, CSP to BP2 9/27/1859, revised into CSP's solo voice.
181:43 Chief ordered him: BP2 to JoLeC 16 X 1859; *BPH*, ADB to BP2 10/24/1859.
182:2   writing metaphysics: *MS* 921.
182:8   Coast Survey: *NARG* 23 VIII, Civil Assistants H to W, p. 220, ADB to CSP 10/28/1859.
182:9   with my party: See also *NARG* 23 OGS Personnel Records 1844–1863, p. 302, and Record of Employees, p. 21: "Engaged with Asst. Harris in the triangulation of Isle au Breton sound and vicinity."
182:17 I have the honor: Same source as previous note.
182:29 I haven't yet written: *MS* VB1a(4)#1, CSP to BMP 11/24/1859.

183:21 1909 Jan 28: *MS* 706:26–27.

183:26 on the tenth: CSP wrote here, "having set out in October 1859. . . ." But other evidence shows that he actually left on 10 November 1859; see BP2 to JnLeC 13 November 1859: "Charley went South last Thursday [which would have been the tenth]. He stops a day in New York—two or three with the James K. Mills' in Baltimore and a few with the darling Chief in Washington. He is to be stationed in the vicinity of New Orleans in the party of triangulation which is under the command of Harris."

184:2 The views here: *MS* VB1a(4)#1, CSP to SMP 12/11/1859, changed to CSP's solo voice.

184:17 is still aground: *MS* VB1a(4)#1, CSP to BP2 12/15/1859, changed to CSP's solo voice.

184:44 I would like to have: *MS* VB1a(4)#1, CSP to JMP 12/18/1859.

186:6 I just got up: *MS* VB1a(4)#1, CSP to BMP 12/18/1859, changed to CSP's solo voice.

186:24 This style of writing: *MS* VB1a(4)#1, CSP to SMP 12/20/1859.

187:40 of the doctrine: *PW* 73ff., CSP to VW 12/23/1909.

188:32 XX: *MS* 891.

188:37 to pass the time: *MS* 201, combining similar matter from *CP* 4.585, conjecturing that he did it on ship.

189:5 The bad seeing: *MS* VB1a(4)#1, CSP to BMP February 1860, changed to CSP's solo voice.

189:24 When Mr. Harris: *MS* VB1a(4)#1, CSP to SMP 2/18/1860, changed to CSP's solo voice.

190:5 We had a good deal: *MS* VB1a(4)#1, CSP to SMP 3/18/60, changed to CSP's solo voice.

190:25 I was very sorry: *MS* VB1a(4)#1, CSP to SMP 3/25/1860.

191:13 XXI: *MS* 891.

192:9 Emerson's Nature of 1836: *Portable Emerson* extracts from chapter 1 of "Nature" as if copied out by CSP.

192:40 Isle au Breton: *MS* VB1a(4)#2, CSP to SMP 4/2/1860, changed to CSP's solo voice.

193:23 I ought long ago: *MS* VB1a(4)#2, CSP to JMP 4/4/1860.

194:9 My wardrobe: *MS* VB1a(4)#2, CSP to SMP 4/8/1860, changed to CSP's solo voice.

195:2 I was not surprised: *MS* VB1a(4)#2, CSP to JMP 4/10/1860, changed to CSP's solo voice.

195:14 period reference work: *Johnson's Universal Cyclopædia,* ed. Frederick A. P. Bernhard (New York: A. J. Johnson & Co., 1839 and later editions), 2:729.

195:25 his elder brother: F60a:183, JMP to CSP 3/30/1860.

195:27 confided to The Queen: BP to JoLeC 1 IV 1860; on SMP's illness see also F60a:183 and F60b:2, 13, 17–8, 20, 25, 30–31.

195:30 violently wild delirium: The two descriptives added from F60a:183.

196:10 she suffered with: F60b:31 SMP to CSP 4/29/1860. SMP mentioned "Your letters, dear Charley, have been among my greatest comforts . . . & this last week is the only one I think which has not brought us several from you."

196:10 Ben became ill: In the letter mentioned in the previous note.

196:12 and had debated: F60b:20, JMP to CSP 4/20/1860.

196:15 for six months: F60b:31, SMP to CSP 4/29/1860.

196:15 to recover: *BPH*, CEP to relatives in Salem 4/30/1860.

196:22   all hands demanded: Same source as previous note.
196:25   then to Paris: BP2 to JoLeC 26 V 1860.
196:26   assumed by Jem: F60b:35, JMP to CSP 5/2/1860.
196:31   connect him strongly: A great many notes from Ben about his trip during 1860. For representative examples, see F60b:67, 6/10/1860 (hearing Lillie Greenough sing in France, meeting many exemplary persons), F60b:82, 6/30/1860 (Ben's account of the Wilberforce to Huxley debate over Darwin, a debate he witnessed in person).
196:40   study science: F60a:183, JMP to CSP 3/30/1860.
197:8   Jem says: MS VB1a(4)#2, CSP to SMP 4/23/1860.
197:33   I am delighted: MS VB1a(4)#2, CSP to JMP 4/23/1860.
198:31   Greenough, Anna: Falpha:Greenough. Charley's principal ultimate hope for news of Lillie would have been by way of Ben, but he had not yet departed for Europe. Yet later Ben did meet his former Agassiz School pupil Lillie and her future husband, Moulton, when he traveled to France, as mentioned four notes above.
199:3   the writer: This account is adapted from the (probably autobiographical) introductions to Anna Lillie [Greenough] [Moulton] Hegermann-Lindencrone, *In the Courts of Memory: 1858–1875 from Contemporary Letters* (New York: Harper & Brothers, 1912), and *The Sunny Side of Diplomatic Life, 1875–1912* (New York: Harper & Brothers), 1914, especially the latter, which is a fuller account.
199:26   In 1859: Falpha:Greenough, MEH to HPE.
199:42   as her memoirs: *In the Courts of Memory*.
200:5   new home next door: Ketner and Kloesel, eds., *Peirce, Semeiotic, and Pragmatism*, 404.
200:10   letter to her mother: *In the Courts of Memory*, 1–4.
201:42   frontispiece portrait: Preceding paragraph adapted from *In the Courts of Memory*.
202:2   nineteenth of May: F60:43 (JMP to CSP 5/19/1860), 45 (Stephen Harris to CSP 5/21/1860), 46 (SMP to CSP 5/21/1860).
202:3   met his father: F60:46, BP2 to CSP 5/22/1860.
202:4   at one PM: BP2 to JoLeC 26 V 1860.
202:8   of the departure: Same source as previous note.
202:9   which he reached: F60:45, Stephen Harris to CSP 5/21/1860—CSP's annotation of receipt is "Rec'd Cambridge 1860 May 26."
202:16   under the necessity: NARG 23 1860 VII, Civil Assistants H to Z, p. 254, CSP to ADB 5/19/1860.
202:22   Thursday before last: MS VB1a(4)#2, CSP to SMP 5/20/1860, changed to CSP's solo voice. Days of the week for trip events have been translated into calendar dates.
203:5   I grew up: PPM 164, added punctuation to enhance the conversational aspect.
203:38   XXIII: MS 891.
205:7   THE RULES OF LOGIC: MS 743.
205:35   the mere vinculum: CD: *vinculum* 1, "A bond of union; a bond; a tie."
206:4   back from Louisiana: NARG 23 OGS Personnel Records 1844–1863, p. 302: "1860 $15 pr mo Aid. Resigned June 1st after duty in Sec VIII with Sub Asst Harris."
206:6   Studied Natural History: MS 1634.
206:9   study biology privately: BPH, BMP to BP2 24 June 60: "Charley is studying with Mr. Agassiz now for a while. He is well."
206:12   from Plato: MS 988. There were two axioms labeled "4," so numbers have been adjusted.

208:2   Distinction of Metaphysics: *MS* 921.

208:10   to take: *MS* 921:34.

208:41   we have no thought: Here CSP referenced Corollary III, which is probably given at *MS* 921:39, but omitting it doesn't appear to change the sense of this sentence.

209:1   That will do: *MS* 921:36–37.

209:5   Psychological Treatment: *MS* 921.

209:17   XXV: *MS* 891.

209:37   1860 July 13: *MS* 921.

210:1   XXVIII: *MS* 891.

210:38   Milford, Penn. 1898: *CP* 1.563; compare *MS* 440, also the lectures in *RLT*—this passage is from an early draft of lecture seven.

210:41   Kant points out: shifting to *CP* 4.2; compare *MS* 440, also the lectures in *RLT*—this passage is from an early draft of lecture seven.

211:8   XXXII: *MS* 891.

213:3   Charley's first wife: This section is based primarily on CLB's letters to CSP as preserved by him in a letter file book begun late in 1859 (see *MS* VB1a[4]#1, CSP to BMP 12/18/1859 plus Falpha:Cuddeback). They cover the years 1860–1861 and are located at F60 as a unit, including the 1861 letters. References to these letters within this section will be by date only.

213:5   shipwrights and: Falpha Badger.

213:6   evening of 27 October: 10/28/1860.

213:8   began in verbal: 10/28/1860.

213:9   later placed: evident in a number of later CLB to CSP letters.

214:1   for example Ben: Sydney George Fisher, *The True Benjamin Franklin* (Philadelphia: J. B. Lippincott, 1903).

214:2   Richard Feynman: James Gleick, *Genius: The Life and Science of Richard Feynman* (New York: Pantheon, 1992).

215:1   as far back 1858: 6/30/1860.

215:3   in a special: 1/29/1860.

215:5   embarrassed schooner: a reasonable inference from 1/29/1860.

215:6   by confiding: 1/29/1860; see also 5/6/1860.

215:10   candid letters: 5/6/1860.

215:8   It would give me: 5/29/1860.

215:43   to take Carrie: Based on 10/28/1860, written on Sunday, the next day.

216:5   must be in love: Last sentence from 11/2/1860.

216:12   to be obeyed: 10/28/1860.

216:22   you have asked: 10/28/1860.

216:31   Do you still wish: 11/2/1860.

217:4   Oh Charley: 11/11/1860.

217:33   you have made: 11/23/1860.

217:37   placed in writing: See 11/28/1860.

218:1   It is all: 11/28/1860.

218:20   I am very angry: 12/4/1860.

219:18   which we prefer: vol. 5, p. 693.

220:14   if ever there was:: For an especially good historical medical article on this, see David F. Musto, "Opium, Cocaine and Marijuana in American History," *Scientific American: Medicine*, Special Issue (New York: Scientific American, 1993), 30–37. Compare Dmitri Tymoczko, "The Nitrous Oxide Philosopher," *Atlantic Monthly*,

May 1996, 93–101, which describes the experiences of William James and other contemporaries with nitrous oxide.

220:26 I shall be extremely: 12/11/1860.
220:32 at Charley's: 12/13/1860.
220:36 You will no doubt: 12/18/1860.
221:14 As later writings: 12/12/1860.
221:31 running into June of 1861: 1/10/1861; 1/28/1861; 2/3/1861; 2/5/1861; 2/13/1861; 6/2/1861.
221:34 I want you: 1/28/1861.
221:35 making me sick: 2/13/1861.

Chapter 4

226:22 for his Cambridge: *MS* 619.
229:17 the fall semester: F60b:159, CSP appointed Proctor in the absence of Mr. Jennison, author of *Orthœpy* of O.K. Club fame; see also F60b:162.
229:27 Lawrence Scientific School: F60:16, 18.
229:33 Continuous quantity: *P* 120.
230:18 LII: *MS* 891.
230:34 In my twenties: *MS* L477, CSP to FAW fall/1913 (Falpha:Windship); see also *MS* 649, 650, 681.
232:5 In 1871 I noticed: *The Nation* 13 (7/12/1871): 369; CSP was not the author of this notice. Nevertheless it has been changed to CSP's solo voice.
232:13 LIV: *MS* 891.
232:31 It has long: *MS* 154.
232:35 in Harvard University: Ben Peirce's regular Wednesday afternoon mathematical club, which held its meetings in Ben's rooms on campus (see F60b:161).
233:2 No longer wondered: *MS* 1634.
233:5 the study of logic: Using two sources from *MS* L75.
233:6 occupation ever since: Remainder of this sentence from F62:6, CSP to FM 1/1/1862.
233:16 Miss Zina Fay: F61:8, leaf from CSP diary in ZFP bible.
233:19 Father's 3rd Lecture: William Barton Rogers, *The Life and Letters of William Barton Rogers*, ed. his wife, 2 vols. (Boston: Houghton Mifflin, 1896), 2:64: "[Ben] Peirce is giving a course in the Lowell Institute on 'Mathematics in the Cosmos,' which thus far has been as much theological as anything else."
233:26 The temple of my heart: *MS* 1629b:187.
233:41 Peirce's Lowell Lectures: Orville Dewey, *Autobiography and Letters of Orville Dewey*, ed. his daughter (Boston: Roberts Brothers, 1884), 256. A highly laudatory account of Ben's lectures appeared in the *Boston Daily Courier*, 2/15/1861, p. 2, cols. 2–3.
234:25 I was in town: F61:45, ZF to CSP 3/11/1861. ZF wrote, "Miss Lillie has recovered . . . ," which has been changed here to "She has recovered. . . ."
234:34 who was holding forth: Josiah Parsons Cooke, *Religion and Chemistry: A Re-Statement of an Old Argument*, Revised Edition (New York: Charles Scribner's Sons, 1880). First edition was 1864.
234:42 The time has been: Cooke, *Religion and Chemistry*, 1ff.
235:35 A wonderful singer: *BPH*, CEP to Salem relatives 4/2/1861.
236:7 my dear friend: F61:97, ZF to CSP 6/7/1861.

236:15   what signifies: *CD: roué*, "A man devoted to a life of pleasure and sensuality, especially in his relation to women."

236:37   after returning: Anna Lillie Hegermann-Lindencrone, *In the Courts of Memory: 1858–1875 from Contemporary Letters* (New York: Harper & Brothers, 1912), 16–17.

237:6   rebellious Confederate: Emma Le Conte, *When the World Ended: The Diary of Emma Le Conte* (New York: Oxford University Press, 1957), 86.

237:20   urged Ben: JnLeC to BP2 2/3/1861.

237:27   a passionate fire: F61:153, Mary Towle Palmer, *The Story of the Bee* (Cambridge, Mass.: Riverside Press, 1924), 3.

237:31   I wrote to Columbia: *BPH*, ADB to BP2 4/16/1861.

237:43   All Massachusetts: F61:55, BP2 to ADB 4/30/1861.

238:17   Bache responded: *BPH*, ADB to BP2 5/4/1861.

238:23   conferred with Bache: F61:60, BP2 to ADB 5/20/1861; F61:67, CEP to Salem relatives 5/28/1861: "Ben has gone to Washington"; F61:68, CEP to Salem relatives 6/9/1861: "Ben returned from Washington last Friday, having been there nearly a fortnight. . . . He dined at General Totten's who is next in rank to General Scott. Ben thinks that Scott is a truly wonderful man. . . . I understand that Scott says that the war will be all over by the first of next May."

238:27   As Aunt Lizzie: *BPH*, CEP to Salem relatives 6/9/1861.

238:34   in their new military: For example, F61:60, E. S. Huntington to CSP 5/12/1861: "Why don't you come down [to Fort Independence, Boston Harbor] and see a fort under arms in time of war? I must go to dress parade now"; or F61:66, John B. Noyes to CSP 5/28/1861 concerning CSP's visit to Noyes at Fort Independence where Noyes was in Rifle Company B, Fourth Battalion.

238:34   friend Horatio Paine: F61:93, Horatio Paine to CSP 7/7/1861: ". . . off to Washington—Medical Assistant—rank cadet. . . . Curtis goes too—So goodbye old fellow. H. Paine."

238:41   the action of a sign: *CP* 5.472ff., which is from *MS* 318 1907.

239:36   undertaken for the Coast: F61:71, BP2 to ADB 6/11/1861, also see *P* 10 1862.

240:7   Bache promptly: F61:73, BP2 to ADB 6/18/1861, recording ADB's consent given elsewhere.

240:12   As I hear: F61:79, CSP to ADB 6/19/1861.

240:19   Bache to Ben: *NARG* 23 Superintendent's party VIII, ADB to BP2 7/1/1861.

240:21   until April: *NARG* 23 record of employees, p. 21: "July 1, 1861 to April 1872— aided Prof. Benjamin Peirce, at Cambridge, Mass."; also *NARG* 23 CGS personnel records 1844–1863, p. 302.

240:27   Does my appointment: *NARG* 23 CGS Civil Assistants G to Z III, CSP to ADB 8/16/1862.

240:38   Yours of Aug. 11: *NARG* 23 Civil Assistants G to Z III 1862, ADB to CSP 8/16/1862.

241:8   I know that: F correspondence, FBE to AWB 1954.

241:21   an extended visit: F61:100, ZF to CSP 7/22/1861; see also F61:102, Kate Fay to CSP 7/31/61.

241:22   by way of chemistry: Besides the following extracts, see also F61:107, Laura M. Fay to CSP 10/20/1861; F61:109, LMF to CSP 10/28/1861; F61:111, LMF to CSP 12/26/1861.

241:28   Moon alias Kate Fay: F61:103, Fay sisters to CSP approximately 8/10/1861.

241:33   Views of Chemistry: *MS* 1047.

242:10   INTRODUCTORY TO METAPHYSICS: *MS* 921 (see F61:112, 114, 122, 130).

242:26   distinction of metaphysics: extracted from *MS* 921:34; compare a more formally written version at *MS* 920.

243:1   has been a lesson in logic: *P* 107, republished in *CP* 5.363 or *W*2:243 or *CLL*.

243:7   I remember: *MS* 318 [prag 25] Example 2.

243:25   laboratory of professor: F61:139, Josiah P. Cooke to CSP 8/29/1861.

243:26   admitted in March: F61:36, March 1861.

243:33   Professor Eliot: Using texts and commentary in Ralph Barton Perry, *The Thought and Character of William James*, 2 vols. (Boston: Little, Brown & Company, 1935), 1: chapter 11.

244:3   could not verbally defend: This sentence adapted from Perry, *Thought and Character of William James*, 1:474, beginning, "He adds that 'when a maturer companion, Mr. Charles S. Peirce. . . .'"

244:6   made an estimate: James, *The Letters of William James, Edited by His Son Henry James* (Boston: Atlantic Monthly Press, 1920), 1:31, changed to present tense.

244:13   Agassiz is: Combining elements of two letters by WJ of 9/16/1861 and 12/25/1861, in Perry, *Thought and Character of William James*.

244:35   Miss E. M. Hight's school for girls: *Cambridge Chronicle* 8/31/1861, p. 3, col. 1; F61:158, Ellen M. Hight to CSP approximately 11/8/1861; F61:167, Hight to CSP 11/27/1861; F61:170, Hight to CSP 11/29/1861.

244:40   second in command: *BPH*, CEP to Salem relatives 11/10/1861. On Captain Davis in the Civil War naval battle at Port Royal, see a good description of the engagement in *The American Annual Cyclopædia and Register of Important Events of the Year 1861* (New York: D. Appleton, 1870, 1: 289ff.; see also the *Dictionary of American Biography* article on Admiral C. H. Davis, 5:106ff. The account here is adapted from those sources.

245:17   This little thing: F61:170, ZF to CSP approximately 12/1/1861.

246:8   Lesson of the Year: *MS* 891.

246:36   I arrived: *MS* VB1a(4)#2, CSP to SMP January 1862.

247:11   an excellent time: *MS* VB1a(4)#2, CSP to JMP 2/1/1862.

247:12   Miss Amy: Zina's sister, Amy Fay, the noted concert pianist whose teacher was Liszt, author of the letters collected later by Zina and published as *Music Study in Germany*. See also *More Letters of Amy Fay: The American Years, 1879–1916*, ed. Sister Margaret William McCarthy (Detroit: Information Coordinators, 1986) and Norma Pereira Atkinson, *An Examination of the Life and Thought of Zina Fay Peirce, an American Reformer and Feminist* (Ann Arbor, Mich: University Microfilms no. 8401286, 1983).

247:22   mathematical computation: *RLT* lecture four, 165ff.

248:19   I have: *CP* 8.385.

248:28   LXII: *MS* 891.

248:41   Notebook V: F62:4, see Perry, *Thought and Character of William James*, 1:215.

249:15   I abominate: *MS* L 408.

249:23   years ago I read: *CP* 2.21.

249:30   Ever since Wundt: *CP* 7.597.

249:35   LXIII: *MS* 891.

249:42   The several methods: These are the concluding lines of "The Fixation of Belief" (*P* 107, the first line has been altered to provide context for the remark), first published in 1877. Drafts of the paper existed much earlier.

250:19   Ben confided: F62:33, BP2 to ADB 3/27/1862.

250:37 eight days: *BPH,* ADB to BP2 4/3/1862.

250:39 should be captivated by a Fay: Surely a punning allusion to Middle English *fay,* CD: "a fairy."

251:1 less for difference: Colloquial language among mathematicians concerning whether an expression is positive or negative—in the elaborate hand calculations required in astronomy in that period, keeping the sign while a laborious calculation unfolded was often a source of error.

251:4 Ben confided further: F62:39, BP2 to ADB 4/13/1862.

251:28 The matter: Sentence added from F62:41, BP2 to ADB 4/14/1862.

251:30 "the Fay" later: F62:46, ADB to BP2 4/23/1862.

251:32 her estimation: *BPH,* CEP to Salem relatives 4/9/1862.

252:40 as her fellow: This account of ZFP is adapted from Atkinson, *Examination of the Life and Thought of Zina Fay Peirce,* chapter 1.

253:28 the groom had: F62:120, BP2 to ADB 10/12/1862.

254:7 couple were married: F62:121, Marriage License, St. Albans Vermont 10/16/1862; see also divorce decree of 1883 in Preston Tuttle Collection (Institute for Studies in Pragmaticism) CSP photo folder, plus *BPH,* CEP to Salem relatives 10/14/1862.

254:11 returned to winter: *BPH,* CEP to Salem relatives 10/14/1862.

254:13 his confidence: F63:90, BP2 to ADB 5/17/1863.

254:18 such was: Appendix D in Havelock Ellis, and John Addington Symonds, *Sexual Inversion* (London: Wilson & Macmillan, 1897), 273ff., is entitled "Letter from Professor X." Professor X is identified as "an American of eminence, who holds a scientific professorship in one of the first universities of the world." In Jonathan Katz, *Gay American History: Lesbians and Gay Men in the U.S.A.* (Toronto: Fitzhenry & Whiteside, 1976), 353, in a letter of 5/20/1891 from Symonds to Dakyns, one finds the following:

> I [Symonds] have received a great abundance of interesting & valuable communications. . . .
>
> The oddest information sent me has come from (1) America, in the shape of sharply-defined acute partisanship for Urningthum. . . .

Writing to Edmond Gosse (Katz, 353–354) on 6/22/1891, Symonds mentioned his new American ally:

> I found a fierce & Quixotic ally, who goes far beyond my expectations in hopes of regenerating opinion on these topics, in a Prof. Pierce (?) of Cambridge Mass. He ought to be in Europe now. . . . If he crosses your path in London, look after him, & mention me. I hear he professes Mathematics.

James Mills Peirce had been professor of mathematics at Harvard for some time, and he traveled to Europe in 1891. Writing to T. S. Perry from the Isle of Wight on 7/13/1891, James Mills Peirce stated:

> Clifford and I had a charming day walking in the New Forest. We are on this Isle for a day or two. . . . I had a pleasant letter from Symonds just before sailing, asking me to go to see him. I mean to accomplish that if possible.

Charles Peirce was never a professor of mathematics and did not travel to Europe in 1891. Symonds's other American ally was Thomas Sergeant Perry (Katz, 336) who was a close friend of James Mills Peirce.

As Katz summarizes (629), Professor X has been variously identified as Benjamin Osgood Peirce by the editor of Symonds's letters and as Charley Peirce by Leon Edel, the biographer of Henry James the novelist. But Katz agrees that the only possibile identification for Professor X is James Mills Peirce.

See also the entry for JMP in *Dictionary of American Biography,* vol. 10.

254:23   sensible & agreeable: *BPH,* CEP to Salem relatives 7/15/1862.

254:25   she is lady-like: *BPH,* CEP to Salem relatives 11/1/1862.

254:26   earthly blessings: *BPH,* CEP to Salem relatives 12/1/1862.

254:28   The Chemical Theory: *P* 11.

254:31   had been founded: Robert V. Bruce, *The Launching of Modern American Science, 1846–1876* (New York: Knopf, 1987).

255:19   remark by Juliette: See, p. 32.

255:20   comment from *HUP,* JP to JHW 1/15/1921.

255:23   the highest diplomatic: "diplomatic" added.

255:43   advice from Sherlock: Sebeok and Umiker-Sebeok, *"You Know my Method": A Juxtaposition of Charles S. Peirce and Sherlock Holmes* (Bloomington: Gaslight, 1980), 40.

256:1   dangerous it always is: Sir Arthur Conan Doyle, *The Complete Sherlock Holmes* (Garden City, N.Y.: Doubleday, 1930), 272.

256:3   I make a point: Doyle, *Complete Sherlock,* 407.

256:4   a capital mistake: Doyle, *Complete Sherlock,* 163.

256:10   two-volume biography: Henry James, *Charles W. Eliot: President of Harvard University 1869–1909* (Boston: Houghton Mifflin, 1930).

256:27   were tessellated: See *CD* 6250.

257:5   only five years: This account adapted from Hugh Hawkins, *Between Harvard and America: The Educational Leadership of Charles W. Eliot* (New York: Oxford University Press, 1971); James, *Charles W. Eliot;* Max H. Fisch, *Peirce, Semeiotic, and Pragmatism: Essays by Max H. Fisch,* ed. Kenneth Laine Ketner, and Christian J. W. Kloesel (Bloomington: Indiana University Press, 1986); Eugen Kuehnemann, *Charles W. Eliot: President of Harvard University* (Boston: Houghton Mifflin, 1909).

257:6   Samuel Atkins Eliot: Kuehnemann, *Charles W. Eliot,* 72.

257:10   classmate, Jem: Charles W. Eliot, *Harvard Memories* (Cambridge: Harvard University Press, 1923), 86.

257:25   a ruthless autocrat: Kuehnemann, *Charles W. Eliot,* 80; Ketner and Kloesel, eds., *Peirce, Semeiotic, and Pragmatism,* 38; see also Hawkins, *Between Harvard and America,* 17.

257:32   Mrs. Bull's home: For the history of Peirce's 1898 lectures at the Cambridge Conferences held in Mrs. Bull's home, see the introduction to *RLT.*

257:40   single greatest disappointment: James, *Charles W. Eliot,* 94ff.

258:10   as acting dean: In the same work at p. 94.

258:35   remold Harvard: Hawkins, *Between Harvard and America,* 25; Edward Lurie, *Louis Agassiz: A Life in Science* (Chicago: University of Chicago Press, 1960), 327.

258:41   But by 1859: Hawkins, *Between Harvard and America,* 20ff.

259:5   instigated by C.W.E.: F63:42, BP2 to ADB 3/6/63.

259:13   the first chemist: Lurie, *Agassiz*, 330; Bruce, *Launching*.

259:17   pathetic and creditable: C. L. Jackson quoted in James, *Charles W. Eliot*, 103–4.

259:22   In June 1863: Lurie, *Agassiz*, 330.

259:30   he saw as: Hawkins, *Between Harvard and America*, 26; James, *Charles W. Eliot*, 98ff.

259:30   Hill tried a second scheme: Hawkins, *Between Harvard and America*, 27.

259:33   It was the greatest: James, *Charles W. Eliot*, 112.

259:35   victimized by that damned Swiss: Hawkins, *Between Harvard and America*, 27. Storer also voiced an opinion about President Hill's "Mad Scheme" of creating a university by filling professorships with the most creative minds available, even if they belonged to "outsiders" (from Hawkins, 27).

260:11   correspondence in Widener: F63:100, BP2 to ADB 5/27/1863. Ben added: "Oh! if we fail of Gibbs! the prospect of science in this vicinity is very dark in the next generation. . . . Above all, there is such a total indifference to honour and honesty!" See also A. Hunter Dupree, *Asa Gray: 1810—1888* (Cambridge: Belknap Press of Harvard University Press, 1959), 320. Compare F63:113, BP2 to ADB, 6/24/1863 (Ben's view that while publicly supporting merit as a basis for appointment, Eliot had privately urged the principle of "appropriate" selection among his political supporters) and *BPH*, ADB to BP2 8/5/1863 (ADB's view: "What a triumph for science! . . . So may it ever be that true men win and intriguers lose!").

260:18   What then became: James, *Charles W. Eliot*, 112ff.; see Hawkins, *Between Harvard and America*, 28ff. for something Eliot did *not* undertake, namely, participation in the Civil War. Massachusetts Governor John A. Andrew offered Eliot a commission as a lieutenant colonel of cavalry in a newly formed regiment. Despite being a good horseman, Eliot—like Charley—declined to be a part of the war, despite having described it as "the great war which we are waging for freedom." Having said that, in September 1863 he left for Europe for two years (Hawkins, 28).

260:29   Although perhaps: Gay Wilson Allen, *Waldo Emerson: A Biography* (New York: Viking, 1981), chapter 15.

261:8   Senatus Universitatis Cantabrigiensis: *MS* 1642, copy in Preston Tuttle Collection, Institute for Studies in Pragmaticism.

261:21   My method: *CP* 6.604; the critic was Paul Carus.

261:30   treatise about: Charley was probably the first American historian of science. His thoroughgoing work in the field (which is full of implications for contemporary issues) recently has been collected and reconstructed by Carolyn Eisele in a marvelous pair of volumes—*HP*.

263:1   Miss Maria: *CP* 6.507.

263:3   is there pointed: Continuing with *CP* 6.287.

263:22   had struggled against: F63:119, 130, 132, 134, 146; F64:5.

263:25   God bless: F63:98, BP2 to ADB 5/27/1863.

264:4   My dear: F63:107, BP2 to BMP 6/7/1863.

264:13   Rustication: Samuel Eliot Morison, *Three Centuries of Harvard: 1636–1936* (Cambridge: Belknap Press of Harvard University Press, 1936), 177, also 41 and 113.

264:21   when he instituted: Morison, *Three Centuries*, 306, 333–334, 391.

264:22   prominent in participation: For example, see F63:134, 153.

265:6   ELEVENTH ANNUAL REUNION: *Cambridge Chronicle* 11/12/1863.

265:19   on the fourteenth reported: *Cambridge Chronicle* 11/14/1863.

265:25   I had undertaken: F63:156, 11/12/1863.

266:28   LADIES AND GENTLEMEN: *P* 12. The published version was a long extract; as given here it has been compressed even further.

272:27   I came substantially: *MS* 660.

272:36   Natural History of Words: *MS* 1137:40.

273:8   Word reached Charley: F65:15, CSP to FEA 2/5/1865.

273:42   practitioner of Socratic Maieutic: *CD* 3581, CSP's definition of *maieutic*.

274:20   onset of genuine learning: See Weil, "School Studies," in Simone Weil, *The Simone Weil Reader*, ed. George A. Panichas (New York: David McKay, 1977). Compare CSP's first rule of logic (and related matters) in *RLT*.

275:39   When my husband and I: JP to Governor Gifford Pinchot 9/4/1934, Library of Congress manuscript division, Pinchot papers.

276:30   destroy some of Peirce's correspondence: in F, Hartshorne letter folder, Hartshorne wrote: "R. B. Perry gave me these letters, but with emphatic instructions to 'burn them, and I mean burn them.' However, I am letting the burning be with you." This letter is followed by a memorandum dated May 6, 1956, which gives more details about the material.

276:32   Bill James first met Peirce: Perry, *Thought and Character of William James*, 1:211.

276:34   They talked philosophy to some extent: Above, pp. 248–49 (WJ notebook entries on conversations with CSP).

276:35   James had resolved to go on into Harvard Medical: Perry, *Thought and Character of William James*, 1:216.

276:37   quite the academic joke: Gay Wilson Allen, *William James: A Biography* (New York: Viking, 1967), 99.

276:38   a biological expedition: Perry, *Thought and Character of William James*, 1:217.

276:41   resume active discussion: James, *Letters*, 1:53.

276:42   start their own private school: As early as 1861 Charley began teaching privately. Perhaps we have a record of his first pupil. E. N. Horsford, Professor of Chemistry at the Lawrence Scientific School, wrote the following to JMP (F61:8 1/12/1861): "It occurs to me that possibly your brother might like to give instruction as a private tutor in mathematics. If you think he would, will you please introduce the bearer [identified by CSP's handwritten annotation as William Wheelwright, see p. 233 above], who wishes to prepare himself for Mr. Eustis' department of the Scientific School."

In 1861 he also taught at Ellen Hight's school for young ladies in Cambridge (see F61:58, Hight to CSP 11/8/1861, and related letters).
Zina and Charley hoped to start a private school (see *BPH*, ADB to BP2 6/9/1862) and continued to offer private lessons. In 1866 they proposed to open a private school in Cambridge (F66:4; F66:37: "Charley & Zina are getting out their circular prospectus for their school"; F66:71), or in New York City (F66:13). James attended CSP's Lowell Lectures in 1866. So perhaps the convincing occurred just after James returned from the Agassiz expedition when William was particularly primed with tendencies toward philosophy.

James's first book in philosophy, *The Will to Believe* (1896), was dedicated "To My Old Friend, CHARLES SANDERS PEIRCE, To whose philosophic comradeship in old times and to whose writings in more recent years I owe more incitement and help than I can express or repay." That is a very strong dedication, such as a pupil addresses to his master. Juliette might have been right.

277:39   moving into 20 Quincy: Perry, *Thought and Character of William James*, 1:227. Charley's mother recorded the event in one of her newsy letters to Benjamin in

Paris (SMP to BMP 10/9/1866): "The Thies's have just been in to take leave. They all go to Europe tomorrow. . . . They have let their house to Mr. Henry James. The family will be pleasant neighbors & Mr. James a great addition to Cambridge. Miss Maria Fay [Zina's sister, just returned from Paris] has been passing a few days at Charley's. She looks quite Parisian & doesn't she regale one with the celebrity of *Madame Moulton* [Lillie Greenough among the court in Paris] & the Lords & Dukes & Noble Princes . . . ?"

277:42 Charles became an intimate: Perry *Thought and Character of William James*, 1:533.

279:1 In the sixties: CSP to his former student Christine Ladd-Franklin (after 1903), in *O* 1243.

280:8 at Mrs. Bull's: *RLT* introduction.

280:9 began reading Schröder's: Ernst Schröder, *Vorlesungen über die Algebra der Logik (exacte Logik)* (Leipzig: Drei Bänder, 1890), 1:710.

280:14 Peirce, Charles: With special thanks to Joseph Morton Ransdell for calling this to my attention.

280:39 become a student: See *CP* 5.477, 4.155, and 4.547. Charles Grassman, a neighbor of the Peirces in Milford, told Fisch in 1966 that gypsies were often in Milford, that Juliette was intimate with them, and that he thought Juliette was a gypsy herself (Falpha:gypsies).

280:40 nineteenth century books: See the bibliography for the works of George Borrow and of Charles G. Leland.

280:42 Professor Walter Starkie: See bibliography for the works of Starkie.

281:13 to others conversant: Borrow, *Romano Lavo-Lil: Word-Book of the Romany or, English Gypsy Language* (London: John Murray, 1919), 185.

281:25 began its migration: Konrad Bercovici, *The Story of the Gypsies* (New York: Cosmopolitan Book, 1931; Angus M. Fraser, *The Gypsies* (Oxford: Blackwell, 1992); Bart McDowell, *Gypsies: Wanderers of the World* (Washington, D.C.: National Geographic Society, 1970).

281:28 conversing fluently: Walter Starkie, *Spanish Raggle-Taggle: Adventures with a Fiddle in North Spain* (London: John Murray, 1934), 472.

281:35 Laches chibeses: Starkie, *Spanish Raggle Taggle*, 269.

282:7 Pope had placed: Fraser, *Gypsies*.

282:9 were the prototypes: Fraser, *Gypsies*.

282:11 they entered Europe: Fraser, *Gypsies*.

282:12 the great: Fraser, *Gypsies*; Starkie, *Spanish Raggle Taggle*.

282:17 travelling by ship: *MS VB1b*, CSP to JP 1/1/1890, and related letters.

282:36 he told me: F correspondence: Victor Lenzen to MHF "The Identity of Juliette" 1/13/1973. This will be referenced as VLIJ. In that document and in related materials, Lenzen summarized his "Bacourt hypothesis" for Fisch in 1973. At first Lenzen also suggested that JP might have been a gypsy but later changed his mind.

282:40 Juliette Annette Froissy: VLIJ.

282:40 in all likelihood: VLIJ.

282:42 command of literary: VLIJ. See also *MS VB1a(4)#4*, CSP to BP2 8/17/1879—CSP has loaned two volumes of a French work to Madame Pourtalais (JP).

283:8 women of their bands: Starkie, *Spanish Raggle Taggle* throughout.

283:23 formed with that vampire: See p. 14.

284:2 Admiral Charles Henry Davis: *National Cyclopædia of American Biography*, 4:166.

284:9 Hodie Uxor: *MS 1623*, CSP's diary entry for Tuesday 1/6/1914: "Epiphany. Hodie Uxor L annos nata est": "Today is my wife's fiftieth birthday." A confirmation from another person is at Falpha:Juliette, wherein Mrs. Laura McLaughlin in a letter of 11/24/23 to George Derby (JP's minister in Milford) said Juliette will be sixty in February of 1924.

284:22   Marquis having proceeded them: *New York Times* for 11/23/1876 (via VFL–MHF in F76:111): "Madame la Marquise de Chambrun has arrived from Havre." The Marquis had arrived 7/6/1876 (F76:82).

284:28   nearer to his pendulum: F76:103, CSP to J. E. Hilgard 10/14/1876 (CSP informing the Coast Survey office that until further notice he is staying in the Brevoort House in New York City). See also F76:111, CSP to CPP 11/18/1876 (CSP writing up his operations abroad from the trip to Europe from which he had just returned).

284:30   found himself at home: F77:57, CSP to WJ 5/1/1877.

284:33   at Stevens Institute in Hoboken: *NARG* 23 Assistants N to Z 1876, CSP to Patterson 10/10/76; *NARG* 23, Patterson to CSP 10/13/1876, CSP to rent but Congress must approve; F76:96. Zina refused to accompany CSP to New York City during October 1876 where he had been ordered by the Coast Survey, despite his letter requesting her to do so. CSP was then conducting gravity studies at Stevens Institute in Hoboken. At *MS* VB1b there is a loving letter from CSP in New York City to ZFP in Cambridge, requesting her to join him (10/1/1876).

284:36   Roy wanted to see: F77:8, CSP to Gilman 1/13/1878.

285:5   Adolphe Fourier: VLIJ.

285:6   French monarchist: Adolphe Fourier de Bacourt, *Souveniers of a Diplomat* (New York: Holt, 1885).

285:11   Polk appointed Bancroft: Russel B. Nye, *George Bancroft: Brahmin Rebel* (New York: Knopf, 1945), 159.

285:23   the musical type: Bertha B. Quintana, and Lois Gray Floyd, *!Que Gitano! Gypsies of Southern Spain* (New York: Holt, Rinehart & Winston, 1972), chapter 4.

285:25   committed afficionado: Quintana and Floyd, *¡Que Gitano!*; Jan Yoors, *The Gypsies of Spain* (New York: Macmillan, 1974), 141–143. The latter reference particularly illustrates the passion of an afficionado.

287:25   All Gypsy women: Starkie, *Spanish Raggle Taggle*, 286. Wendell Phillips Garrison, who in later years was editor of *The Nation* (for which journal Charley wrote), mentioned in a letter (9/6/1902) to Peirce (Falpha:Gipsy, see also Falpha:gypsy) after having visited the Peirces in Milford: "My late lamented friend Dean Sage, who loved all outdoors and was a great Borrovian [an admirer of George Borrow, the English Gypsy scholar], went daft on the gipsies who haunted Albany for a time. As for fortune-telling, your wife did me up brown on your porch one day, with tales of deception & perhaps matrimony which I did not take down in shorthand. I have more respect for palmistry than for cards. . . ." See also VLIJ.

287:27   support of the Red Cross: *MS*Vdelta, Alfred Marvin to Albert W. Staub 11/20/1917. This is a remarkable letter, worthy of some extracts here:

> I am enclosing . . . 80 dollars from Mrs. Juliette Peirce of Milford. . . . I wish to say a few words for this wonderful little lady. . . . She is a French pensioner but throughout the war has steadfastly turned back her annuity to the old friends at home, who are destitute and has lived, we know not how, that they might be sustained. . . . She has sacrificed all luxuries . . . and has for some weeks at Milford and Matamaros . . . and Port Jervis, N.Y., been occupied in "Telling Fortunes" from a pack of cards once the property of the Empress Josephine, consort of Napoleon and these cards are encased in an inlaid box

presented for that purpose by the emperor to his wife, and Mrs. Peirce has faithfully and steadfastly sat at her task with the result contained herein.

287:28   she gave readings: For example, this letter (among many like them): *MS* Vdelta, Mrs. Elsie Barnes to JP 7/12/1925: "Last Sunday morning I and two other ladies went to consult you by your famous cards. . . . I was the first to go in to see you & you told me I had a loss where I had left my things. Well when I returned to the hotel here my suitcase . . . was missing. . . . I send a piece of my hair you might tie round your finger [while handling the cards]." See also Mrs. M. P. Mooney to JP 6/10/1925.

287:37   the outside as *duke*: For example, Fraser, *Gypsies*. Commonly mentioned in the scholarly literature on gypsies.

287:43   Gypsy choral groups: Fraser, *Gypsies*, 205ff.

288:18   an inbred suspicion: For example, Fraser, *Gypsies*.

288:20   what was described: *MS* VB1a(2), SMP to JP 10/8/1883: ". . . terrible strain upon your nervous system which has brought this Hysterical Attack upon you. . . ." At *BPH*, SMP to HPE 11/23/1883: ". . . her doctor insists that she must [keep to her bed] the first four days of her 'times.'" And at *BPH*, SMP to HPE 11/27/1883: "The jar of carriages [JP] has to avoid as much as possible—poor thing! This delicacy is certainly genuine."

288:25   George Bancroft: M. A. DeWolfe Howe, *The Life and Letters of George Bancroft*, 2 vols. (New York: Charles Scribner's Sons, 1908), 2:64—Bancroft converses with Bacourt 4/12/1847.

288:41   a great friend: *PW* 113, where CSP stated, "Bancroft had been very intimate with my mother's family, as in his old age he was a great friend of my wife here." See *MS* VB1a(2), SMP to CSP 11/30/1881: Bancroft writes SMP, and Bancroft is a friend of her parents.

289:1   among the original mentor group: *MS* VB1a(2), SMP to CSP early 1877: "I could not put into effect my plan of going to see your friend Madame P. Your father went however & was much pleased with his visit—he found her looking sweetly & appearing happily fixed in her new lodgings. I was sorry I could not have gone myself."

289:8   Would Mademoiselle consent: *MS* Vgamma, CSP to JP early 1877.

289:19   members of the Peirce: *BPH*, JP to BP2 12/31/1878, new year wishes to BP2 family and a similar note to Bertie Peirce; *MS* VB3b#2, BP2 to CSP 7/31/1879; *MS* VB1a(4)#4, CSP to BP2 8/17/1879, Madame Pourtalais and Mrs. Grey will visit CSP in Ebensburg at CSP's gravity station; *MS* VB1a(4)#4, CSP to CEP 9/15/1879, CSP has a big house in Ebensburg full of visitors; *MS* VB1a(2), SMP to CSP 9/18/1879, Madame Pourtalais at Ebensburg to get a change of air for her health; F79:223, SMP to CSP11/3/1879, SMP received a sweet letter from Madame Pourtalais; *MS* VB1a(2), SMP to CSP 11/30/1881, Madame Pourtalais is ill and presumably CSP is helping to care for her; *MS* VB1a(2), SMP to CSP 5/7/1882; *MS* VB1a(2), SMP to CSP 6/11/1882, SMP's good wishes to Madame Pourtalais; *MS* VB1a(4)#8, CSP to SMP 8/29/1882, Madame Pourtalais is in Montreal with her maid and goes on to Quebec, her health continues dubious; *MS* VB1a(4), CSP to JMP 10/4/1882, CSP is in agony over Madame Pourtalais's health.

289:37   cosmopolitan scholars and diplomats: Nye, *Bancroft*, 280.

289:39   political aspect of national: Nye, *Bancroft*, 282.

289:42   she was receiving about 18,000: VLIJ.

290:2   On it these words: *MS* VB1b, CSP to JP 4/22/1890.

290:15   He was very busy: For an example from among the many letters (F76 and F77) on CSP's gravity experiments, see *NARG* 23 Assts H to Q CSP to Patterson 1/24/1877.

290:22   until some years: *MS* VB1a(4)#4, CSP to BP2 8/17/1877.

290:25   thirteenth of September 1877: F77:113, VFL to MHF, citing *New York Times*.

290:27   eighteen November 1877: F77:149, VFL to MHF, citing *New York Times*.

290:28   42 Seventh Street: F77:163, *New York City Directory* 1877–1878.

290:34   a list of years: Falpha:Juliette, from *MS* 278 D3 on a verso, the city names have been added based on correspondence.

291:6   entirely chaste: *MS* VB1a(4), CSP to ?? not dated but after 6/2/1881 (the date of HHDP's marriage): "Madame Pourtalais and I have not been indulging in wantonness. . . . My father, who really did know the world, was with her."

291:8   kept to her bed: *BPH*, SMP to HPE 11/23/1883; *BPH*, SMP to HPE 11/27/1883, JP's delicacy is certainly genuine, she speaks english imperfectly, SMP is sure there has been much less impropriety than has been supposed between them, her cheeks are hollow and she is deathly pale.

291:18   Mrs. Peirce moved: F82:9, CSP diary, other January entries.

291:23   had provided Madame: *MS* VB1a(4)#8, CSP to SMP 1/24/1882; CSP discussed the events of the trial in this letter.

291:29   1324 Riggs Street: F83:9, *Boyd's Directory of the District of Columbia* 1883.

291:30   occupied by March: F82:25, 34, CSP diary March.

291:31   Baltimore Circuit Court: *MS* VB1a(2), SMP to JP 4/24/1883.

291:34   welcoming her: F83:33, SMP to JP 3/16/1883.

291:36   in a civil ceremony: F83:54, marriage certificate New York, NY—"I, John H. Seaman, an Alderman of the City of New York, do hereby certify, that on the twenty-sixth day of April A.D. 1883, at the City Hall in the City of New York, I duly performed the marriage ceremony between Mr. Charles Sanders Peirce, of Baltimore, Maryland, United States, and Mrs. Juliette Annette Pourtalai, of Washington, D.C., United States."

291:37   had been ordered: F83:60, VFL to MHF Steamship Labrador from New York to Le Havre on 5/2/1883, on board were C. S. Peirce and Mrs. Peirce; *NARG* 23 (F83:53), Hilgard to Secretary of the Treasury, requesting authority to send CSP to England, Switzerland, and France on gravity and spectrum meter work.

293:13   is inside of you: Roy's ideas here are like those expressed in the Gospel of Thomas, see *The Nag Hammadi Library in English*, ed. James M. Robinson (New York: Harper & Row, 1977), 118, logion 3 of "The Gospel of Thomas"; also similar to themes in CSP's work, for example at *P* 26, 27, and 41 (the notion of external signs).

293:31   As I am going: F65:15, CSP to FEA 2/5/1865; compare F65:33, CSP to FEA 3/2/1865.

294:18   elementary kinds of reasoning: *CP* 8.227.

294:21   February through: See *W*2:162–302.

294:23   Deduction: not <u>necessary</u>: *MS* 754:05, the terminology has been adjusted to abduction (guessing), induction (sampling), deduction (entailment), which will be standard in this work.

294:44   lectures fell through: F65:40, CSP to FEA 3/17/1865.

295:6   Reports to Overseers: F65:1, 2:117; see also Ketner and Kloesel, eds., *Peirce, Semeiotic, and Pragmatism*, 115, Fisch's summary of the evidence in support of the lecture series having been given.

295:11   especially since he was: Morison, *Three Centuries*, 304ff.

295:12   The evidence also shows: F65:41, BP2 to W. L. Gage 3/21/1865.

295:23   I had previously confirmed: Ketner and Kloesel, eds., *Peirce, Semeiotic, and Pragmatism*, 376–400, where Fisch gives the arguments; also Eisele's essays in *Studies in the Scientific and Mathematical Philosophy of Charles S. Peirce: Essays by Carolyn Eisele*, ed. Richard M. Martin (The Hague: Mouton, 1979); Ketner's essays in the appendix of *A Thief of Peirce: The Letters of Kenneth Laine Ketner and Walker Percy*, ed. Patrick H. Samway, S.J. (Jackson: University Press of Mississippi, 1995).

295:28   I ask your attention: *P* 16, W1:162ff. Only an outline is given here. See also F65:39 3/17/1865.

297:3   Perhaps the most: W1:223.

297:9   I shall establish: W1:289.

297:26   I have wearied you: W1:302.

298:6   When Mill's: F65:44, autobiographical scrap in *MS*.

298:20   LXIX: *MS* 891.

299:19   Certes, Wyttynys, la premiere manifestation:
The French passage is composed from a number of sources in Peirce's works that are cited within curly brackets { } in the following English version. The first two sentences have been added.

> *To be sure, Wyttynys, the first appearance of one's scientific independence is an event that can well be noted as a distinct, even remarkable, phenomenon, perhaps even a grace. Usually it is preceded by a period of particularly intense study, that having been my condition for two prior years. Indeed, from* {begin extract from *MS* 867:02} *the moment when I could think at all, until now, I have been diligently and incessantly occupied with the study of methods of inquiry, both those which have been and are pursued and those which ought to be pursued. I was thoroughly grounded not only in all that was then known of physics and chemistry, but also in the way in which those who were successfully advancing knowledge proceeded. I have paid the most attention to the methods of the most exact sciences, have intimately communed with some of the greatest minds of our times in physical science, and have myself made positive contributions. I am saturated through and through with the spirit of the physical sciences. I have been a great student of logic, having read everything of any importance on the subject, devoting a great deal of time to medieval thought, without neglecting the works of the Greeks, the English, the Germans, the French, etc., and have produced systems of my own both in deductive and in inductive logic. In metaphysics, my training has been less systematic; yet I have read and deeply pondered upon all the main systems, never being satisfied until I was able to think about them as their own advocates thought.*
>
> *My philosophy* {begins extract from *MS* 867:04} *may be described as the attempt of a physicist to make such conjecture as to the constitution of the universe, as the methods of science may permit, with the aid of all that has been done by previous philosophers. I support my propositions by such arguments as I can. Demonstrative proof is not to be thought of. The demonstrations of the metaphysicians are all moonshine. The best that can be done is to supply a hypothesis not devoid of all likelihood, in the general line of growth of scientific ideas, and capable of being verified or refuted by future observers.*
>
> *I recall* [Peirce did not write this paragraph; it has been supplied for continuity] *mid May of 1865, near the end of the horrible war, strolling and smoking along the Charles, a pleasant walk then from my lodgement at 2 Arrow Street. It was my habit with*

such excursions to carry a notebook on the chance an idea should strike me, and one such entire web of thought did stand forth late that afternoon, demanding to be recorded. The feeling was so abrupt and discontinuous that I remember marking the onset of my notes with a single largely written word

BEGUN.

That was to record the rather distinct feeling that my own thoughts had arisen for the first time. My pencil, with a will of its own, fairly flew through my little note book, furiously filling it completely in a matter of minutes. Cum saccus rumpitur aqua fluit: When the sack breaks water flows. The next few years as I began to produce distinct results in the logic of science, consequently to publish them in the late sixties, I referred back to those basic rough but seminal notes on what I then called teleological logic.

Wyttynys, never forget that {extracted from CP 1.11 f} my work is meant for people who want to find out; people who want philosophy ladled out to them can go elsewhere. There are philosophical soup shops at every corner, thank God!

The development of my ideas has been the industry of many years. In the course of this ripening process, I used for myself to collect my ideas under the designation fallibilism; and indeed the first step toward finding out is to acknowledge you do not satisfactorily know already.

Indeed, out of a contrite fallibilism, combined with a high faith in the reality of knowledge, and an intense desire to find things out, all my philosophy has always seemed to me to grow.

301:10   1865 May 14: *MS* 802.

302:24   the 1877–1878 articles: *P* 107, 119–123.

302:40   a word ugly enough: *P* 1078: "What Pragmatism Is" 1905.

303:24   as finally published: Kenneth Laine Ketner, "A Brief Intellectual Autobiography by Charles Sanders Peirce," *American Journal of Semiotics* 2 (1983): 61–83, one of CSP's better autobiographical statements. This edition of it includes bibliographic keys to *CB*, providing a tour through CSP's publications with Charley himself as guide.

303:28   I am much given: Ketner, "A Brief Intellectual Autobiography," 69ff.

303:39   in a speech: *O* 677.

304:3   Agassiz's expedition in Brazil: James, *Letters*, 1:56, 71.

304:4   The very next sentence: Ketner, "A Brief Intellectual Autobiography," 69.

304:11   I divide: Ketner, "A Brief Intellectual Autobiography," 69–70.

304:40   That which embodies: Ketner, "A Brief Intellectual Autobiography," 71,73.

304:41   the general properties: Ketner, "A Brief Intellectual Autobiography," 73.

306:3   from his reading: See especially George Boole, *An Investigation of the Laws of Thought* (1854; reprint, New York: Dover, 1953), chapter 2 ("Signs and Their Laws").

306:8   Topics of the Nation Article on Pragmatism: Outline topics are from *MS* 317; content is from *MS* 318, using as CSP's basic final run sheets 1–12, 125–135, 49, 136ff.

307:10   The philosophical: *MS* 318, the run starting at sheet 125.

307:41   The monstrous: this and the next two sentences are from *MS* 319:03.

308:14   Illustrations of the Logic: *P* 107, 119–123.

308:32   Pragmatism is: this and the next sentence are from *MS* 320:27.

308:39   the experimental method: Compare *MS* 320:29.

309:3   Thomas Beddoes: this sentence is from *MS* 320:29.

309:4   it is the procedure: See Arthur Franklin Stewart, "Peirce, Beddoes, and

Pragmatistic Abstraction: An Introduction," *Southwest Philosophical Studies* 13 (1991): 75–88.

309:4   To you, at: *MS* 322:13.5.

309:12   By their fruits: *The Gospel According to Saint Matthew* 7:16, 20.

309:29   I might offer: Changing to *MS* 318:50ff.

311:31   Since the most acute: Skipping to *MS* 318:67.

312:15   This requaesitum: *MS* 318:70.

312:19   So much: Moving to *MS* 318:79.

312:20   awakened or otherwise: The last three words are from *MS* 322:09.

312:24   the meaning of the command: This sentence from *MS* 322:09.

312:35   I am now: Moving to *MS* 318:81.

312:42   To summarize: This paragraph is from *MS* 322:10.

313:26   So keep trying: The following works provide a good introduction to Peirce's system of science and to his semeiotic: Kenneth Laine Ketner, "Charles Sanders Peirce," in *Classical American Philosophy*, ed. John J. Stuhr (New York: Oxford University Press, 1987); Samway, ed., *Thief of Peirce*; *RLT* (Peirce's 1898 Cambridge Conferences Lectures in which he gave a popular account of his approach); E. T. Nozawa, "Introduction to Charles Sanders Peirce and the Peircean System of Science and Peircean Semeiotic," *Gaciac Bulletin* 20 (May 1997): 1–6. See also the list of books arising from the 1989 Peirce Congress as listed in Kenneth Laine Ketner, ed., *Peirce and Contemporary Thought: Philosophical Inquiries* (New York: Fordham University Press, 1995), xiv n.1.

314:12   Charley put a paragraph: F65:163, H. P. Bowditch's notes of BP2's lectures, placed into CSP's voice; the course of fourteen lectures ended on 1/18/1866.

315:22   the Le Contes were: This account is drawn from Joseph Le Conte, *'Ware Sherman: A Journal of Three Months' Personal Experience in the Last Days of the Confederacy* (Berkeley: University of California Press, 1937); Lester D. Stephens, *Joseph Le Conte: Gentle Prophet of Evolution* (Baton Rouge: Louisiana State University Press, 1982); and the BP2 to Le Conte correspondence file in F.

315:33   who was still in charge: Stephens, *Joseph Le Conte*, 107.

316:35   Private Thoughts LXX: *MS* 891.

316:40   I can hardly: F66:95, BP2 to J. Anderson in England 12/2/66.

316:43   a tour of a year: F66:89, JMP to BMP 11/19/1866.

317:12   I address you: W1:358ff.

318:38   we are repeatedly: W1:390ff.

319:33   Those capitalists who: W1:405ff.

320:31   Beware of a: W1:440ff.

320:41   entering the second half: W1:454ff.

321:25   I here announce: W1:465ff.

322:14   at the last: W1:471ff.

324:2   philosophy is: W1:490ff.

324:37   We have already seen: W1:494ff.

325:19   the word electricity means: W1:498ff.

325:29   The necessary and true: W1:500ff.

325:34   I announce to you: W1:502ff.

325:37   nec ad melius: Neither to live better, nor to discourse more pleasantly.

326:1   been in 1866: *CP* 1.562.

326:3   On the Logic: Augustus DeMorgan, "On the Syllogism, No. IV, and the Logic of Relations," *Cambridge Philosophical Transactions* 10: 331–358.

326:24   THREE PAPERS: F67:1 1867.

326:41   It is true: F67:1, CSP to Christine Ladd-Franklin 10/28/1904.

327:8   When I was in the twenties: F64:104, autobiographical scrap from *MS*.

327:27   or the science: *MS* 655:24–25.

328:5   DEFINITION 3rd DRAUGHT 1: *MS* 645.

331:39   Proceedings of the American Academy: *P* 32, read on 14 May 1867, published in the *Proceedings* for 1867, 7:287–298, which appeared in print in 1868.

336:7   I come now to: *CP* 8.331.

336:28   Though a life-long student: *P* 513.

338:17   It is also: This sentence has been added.

342:27   Of or pertaining: *CD Supplement*, 11 (1909), 217.

342:31   In the phenomenology: *CD Supplement*, 11 (1909), 475.

343:5   The mode of being: *CD Supplement*, 12 (1909), 1189.

343:12   Thirdness: The mode of being: *CD Supplement*, 12 (1909), 1344.

344:1   In classification: *MS* 292:34ff., compare 292:98.

344:18   using the procedures: Compare CSP's excellent description of his early method at W1:515.

344:19   his '67 article: *P* 32.

345:7   inspired by Boole: Robert W. Burch—in *A Peircean Reduction Thesis: The Foundations of Topological Logic* (Lubbock: Texas Tech University Press, 1991)—presents this interpretation; see also Helena M. Pycior, "Peirce at the Intersection of Mathematics and Philosophy: A response to Eisele," *Peirce and Contemporary Thought,* ed. Ketner.

345:11   guess at Emerson's Riddle: See Allen's interesting discussion (in *Waldo Emerson,* 478) of Emerson's poem "The Sphinx" (1841). Does the theme of this poem harmonize with Shakespeare's evocation, "His glassy essence"?

345:21   mathematics in Peirce's conjecture: Burch, *A Peircean Reduction Thesis;* for a nontechnical introduction to the matter see Samway, ed., *Thief of Peirce,* 195–219, 240–250 (on Peirce's hypothesis that the fundamental stuff of the cosmos is relation).

345:24   Peirce helped to found: Ketner, "The Early History of Computer Design" (with the assistance of Arthur F. Stewart), *The Princeton University Library Chronicle* 45 (1984): 187-224, and "Peirce and Turing: Comparisons and Conjectures," *Semiotica* 68 (1988): 33-61 (these two articles were intended to form a small book).

345:30   even claimed: Inscribed in Ketner's copy of Percy's novel *The Thanatos Syndrome*— "For Ken Ketner with best wishes and thanks from a fellow Cenopythagorean. Walker 11/5/87." See also Percy's Jefferson Lecture before the National Endowment for the Humanities in Percy, "The Divided Creature," *The Wilson Quarterly* 13 (1989): 77-87.

345:41   It is my fate: *MS* Vzeta, CSP to J. M. Hantz 3/29/1887.

346:29   in that passage: p. 255.

346:38   an emotional: Perhaps the prime example of an emotional interpretant is the eureka feeling. For an excellent discussion of CSP's understanding of emotion, see David Savan, "Peirce's Semiotic Theory of Emotion," in *Proceedings of the C. S. Peirce Bicentennial International Congress,* ed. Ketner et al.

347:16   words of Benjamin Peirce, Senior: p. 69.

347:37   flat in Somerville, filled: Martin Buber, in his magnificent discussion of the phenomenology of religious experience, exhibits the inner sense of firmament in *I and Thou,* trans. Walter Kaufmann (New York: Charles Scribner's Sons, 1970), 59.

Buber's hypotheses are sometimes identified as "Relationism," which tends to bolster one's guess that they are close to those Charley advanced. Compare *HP2*:685–696.

If we read Genesis in the Old Testament (using the King James version) as Charley and Ben read it—which is perhaps the same way that Buber read it—then the events of "the second day of creation" would have special meaning for the brethren of the Florentine Academy.

348:24   But remember Ion:

> SOCRATES: I perceive, Ion; and I will proceed to explain to you what I imagine to be the reason of this. The gift which you possess of speaking excellently about Homer is not an art, but, as I was just saying, an inspiration; there is a divinity moving you, like that contained in the stone which Euripides calls a magnet, but which is commonly known as the stone of Heraclea. This stone not only attracts iron rings, but also imparts to them a similar power of attracting other rings; and sometimes you may see a number of pieces of iron and rings suspended from one another so as to form quite a long chain: and all of them derive their power of suspension from the original stone. (*Ion. The Dialogues of Plato*, trans. Benjamin Jowett [New York: Appleton, 1898])

Bibliography

Abbott, Katharine M. *Old Paths and Legends of New England*. New York: G. P. Putnam's Sons, 1909.

Abbott, John S. C. *Kings and Queens; or, Life in the Palace: Historical Sketches of Josephine and Maria Louisa, Louis Philippe, Ferdinand of Austria, Nicholas, Isabella II, Leopold, Victoria, and Louis Napoleon*. New York: Harper & Brothers, 1855.

Agassiz, Louis. *Methods of Study in Natural History*. Boston: Houghton Mifflin, 1889.

———. *Essay on Classification*. First American Edition 1857. Cambridge: The Belknap Press of Harvard University Press, 1962 edition, edited by Edward Lurie.

Ahlstrom, Sydney, and Bruce Mullin. *The Scientific Theist: A Life of Francis Ellingwood Abbot*. Macon: Mercer University Press, 1987.

Albanese, Catherine L., editor. *The Spirituality of the American Transcendentalists*. Macon: Mercer University Press, 1988.

Allen, Gay Wilson. *Waldo Emerson: A Biography*. New York: Viking, 1981.

———. *William James: A Biography*. New York: Viking, 1967.

The American Annual Cyclopædia and Register of Important Events of the Year 1861. Volume 1. New York: D. Appleton, 1870.

Anderson, Nicholas Longworth. *The Letters and Journals of General Nicholas Longworth Anderson: Harvard, Civil War, Washington, 1854–1892*. Edited by Isabel Anderson. New York: F. H. Revell, 1942.

Archibald, Raymond Claire. *Benjamin Peirce 1809–1880: Biographical Sketch and Bibliography*. Chicago: Open Court, 1925.

Atkinson, Norma Pereira. *An Examination of the Life and Thought of Zina Fay Peirce, an American Reformer and Feminist*. Ann Arbor, Mich.: University Microfilms no. 8401286, 1983 (Ph.D. diss., Ball State University).

Bacourt, Adolphe Fourier de. *Souveniers of a Diplomat: Private letters from America during the administration of Presidents Van Buren, Harrison, and Tyler, by the Chevalier de Bacourt, minister from France, with a memoir of the author by the Comtesse Mirabeau*. New York: Holt, 1885.

Bail, Hamilton Vaughan. *Views of Harvard: A Pictorial Record to 1860*. Cambridge: Harvard University Press, 1949.

Baring-Gould, Sabine. *Curious Myths of the Middle Ages. Reprint of essays originally published in 1866–68*. New Hyde Park, N.Y.: University Books, 1967.

Bercovici, Konrad. *The Story of the Gypsies*. New York: Cosmopolitan Book, 1931.

Boole, George. *An Investigation of the Laws of Thought, on which are founded the Mathematical Theories of Logic and Probabilities*. 1854. Reprint, New York: Dover, 1953.

Borrow, George. *The Bible in Spain: or, The Journeys, Adventures, and Imprisonments of an Englishman in an attempt to Circulate the Scriptures in the Peninsula*. London: John

Murray, 1842. First edition was 1842; many printings and editions through 1914.

———. *Romano Lavo-Lil: Word-Book of the Romany or, English Gypsy Language*. London: John Murray, 1919.

———. *The Romany Rye, With an Introduction by Walter Starkie*. London: Cresset, 1948.

———. *The Zincali: An Account of the Gypsies of Spain*. London: John Murray, 1907.

Bowen, Catherine Drinker. *Yankee from Olympus: Justice Holmes and His Family*. Boston: Little, Brown & Company, 1944.

Bruce, Robert V. *The Launching of Modern American Science 1846–1876*. New York: Knopf, 1987.

Buber, Martin. *I and Thou*. Translation of *Ich und Du* by Walter Kaufmann. New York: Charles Scribner's Sons, 1970.

Burch, Robert W. *A Peircean Reduction Thesis: The Foundations of Topological Logic*. Lubbock: Texas Tech University Press, 1991.

Cadwallader, Thomas C. "Charles S. Peirce (1839–1914): The First American Experimental Psychologist," *Journal of the History of the Behavioral Sciences* 10 (1974): 291–298.

———. "Peirce as an Experimental Psychologist," *Transactions of the Charles S. Peirce Society* 11 (1975): 167–186.

Carpenter, Frederic Ives. *Emerson and Asia*. Cambridge: Harvard University Press, 1930.

Clarke, James Freeman. *James Freeman Clarke: Autobiography, Diary, and Correspondence*. Edited by Edward Everett Hale. Boston: Houghton Mifflin, 1891.

Colapietro, Vincent M. and Thomas Olshewsky, editors. *Peirce's Doctrine of Signs: Theory, Applications, and Connections*. Berlin: Mouton de Gruyter, 1996. Essays from the Peirce Sesquicentennial International Congress, Harvard 1989.

Cooke, Josiah Parsons. *Religion and Chemistry: A Re-statement of an Old Argument*. Revised Edition. New York: Charles Scribner's Sons, 1880. First edition was 1864.

Crowninshield, Clara. *The Diary of Clara Crowninshield*. Edited by Andrew Hilen. Seattle: University of Washington Press, 1956.

Daniels, George H. *American Science in the Age of Jackson*. New York: Columbia University Press, 1968.

Day, Gardiner Mumford (Rector of Christ Church, Cambridge, 1941). *The Biography of a Church: A brief History of Christ Church, Cambridge, Massachusetts*. Cambridge: Riverside, 1951.

Debrock, Guy and Menno Hulswit, editors. *Living Doubt: Essays Concerning the Epistemology of Charles Sanders Peirce*. Dordrecht: Kluwer, 1994. Essays from the Peirce Sesquicentennial International Congress, Harvard 1989.

De Morgan, Augustus. "On the Syllogism, No. IV, and the Logic of Relations," *Cambridge Philosophical Transactions* 10: 331–358 (read April 23, 1860, dated at the end as November 12, 1859).

Dewey, Orville. *Autobiography and Letters of Orville Dewey, Edited by his Daughter* [Mary E. Dewey]. Boston: Roberts Brothers, 1884.

Dictionary of American Biography. New York: Charles Scribner's Sons, 1930.

Dictionary of Scientific Biography. Edited by Charles Coulston Gillispie. New York: Charles Scribner's Sons, [1970–1980].

Doyle, Sir Arthur Conan. *The Complete Sherlock Holmes*. Garden City, N.Y.: Doubleday, 1930.

Dupree, A. Hunter. *Asa Gray: 1810–1888*. Cambridge: Belknap Press of Harvard University Press, 1959.

Eco, Umberto. *The Name of the Rose* [*Il nome della rosa*]. New York: Warner, 1984.

Eco, Umberto, and Thomas A. Sebeok, editors. *The Sign of Three: Dupin, Holmes, Peirce.* Bloomington: Indiana University Press, 1983.

Eisele, Carolyn. "Benjamin Peirce [Junior]." In *Dictionary of Scientific Biography.* Edited by Charles Coulston Gillispie. New York: Charles Scribner's Sons, [1970–1980], 10:478–481.

———. "Charles Sanders Peirce." In *Dictionary of Scientific Biography.* Edited by Charles Coulston Gillispie. New York: Charles Scribner's Sons, [1970–1980], 10:482–488.

———. *Studies in the Scientific and Mathematical Philosophy of Charles S. Peirce: Essays by Carolyn Eisele.* Edited by Richard M. Martin. The Hague: Mouton, 1979.

Eliot, Charles W. *Harvard Memories.* Cambridge: Harvard University Press, 1923.

———. *Charles W. Eliot and Popular Education.* Edited by Edward A. Krug. New York: Columbia Teachers College Bureau of Publications, 1961.

Ellis, Havelock, and John Addington Symonds. *Sexual Inversion.* London: Wilson & Macmillan, 1897.

Emerson, Ralph Waldo. *The Portable Emerson.* Edited by C. Bode. New York: Penguin, 1981.

The Encyclopedia Britannica. 13th edition. London: Encyclopedia Britannica, 1926.

Esposito, Joseph L. *Evolutionary Metaphysics: The Development of Peirce's Theory of Categories.* Athens: Ohio University Press, 1980.

Fay, Amy. *More Letters of Amy Fay: The American Years, 1879–1916.* Edited by Sister Margaret William McCarthy. Detroit: Information Coordinators, 1986.

Ferguson, Moira, and Janet Todd. *Mary Wollstonecraft.* Boston: Twayne, 1984.

Fisch, Max H. *Peirce, Semeiotic, and Pragmatism: Essays by Max H. Fisch.* Edited by Kenneth Laine Ketner, and Christian J. W. Kloesel. Bloomington: Indiana University Press, 1986.

Fisher, Sydney George. *The True Benjamin Franklin.* Philadelphia: J. B. Lippincott, 1903.

Fraser, Angus M. *The Gypsies.* Oxford: Blackwell, 1992.

Friend, Julius W., and James Feibleman. *The Unlimited Community: A Study of the Possibility of Social Science.* London: George Allen & Unwin, 1936.

Gallie, W. B. *Peirce and Pragmatism.* New York: Dover, 1966.

Gleick, James. *Genius: The Life and Science of Richard Feynman.* New York: Pantheon, 1992.

Gordon, Linda. *Woman's Body, Woman's Right: A Social History of Birth Control in America.* New York: Grossman, 1976.

Grellmann, H. M. G. *Dissertation on the Gipseys.* London: William Ballintine, 1807.

Hale, Edward Everett. "My College Days," *Atlantic Monthly* 71 (1893): 355–363.

———. *A New England Boyhood.* New York: Cassell, 1893.

———. "'Tis 60 years Since' at Harvard," *Atlantic Monthly* 78 (1896): 496–505.

Hammett, Dashiell. *The Maltese Falcon.* New York: Vintage Crime, 1992.

Handlin, Lilian. *George Bancroft: The Intellectual as Democrat.* Cambridge: Harper & Row, 1984.

Hatfield, James Taft. *New Light on Longfellow.* Boston: Houghton Mifflin, 1933.

Hawkins, Hugh. *Between Harvard and America: The Educational Leadership of Charles W. Eliot.* New York: Oxford University Press, 1971.

Hegermann-Lindencrone, Anna Lillie [Greenough] [Moulton]. *In the Courts of Memory: 1858–1875 from Contemporary Letters.* New York: Harper & Brothers, 1912.

———. *The Sunny Side of Diplomatic Life, 1875–1912.* New York: Harper & Brothers, 1914.

Henderson, Harold. *Catalyst for Controversy: Paul Carus of Open Court.* Carbondale: Southern Illinois University Press, 1993.

Higginson, Thomas Wentworth. "How I was Educated," *Forum* 1 (1866): 172–182.

Hill, Thomas. [Review of three books on creation]. *Christian Examiner* 59 (1855): 375–398.

Hoar, George Frisbie. *Autobiography of Seventy Years.* Vol. 1. New York: Charles Scribner's Sons, 1903.

Houser, Nathan. "The Fortunes and Misfortunes of the Peirce Papers." In *Signs of Humanity.* 3 vols. Edited by Michel Balat and Janice Deledalle-Rhodes. New York and Berlin: Mouton de Gruyter, 1992, 3:1259–1268.

Houser, Nathan, Don D. Roberts, and James Van Evra, editors. *Studies in the Logic of Charles Sanders Peirce.* Bloomington: Indiana University Press, 1997. Essays from the Peirce Sesquicentennial International Congress, Harvard 1989.

Howe, M. A. DeWolfe. *The Life and Letters of George Bancroft.* Two volumes. New York: Charles Scribner's Sons, 1908.

James, Henry. *Charles W. Eliot: President of Harvard University 1869–1909.* Boston: Houghton Mifflin, 1930.

James, Mary Ann. *Elites in Conflict: The Antebellum Clash over the Dudley Observatory.* New Brunswick: Rutgers University Press, 1987.

James, William. *The Letters of William James, edited by his son Henry James.* Boston: Atlantic Monthly Press, 1920.

———. *Philosophical Conceptions and Practical Results.* A reprint from *The University Chronicle* [University of California] September 1898. Berkeley: University of California Press, 1898.

———. *Varieties of Religious Experience: A Study in Human Nature, Being the Gifford Lectures on Natural Religion Delivered at Edinburgh in 1901–1902.* Cambridge: Harvard University Press, 1985.

———. *William James: Selected Unpublished Correspondence 1885–1910.* Columbus: Ohio State University Press, 1986.

Johnson's Universal Cyclopædia. Frederick A. P. Bernhard editor-in-chief. New York: A. J. Johnson & Co., 1839 and later editions.

Katz, Jonathan. *Gay American History: Lesbians and Gay Men in the U.S.A.* Toronto: Fitzhenry & Whiteside, 1976.

Ketner, Kenneth Laine. "Peirce and Turing: Comparisons and Conjectures." *Semiotica* 68 (1988): 33–61.

———. "Pragmaticism Is an Existentialism?" In *Frontiers in American Philosophy.* Edited by Robert W. Burch and Herman J. Saatkamp, Jr. 2 vols. College Station: Texas A&M University Press, 1991, 2:105–111.

Ketner, Kenneth Laine, with the assistance of Arthur F. Stewart. "The Early History of Computer Design: Charles Sanders Peirce and Marquand's Logical Machines" *Princeton University Library Chronicle* 45 (1984): 187–224.

Ketner, Kenneth Laine, with the assistance of Claude Ventry Bridges and Arthur Franklin Stewart. *A Comprehensive Bibliography of the Published Works of Charles Sanders Peirce, with a Bibliography of Secondary Studies.* 2d edition, revised. Secondary bibliography by C. J. W. Kloesel and J. M. Ransdell. Bowling Green, Ohio: Philosophy Documentation Center, 1986.

Ketner, Kenneth Laine, editor. "A Brief Intellectual Autobiography by Charles Sanders Peirce," *American Journal of Semiotics* 2 (1983): 61–83.

———. *Peirce and Contemporary Thought: Philosophical Inquiries.* New York: Fordham University Press, 1995.

———. *Reasoning and the Logic of Things: The Cambridge Conferences Lectures of 1898 by Charles Sanders Peirce.* With an introduction by Kenneth Laine Ketner and Hilary

Putnam. Cambridge: Harvard University Press, 1992. Contains Putnam's presidential address from the Peirce Sesquicentennial International Congress, Harvard 1989.

Ketner, Kenneth Laine, Joseph M. Ransdell, Carolyn Eisele, Max H. Fisch, and Charles S. Hardwick, editors. *Proceedings of the C. S. Peirce Bicentennial International Congress.* Lubbock: Texas Tech University Press, 1981.

Kevelson, Roberta, editor. *Peirce and Law: Issues in Pragmatism, Legal Realism, and Semiotics.* New York: Peter Lang, 1991. Essays from the Peirce Sesquicentennial International Congress, Harvard 1989.

King, Moses. *Benjamin Peirce: A Memorial Collection.* Boston: Rand, Avery, & Company, 1881.

Kloesel, Christian Johann Wolfgang. "Bibliography of Charles Peirce, 1976 through 1981." In *The Relevance of Charles Peirce.* Edited by E. Freeman. LaSalle, Ill: Monist Library of Philosophy, 1983.

———. "Charles Peirce and the Secret of the Harvard O.K." *New England Quarterly* 52 (1979): 55–67.

Kuehnemann, Eugen. *Charles W. Eliot: President of Harvard University (May 19, 1869—May 19, 1909).* Boston: Houghton Mifflin, 1909.

Kuklick, Bruce. *The Rise of American Philosophy: Cambridge, Massachusetts 1860–1930.* New Haven: Yale University Press, 1977.

Layman, Richard. *Shadow Man: The Life of Dashiell Hammett.* New York: Harcourt Brace Jovanovich, 1981.

Lawrence, Robert Means. *Old Park Street and Its Vicinity.* Boston: Houghton Mifflin, 1922.

Le Conte, Emma. *When the World Ended: The Diary of Emma Le Conte.* New York: Oxford University Press, 1957.

Le Conte, Joseph. *The Autobiography of Joseph Le Conte.* Edited by D. Armes. New York: D. Appleton, 1903.

———. *'Ware Sherman: A Journal of Three Months' Personal Experience in the Last Days of the Confederacy.* Berkeley: University of California Press, 1937.

Leland, Charles G. *The English Gipsies and Their Language.* New York: Hurd & Houghton, 1873.

Lenzen, Victor F. *Benjamin Peirce and the U. S. Coast Survey.* San Francisco: San Francisco Press, 1968.

———. "Reminiscences of a Mission to Milford, Pennsylvania," *Transactions of the Charles S. Peirce Society,* 1 (1965): 3–11.

Lewis, R. W. B. *The Jameses: A Family Narrative.* New York: Farrar, Straus & Giroux, 1991.

Liszka, James Jakób. *A General Introduction to the Semeiotic of Charles Sanders Peirce.* Bloomington: Indiana University Press, 1996.

Longfellow, Henry Wadsworth. *The Poetical Works of Henry Wadsworth Longfellow.* New York: AMS, 1966.

Lopez, Enrique Hank. *The Harvard Mystique.* New York: MacMillan, 1979.

Lowe, Victor. *Alfred North Whitehead: The Man and His Work.* 2 vols. Baltimore: The Johns Hopkins University Press, 1985, 1990.

Lowell, Anna C. *Seed-Grain for Thought and Discussion.* 2 vols. Boston: Ticknor & Fields, 1856.

Lurie, Edward. *Louis Agassiz: A Life in Science.* Chicago: University of Chicago Press, 1960.

McDowell, Bart. *Gypsies: Wanderers of the World.* Washington, D.C.: National Geographic Society, 1970.

Madden, Edward H. *Chauncey Wright and the Foundations of Pragmatism.* Seattle: University of Washington Press, 1963.

Manning, Thomas G. *U.S. Coast Survey vs. Naval Hydrographic Office: A 19th–Century Rivalry in Science and Politics.* Tuscaloosa: University of Alabama Press, 1988.

Marling, William. *Dashiell Hammett.* Boston: Twayne, 1983.

Miller, R. H. "Hammett's *The Maltese Falcon,*" *Explicator* 54 (1996): 173–174.

Moore, Edward C., editor. *Charles S. Peirce and the Philosophy of Science: Papers from the Harvard Sesquicentennial Congress.* Tuscaloosa: University of Alabama Press, 1993. Essays from the Peirce Sesquicentennial International Congress, Harvard 1989.

Moore, Edward C. and Richard S. Robin, editors. *From Time and Chance to Consciousness: Studies in the Metaphysics of Charles Peirce.* Oxford: Berg, 1994. Essays from the Peirce Sesquicentennial International Congress, Harvard 1989.

Morison, Samuel Eliot. *Three Centuries of Harvard: 1636–1936.* Cambridge: Belknap Press of Harvard University Press, 1936.

Musto, David F. "Opium, Cocaine and Marijuana in American History," *Scientific American—Medicine,* Special Issue. New York: Scientific American, 1993, 30–37.

National Academy of Sciences, Committee on the Preparation of the Semi-Centennial Volume. *A History of the First Half-Century of the National Academy of Sciences 1863–1913.* Washington: Lord Baltimore, 1913.

National Cyclopædia of American Biography. New York: James T. White & Company, 1900.

Nicolson, Harold. *Sainte-Beuve.* London: Constable, 1957.

Norton, Charles Eliot. *Philosophical Discussions by Chauncey Wright.* New York: Henry Holt, 1877.

Nozawa, E. T. "Introduction to Charles Sanders Peirce and the Peircean System of Science and Peircean Semeiotic," *Gaciac Bulletin* 20 (May 1997): 1–6.

Nye, Russel B. *George Bancroft: Brahmin Rebel.* New York: Knopf, 1945.

Odgers, Merle M. *Alexander Dallas Bache: Scientist and Educator 1806–1867.* Philadelphia: University of Pennsylvania Press, 1947.

Palmer, Mary Towle. *The Story of the Bee.* Cambridge: Riverside, 1924.

Parkman, F. Review of *Catalogue of the Library of Harvard University in Cambridge, Massachusetts, Christian Examiner* 8 (1830): 321–25.

Parret, Herman, editor. *Peirce and Value Theory: On Peircean Ethics and Aesthetics.* Amsterdam: John Benjamins, 1994. Essays from the Peirce Sesquicentennial International Congress, Harvard 1989.

Paton, Lucy Allen. *Elizabeth Cary Agassiz: A Biography.* New York: Arno, 1974.

Peabody, Francis G. *Harvard in the Sixties: A Boy's Eye View. Some Reminiscences contributed to the Cambridge Historical Society at its meeting of March 12, 1935.* Cambridge, 1935.

Peirce, Benjamin [Senior]. *A History of Harvard University, from its Foundation, in the year 1636, to the period of the American Revolution.* Cambridge: Brown, Shattuck, & Company, 1833. Library of American Civilization, microform edition, LAC 13038.

Peirce, Benjamin [Junior]. *Peirce's Course of Instruction on Pure Mathematics for Use of Students in Harvard University.* Boston: James Munroe & Company, 1835– . A series of volumes on mathematical topics.

Percy, Walker. "The Divided Creature," *Wilson Quarterly* 13 (1989): 77–87.

———. *Lost in the Cosmos.* New York: Washington Square, 1984.

———. *The Message in the Bottle: How Queer Man Is, How Queer Language Is, and What One Has to Do with the Other.* New York: Farrar, Straus & Giroux, 1975.

———. *Signposts in a Strange Land.* Edited by Patrick H. Samway, S.J. New York: Farrar, Straus & Giroux, 1991. Interviews with Percy.

Perry, Ralph Barton. *The Thought and Character of William James.* 2 vols. Boston: Little, Brown & Company, 1935.

Phillips, James Duncan. *Salem and the Indies: The Story of the Great Commercial Era of the City.* Boston: Houghton Mifflin, 1947.

————. *Salem in the Eighteenth Century.* Salem: Essex Institute, 1969.

Plato. *The Dialogues of Plato.* Translated by Benjamin Jowett. New York: Appleton, 1898.

Potter, Vincent G. *Peirce's Philosophical Perspectives.* Edited by Vincent M. Colapietro. New York: Fordham University Press, 1996.

Putnam, Hilary. "Peirce the Logician." *Historia Mathematica* 9 (1982): 290–301.

Quintana, Bertha B., and Lois Gray Floyd. *!Que Gitano! Gypsies of Southern Spain.* New York: Holt, Rinehart & Winston, 1972.

Reid, Bill. *Big-Time Football at Harvard, 1905: The Diary of Coach Bill Reid.* Edited by Ronald A. Smith. Urbana: University of Illinois Press, 1994.

Reingold, Nathan, editor. *Science in Nineteenth-Century America: A Documentary History.* New York: Hill & Wang, 1964.

Robinson, James M., editor. *The Nag Hammadi Library in English.* New York: Harper & Row, 1977.

Rogers, William Barton. *The Life and Letters of William Barton Rogers,* edited by his wife [Emma Savage Rogers]. Two volumes. Boston: Houghton Mifflin, 1896.

Royce, Josiah. *The Problem of Christianity.* New York: Macmillan, 1913.

————. *War and Insurance: An Address Delivered before the Philosophical Union of the University of California at Its Twenty-Fifth Anniversary at Berkeley California, August 27, 1914.* New York: Macmillan, 1914.

Samway, Patrick H., S.J. *Walker Percy: A Life.* New York: Farrar, Straus & Giroux, 1997.

Samway, Patrick H., S.J., editor. *A Thief of Peirce: The Letters of Kenneth Laine Ketner and Walker Percy.* Jackson: University Press of Mississippi, 1995.

Savan, David. "Peirce's Semiotic Theory of Emotion," in *Proceedings of the C. S. Peirce Bicentennial International Congress.* Edited by Kenneth Laine Ketner and others.

Schiller, Friedrich. *The Æsthetic Letters, Essays, and The Philosophical Letters of Schiller.* Translated by J. Weiss. Boston: Charles C. Little & James Brown, 1845.

————. *On the Æsthetic Education of Man, in a Series of Letters.* Translated with an introduction by Reginald Snell. New Haven: Yale University Press, 1954.

Schröder, Ernst. *Vorlesungen über die Algebra der Logik (exacte Logik).* Drei Bänder: Leipzig, 1890–.

Sebeok, Thomas A., and Jean Umiker-Sebeok. *"You Know my Method": A Juxtaposition of Charles S. Peirce and Sherlock Holmes.* Bloomington: Gaslight, 1980.

Shakespeare, William. *The Complete Illustrated Shakespeare.* Edited by Howard Staunton. New York: Park Lane, 1979.

Singer, Milton. "A Tale of Two Amateurs Who Crossed Cultural Frontiers with Boole's 'Symbolical Algebra'," *Semiotica* 105 (1995): 7–186.

Smith-Rosenberg, Carroll. *Disorderly Conduct: Visions of Gender in Victorian America.* New York: Knopf, 1985.

Starkie, Walter. *In Sara's Tents.* New York: E. P. Dutton, 1953.

————. *The Road to Santiago: Pilgrims of St. James.* London: John Murray, 1957.

————. *Spanish Raggle-Taggle: Adventures with a Fiddle in North Spain.* London: John Murray, 1934.

Stephens, Lester D. *Joseph Le Conte: Gentle Prophet of Evolution.* Baton Rouge: Louisiana State University Press, 1982.

Stevens, W. Le Conte. "Sketch of Prof. John Le Conte," *Popular Science Monthly* 36 (1889): 112–120.

Stewart, Arthur Franklin. "Peirce, Beddoes, and Pragmatistic Abstraction: An Introduction," *Southwest Philosophical Studies* 13 (1991): 75–88.

Stewart, Arthur Franklin, editor. *Religious Dimensions of Peirce's Thought.* Beaumont: Lamar University Center for Philosophical Studies, to appear. Essays from the Peirce Sesquicentennial International Congress, Harvard 1989.

———. *Contemporary Essays on Charles S. Peirce.* Beaumont: Lamar University Center for Philosophical Studies, to appear. Essays from the Peirce Sesquicentennial International Congress, Harvard 1989.

Stuart-Wortley, Lady Emmeline. *Travels in the United States, etc. During 1849 and 1850.* New York: Harper & Brothers, 1851.

———. *Wanderers: Episodes from the Travels of Lady Emmeline Stuart-Wortley and Her Daughter Victoria, 1849–1855.* Edited by Nina Cust. London: J. Cape, 1928.

Stuhr, John J., editor. *Classical American Philosophy.* New York: Oxford University Press, 1987 (pages 13–92: "Charles Sanders Peirce," introductory essay and readings prepared by K. L. Ketner).

Swedenborg, Emanuel. *A Treatise on the Nature of Influx: or, of the Intercourse between the SOUL and BODY Which is supposed to be either by PHYSICAL INFLUX, or by SPIRITUAL INFLUX, or by PRESTABLISHED HARMONY.* Translated from the Latin by the Rev. Thomas Hartley, D.D. Boston: I. Thomas & E. T. Andrews, 1794.

———. *Angelic Wisdom Concerning the Divine Love and the Divine Wisdom.* New York: Swedenborg Foundation, 1971. First U.S. edition and English translation was 1851.

Symons, Julian. *Dashiell Hammett.* San Diego: Harcourt Brace Jovanovich, 1985.

Tharp, Louise Hall. *Adventurous Alliance: The Story of the Agassiz Family of Boston.* Boston: Little, Brown & Company, 1959.

Tymoczko, Dmitri. "The Nitrous Oxide Philosopher," *Atlantic Monthly,* May 1996, 93–101.

Vera, Augusto. *Introduction a la philosophie de Hegel,* Paris 1855.

Virgil (Publius Vergilius Maro). *The ÆNEID.* Translated into English by Frank O. Copley. Indianapolis: Bobbs-Merrill Co., 1965.

———. *The Æneid of Vergil.* Edited with introduction and notes by R. D. Williams. New York: Macmillan Education Limited, 1972.

Ward, Gerald W. R. *The Peirce-Nichols House.* Historic house booklet number 4. Salem, Massachusetts: Essex Institute, 1976.

Weil, Simone. *The Simone Weil Reader.* Edited by George A. Panichas. New York: David McKay, 1977.

Whitehead, Alfred North. *A Treatise on Universal Algebra with Applications.* New York: Hafner Publishing Company, 1960.

Wright, Chauncey. *Letters of Chauncey Wright, with some account of his life by James Bradley Thayer.* Cambridge: John Wilson & Son, 1878.

———. *The Philosophical Writings of Chauncey Wright: Representative Selections.* Edited by Edward H. Madden. New York: Liberal Arts, 1958.

Yoors, Jan. *The Gypsies of Spain.* New York: Macmillan, 1974.

Index

Note: Page numbers in italics refer to figures. Notes are referenced by page and line (e.g., 361*n*.10:40 indicates the note to page 10 line 40 that appears on page 361). Abbreviation of names follows the list on pp. 359-360.

Abbot, Ezra, 141
Abbot, Francis Ellingwood ("Frank"), 155, 157, 279, 293, 294
Abbot, Sibley, 141
Abbott, John C.: *Kings and Queens; or, Life in the Palace, 100,* 213
abductive (retroductive) reasoning, 248, 266, 294
Abelard, Peter, 62
accidents, responsibility for, 73
Adams, John Quincy, 91
aesthetics, 136
Agassiz, Alexander, 200
Agassiz, Elizabeth Cabot Cary, 200, 201
Agassiz, Louis, 89, 93–94, 95, 99, 105, 112, 118, 126, 140, 200, 206, 229, 234, 244, 258, 259, 263, 276, 304, 315, 343
Agassiz School for Young Ladies, 200, 251, 253
agrarianism, 126
Alexander, Stephen, 173, 175
algebra, 337
American Academy of Arts and Sciences, 99, 118; CSP's lectures at, 326–338
American Association for the Advancement of Science (AAAS): meetings of, 95, 102, 105, 106, 109, 112, 127, 169; CSP's reporting of, 172–178
American Journal of Science and Art: "The Chemical Theory of Interpenetration" (CSP), 254–255
American Philosophical Society, 90, 160
Ames, Felham Warren, 157
"Anacreontic Valentine" (CSP), 168–169
Analytic Mechanics (BP2), 69, 104
Anderson, Maj. Robert, 127
Andover Academy (Andover, MA), 68, 69

anthropological logicians, 318
Apelt, Otto, 296
"Apology of Socrates, The" (CSP), 206–207
Appleton, W. H., 308
apprehension in intuition, theory of, 293
Arabian Nights stories, 73
architectonical method, 262
argument from authority, 334
Arisbe (Milford, PA), 31, 47, 48, 49, 50, 52, 66, 362*n*.31:35
Aristotle, 62, 72–73, 233, 247, 296, 307, 318, 324
Armsby, Dr. James, 115
Atkinson (a student), 243
Augustine (saint), 296

Babbage, Charles, 196
Bache, Alexander Dallas ("The Chief"): on Civil War, 237, 238; death of, 238, 315; in Florentine Academy, 90–92, 95, 118; as friend of Peirce family, 87, 102, 108, 109, 124; at meetings of AAAS, 112, 173; reaction to CSP's first marriage, 250–251, 254; as superintendent of Coast Survey, 89, 91, 116, 124, 180, 182, 239–240. *See also* "Florentine Academy"
Bache, Mrs. Alexander Dallas, 179
Bacon, Sir Francis, 267, 271, 295, 296
Bacourt, Adolphe Fourier de, 9, 285, 286–287, 288
Badger, Caroline Louise ("Carrie," first wife of CSP): correspondence of, 213, 215–221; courtship of, 213, 215–216; and opium use by CSP, 218–220; secret marriage of, 213, 216–219; and separation from CSP, 217, 220–222; and turmoil over affair, 216–217, 220; and written marriage agreement, 217, 220–222
Badger, John L., 213
Badger, Maggie, 216
Baldwin's Dictionary, 19
Bancroft, George, 76–77, 89, 91, 201, 285, 288, 289
Barnes, Elsie, 390*n*.287:28

Author photograph by Hershel Womack

KENNETH LAINE KETNER is the Charles Sanders Peirce Professor of
Philosophy at Texas Tech University and the director of its Institute for
Studies in Pragmaticism. He is editor of several works by and about Peirce
and was co-organizer for the Charles S. Peirce International Congress held at
Harvard in 1989. He is also one of the two principals in a noteworthy volume
of correspondence with Walker Percy (*A Thief of Peirce: The Letters of Kenneth
Laine Ketner and Walker Percy*, published in 1995).

HIS GLASSY ESSENCE

was composed electronically
using Palatino and Optima type faces with displays in
Bernhard Modern and Type Embellishments One.
The book was printed on 60#
Glatfelter Supple Opaque Recycled Natural paper
and was Smyth sewn and cased in Pearl Linen cloth
by Thomson-Shore, Inc.
The dust jacket was printed in four colors by
Vanderbilt University Printing Services.
Book and jacket design are the work of Gary Gore.
Published by Vanderbilt University Press
Nashville, Tennessee 37235

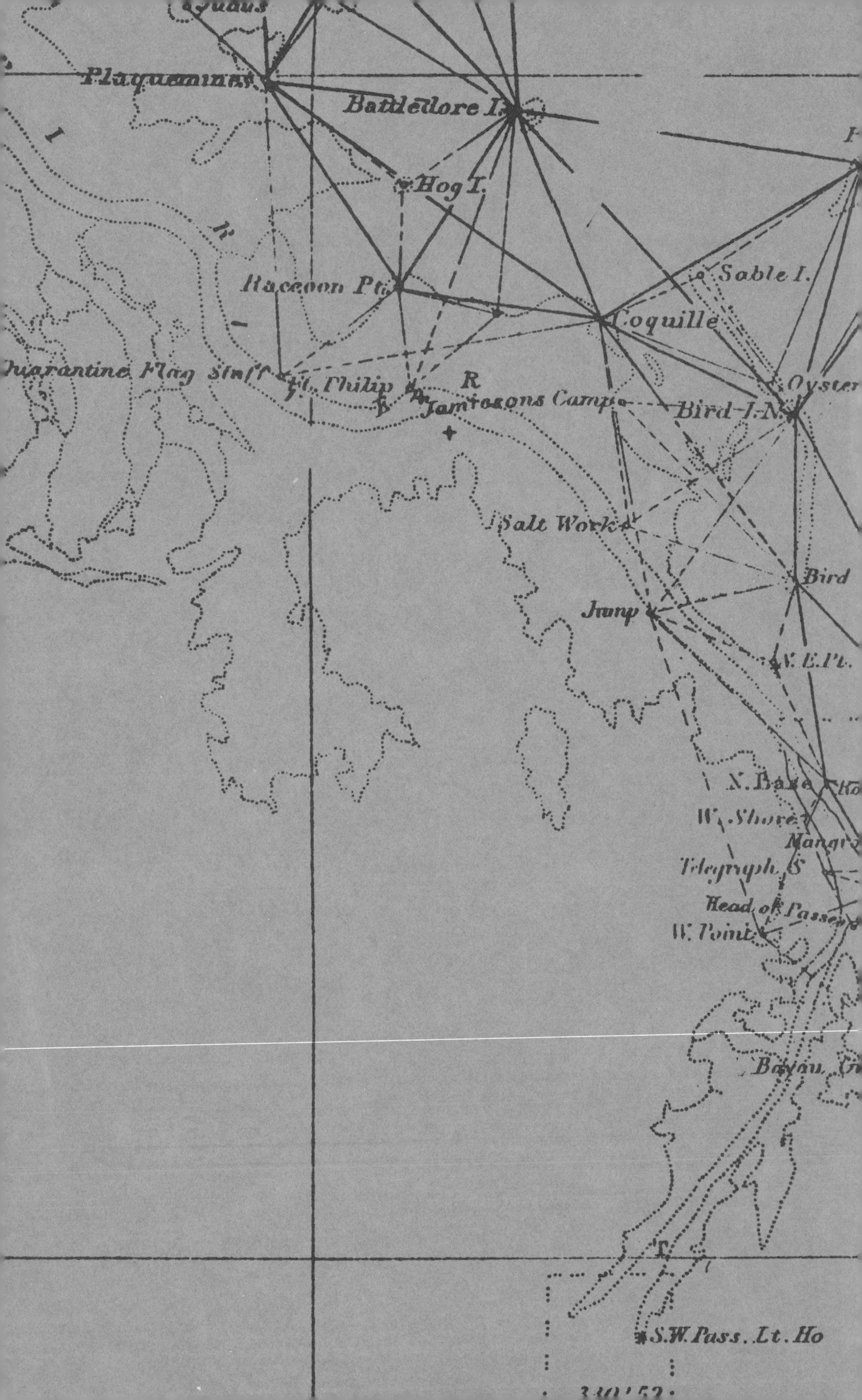

Plaquemines
Battledore I.
Hog I.
Raccoon Pt.
Sable I.
Coquille
Quarantine Flag Staff
Ft. Philip
R
Jamiesons Camp
Bird I. N.
Salt Works
Bird
Jump
N. E. Pt.
N. Base
W. Shore
Telegraph S
Head of Passes
W. Point
S.W. Pass. Lt. Ho